Just Tell Me When to Cry

Just Tell Me When to Cry

A Memoir

Richard Fleischer

Carroll & Graf Publishers, Inc.
New York

Copyright © 1993 by Richard Fleischer

First Carroll & Graf edition 1993

Carroll & Graf Publishers, Inc.
260 Fifth Avenue
New York, NY 10001

Library of Congress Cataloging-in-Publication Data

Fleischer, Richard.
    Just tell me when to cry : a memoir / Richard Fleischer.
    —1st Carroll & Graf ed.
        p.   cm.
    Includes index.
    ISBN 0-88184-944-8 : $21.00
    1. Fleischer, Richard.   2. Motion picture producers and directors—
United States—Biography.   I. Title.
PN1998.3.F6A3   1993
791.43'0233'092—dc20   93-7979
    [B]   CIP

Manufactured in the United States of America

For
Saul David, who had the faith;
Knox Burger, who kept the faith;
and
Mickey, who did all of the above
and who lived it all with me.

Fade In

Recently one of the most distinguished public relations men in the business introduced me to a friend of his by saying, "There isn't a book about Hollywood in which his name doesn't appear." Well, PR people are given to hyperbole and I modestly waved it aside at the time. But I've been thinking about it and have come to the realization that he was right. I don't believe you can pick up a book that factually covers Hollywood from 1945 to the present without finding my name in it. It's not all that surprising when you realize that I've directed forty-seven feature films, one third of which have been honored with awards of one sort or another including, in various categories, twenty-five Academy Award nominations and eight Academy Awards. Also, along the way, some of my films, such as *Twenty Thousand Leagues Under the Sea* and *The Vikings*, have entered the hallowed pantheon of movie classics. Others have become classics of their genre, such as *Fantastic Voyage* and *Soylent Green* in science fiction; *The Narrow Margin* in *film noir*; *Compulsion* in courtroom drama; and still others, such as *The Boston Strangler* and *The New Centurions*, are considered watershed pictures of their type.

Movies are a funny business. For some reason it is almost impossible to tell a serious story about the film industry without everyone laughing. The worse the disaster, the more hilarious it becomes. You can tell of careers being ruined, fortunes being lost, people being injured, or worse, and the reaction is always laughter. The trouble, I suppose, is that while it's a serious business, it seems too ridiculous to be taken seriously. After all, it's only moving shadows on a silver screen.

The stories I have to tell are mostly funny. Some of them even seemed funny at the time they were happening. But underneath the bizarre craziness there is something else. It is an insider's look at the inside of the movie business. This is the way it really is, this is the way it works. My purpose was not to glamorize Hollywood, or to deglamorize it, but to tell it straight arrow as it happened to me.

On ancient maps, the uncharted areas were sometimes marked, "Here there be Monsters." If anyone was foolhardy enough to try to make a map of the movie business, such a legend wouldn't be out of place. Monsters do exist, and I've written about some of them. But there are Monsters and there are Monsters. Some are horrible and others are sort of lovable.

I haven't tried to be deliberately harsh about some of the personalities in this book, just truthful. They're a quirky lot, these movie folk, but that's what makes them special. You shouldn't expect logical or conventional decorum from the supertalented. Let's face it: Good behavior is the last refuge of mediocrity.

This book is not a collection of thrice-told stories, or tales you've heard before, nor is it a ". . . and then I directed . . ." book. What it is, I hope, is a record of what it's like working with the moguls, monsters, superstars, greats, near-greats, and ingrates of Hollywood: the John Waynes, Rex Harrisons, Darryl Zanucks, Howard Hugheses, Kirk Douglases, Orson Welleses, and all the otherses.

I wanted to write a book from the perspective of an active participant in some pretty mad shenanigans, as a close-up observer of some of Hollywood's most delightfully despicable, lovably hateful, admirably deranged characters.

And that's what I did.

I

"John Wayne hasn't shit yet."

Those were the first words I ever heard spoken on a sound stage. They were my introduction to the magic and the glamor of Hollywood.

It was early 1945. I was twenty-seven years old and was being shown around RKO Radio Pictures Studios by my new boss, Sid Rogell.

I had actually arrived in town the day before with my very pregnant wife, Mickey, having driven across the country from New York. I wanted to check in at the studio as soon as I got there, but a picket line, or rather a picket circle, prevented that. There was an industry strike going on, and pickets had formed a circle in front of the main gate so that you couldn't drive into the studio without going right through it.

We tried that. When we got right in the center of the circle, feeling a lot like General Custer at Little Big Horn, the drive shaft fell out of the car.

The pickets pushed us through the studio gates and I didn't bother to check in that day. Instead I called the AAA and we were towed ignominiously away.

The following day I taxied to the studio and met Sid Rogell. There were two production units at every studio at that time. One unit made A pictures—big budgets, long shooting schedules, expensive stars. The other unit made the B pictures, or programmers. They were the opposite in every way and were meant to fill the bottom half of a double feature program. Still, every once in a while a nifty B picture got made. Rogell was in charge of the B unit and ran it with all the humanity of a tyrant.

One of the series that Rogell's unit churned out was Dick Tracy, and he looked just like him. He had the same sharply broken nose and jutting chin. Physically, though, he was a solid, stocky square and looked like a short football player who never took off his shoulder pads. He walked like an athlete nursing a bad back, which he frequently had, but insisted on running up all stairs two at a time.

Rogell greeted me warmly. He'd heard about my grand entrance the day before and said, "You should have run over a couple of those bastards." We chatted amiably about the strange good fortune that had brought me out to the Coast. I had organized a group of students from the Yale Drama School, where I was also enrolled, to do a summer of theater-in-the-round in New England. An RKO talent scout named Arthur Willi caught one of the shows I'd directed, sought me out after the performance, and said, "Young man, how would you like to come to Hollywood and direct movies?" Just like that. Even Cinderella never had it so good.

It was three years before I started the contract. RKO, it seems, was in the middle of one of its almost continuous management upheavals at the time that Arthur Willi touched me with his magic wand. Since I had a seven-year contract, with an option every six months, he felt that if I went to the Coast I'd surely be lost in the shuffle and would find myself back in New York at the end of the first option period. He advised staying put until things quieted down in Hollywood and got me an interim job at RKO Pathé News in New York. I'd had terrible stomach butterflies about leaping into the Hollywood scene with no movie experience and, since there were no film schools in existence, I embraced the Pathé job with open arms, eyes, and ears. It was a humble beginning, $35 a week as assistant title writer, but at the end of three years I was head writer for the newsreel, had written and directed many documentary films, was producing and editing a series of my own called *Flicker Flashbacks*, and was knocking down a cool $100 a week.

Because of my Pathé film training, when the big finger eventually beckoned me to Hollywood I was considerably better prepared to start making movies than most of the newcomers who made the cross-country trek. My boss at Pathé offered to meet the $150 a week I'd be making as a big-time movie director in Hollywood if I stayed. It was tempting but, no, this young man was going West.

Virtually everyone who worked for any of the so-called majors (Twentieth Century-Fox, Warner Brothers, Columbia, Paramount, MGM, and RKO) was under long-term contract to that studio. Even the stars. And here I was with a studio contract, too, just like Fred Astaire and Ginger Rogers. Well, I wasn't way up there in salary as they were, but we were fellow contractees at the same studio, and that was heady stuff. True, $150 per wasn't too great for Hollywood, even at that time, but it was only the beginning. If I survived the entire seven years of my contract I'd be earning the totally inconceivable sum of $1,250 a week.

The studio system, with its long-term contracts, was meant to engender a sense of security among its employees. After all, they had to pay you every week, whether you were actually working or not. And there were periodic raises, too. Being under contract sounded just great. But the system had a few minor flaws that sort of took the bloom off the rose. Like, at the end of every six-month period they had the option of dropping the contract. Usually this happened when the salary got higher than the studio thought you were worth.

Fair enough. But it worked the other way around, too. Sometimes neophyte actors and directors, who were under contract, became stars, and the studio had them for a paltry salary. Also, it was common practice among independent producers, as well as studios, to loan out the services of these valuable personalities to other companies for tens, or even hundreds, of thousands, of dollars. The contract owner pocketed the difference. It was a source of great profit to the owners and of great resentment by the personalities involved. A prime practitioner was the famous independent producer of *Gone With the Wind*, David O. Selznick. Ingrid Bergman was under contract to Selznick, during which period he loaned her out eight times. For her role in *Gaslight*, for which she won an Oscar, Selznick received $253,750, but he paid Bergman just over $75,000.

And there was another downside to being under contract: loss of control. There was no right to pick and choose. The studio chiefs did it for you, whether you liked it or not. As a director, they told you who would write your screenplay, act in it, photograph it, compose the music for it. Actors were forced into films they didn't want to do and loaned out against their will.

Anyhow, I was very happy to be sitting in Sid Rogell's office at RKO, in Hollywood, that spring morning with that lovely contract in my pocket, trying to appear older than I looked or felt. Rogell thought it would be a good idea if he showed me around. The first thing he wanted me to see was what he referred to as my suite of offices. A suite? I'd heard about these Hollywood offices. Ankle-deep carpets, lush casting couches, maybe a well-stocked bar behind a sliding mahogany panel.

Whatever it was I was expecting, I didn't get it. The suite turned out to be three barren rooms in one of the ramshackle wooden buildings of which the studio was mostly composed. It looked like a police station in a run-down precinct.

The suite was not mine alone, however. The front room was a secretary's office. The remaining two rooms were to be shared with two other young directors, Mark Robson and Robert Wise. (Both were to become important, respected directors, with Robson directing *Valley of the Dolls* and Wise directing *The Sound of Music* and *West Side Story*.) Being good friends, Robson and Wise decided to share one of the rooms together, leaving me an entire office to myself.

The studio was humming with activity. It was the Golden Age of RKO, and every stage was crammed with famous stars and directors. Rogell wanted me to see it all, so we started with a big John Wayne production that was shooting on a nearby sound stage.

It was about ten-thirty in the morning when we walked on the set. I was impressed. Although we were inside a sound stage, the set was the exterior of a large ranch house. There was plenty of real dirt in which real trees stood and real plants grew. Several horses were tethered to a hitching post. It looked as authentic as could be. But something was wrong. Even I knew that.

It was too quiet. Nothing was happening. The crew, and it was a large one, was lounging. Small groups were sitting around, talking in subdued tones, and playing cards. To Rogell, as I learned later, this was anathema. Nothing like this could ever happen on one of his productions. The activity on the sets of his pictures amounted to controlled chaos. When a scene wasn't actually being shot the crew looked like it was participating in a Chinese fire drill as they raced about moving walls, cables, lights, and cameras in preparation for the next setup. Once, when a director fell two days behind schedule, Rogell rushed down to the set, snatched the script from the director's hands, and ripped out a fistful of random pages. He shoved the script back into the director's chest and said, "Here! Now you're two days ahead."

Even though it wasn't his production, the scene that greeted him on the Wayne set was intolerable. The assistant director on the show had spotted Rogell and knew what was going on in his mind. That's when he came over and offered his cryptic, or craptic, explanation, "John Wayne hasn't shit yet."

"What the fuck is that supposed to mean?" Rogell asked.

"Well, you see," the assistant director clarified, "the Duke can't work until he has a bowel movement. Looks like he's constipated today. He usually shits much earlier than this." He pointed to a large trailer parked near a stage wall. "As soon as he comes out of his dressing room we'll go to work."

"You mean," Rogell said, aghast, "you've been waiting for him to come out since eight o'clock this morning?"

"That's right," the assistant director assured him and ambled away.

Rogell looked at his watch and said, "Jesus Christ." I stood there and marveled at the glamor of Hollywood.

We stood around for a while. Rogell showed me the set. Every couple of minutes we'd glance over at the dressing room and wonder what was going on in there.

We were on our way off the stage when there was a flurry of action. There must have been some prearranged signal to alert the crew. Bells rang. A voice yelled out, "Hit 'em all!" and the huge arcs sputtered to life. Lights all over the place flicked on. The crew scattered to their various posts.

The assistant director came running over to us. "He's shit! He's shit!" he announced excitedly and dashed off. Our eyes were riveted to the dressing room door. Nothing happened for a few minutes. Then the door opened and out he stepped. Duke Wayne. Big as life. Big as all outdoors. Big as the wheat fields of Kansas, the oil fields of Texas. America's hero. He strode toward the set, greeting his friends on the crew. Soon he was lost to view, surrounded by the director, the camera, and its crew, electricians, wardrobe people, and anyone else who was trying to look busy.

The episode gave me pause. What I had witnessed was a display of unadulterated, raw power. Who else could halt production for hours, at great cost to the studio, by peristalsis alone? It was too awesome to think about. This was not someone you wanted to offend.

I wouldn't. Not me.

My next brush with the Wayne mystique came nine years later.

I was sitting on the fantail of a motor cruiser about a mile and a half off the western tip of New Providence Island, in the Bahamas, eating a banana. It was lunchtime and a banana was about all I could handle, tied up as I was in one of the rubber suits we used for Aqua-Lung activities. It was 1954, and the wet suit was still unknown to most of us who needed to breathe underwater.

The reason we were out there at all was because we were scouting underwater locations for Walt Disney's *Twenty Thousand Leagues Under the Sea*. We had been told that the coral reef off Lyford's Cay was fantastically beautiful. And so it was. There were six of us, all told; in addition to me, there was Fred Zendar, water expert; Till Gabbani, underwater cameraman; two stuntmen/lifeguards; and a studio location manager. We'd looked all over the Bahamas, and this was by far the best spot.

A small rowboat with a tiny outboard motor drifted near us. Two young Bahamian men were aboard. They had some fishing gear with them, but they seemed much more interested in us than in fishing. Whenever we looked at them they gave us shy smiles. We offered them a couple of box lunches, so they came alongside.

We learned that they had come from the tiny town of Spanish Wells, on an island hardly bigger than the town, in the outermost region of the outermost islands. We had been there the week before, in fact, and were impressed by its remoteness and unique simplicity.

It was quite a trip for these two young men to make in that minuscule open boat. It had taken us a day and a half in our cruiser that could sleep eight. And we had come close to capsizing in a terrible storm. It was daunting even to contemplate how they made such a voyage. More than that, we wondered why. Surely not for the fishing. The sole occupation of Spanish Wells was fishing.

The English dialect spoken by the Bahamians is charming but almost completely unintelligible. These young fellows, coming from such a remote spot, far out of the main tourist stream, had a patois that was close to impenetrable.

"What are you doing so far from Spanish Wells?" I asked them. They replied in a musical, liquid mumble. I deciphered it to be that they'd come to their capital city, Nassau, to see a movie.

We were all very impressed. They had to be real movie fans to make such a tough journey just to see a movie. It would be interesting, I thought, to find out who they thought of as stars. "Did you ever hear of Kirk Douglas?" I asked them. Kirk was playing the lead in our film.

They looked puzzled. "Whoozee, mon?" they asked.

"An actor," I told them. "Okay," I went on, "how about James Mason?"

Their response surprised me. They became emotionally agitated. "No, no," they said vehemently. "We doan like im. He bahd mon . . . bahd mon."

I was shocked. Why should they react this way to James Mason?

"Why do you think he's such a bad man?" I asked them. "What did he do?"

"He kill dot mon," they shouted passionately. "Dot's whateedo. He bahd mon, bahd mon." They were pointing their forefingers at me as though I were somehow an accomplice to this murder.

It didn't make any sense to me. I turned to my friends for help. Freddie Zendar came up with the answer. "Oh, yeah," he said in his Swiss accent, "I saw that picture. Mason plays a real nasty villain and he kills one of the nice guys."

"It was only a movie," I explained to the natives in the little boat. "James Mason was only play-acting. He didn't kill anybody. It was only make-believe."

They weren't convinced and shook their heads in disbelief. "Bahd mon," they repeated, "bahd mon."

"Tell me," I asked them, "who's your favorite actor?"

Their reply was unhesitating and definite. "John Wayne!" they cried in unison. "John Wayne!"

Again I was impressed. This time it was not by the two men in the boat, but by the fame of John Wayne. At that moment I realized that there probably wasn't anyone in the whole world who didn't know what he looked and sounded like. These two came from the edge of nowhere, and they knew.

My curiosity made me ask one more question. "Why," I asked, "do you like John Wayne so much?"

They seemed astonished that I should ask a question with such an obvious answer. They looked at me with wide-eyed wonder and said, "Becauseetalkjuslikeusmon."

It was amazing, I thought, how people identified with this man. This was true stardom. This was Power with a capital P. Without even being aware of it, he could influence lives.

Little did I know how much.

Buddy Adler was head of production at Twentieth Century-Fox in 1959, and we were good friends. The reason for that was because I had played an important part in his reaching this exalted position. Four years earlier I had directed his, and my, first picture for the studio, *Violent Saturday*. Buddy was the producer. Besides being the first CinemaScope picture ever made for under $1 million, it was a damn good movie. Darryl Zanuck, the studio's big boss, was very taken with it, and we—Buddy and I—became sort of heroes.

The direct result of this minor triumph was that I was given a five-year directing contract and Buddy became Darryl's most favored producer. When Adler produced *Love Is a Many-Splendored Thing* the same year, he was well on his way to being Zanuck's successor, which is what happened when Darryl Zanuck left the studio to become an independent producer in 1956.

Critical acclaim and a successful movie are a combination that never hurt anybody, and it didn't hurt me. Since my first picture with Buddy I'd been blessed with a run of films with that winning combination. When I completed Richard Zanuck's first picture, *Compulsion*, in 1959, I knew I had made my best film by far. At this moment I was riding high, feeling good. Not a cloud in the sky. Top of the world, Mom.

Then Buddy Adler asked me to come to his office.

Buddy Adler's appearance ran counter to the popular stereotype of a studio chief. He was tall and thin, for a start. A shock of wavy white hair over a craggy, theatrically handsome face. Tonsorially immaculate, he had a gray look, instead of the usual Hollywood tan, as though he'd just left the barber's chair. Because of the white hair, the pale face, and the light color of his clothes, he always struck me as an *éminence grise*.

He gave me the usual warm and friendly greeting as I entered his office. Then he got right to the point. "Dick," he said, "I've got a wonderful assignment for you. A real plum."

"Sounds great. What is it?"

"The next John Wayne picture."

My heart gave a little jump. John Wayne! Doing a picture with John Wayne was important.

"Thank you, Buddy," I said. "That's wonderful. What's it about?"

"It's an action-adventure story called *North to Alaska*, and it's just great. It's terrific. You'll love it."

"When can I see the script?"

"There's no screenplay yet. The boys are working on a treatment and they're doing a sensational job."

"Well, I'd like to know a little more about it. Isn't there anything I can read?"

"Not really, but the boys have an office right across the hall. Why don't you go there and let them tell you the story. I told them you'd be coming over."

"Okay," I said. "Sure."

"Come back here when you're finished," he said as he saw me to the door. "It's a helluva story. You'll love it."

"The boys" were John Lee Mahin and Martin Rackin, two well-established writers who knew the Hollywood ropes like sailors on a clipper ship. Mahin, particularly, was an experienced pro. Marty Rackin was a real character. He was a fast-talking, breezy, nervous, con-man type who blinked his eyes a lot. You always had the feeling that he was some sort of a street-corner shell-game operator keeping an eye open for the cops.

Mahin sat slouched glumly in an armchair while Marty went into his pitch. He told a mundane story, which he embellished with appropriate gestures. If you weren't too critical or demanding it sort of held together, in its plodding way. At least I could follow it. But my mind was one jump ahead. I could see that this story was heading for a dead end, a cul-de-sac, at about the midway point. I was curious as to how they would resolve it.

When Rackin reached that very point, he stopped.

"What happens then?" I asked.

"That's as far as we've gotten."

"You've got a problem."

"No, no, no, no," he said, dismissing my remark with a wave of his hand. "We'll lick that. We've practically got it licked now, haven't we, John?" Mahin nodded slowly, contemplatively.

I thanked the boys and returned to Buddy's office.

"Well," he asked, "what do you think?"

"I think they've got a problem. Right in the middle of the second act."

"No, no, no, no," Buddy said. "The boys are very clever. Whatever it is, they'll lick it. Don't worry about it."

"I'll worry about it."

"Charlie Feldman wants you to have lunch with him at his house a week from today," he went on. "Capucine will be there, and he wants you to meet her. She's going to play the lead opposite Wayne."

I felt the control of my destiny slipping out of my hands.

"Sure," I said. "I'll be there."

Famous Artists was one of the most powerful talent agencies at that time, and Charles K. Feldman was its head. His connections were many and powerful; he represented Buddy Adler and was the shadow government of Twentieth Century-Fox, running it, unofficially, in tandem with Adler; he represented, among many other important stars, John Wayne; he was the agent and boyfriend of the very beautiful but not very talented French actress Capucine; and, by some strange coincidence, he represented the two writers, Rackin and Mahin. I was no stranger to Feldman, either, since I was also represented by his agency. Because of *Compulsion*, I was, in fact, the hot client of the week. It was the reason, obviously, that I was being given this prize John Wayne assignment.

I met Charlie at his home in Bel Air on the appointed date, and he filled me in on a few details before lunch.

"Wayne's got director approval," he told me, "but that's no problem. If Buddy and I recommend you I'm sure he'll go along."

"Great," I said.

"We haven't talked to him about you yet, because he's on his yacht somewhere in Mexico and it's hard to reach him. He calls us by radiophone every couple of days. Next time he does we'll get you set with him."

"That's fine, Charlie, but maybe you shouldn't rush things too much."

"What do you mean?"

"Don't get me wrong. I really appreciate your giving me this opportunity. It's a wonderful break. But I haven't decided whether I want to do this picture."

"Why not?" he asked, truly perplexed.

"Because I don't know what the story is. When I talked to Rackin and Mahin last week they were only able to tell me half of it. And they were hung up on a big plot point. How can I say I'll do a picture if I don't know what it's about?"

"Oh, well, that's no problem," he said with a laugh. "You be here ten o'clock tomorrow morning. I'll have the boys over and they'll tell you the story."

"The whole story?"

"Of course."

"From beginning to end?"

"The whole thing, and it's great. You'll love it. The boys have done a terrific job."

"Well, I'm certainly anxious to hear it."

"And after you've heard it, you can make up your mind about whether you want to do it."

"Sounds fair to me," I said. Indeed, it was fair. Couldn't be fairer.

Capucine made her appearance at that point. She was singular in name and beauty.

Our lunch was pleasant enough, if somewhat strained. It was supposed to be a "get acquainted" lunch, but there wasn't that much to get acquainted with. Her English, like her experience, was minimal. In fact, she spoke hardly at all. I felt that in her case still waters ran shallow. Although she was beautiful, there was no spark of personality to back it up. I wondered how this bland, rather shy beauty was going to portray a spirited prostitute in an Alaskan whorehouse opposite John Wayne. It worried me.

I came away from that luncheon with one strong impression, however.

Charlie was madly in love with her.

The following morning I arrived at Feldman's house promptly at ten o'clock. The boys had not yet arrived. Charlie greeted me effusively at the door and practically pulled me into the house.

"Congratulations!" he exclaimed. "Congratulations!"

"Thank you. What did I do?"

"You're all set with John Wayne. He's approved you, just like I said he would."

"But . . . but I don't understand," I stammered. "What about our agreement? I was supposed to hear the whole story before I made up my mind."

"Well, Duke phoned early this morning from the yacht, and I thought I'd save us all some time and trouble, so I told him all about you and he said okay. You're all set. Isn't that great?"

"No, it isn't great," I replied, steam beginning to rise from my collar. "It's terrible. What if I don't like the story? What if I don't want to do it?"

"You're committed now. You have to do it."

"I didn't make any commitment."

"The whole thing is academic anyway," Charlie said deprecatingly. "The boys will be here any minute, and you'll hear the story. They've licked all the problems. Believe me, you'll love it."

"I sincerely hope so," I said.

The boys arrived just about on cue. Charlie gave them the good news about my being approved by Duke Wayne and ushered the three of us into the study. Charlie had to make some phone calls and excused himself. As he closed the door he said, "Dick's concerned about the story, but I told him he's got nothing to worry about. Right?"

"Oh, sure, sure, Charlie," Rackin said with a nervous half laugh, his eyes blinking even more than usual. "It's great."

Mahin assumed his pose of deep contemplation on the sofa, and Marty Rackin went into his act. He started at the beginning and told the same story I'd heard the week before, with the same gestures.

Inexorably we came to the dreaded spot in the middle of the second act. That's when Marty stopped talking.

"What happens next?" I queried.

"We don't know. We've got a bit of a problem right there."

"It's the same problem you had last week."

"Yeah, but we're working on it. We've almost got it licked, haven't we, Johnnie?"

Mahin slowly nodded his head in agreement.

I was beginning to feel sick. I'd been lied to, deceived, manipulated. It was unbelievable. It was also clear that Charles K. Feldman, the dean of agents, the power behind the throne, the mastermind of the whole project, had never even heard the story.

Charlie was waiting expectantly as we came out of the study.

"Well," he asked, "what do you think?"

"I think the story is in the same trouble it was in a week ago," I answered. "Nothing's been solved. Nothing's been licked. And I still don't know what the hell this story is about."

Charlie elaborately lit a big cigar.

"I told you not to set me with Wayne before I'd made up my mind," I went on. "Well, I've made up my mind. Next time you speak to him you can tell him that I'm not doing the picture."

"I can't do that," Charlie said, taking a long pull on the cigar.

"Why not?"

"If he hears that you don't want to do it, we're liable to lose him."

"Are you saying that John Wayne would drop out of a movie because I don't want to do it?" I asked incredulously. "He never even heard of me until an hour ago."

"No, it isn't that, exactly. You see, Wayne gave us a commitment to do this picture, but he only knows the title. We never told him the story. He's been going along on good faith and trust."

I was astounded. Wayne hadn't heard the story either.

"If he hears you don't want to do it, he'll become suspicious that there's something wrong with it and will want to see the script."

"What script?" I asked, bewildered.

"There isn't any. You know that. But he thinks we're almost finished with it. We've been keeping him happy with reports about how well it's going. If he finds out there isn't any screenplay, we'll lose him." He produced a large cloud of cigar smoke. "And I can tell you one thing," he went on, "we're not going to lose him." There was an edge to his voice that chilled me.

I looked at the three of them sitting there. Here were dedicated exponents of the saying "To make a living, craftiness is better than learnedness," practicing their philosophy with a vengeance. The two writers may have been forced into this manner of survival by their own ineptness. Charlie Feldman didn't know there was any other way. He was no Zanuck, or Goldwyn, or Cohn. He didn't have their theatrical instincts, their sense of story values. He knew nothing of scripts, or construction, or character development, and didn't want to. But he was calling the shots at Fox, manipulating Buddy Adler's strings. And all with a professional, confident cynicism. He thought nothing of this shabby deceit of his good friend and top client who had placed his trust in him. It was good business, and no rising director with some cockamamie sense of ethics was going to interfere with it.

It seemed pointless to carry the discussion any farther. Charlie Feldman was not about to give me any tea and sympathy.

"I'd better have a talk with Buddy Adler," I said.

"That's a good idea," he agreed.

Buddy gave me tea and sympathy when I got to his office. He was very understanding.

"Charlie shouldn't have jumped the gun like that," he told me. "It puts us all in a bad spot."

"Particularly me," I said. "I wouldn't want Wayne to think I don't want to do the picture because I don't like him. I don't need him as an enemy."

Buddy nodded in understanding.

"I know how you feel about the story," he said, "and you're right. We do have a problem." He paused for a moment, then he said, "Will you do me a favor? A big, personal favor?"

"If I can, of course I will."

"Work on it with the boys. You're very good at story construction, and they need all the help they can get. Will you do this for me?"

"Okay, Buddy, if that's what you want. But that doesn't mean I'm committed to doing the picture."

"No. But maybe you'll feel differently about it by the time you're finished."

"Maybe."

"There's one other thing."

"Yes?"

"Wayne is due back from Mexico in a couple of weeks. If we can show him a completed treatment and some pages of screenplay, we can keep him on the hook."

"If you say so."

"The point is you and the boys will have to work seven days a week to do it. You'll have to give up your weekends."

"Okay. I'll do my best."

"I know you will. Thanks."

If "What Kind of Fool Am I?" had been written at that time, a heavenly chorus would have been humming it in the background.

My marathon meetings with the boys didn't go well at all. The sticking point remained stuck. We approached it from every angle. We thrashed it out over and over again. I made suggestions they couldn't accept. Rightfully. They made suggestions that I blew out of the water.

We hammered at it twelve hours a day. Sent out for lunch. Spent Saturday and Sunday in the office. No progress. I knew it was hopeless, but I never said so to them. I worked as hard as they did to find a solution.

Toward the end of the second week Adler asked me to come to his office. I wasn't at all prepared for what he had to say.

"You know Wayne is liable to show up almost any time now, and you're not making any progress."

"I know."

"The boys tell me it's your fault."

It took a moment for the words to register. When they did, I was staggered.

"My fault?"

"That's right. They say you're putting up roadblocks all the time. Not letting them get ahead on the story. You throw out every suggestion they come up with. You're the reason they're not making any headway."

I sat there with my mouth open in shock. It was treachery, pure and simple. The Hollywood stab in the back in all its sleazy glory.

I was boiling.

"Those bastards are blaming me for their own inadequacies," I said angrily. "They're the writers. They should come up with the solutions."

"Here's what I want you to do," Buddy said. "I want you to go home and not come into the studio. I don't want you to work with the boys anymore. When the script is finished we'll send it to you."

Buddy was sitting behind his big desk in an oversize leather chair. I walked over and faced him. "Don't bother sending me any script," I said. "I'm not doing this picture."

"Are you refusing?"

This was dangerous territory. I was under contract. If I refused outright there could be serious consequences. Studios could do nasty things to people who flatly refused to do what they were told. They could put you on suspension and stop paying you and not let you work for anyone else. Things like that. The trick was to refuse without actually, legally, using the word. "No," I said. "I'm not refusing. But I'm not going to do the picture, anyhow."

"How are you going to do that?"

"Because I'm going to get very sick."

"I'll get you a doctor."

We stared at each other for a moment.

"I'm going to come in here and throw up on your desk."

"I'll wipe it off."

Obviously I wasn't going to win this exchange. There was nothing left but for me to go home.

When I came out of Adler's office I crossed the hall to where the boys were working. I walked past the secretary to their office door and stuck my head in.

"Hey, fellas." They both looked up. "You're a couple of pricks," I said, and left.

By the time I got home I was seething with a fine mixture of anger, indignation, and outrage. I needed help. I needed advice. I needed an agent.

Charlie Feldman, as head of Famous Artists, was theoretically my agent. Some agent. I wasn't about to turn to him for help. The man at the agency who was my personal representative and close friend was Phil Gersh. Formally my agent there had been Ray Stark, but he'd wandered off to different and greener pastures. Gersh replaced him and was his match in every way. Aggressive, knowledgeable, he seemed to have an inside line to every studio and producer in town. A bantam fighting cock, he'd kill for his client if he had to. I phoned him and gave him the tawdry details.

Phil was as disgusted by what had happened as I was.

"You really want to get off this picture?" he asked after a moment's Machiavellian thought.

"You bet. I'll do anything to get off."

"Well, I know one way. It's dangerous, but it's sure-fire."

"What is it? Tell me what to do."

"You know how nuts Charlie is about Capucine?"

"Of course."

"All you have to do is to call Buddy Adler and tell him you don't think she's right for the part. You'll be off the picture in two minutes."

"You really think that'll work?"

"Guaranteed. Buddy will immediately tell Charlie, Charlie will explode, and you'll be off the picture."

"I'll do anything."

I followed Gersh's advice.

In two minutes I was off the picture.

In three minutes I was on suspension.

North to Alaska eventually got made. Henry Hathaway, yet another Feldman client, directed it. I don't know if they ever solved the story problem because I never got around to seeing the picture. The reviews, while bland for a John Wayne movie, all mentioned a slam-bang barroom brawl that Hathaway must have incorporated. Maybe it distracted the audience enough so the hole in the middle of the second act wasn't all that noticeable.

By the time the picture was released I had already moved my family to Europe and determined to live there permanently. I'd had enough of the Rackins, the Mahins, the Feldmans, and the Adlers. The uprooting of my family and the changing of the whole course of my career was directly linked to the John Wayne episode. He had traumatically changed my life, and I'd never even met the man.

That was yet to come.

The Castellana Hilton, in Madrid, was unquestionably the dirtiest hotel in the chain. I hated every minute I had to stay there. But that was where everyone in the ill-fated Samuel Bronston Company stayed. Besides, the Ritz didn't take in movie people. No matter who. Not even John Wayne. Which was probably why he, too, was staying at the Dirty Hilton.

Samuel Bronston was one of the first independent producers of big-budget, American-style movies in Europe. John Wayne and I were both working for the Bronston Company, but on different projects. He was doing *The Circus Story*, and I was preparing *Nightrunners of Bengal*.

It was now 1963, and I'd been living in Europe four years. My home was in Rome, but for this film I had to commute to Madrid every two weeks. In all the many visits to Madrid I'd made in the past several months, though, our paths never crossed. Whenever I was in town Wayne was either away on location, or shooting nights, or something.

Until one night.

I was having a predinner martini in the lobby of the hotel at about ten o'clock one evening with Phil Yordan, Sid Harmon, and several other people connected with the Bronston Company. It was all very casual and unplanned. We were trying to decide where to eat.

If we'd made up our minds a minute earlier, I would have missed him. But we didn't. The elevator doors opened at the other end of the room and out stepped Sam Bronston and his wife and big John Wayne and his beautiful wife, Pilar. I hoped they'd continue on out the front door. No such luck.

Sam Bronston saw us immediately and herded his group over to where we were sitting. Greetings were given and introductions made. There were now about twelve of us, so the names passed around pretty quickly and confusingly. Duke Wayne and I finally shook hands. It was a moment of no apparent significance to him.

Everyone found a seat. Drinks were ordered, peanuts eaten, conversation flowed easily with a lot of hearty laughter from Duke. I began to relax. There was absolutely no sign of recognition of my name on his part. Why should there be? He'd probably heard it maybe twice, four years ago. Since then he'd doubtless met thousands of people.

The chitchat continued for another hour. We were all having a good time. Wayne was charming and pleasant and paid no more attention to me than to anyone else. I seemed to be just another face in the crowd, and grateful for it.

At the fashionable hour for dining in Spain, eleven o'clock, Sam Bronston suggested we all have dinner together in the hotel. We were led to a large, round table by the *maître d'* and placed ourselves around it haphazardly, with no particular seating arrangement in mind. As luck would have it, I wound up sitting next to Duke Wayne.

I had just sat down and was unfolding my napkin when he turned to me, a pleasant smile on his face.

"So you're the fella who didn't want to make a movie with me," he said.

I froze. He had known who I was all along. Those bastards in Hollywood had really done it to me. But good. They had given Wayne precisely the impression I didn't want him to have—that I didn't want to do the picture not because of the story, but because of him.

"No, Duke," I replied, meeting his stare. "I'm the fellow who didn't want to make a bad John Wayne movie."

Duke laughed. He wasn't acting. It was a sincere laugh. "You were right," he said. "I shouldn't have made that picture, either."

We came away from dinner liking each other a lot.

A nice relationship developed over the next few weeks. If he spotted me going through the lobby, I'd get a shout and a wave to join him. We managed to have dinner together a couple of times before I had to leave.

When I left for Rome I felt I'd made a friend.

But there was a postscript to the Wayne in Spain experience.

Nine years later, in Hollywood, I was offered another John Wayne movie to direct. This time I liked the project. Katharine Hepburn was the costar, and the highly esteemed Hal Wallis would produce. The story was good, too. With a combination like that, what was not to like? I accepted with pleasure.

Just as before, Wayne had director approval. I couldn't see any problem there. Our little misunderstanding had been cleared up, hadn't it? We were on friendly terms, weren't we? He did smile upon me, and shake my hand, and break bread with me, didn't he? Surely his approval was a foregone conclusion. Wrong.

Wayne would have none of me. He adamantly refused to give his approval.

Hal Wallis couldn't understand it. He tried over and over to get him to change his mind. Wayne wouldn't budge. Nor would he give a reason. Hal was forced to withdraw his offer. It would have been an important assignment for me. I'd had my heart set on doing it.

John Wayne's revenge. It had taken fourteen years, but he got it. I had broken an unwritten law: No varmint turns down a John Wayne picture. When you do that, pard, you're hurtin' his feelin's and woundin' his pride. And there's no forgivin' that. Ever.

I was the victim of a massive case of pique. It was petty. It was small. It was mean. It was Duke Wayne.

Once again my life and my career had been influenced by this man I'd rarely seen and hardly knew. My instincts about him had been right, though.

This was not someone you wanted to offend.

II

Sid Rogell, the tough-as-nails head of RKO's B picture unit, could have squashed me like a bug underfoot when I first went to work at the studio. There wouldn't be enough left of me to scrape up and send back to New York. But he didn't do that. For whatever reason, Rogell took a liking to me and became my friend. More than a friend, my mentor. I became his protégé, and he turned me from a Yale Drama School graduate into a Hollywood survivor. It is why I am sometimes called, by those I have worked with, The Iron Butterfly.

Every day, without fail, I'd get a phone call from him at ten-thirty in the morning. "Shall we inspect the property?" he'd ask. I'd meet him outside my office and we'd walk for coffee to a tiny diner that was parked just outside the studio auto gate. Then we'd make a tour of the stages. I sat in on almost every conference he had in his office and attended every production meeting.

Production, or budget, meetings consisted of the producer, the director, and the heads of every department, along with their first assistants, sitting around a long table facing Rogell at the head. I sat in a chair to his right and a little behind him, like a royal consort, and never opened my mouth. I was just there to observe. The point of the meeting was for the director to discuss every single scene in the picture, how he was going to shoot it, how much time it would take. Wardrobe. How many changes for each actor? Will any get torn or dirty? How many replacements will you need? Extras. How many men, how many women? Ages? How about kids? What sex and age? You want animals? Horses, dogs, cats? How many of each? How long will you use them? A zillion questions, all of them needing instant answers.

Rogell's job was adversarial. He was there to challenge the director on anything that seemed superfluous or extravagant. A camera crane? What for? Six costume changes for the leading lady? She gets three and you can double them. A hundred people for a mob scene? On that set? Shit, you can do it with thirty-five and you don't need them for two days. You can get rid of them in one. Who the fuck do you think you are, deMille? Rogell's decisions were law, and there was no appeal.

The first one of these production meetings Rogell took me to was a jolt. Sid would time his entrance so that everyone was seated and waiting for him. Not for long, maybe two minutes. Just enough to make a dramatic entrance. Rogell was too conscious of the cost of time to spend more than was absolutely necessary. I was not only excited about the idea of attending a production meeting, but also this one, for me, was something special. The director of the picture about to be dissected was Harold Clurman. For theater people, this was a name to reckon with. Along with Cheryl Crawford and Lee Strasberg, he was a founder of the fabled Group Theater. For drama school students he was one of the legitimate theater's gurus. A veritable icon. It would be an honor to be in the same room with him.

Rogell made his entrance, sat down, and said, "Well, the first thing we're going to do today is kick the director right in the balls." My guru? My icon? "You don't have forty days to shoot the picture. You've got thirty."

My eyes were fixed on Clurman. He had no reaction whatsoever. He just stared at Rogell. "Scene one," Sid read from the pile of breakdown sheets in front of him, without looking up. "Exterior. Newsstand. Night. Rain." Now he looked up at Clurman. "Rain? You know how much fucking rain costs? You know about special-effects guys, and the rigging, and the time it takes? What do you want rain for?"

"For the mood," Clurman answered. "It's the opening of the picture."

"Fuck the mood. No rain. Now, how many people do we see in the street?"

"Wait a minute. Just a minute," Clurman said, holding up his hand. Here it comes, I thought. A big fight, for sure. You can't just run roughshod over such a distinguished theater man. "Okay, no rain," he said. "How about dust? Lots of dust blowing everywhere. Can we afford dust?"

My guru. My icon.

Those production meetings showed Rogell's pleasanter side.

Meetings in his office with writers brought out the worst in him. A writer needed a black belt in karate just to get through one of those meetings. It wasn't that he hated all writers. He treated fairly decent writers with great respect. It was the second-raters, the hacks, who infuriated him. However, since most of the writers his unit could afford were not all that great, there were very few meetings where he didn't lose his temper, sometimes violently.

I was in his office one day when a writer who was working on one of my films showed up. He had delivered his completed screenplay the night before to me and, since Sid was away from his office for the moment, to Rogell's secretary. Sid and I had read it and we were underwhelmed. The writer, a man of some modest name in the field, bounced into the office. "Well," he asked brightly, "did you read the screenplay I delivered?"

Rogell picked the script up off his desk with his thumb and forefinger and held it away from him as though it had an overpowering stench. "If you're talking about this piece of shit," he said, "yeah, I read it."

The writer made a terrible mistake. He got angry. "What do you mean, 'shit'?" he sputtered. "I delivered a goddamn good screenplay."

"You shouldn't even be allowed to deliver milk to somebody's doorstep, you idiot," Sid yelled, rising from his desk and coming toward him threateningly. The writer was a skinny little wretch. Rogell was twice his width.

"I demand to know what's wrong with it," the wretch shouted.

Rogell grabbed him by his collar at the nape of the neck. "Get out of my office, you son-of-a-bitch," he roared, "you're fired." Then he frog-walked him to the door and threw him out.

One Christmas Eve Sid asked me to stop by his office for a traditional holiday drink. We had just toasted each other and taken our first sip when the intercom buzzed. Sid answered it, and his secretary announced the presence of a fairly well-known writer in the outer office. He told her to send him in. The writer entered the office beaming.

"Sid," he said, "thanks for asking me to come up, but I can't stay. I just got a call from the hospital. My wife's had a baby. A girl!"

"Great!" said Sid, coming over to shake his hand. "Congratulations! How about a quick drink?"

"I'd love to," the writer responded, "but I've got to get right over there."

Rogell was very understanding. "Sure, I know how it is. You be on your way." He slapped his shoulder and led him toward the door. "And give my best to your wife and daughter."

"You bet," said the writer as he left. "And, hey, Merry Christmas to you both!"

"Merry Christmas!" we echoed back.

As soon as the door shut, Rogell turned to me. "That son-of-a-bitch!" he said from behind clenched teeth. "That dirty son-of-a-bitch!" I looked at him with raised eyebrows. "I didn't ask him up here for a drink," he explained irritably. "I wanted him to come up here so that I could fire him. How can I do that after he tells me his wife's had a baby on Christmas Eve?" I tried to look compassionate about the problem caused by this thoughtless writer. Then he went on. "*Now* I'll have to wait until after New Year's, goddamn it."

RKO was known as the biggest small studio or the smallest big studio in Hollywood. That wasn't always so. It was formerly known, in 1926, as Film Booking Offices of America, or FBO, and boasted such stars as Anna Q. Nilsson, Warner Baxter, and Irene Rich. The owner was Joseph P. Kennedy, father of John, Robert, and Edward. At best, FBO was a small-time outfit. Until sound. The "talkies" hit the industry with a monumental impact. Small movie companies that were unable to meet the large financial demands of converting to sound were wiped out. But luck, Providence, call it what you will, intervened in the case of FBO. David Sarnoff, president of Radio Corporation of America, or RCA, was looking for a way to introduce his newly developed sound system into the movie industry. Since Western Electric had gotten in first and sold its own sound system to all the big studios, Sarnoff wasn't left with too many choices. He chose FBO and bought a large interest in it. FBO now had considerable financial strength but lacked one essential playing card: theaters in which to showcase their new "squawkies," as they were sometimes called. The Keith-Albee-Orpheum (KAO) circuit of seven hundred vaudeville theaters seemed just the ticket. On October 23, 1928, a giant merger among RCA, FBO, and KAO was confirmed and, with a bow toward Sarnoff, the official name became Radio-Keith-Orpheum, or RKO.

When I arrived in Hollywood there were lots of stars with deals at RKO. Walk on to any sound stage and you'd probably see Bing Crosby, Ingrid Bergman, Cary Grant, John Wayne, Fred Astaire, Ginger Rogers, you name them. When it came time for me to direct my first picture, *Child of Divorce*, in 1946, I got as my star

Sharyn Moffett. It could have been worse. She was a ten-year-old actress the studio hoped would turn into a Shirley Temple or a Margaret O'Brien, a metamorphosis devoutly to be wished. Actually she was a good little actress, better than most of the adults around her. The chrysalis, however, stubbornly refused to turn into a butterfly. She never did fly.

The movie turned out remarkably well. In their book *The RKO Story*, Richard B. Jewell and Vernon Harbin comment: "It is seldom that one finds an RKO picture whose only flaw was an excess of artistic integrity." As a reward for displaying so much artistic integrity, I was given a second Sharyn Moffett vehicle to direct. This one was an unabashedly sentimental potboiler about a small girl and her dog named Banjo, which was also the title of the picture. Very little room for artistic integrity here. I took a trip to New York when the picture was finished shooting and the editor was working on the first assembly of the film. To cheer me up he took a scene from the picture, cut it up into dozens of celluloid banjo picks, and mailed them to me in an envelope with a note, "This is the best I could do with this scene." It made me feel really good.

Not many of the B pictures churned out by the Rogell unit were ever previewed. They were manufactured and dumped into the theaters owned by RKO. It didn't make any difference how good or how bad they were, they had their home on the lower half of a double bill guaranteed. The only screening they got before release was in a projection room at the studio for Rogell and a few other people. I attended all of these screenings sitting next to him. About halfway through, he'd fall asleep. Either the lights coming on, or the obligatory noisy chase and shoot-out at the end of the picture would wake him. Sid would stand, say two words—"Ship it"—and leave.

Occasionally, though, a Rogell picture that wasn't run-of-the-mill would get a public preview in a regular movie house. These were always held at the Pantages Theater in downtown Los Angeles. The audience there was considered to be typical of the moviegoing public for which these low-budget pictures were intended, not too sophisticated or discriminating. We previewed *Child of Divorce* there and it played beautifully. My wife, Mickey, told me that after the showing all the usherettes were in the ladies' room, crying.

Banjo was supposed to be previewed at the Pantages, but at the last minute Rogell came down with a bad back. He was in a lot of pain, too much to make the long trip to downtown L.A. He de-

creed, therefore, that the picture would be previewed at the Bruin
Theater in Westwood Village, which was less than five minutes
from his home.

I had no objection to this because I hadn't been in Hollywood
long enough to know any better. Westwood Village was the location
of UCLA. It was a "college town," and everyone, except me, knew
what that meant: pseudosophisticated, smart-alecky, supercritical
audiences. Major studios always previewed their biggest, most star-
laden superproductions in the Village. There were only two theaters
there, the Bruin and the Village (there are now about a dozen), and
when they had a preview they'd put a big sign on a stand in front of
the theater that read "MAJOR STUDIO PREVIEW TO-
NIGHT," and would hike the price of admission by 50 percent.
Rogell should have known better, but the pain must have clouded
his mind.

After my good experience with the preview of my first movie, I
was looking forward to the second. *Banjo*, I felt, was an audience
picture. The crowd at the Pantages surely would have loved it, so
why not everywhere else? Mickey and I were in a festive mood and
decided to splurge. Before going to the theater we went to the
Brown Derby, in Beverly Hills, for dinner.

The restaurant was crowded, our table wasn't quite ready, and
the *maître d'* asked us to have a seat at the bar for a few minutes. We
found two empty stools next to an elderly, white-haired, dignified
gentleman and sat down. Our spirits were high, our mood was
merry, and small things made us laugh. After a minute or so, the
elderly gentleman turned toward us. "Excuse me," he said with a
smile. "I don't mean to be intrusive, but it's so nice to see young
people having a good time. I'm really enjoying watching you. May I
buy you a drink?"

We thanked him, accepted his offer, and he motioned the bar-
tender. After we'd ordered, he said, "You seem so happy about
something. I'd like to know what it is."

"Well, I'm a movie director and we're having a preview tonight
of my second picture."

"Why, that's wonderful. I can understand how you feel. I used
to be in that business myself."

"Really? That's very interesting." I scanned his face. He looked
vaguely familiar, but I couldn't place him. "Just what part of the
business were you in?"

"Oh," he replied, depreciatingly, "I was known for my voice."

For his voice. An actor? A singer? Again, I studied his face, but it revealed nothing. "Would you mind telling me, sir, what your name is?"

"D. W. Griffith."

And indeed it was. One of the series of shorts that I made for Pathé News before coming to Hollywood was called *Flicker Flashbacks*. It had to do with movies made in the very early days of picturemaking, and D. W. Griffith appeared as a young actor in some of them. The face clicked into place in my mind. Narrow and boney, with a patrician, hooked nose and piercing eyes, it was he, all right. But he wasn't famous for his acting roles. Griffith, in the early days, was a giant among filmmakers, perhaps the most famous director who ever lived. His films, such as *Birth of a Nation* and *Intolerance*, took the world by storm. The name D. W. Griffith became synonymous with the movie industry. If ever there was a legendary figure in motion pictures, it was this man.

When we left him to go to our table, we shook hands and he wished us well with the preview. I was walking on air. *D. W. Griffith*. It was an omen, a sign. Meeting D. W. Griffith on the night of a preview! It could only mean one thing: good luck. Tonight was going to be our night.

There was a big crowd in front of the Bruin Theater in Westwood Village. The big sign was in place. MAJOR STUDIO PREVIEW TONIGHT. As was customary, neither the name of the picture nor the studio that produced it were announced. The audience was paying extra and going in blind, not knowing what to expect.

The inside of the theater was jammed with college kids. Completely sold out. Everyone was talking and moving about. There was an air of excited anticipation. We found the roped-off section near the back of the house where our seats were and sat down next to Sid Rogell.

The lights dimmed. The audience settled down and grew hushed. The curtains parted from the screen and on came the RKO Radio Pictures trademark, a slowly turning globe of the world, with a huge radio pylon on the North Pole sending out Morse code signals that took the shape of lightning streaks.

As though it had been organized, the audience let out a groan. This was not one of the major majors, but the least of them. RKO wasn't good enough for the sophisticated college crowd. Then the titles started: RKO Radio Pictures Presents: (dissolve to) BANJO. (A bigger groan from the audience, but they still had hope. Dissolve to) starring SHARYN MOFFETT. The audience went mad. Pandemonium broke out. The entire audience rose to its feet and started pushing toward the aisles. They were screaming "NO! NO!" at the screen. The ushers, three abreast, rushed into the aisles yelling, "You can't get your money back after you've seen the title!" and started pushing the surging crowd back. It was utter chaos. Cursing, yelling, screams, shouts. They were a furious lynch mob looking for a victim.

It took several hectic minutes before they sat down again to watch the picture. It was the fashion in those days to greet each star or popular actor's first appearance in a preview movie with a round of applause. This film would be no exception. Every actor, no matter how minuscule the part, received a huge hand (and a laugh). Jacqueline White and Walter Reed, the adult leads, got applause like they had never gotten before and would never get again. And Sharyn Moffett got an absolute ovation.

Sid Rogell leaned over to me and whispered, "Don't worry about it. It'll take them a few minutes before they get caught up in the story. Then they'll settle down and be quiet." I thought for a moment he might be right. After about ten minutes there seemed to be a lull, they were almost quiet. Then a Western Union boy appeared on the screen, to deliver a telegram. Wild cheers and applause for the Western Union boy. A moment later there was a close shot of a bird in a bush. Another ovation, the kind reserved for maybe Greta Garbo. They talked back to the screen. They answered lines of dialogue with their own. When the scary swamp scenes came on, they went out of their minds with screaming mock fright.

When the picture was over the audience stood up en masse, hissing and booing the screen. They walked up the aisles backward, still hissing and booing the screen. I hid the velvet rope that blocked off our seats in the hope of not calling attention to ourselves and tried not to look like I was part of the studio people. Nobody paid any attention to us. They were too busy hissing and booing and walking out backward.

No one escaped the disaster of *Banjo* unscathed. Sharyn Moffett got fired; the dog who played Banjo got fired; the producer, Lilly Hayward, got fired. I was the only one who didn't, because I was under studio contract. But it was several months before Rogell would even speak to me or before we started to "inspect the property" again.

If only we had previewed at the Pantages. But then, Sid Rogell had a bad back. Still, I couldn't complain. I did get to meet D. W. Griffith, a lucky omen if ever there was one.

After the fiasco of *Banjo* it wasn't too difficult for Stanley Kramer to arrange a loan-out for my services from RKO. Sid Rogell was only too glad to get rid of me for a while. Stanley Kramer was not then *Stanley Kramer*. He was a brand-new, independent producer about to make his first movie, *So This Is New York*. It was to be an avant-garde, sardonic comedy based on Ring Lardner's book *The Big Town*. The screenplay was cowritten by his partner, Carl Foreman, and Herbert Baker, a young, rotund schoolmate of mine from Yale. Kramer had seen my first picture, *Child of Divorce*, was very impressed, and with Baker's enthusiastic urging offered me the job. Naturally, I leapt at it.

The team of Kramer and Foreman was a good one. They were both in their midthirties, well-educated, fiercely socially conscious, had forceful personalities, and had put in lengthy apprenticeships in the industry. Kramer started as a swing-gang laborer on a studio back lot and finally became a film editor. Foreman had put in time doing circus and carnival exploitation and free-lance writing. They had paid their dues before forming a company and becoming independent producers. There was a lot of Spencer Tracy about Kramer. He had the same weatherbeaten, bushy eyebrowed look and even sounded somewhat like him. Years later he directed Tracy in several movies and almost turned into a Tracy clone. Foreman had a more rawboned look. He was about six feet tall, with a rough, pockmarked face, wide features, and prematurely thinning hair. They were two terrific guys.

When *So This Is New York* was finished and I had returned to RKO serfdom, there was a long hiatus for the Kramer Company, and Carl needed a job. He had an idea for an original story called *The Clay Pigeon*, and I convinced Rogell to hire him to develop it into a screenplay.

Carl and I both lived in the San Fernando Valley at that time, so we drove to and from work together every day. It was on one of those drives that Carl came up with an interesting suggestion. He said, "Look, since we have to spend almost two hours a day in the car, why don't we use that time to develop a story idea I've got in mind?" I said, "Sure, why not?" and I asked what the idea was. It was, he told me, about a small-town sheriff who had exactly one hour to prepare for a showdown with some killers who were coming to get him. So over the next eight weeks, Carl and I developed the story and the characters for *High Noon*. (Carl had forgotten to mention that his idea was based on a story that had been published in *Collier's*. It's strange how ego sometimes gets in the way of memory.)

When the script of *The Clay Pigeon* was finished, Rogell called me into his office. "This is pretty poor stuff," he said, gazing into an apparently clouded crystal ball. "I don't think your friend is going to amount to much as a writer." He then proceeded to replace the future author of such screenplays as *High Noon*, *The Bridge on the River Kwai*, and *The Guns of Navarone* with Lilly Hayward, the author of *Banjo*. My RKO contract eventually kept me from directing *High Noon*, although I did get to do *The Clay Pigeon*. It was not what could be called a good trade-off.

III

Two topics in 1947 caught and held public interest. One was the start of the House Un-American Activities Committee's frightful investigation into Communist infiltration of Hollywood. The other was Howard Hughes.

Five years earlier, on November 16, 1942, the Kaiser-Hughes Corporation entered into an $18 million contract with the federal government to build three flying boats to aid the war effort. They were to be the biggest-by-far aircraft ever built, designed to carry seven hundred passengers or sixty tons of equipment each, and, to save precious war materials, were to be made entirely of plywood.

Now the war was over, the money spent. Only one plane had been built, and it had not yet flown. The press dubbed it the *Spruce Goose*. The government, convinced it would never fly, dubbed it a dodo, and on July 28, 1947, the Special Senate Committee Investigating the National Defense Program began an inquiry. The contrast between this investigation and the obscenity being conducted by the House Un-American Activities Committee couldn't have been greater. On the one hand you had writers, actors, and producers being browbeaten and humiliated; on the other, you had a dashing, handsome multimillionaire hero, a flamboyant moviemaker, a test pilot who held the land speed record, the transcontinental speed record, the around-the-world speed record, who had survived three highly publicized, spectacular airplane crashes, making an absolute hash, a laughingstock, out of his interrogators. It warmed the cockles of the heart and delighted the public.

Still, as much as everyone was rooting for Hughes, a basic skepticism remained about the *Spruce Goose*. Would it fly? It was a subject of general discussion and debate. How could anything with a tail eight stories high, a wingspan longer than a football field, a hull thirty feet tall, and two hundred eighteen feet long and weighing four hundred thousand pounds possibly fly? There was a lot of doubtful head-shaking.

The head-shaking, as well as the Senate investigation, came to rather an abrupt halt when, on November 2 of that year, with Hughes at the controls, the *Spruce Goose* flew. It didn't fly high and it didn't fly far but, by God, it flew. It was supposed to be a demonstration taxi run for the press, but Hughes apparently couldn't resist the temptation. He lifted it about seventy feet above the water and flew it for a mile.

Just a little over six months after the Special Senate Committee Investigating the National Defense Program called an embarrassed halt to its hearings, Robert Wise and I were in Sid Rogell's office at RKO. It was early evening of May 10, 1948, and we were comfortably seated, sipping an end-of-day scotch before going home, when the desk phone rang. Sid answered it and sat there listening, expressionless. It didn't seem like much of a conversation because after only a few seconds he said, "Okay. Thanks," and hung up.

"Well, gentlemen," he said to us, leaning back in his swivel chair, "Howard Hughes has just bought the studio."

Bob and I stared at him for a long, unbelieving moment. There was only one thing I could think of to say. It was the first thing you usually thought of whenever Hughes's name was mentioned.

"He'll never get it off the ground."

Unfortunately, I was right.

Whenever new management takes over any company, whatever the field, a shiver runs up the spine of all the employees. What ran up our spines was a shock wave that registered 6.2 on the Richter scale. The ordinary workers, the grips, electricians, plasterers, secretaries, as well as management were naturally concerned about their jobs. N. Peter Rathvon, the president of the studio, issued a calming, reassuring statement that Mr. Hughes was not considering any wholesale replacements or firings. Those on the creative side, however, were filled with anxiety and trepidation, for Hughes's reputation as an interferer, a meddler, a tamperer went before him like a bad sore throat precedes a nasty cold.

Dore Schary was the head of production at the studio and doing a wonderful job. He had put exciting and challenging projects into work, such as *Crossfire*, *The Boy with Green Hair*, and *I Remember Mama;* had filled the roster with the most promising new talent in Hollywood; and, in the short time he'd been there, had made RKO the second most important studio in the ranks of the Big Six. However, fears about Hughes were anything but unfounded.

On June 30, barely more than six weeks after Hughes took over, Dore Schary resigned. By the end of summer more than seven hundred employees had been fired.

At the time of the takeover I was working with Carl Foreman on *The Clay Pigeon,* a small picture for the Rogell unit. We were driving to the studio together one morning when Carl said, "Did you see the Howard Hughes press announcement in today's paper?" I hadn't. "Well," said Carl, "he says he's going to devote the entire output of the studio to films of sex and violence."

"I've got a great title for his first movie," I said.

"What's that?"

"*Bang!* **Bang!**"

While the studio was falling apart all around us, nothing seemed to affect the B picture unit. We steamed right along churning out our little movies with no interference from anyone. Others were not so lucky. Hughes's meddling was becoming intolerable. He seemed to be obsessed with changing the ends of pictures, earning himself the reputation of being an anal erotic. He screened every film made in the studio in a private projection room off the lot. This was his privilege as well as his duty. However, since he had no sense of time, the films sat in his projection booth for months before he got around to looking at them. Independent producers were getting fed up and began leaving the studio at an alarming rate. Forty-nine pictures had been planned for 1949. Only twelve were made, three of which were mine. Single-handedly I had directed 25 percent of RKO's entire output.

Then, in 1950, a miracle happened. I made a good picture. It was more than a good picture. It was really kind of terrific. *The Narrow Margin* was shot in thirteen days, and everyone who saw it at the studio was convinced it was my breakthrough film. When it was eventually released, *Time* magazine devoted its entire Cinema section to a rave review and a long, in-depth feature article about Stanley Rubin, the producer, and me, calling us Hollywood's bright new hopes for the future.

The picture was so good, in fact, that it finally came to the attention of Howard Hughes, who promptly put it in his projection booth, where it sat for more than a year.

IV

During the period when my picture disappeared into the black hole of Howard Hughes's projection room, some major events took place at RKO. One of them really rocked me. Sid Rogell got fired. Hughes had designated him to be the executive producer for the entire studio, which meant he was one of the very few people who had direct contact with Hughes. It also meant that Hughes, as was his practice, would call him on the phone at two or three in the morning to discuss business. Sid didn't take kindly to this. He had a notoriously short wick to begin with, and it wasn't too long before he blew up. One night he told Hughes what he thought of these intolerable interruptions of his sleep. The next day he was fired. Hughes brought in a veteran Hollywood producer, Samuel Bischoff, to take his place.

None of this caused much of a stir in the industry. It was normal studio comings and goings. What did cause major excitement, however, was the appearance on the lot of the independent producing team of Wald and Krasna. Hughes had signed them to produce sixty pictures in five years. It was a $50 million deal and was the biggest independent transaction in movie history. Besides, it was announced to the press, Hughes had promised them complete autonomy. Promises, promises. A couple of years later they asked for, and got, their release from their contract. Samuel Bischoff left a year before that.

In the meantime we lived in the rosy glow of a false dawn of hope and promise at the studio. I missed my mentor-tormentor, Sid Rogell, but the Wald-Krasna team was showing signs of doing for me what Sid was never able to do, give me an A picture.

Jerry Wald and Norman Krasna, the Whiz Kids, as they were affectionately called (because of their initials), were highly respected in the industry. Wald, a flamboyant, exuberant, fat man, had spent the past eighteen years at Warner Brothers and was their top producer. Krasna, small, thin, and completely bald, was in the highest echelon of comedy writers and considered a star. (He was sensitive about his baldness and referred to other people's hair as "that unsightly growth on your head.")

As part of their indoctrination, Hughes had shown them the hoard of unreleased films he had squirreled away in his projection room. They were very much taken with my little picture *The Narrow Margin*, and immediately wanted to meet me and the producer, Stanley Rubin.

It was impossible to have a meeting with Jerry Wald that was anything but frantic. Krasna was calm and subdued. Wald was a mountain (literally) of wild energy, wild statements, and wild hyperbole. He never sat down, but paced all over the room, talking nonstop, arms gesturing and flailing. He had a deep-rooted mania for publicity, and there was a ceaseless flow of fanciful press releases from his office. He made up titles of pictures, attached the biggest star names in town to them, and gave them to a gullible, eager press who unhesitatingly printed everything. If a star bothered to deny it publicly, which rarely happened, Wald would get his name mentioned all over again. Two for one.

His office filing cabinet became a standing joke. If you mentioned any kind of story idea to Jerry, no matter how weird, outlandish, or esoteric, he'd say, "Wait a minute! We've been working on that. Look. I'll show you!" and run to the cabinet and pull a piece of paper out of a file. Waving it around in the air triumphantly, he'd say, "See? I told you. Here it is. The same story." Then he'd jam it back into its folder and slam the drawer.

Wald and Krasna were wildly enthusiastic about the future of Stanley Rubin and me at the studio. We were the kind of new talent they were looking for, they told us. No more B pictures for us. Only important things from now on. Were we familiar with the Orson Welles material he'd shot years ago of the Rio Carnival? We'd heard of it. It was legendary. Well, why don't you two guys screen it and see if you can come up with a story idea that can incorporate that film? You'll be real heroes if you do, and we'll make a big, big picture out of it. Sure, we said, we'd love to see the Welles film and give it a whirl.

Rubin and I spent the better part of a week looking at a ton of completely underexposed, poorly photographed, totally unusable footage of the famous Rio Carnival. We taped a book of matches to a memo and sent it to W-K. The memo read: "Is there fire insurance on the Welles film?"

Wald-Krasna presented another project to us. The great Al Jolson was reaching the end of a long and fabulous career. A successful film, *The Jolson Story*, had already been made about him. Now W-K wanted to make a film *with* him. He was still a star, a big name, and it would be his last hurrah. They had a commitment from Jolson to do such a film, and they wanted Rubin to produce it and me to direct it. It would be our break into the big time.

There was one minor problem, however. They didn't have a story. Not only that, but Jolson was presently touring Korea entertaining the troops and was due in Hollywood in less than a week. They had promised him a complete story synopsis on his arrival. The commitment depended on it. No synopsis, no Jolson. In fact, our big break depended on it. No synopsis, no Jolson, no picture. Rubin and I vowed not to let this opportunity slip away from us. Wald and Krasna weren't just dangling a carrot in front of our noses, it was a filet mignon. I suggested we recruit a good friend of mine, Herbert Baker, a young and promising comedy writer, to help us out.

We held a story conference in Wald's office to decide on what the basic concept of the story would be. There were five of us there —Wald, Krasna, Baker, Rubin, and myself—and it was a typical Jerry Wald conference. He had the knack of getting everyone talking at once. We were all pacing and talking frenziedly to each other, while a hundred bad ideas per minute cascaded out of Wald's mouth. The room sounded like a raucous bar at the height of the happy hour.

Suddenly Wald walked out of the room into his secretary's office and shut the door. Instantly the tumult and the shouting died. An exhausted quiet descended on us and we had a chance to ruminate in silence. It wasn't long before the door flew open and Wald burst in. He looked at us for a moment, surprised by the restful calm. "Well," he said, "what's holding up the confusion?"

By the end of the day we had settled on the highly original idea of some sort of USO story, Jolson entertaining the troops, that sort of thing. And we promised—Rubin, Baker, and I—that we'd work twenty-four hours a day if we had to, and deliver a full, completely worked out story synopsis before Jolson arrived, in four days' time.

We decided to work at Herbie Baker's house in the San Fernando Valley. We knew we were dealing with a cornball concept, and we were trying to pump some freshness and inventiveness into it. Naturally it took longer than we thought, so we worked very late every night, and subsisted on coffee and deli sandwiches. I didn't care how late we worked. Nothing was going to stop me from making a movie with Al Jolson. My big break.

We kept getting reports from Wald-Krasna about Jolson's progress. He was on Guam. He was on Wake Island. Getting closer all the time. He was in Hawaii. Next stop, L.A. To make the deadline we worked straight through the final thirty-six hours. By eight o'clock in the morning on the day we had promised to deliver, we had it finished. We were exhausted, groggy, but happy. Rubin put the pages in his briefcase. He was going directly to the studio to have them copied. We said our good-byes and I opened the front door to leave. The morning newspaper was on the doorstep and I glanced down at it. It had a big, black headline, the kind reserved for an announcement of war or some other calamity. My eyes zoomed in on it. It said: "JOLSON DEAD!"

He never made it out of Hawaii. A heart attack ended his trip and my big break. I picked up the paper and read the details. It was fascinating. He was on his way back to Hollywood to make his last picture, it said. Jerry Wald and Norman Krasna were the producers, and they were shocked and stunned. The one saddened most by this terrible news, however, was the world-famous director John Ford. Yes, Ford was quoted as saying, he was signed by Wald-Krasna to direct Jolie's last picture. It would have been the last hurrah for both of them.

Hooray for Hollywood!

V

Word finally filtered down to me that Hughes had run *The Narrow Margin*. He had run it several times. He was delighted with it. It was his favorite picture. I was feeling pretty good.

Then came an ominous rumble.

Hughes was so impressed with this little film that he wasn't going to bother about fiddling around with the end of it. What he was contemplating doing was remaking it in its entirety—make an A film out of it, with stars. Instead of Charles McGraw and Marie Windsor playing the leads, it would be Robert Mitchum and Jane Russell. Instead of the picture costing $230,000, it would now cost $1 million. Instead of being the tightly wrought gem of a *film noir* we all believed it to be, it would now become—well, something else. I looked on this matter with one downcast and one upturned eye, not knowing whether I should laugh or cry. Mostly I was concerned that if Hughes did carry out his plan to inflate the picture with stars, he'd get someone else to direct it.

My fears were not without foundation. I had been at the studio for most of the seven years called for in my contract and, although I'd shown great promise, I hadn't broken out of the B picture ranks. If Hughes decided to remake *The Narrow Margin* he could very well feel that I wasn't yet ready to be trusted with the direction of the two most valuable stars on the RKO roster, Robert Mitchum and Jane Russell. For years I'd been frustratingly close to making the switch to A pictures. I'd been promised my big break over and over again, but it always eluded me because of the revolving-door procession of various heads of production. They were the only ones who could bring about such a change, but none of them ever stayed long enough to do so. In the past six years I'd counted fourteen heads of production. It got so that we started calling them Officer of the Day.

My experience with these new executives was always exactly the same. Shortly after they were installed I'd get called in to meet them. "Oh, yes," they would say, "I've heard a lot about you. They tell me you're very good. Well, I'm going to see that you get a big picture very soon." A few months later I'd be back in the same office listening to the same speech from another executive.

The only way I could achieve my break, other than the sort of field promotion dispensed by the head of the studio, would be to make a smashing B picture, a so-called sleeper, that would garner plenty of critical acclaim and a healthy box office. There was almost no chance of that happening with the kind of movies produced by the B unit. But Venus must have been in the House of Mars, and the planets lined up correctly on my horoscope, because *The Narrow Margin* looked like it had the potential of doing just that. However, the key to my future was now in Hughes's hands, and he was threatening to drop it down the drain.

There were no discernible signs of production life at RKO during the long, nervous wait while Hughes was making up his mind about what to do with the picture. Everyone who was still left at the studio was under contract. Producers, directors, writers, cameramen, actors were all under contract. Even the seventy-piece studio orchestra. As these contracts expired, of course, the people were let go. In the meantime, those who remained had to be paid whether or not there was work for them to do. When there wasn't any production, this overhead cost was ruinous. It was the job of the new studio executive producer, Sam Bischoff, to come up with a small picture, it didn't seem to matter what it was, to keep the contract people occupied and earning their keep.

Bischoff called me into his office and handed me a script. "Here," he said, "this is your next picture." There was nothing extraordinary about this manner of handing out picture assignments to contract directors, or to anyone else, for that matter. This was the way it was done. No fuss, no muss, no argument. Just do it.

I didn't object to getting a picture assignment, but I was determined that it had to be as least as good as *The Narrow Margin*. I'd finally gotten my foot on the bottom rung of the ladder that would help me climb out of the B picture pit, and I wasn't about to slip back in. Unless it was sheer desperation time, there would be no more B's for me. There was no question that they were a terrific training ground, but I was trained enough, and making too many of them could be a dangerous thing. I was well aware of what happened to a director named William Berke.

Berke was known as the King of the B's. For years and years he had made nothing but pictures with ten- or twelve-day shooting schedules, minuscule budgets of about $100,000, and no stars. Without bothering with editing or any postproduction chores, and with such short shooting schedules, he was able to squeeze in eight or ten pictures a year. And he was going nuts. He begged and pleaded with the powers-that-be to give him a big picture, something with a fifty- or sixty-day shooting schedule, with a lavish budget of, say, $700,000 or $800,000, and stars, but he was ignored and he kept on doing those "twelve-day wonders."

Finally, at long last, a friend of his came into power at RKO. Berke besieged him for a break, for a chance to make good. With enough shooting time and important actors, he was positive he would bring in a winner. The friend took pity on him and gave him the break he was asking for. Berke was given an A picture with a long shooting schedule and stars and he still shot the picture in twelve days.

Under the present circumstances the chances that the screenplay I had just been handed would be something superior were not all that promising. The producer was going to be Lewis Rachmil, whose claim to fame was having been associate producer on all the *Hopalong Cassidy* films ever made. Bischoff told me to read the script immediately and then report to Rachmil's office.

I took the script to my office, read it, and loathed it. It was typical of its genre, a predictable murder mystery involving evil puppets and other characters just as wooden and lifeless, the kind of thing I was now desperately trying to avoid. After *The Narrow Margin*, this would be a hell of a comedown for the breakthrough kid. This script had nothing going for it except schlock.

Rachmil was waiting expectantly for me in his office. "Well, what do you think of it?" he asked as soon as I came in.

"Lew," I said, trying to be kind as I handed him his script, "I'm sorry. I don't like it."

"But are you going to do it?"

"I just told you, Lew. I don't like it." Usually when you said this to a producer it was enough to end the discussion. Who would want a director on a picture who didn't like the script? Also, it was the accepted—in fact, the *only* way—of turning down a project without actually refusing to do it. To refuse outright is to invite suspension.

"I know," he said, "but are you going to do it?"

I was trapped. The only way to turn this thing off was to refuse. It was clear that all the other weasely worded ways were not going to work. I decided to take the plunge. "No, Lew," I said, "I'm not going to do it."

I watched his face slowly turn red. Then, most unexpectedly, he burst into tears. I'd never seen a grown man cry before, and it was acutely embarrassing for both of us. When he turned away to wipe his eyes I slipped out the door.

The next day I was suspended.

Suspension is the most miserable of times and I was, indeed, miserable. Just when my career showed real signs of blossoming, it was stagnating, and there didn't seem to be anything I could do about it except let the suspension run its course. That could be several months. Meanwhile, I was not getting paid and was prohibited from working anyplace else. I was restless, unhappy, frustrated, and not much of a joy to my family. Suspension was working just the way its fiendish designers intended.

As though things weren't bad enough, Stanley Kramer put the cherry on the pie. He wanted me to do an absolutely wonderful project for him called, ironically enough, *The Happy Time*. It was exactly the kind of film I was looking for—a human comedy about a young boy's coming of age. No melodrama, no murders, no evil wooden puppets, but people, warm, human, alive, and funny. The break, the big break, was being held out to me but I was on suspension and there was no way to free my hands to grab it. From this you could go crazy.

In desperation I turned to Sid Rogell. He was still my mentor and I sorely needed him. If he had been around he probably would have been my lifeguard and rescued me from the shark-infested Wald-Krasna waters. And tough as he was, I couldn't see him putting me on suspension after *The Narrow Margin*. I phoned him and made a date for lunch.

Sid came up with a suggestion. "Why don't you write Hughes a letter," he said, "and tell him he's ruining your career?" It seemed like a sensible idea. Straightforward and, like Sid himself, as direct as a battering ram. So I wrote a letter to Howard Hughes and told him he was ruining my career. I also told him why, and how about letting me out of my contract so I could do the Kramer picture? The Hughes headquarters were at 7000 Romaine Avenue, less than a mile from the studio. The letter, registered, was sent there.

Six weeks later, when I'd lost hope of ever hearing anything from anybody ever again, I was asked to come to C. J. Tevlin's office at RKO. Tevlin was the Hughes representative on the lot. "Mr. Hughes was very upset by your letter," he said after I'd come in, saluted, and given my name, rank, and serial number, "so he's making you the following offer." There was a Mitchum-Russell picture, he told me, called *His Kind of Woman* that John Farrow had directed some months earlier. The end needed fixing. Ah, I thought, the anal erotic strikes again. If I would redo the end of the picture, he went on, which wouldn't take more than ten days or two weeks, Mr. Hughes would take me off suspension retroactively, he'd would approve a loan-out for me to do the Kramer picture, and my RKO contract would expire when I finished it.

I was wary. This all sounded a little too good to be true. Even the price he was asking me to pay—fixing up the end of somebody else's picture—wasn't all that bad. I'd get my chance to work with stars at last, and, since I would not be getting any screen credit, there was no risk as far as the final outcome of the film was concerned. If I did a lousy job, John Farrow would get the blame. If I did a great job, I'd be a hero. There was nothing to lose and everything to gain. Still, there was one question I needed answered. What was going to happen to *The Narrow Margin*?

"Mr. Hughes says he's going to release it just as it is," Tevlin replied. That's all I wanted to know. I didn't need to read the script or see the picture he was asking me to fix up. I just wanted to do it and get it over with so I could start work on *The Happy Time*. "Tell Mr. Hughes," I said to Tevlin, "he's got a deal."

A few days later I got a phone call from a young, pleasant-sounding voice telling me that I was talking to Bill Gay. He was to be my contact with Howard Hughes and gave me a phone number where he could be reached at any time of the day or night. He also gave me the routine to be followed: Whenever Mr. Hughes would want to meet I would receive a phone call from Bill Gay alerting me well in advance; from that point on I was to keep him informed of where I was at all times, checking in with him when I arrived anywhere, and checking out with him when I left, giving my next destination; I would, in due course, receive another phone call informing me where and when we would meet.

There were only two places I ever met with Hughes. He maintained offices at the Goldwyn Studios, at Santa Monica Boulevard and Formosa Avenue, where we met at night. By day, it was Bungalow 19 at the Beverly Hills Hotel. That's where my writer, Earl Felton, and I, at eleven-thirty on the morning of December 3, 1950, met Howard Hughes for the first time.

There he was. Tall, thin, handsome. Just like his pictures. Hair parted in the middle, deep creases on either side of the mouth, running from the nose to under the chin. Scraggy. Everything about him needed a sharp edge. His mustache, hair, eyebrows, two-day growth of beard. White, open-necked shirt, clean but slightly frayed at collar and cuffs. Worn-out cotton work pants. Dirty, well-used tennis shoes. It all made him look slightly fuzzy. Until you came to the eyes. The eyes of a flier. Clear, determined, confident. And a dreamer, a visionary. Eyes that held in them distant horizons and limitless skies. It was said that he was driving on Sunset Boulevard at rush hour one evening when he suddenly decided to return to his office. Without even slowing down he made a U-turn. Three cars were smashed and a horrendous traffic jam resulted. When he was asked why he made such a turn he replied, "Hell, I didn't turn. I banked." After you met him you believed the story.

Earl and I introduced ourselves and shook hands, a practice Hughes would give up in later years because of a supremely neurotic fear of germs. He immediately put us on a first-name basis. From then on he became "Howard" to us.

The bungalows at the Beverly Hills Hotel have always been noted for their pleasant, comfortable, understated style. This one was an exception. It was simplicity itself, slightly dowdy, functional, and sparsely furnished. A round table with three straight-backed chairs took up the center of the living room. To the right, as you entered, a couple of not very comfortable easy chairs. The back wall contained a small kitchenette, a powder room, and a door leading to a bedroom. A plain dresser rested against the left wall. On top of the dresser were five small, unopened, Christmas-wrapped packages. They were a source of much speculation for Earl and me because they remained there, untouched, for the many months we were to visit this room. Were they for him or from him? We never found out. It struck us as sad and rather touching.

We settled ourselves around the table and the meeting began, with Howard making probably the greatest understatement of the year. "I'm afraid you'll have to speak up a little," he said. "I've got a slight hearing problem." He was, as a result of one of his airplane crashes, virtually stone deaf.

Felton and I had screened *His Kind of Woman* and agreed with Howard's criticism that the end of the picture, the last half of the last reel, needed more action. As it now stood, the climactic scene took place on the bridge of a yacht anchored in a Mexican bay.

There was a short scuffle between Mitchum and the heavies and that was it. End of picture.

We started working on ideas of how to add more action, more violence. Howard was full of enthusiasm. He was thoroughly enjoying himself. In a few minutes we had made a total wreck of the yacht's bridge. That wasn't enough for Howard. "I want Mitchum to get knocked through the port-side bridge door and make a run for it." But where could he go?

"He could hide in a lifeboat," Earl suggested.

"Yeah," I said, or rather shouted into Howard's ear, "then, if they left a guard behind, right under the lifeboat, Mitchum could jump him."

"Great!" said Howard. "That could be a hell of a fight. And it attracts the others who have gone by, and they come back and Mitchum's got to run again."

And so it went, as we carefully, painstakingly constructed and reconstructed each bit of action, each punch, each gunshot. Hours went by. Hughes put as much concentration into working out the sequence as he must have put into designing airplanes. He was intense, serious, and having a wonderful time.

A bell that sounded like a fire alarm went off in the room. Earl and I jumped two feet out of our chairs. It was a special bell Howard had hooked up to the bedroom phone. It was good and loud so he could hear it. Howard immediately got up and strode to the bedroom to answer it, closing the door behind him.

Earl turned to me. "I'm dying," he said.

"From what?"

"Hunger." I looked at my watch. It was after four, and we'd gotten there at eleven-thirty. Earl was a big lunch man. It was his main meal of the day. He liked his couple of belts of scotch, a steak or a hamburger, all the trimmings, and a nice, rich dessert. Earl eyed the hotel phone in the room. "Do you think I should call room service?"

"Better wait until he comes back and ask him," I advised. "Everything's so goddamned secretive around here. He might throw a fit if you used the phone."

It was a good half hour before we saw Howard again. He loped back to the table and picked up right where we'd left off.

Earl was in extremis. "I'm sorry, Howard, I hate to interrupt you," he blurted out, "but I'm starving to death. Do you think I can get something to eat?"

Hughes looked at him, shocked and deeply concerned. "Of

course!" he exclaimed, leaping to his feet. "I'm so terribly sorry. I'll take care of that right away," he said as he dashed to the phone.

Howard called room service and ordered a glass of milk.

It was almost seven when that first story conference broke up. Earl and I were exhausted, our throats raw from the constant hollering to make ourselves heard, our nerves frayed from the fire-alarm phone bell that would occasionally blast us. As we prepared to leave, Howard put on a display of behavior that I found endearing and moving. Earl was crippled from childhood with polio. He had no use of his legs, but he navigated beautifully with a crutch and a cane. Hughes couldn't be more solicitous about him. He jumped over to pull out his chair, handed him his crutch and cane, helped him into his jacket, ushered him to the door. He literally, as they say, danced attendance on him. These were all things Earl normally hated anybody doing for him and would sometimes lay about him with his cane and deliver a few sharp blows when they tried. Not this time. He was flattered and was all but tugging his forelock as he lurched through the door. Once outside and down the path a bit Earl grabbed his throat with one hand, the other hand outstretched like a thirst-crazed man in the desert. "Whiskey! Whiskey!" he cried out in a hoarse rasp. We made for what he gleefully called the Polio Lounge.

The story conferences continued sporadically, spreading out over a couple of months. The promised ten days to two weeks were long gone. Luckily, Kramer was occupied with *High Noon* and in no rush. Howard was meticulous about every detail. The conferences were long and uninterrupted, except for the phone calls, which lasted from twenty minutes to a full hour. They were a welcome but boring relief. The only other diversion was watching Howard kill an occasional fly that was unfortunate enough to land on the table. Everything would come to a standstill while he stalked it with a rolled newspaper. He was pretty good at it, too, whacking it just hard enough to kill but not squash it. Then he'd scoop it up between two pieces of notepaper, carry it to the powder room, flush it down the commode, wash his hands, and return to the table.

The only other real interruption we ever had was during one long meeting that lasted until dark. There was a loud knock on the door. It was loud enough for Howard to hear, and it startled us. Nothing like this had ever happened before. Howard went to the door, opened it partway, spoke a few hushed words to someone, then slipped outside, shutting the door. We never got a glimpse of who was out there.

We waited about five minutes, listening. There was no sound. Silence. We were beginning to feel uncomfortable, worried. His action had struck us as foolhardy. Finally Earl voiced something that had already formed in my mind. "What do we do if we hear shots?"

"Run like hell," I replied, "and jump out the bedroom window."

"You bastard. You know I can't do that," he growled in mock outrage. "Would you leave a poor, crippled feller behind?"

"Of course I would. One shot and I'm gone. But I'll stop at the desk and ask them to have room service look in on you."

Twenty uneasy minutes went by before we saw Howard again. He went right to the table and continued as though there had been no interruption. It was another minor Hughes mystery.

Robert Fellows was the line producer on the film and had been from the beginning. A rather husky man in his late forties, handsome and with a relaxed, Ivy League look, he was never invited to the daytime story conferences at the bungalow. Apparently Hughes didn't want Bob involved in the creative side of this project and had limited him to the physical production end. The day following the bungalow conferences I would report to him and fill him in on what had taken place.

Even though he had no authority to do so, Fellows decided to start construction immediately on the physical changes as they came up. It would speed things along enormously. He didn't want to ask Hughes for permission to do this. Getting a decision from Hughes might take longer than waiting until all the story conferences were finished. There was no problem in getting this work started. Those in charge at the studio either had no way of reaching Hughes to check or were afraid to ask if they did. Fellows pledged me to secrecy. He decided that if anyone questioned anything we would merely say, "Howard wants it." He was putting his neck in a lovely noose. The trapdoor beneath his feet, however, seemed reasonably secure.

All that had been built of the yacht for the original production was the bridge. It was on Stage 22 in the Culver City lot of RKO and was the biggest stage in Hollywood. A small airplane had taken off, flown, and landed within its walls. The set had been built there because Stage 22 was also a tank. Under its removable wooden floor lay a giant, ten-foot-deep, concrete, swimming pool-like structure. It occupied almost the full length and width of this enormous stage. When it was flooded it became a huge pool in which water sequences could be staged.

The bridge of the *His Kind of Woman* yacht was perched on a high platform, close to one of the stage walls, so that the height perspective would be correct and full advantage could be taken of the expanse of water beneath it. The set looked dinky in that vast space.

As our story conferences progressed, the yacht started to grow. Mitchum hides in a lifeboat? Okay, build some more deck and install a lifeboat. Mitchum takes cover behind some deck housing? Build some deck housing. Mitchum hides behind the smokestack? Build a smokestack. All of this was not merely built. Long shots of a real yacht had been used in the picture. Everything that was now being constructed had to match exactly the same object on the boat already established in the film.

Our set was outgrowing its platform. It was now jammed up against the stage wall with no room to accommodate its rapidly expanding size. And there was no end in sight. New script pages had Mitchum fighting the heavies on the fantail. The studio construction people were appalled. Nothing like this had ever happened to them before. These things were always planned before construction started, they complained, not after. Fellows was implacable. "Howard wants it," he would say. There was nothing for it but to call in house movers. At great expense the set was dragged out into the middle of the tank.

Before we were through we had built the entire yacht, all 150 feet of it, top to bottom, stem to stern, and Hughes never knew it even existed.

The night meetings with Hughes at the Goldwyn Studios were interspersed with the daytime bungalow conferences. Their scheduling was much more capricious. We would go through the usual routine with Bill Gay; the phone call alert; the standing by; the checking in and out; then, far more often than not, a call would come through about ten-thirty or eleven, calling it off. After that we might not hear anything for days, sometimes weeks. Usually the day you were put on alert meant a ruined evening. You couldn't go out to a movie for fear of missing the call. Having friends over was risky. You might have to run out on them. If you had made previous plans to have dinner at a friend's house, you could almost rely on getting called just as you were biting into the shrimp cocktail.

Even when we were off the hook there was an element of risk. My wife, Mickey, and I were having dinner on one of those nonalert evenings at a friend's house. Carl Foreman and his wife were there, too. Just the six of us. The dinner table talk got around to the fact that Lena Horne was performing at the Cocoanut Grove in the Ambassador Hotel and wouldn't it be a kick if we all went down there to see her. It was strictly spur-of-the-moment, and off we went, without reservations, leaving no message behind. None of us had been to the Cocoanut Grove in years.

As we approached the palm-fringed Grove entrance in the lobby of the hotel, the *maître d'* left his post at the door and came directly to me at a half run, ignoring the other two men in our party. "Mr. Fleischer?" he asked, with more than a hint of anxiety tingeing his voice. I nodded in surprise. "Mr. Hughes," he said, "wants you to come to the Goldwyn Studios immediately!" So much for Lena Horne. We were never able to figure out how the *maître d'* recognized me or how I'd been tracked to the Grove.

The Goldwyn office was on the ground floor of a long, shabby, two-story building on the Santa Monica Boulevard side of the studio. A nondescript door in the middle of this depressing structure opened into a narrow, dingy hallway. The first door on the right, un-marked, was the office of one of the richest men in the world.

If the bungalow at the Beverly Hills Hotel lacked something in style, the office at the Goldwyn Studios must have been decorated by *New Yorker* cartoonist George Price, including the single, bare light bulb dangling on a frayed cord from the ceiling. It was a fairly large, square room, its walls covered by what seemed to be an old plastering job that had been abandoned, probably in disgust, before it had been completed. Heavy, dirty curtains were tightly drawn across the window that faced the street inside the studio. Rejects from Goodwill Industries added the final touch in the way of furni-ture; a collapsed and defeated armchair that someone had knocked the stuffing out of; a largish, beat-up desk that, judging from its scars and dents, had seen hard service in a boy's reformatory; four wooden, straight-backed chairs, one of which served as the desk chair, that would have been flattered to be called feeble. One of these chairs, during our first meeting in this room, collapsed under me with a loud crack and I found myself flat on my back surrounded by a thousand toothpicks. Howard thought it was hilarious. He did help me off the floor and dust me off, though. In the wall behind the desk, and a little to its right, was a door that led to who-knows-where? Howard always made his appearance through this door.

Bob Fellows was invited to these meetings, along with Earl and me. We'd get there, having been torn away from the beginning of a delicious dinner somewhere, about forty-five minutes before Hughes showed up. Plenty of time to have at least gotten into the roast beef. When Howard finally did come through that door, he invariably carried with him a carton of milk, a small glass, and a brown paper bag with a sandwich in it. Sometimes there was an apple, too, but we never saw him eat one. He would unfailingly offer to share his meal with us. We would politely turn this kind offer down, protesting that we'd all just come from a fine meal, which was, of course, true. When he laid out his dinner on the desk and started to eat the sandwich, we'd begin.

These meetings were meant to address physical production problems. Hughes would go into great detail about what needed to be constructed. Fellows would take copious notes. I would sit there listening, feeling the sweat roll down my sides from under my arms, knowing that everything Howard was talking about had long since been built. The consequences, should Howard ever find out, were too terrible to contemplate. Whenever Howard would direct his attention to something on his desk, Bob and I would exchange short but significant glances. Bob was courting disaster, but so far, so good.

Over a period of a couple of months, the yacht on Stage 22 grew, bit by bit, script page by script page, to its full size. It was an impressive sight. No one could remember seeing anything like it before. Visitors from other movie companies shooting nearby came to visit it, like tourists.

Howard was carried away with excitement about the sequence. He was inventing. He was creating. He was having a wonderful time. Earl and I got into the swing of things, aiding and abetting. Fellows was having a hard time keeping construction abreast of us. The story took new twists and turns. Fighting and chasing on the decks of the yacht wasn't enough. Howard wanted fighting and chasing inside the yacht, as well. Corridors, the main lounge, the engine room became involved. Soon fighting and chasing weren't enough. Dramatic scenes. He had to have dramatic scenes. Confrontations with the heavies when Mitchum is captured; a nasty German doctor who wants to give him an injection that will destroy his mind; a whipping, torture sequence.

More. He had to have more. Howard was getting hooked on this thing, like an addict. The more we gave him, the more he wanted.

How about Vincent Price, the principal comic relief in the picture, organizing a rescue party? Why not?

How could we leave Jane Russell out of this merriment? No way.

It was during one of our night meetings at Goldwyn Studios. We were discussing the Vincent Price rescue operation. Just exactly how would he and his boatload of Mexican Federales board the yacht anchored out in the bay? Simple. They'd sneak up the boarding ladder, which, by great good fortune, was already lowered.

Howard looked up from the script pages on his desk like an animal suddenly alerted at a water hole. "Wait a minute!" he said, a faraway look in his eyes. He turned to Fellows. "Let me see the stills of the yacht."

"You mean stills of the bridge?" Bob asked. "The set?"

"No, no. Stills of the real yacht," he said. "Full shots. The way it looks in the picture." Bob rummaged around in a folder and came up with the stills.

Hughes studied them carefully for a long time. "I knew it," he finally said. "I knew there was something wrong. The boarding ladder. It's on the wrong side!" He sounded triumphant. Three completely blank stares greeted him as he faced us. Obviously we hadn't a clue as to what he was talking about.

"The boarding ladder on this yacht is on the port side. It should be on the starboard side," he enlightened us. "It's always on the starboard side. I know. I used to own a yacht. How did this come to happen?"

"I don't know, Howard," Bob replied. "Maybe when they were shooting those scenes the action worked better from that side, so they changed it around."

"Well, it's wrong, damn it, it's wrong!" he said. "We can't have a mistake like that in the picture." He studied the stills again. "Anyhow, I'll tell you something," he went on, warming to the subject. "I think this is the wrong yacht for this picture. It's too small. We need a bigger one for all the action we want to play on it."

We couldn't believe what we were hearing.

"What with the ladder on the wrong side . . ." he ruminated. Then he came to a decision. "We'll get another yacht and reshoot everything."

Another yacht! What about the monster we'd built without his knowledge on Stage 22? This complete yacht we'd so carefully matched to the one in the picture had struck a mine. It was blown out of the water. If only it would sink without a trace. I knew it couldn't.

Bob was sitting behind me, a little to my right. I wasn't able to see his reaction. When Howard bent over the desk to study the stills some more, I snuck a look over my shoulder at Bob. He was sitting in his chair in the attitude of Rodin's *The Thinker*—elbow propped on knee, chin resting on the fist of his right hand. His eyes met mine. He didn't change expression. All he did was raise the first finger of the hand on which his chin rested, ever so slightly, so that it covered his lips. It was a tiny move, but it was eloquent.

I certainly wasn't about to say anything, but I couldn't see any way out for Bob. The Great Yacht Scandal surely would have to break. Not only would he be fired, but keel-hauled and flogged through the fleet as well.

I looked over at Earl, on my left. He had a pencil stuck in his mouth and was chuckling to himself. It was a delicious moment, and he savored it. His greatest joy was the painful discomfort of others.

It was Earl who broke the silence. "Howard," he said, "maybe you're making too much out of this ladder thing. I've owned boats and I never knew about that. How many people in an audience are going to pick up on it?"

"Probably not too many," Howard answered. "But it's a mistake. On a yacht, the ladder is always on the starboard side."

"Well," said Earl, "that's something only another millionaire would know."

Hughes burst out laughing. It appeared to be the funniest thing he'd ever heard in his life. He couldn't stop laughing. He kept repeating "only another millionaire would know" and slapping the desk. He tried to continue the meeting, but he couldn't. He kept breaking up. "You're right, Earl. You're right," he finally said, wiping his eyes. "Only another millionaire would know." Then he turned to me. "Do you think we can get away with this size yacht for all the action we've planned?"

"Absolutely, Howard," I hastened to assure him. "Particularly after the action moves inside. Then you really can't judge how big or small it is."

"Okay," he said. "We'll stick with what we've got."

In terms of naval heroes, Lord Nelson came in a poor second to Earl Felton that night.

■ ■ ■

One of the things that kept me occupied for quite a while was trying to find an engine room on a real boat that we could shoot in. Building an engine room set is always a mess. The equipment is heavy, expensive to install, and difficult to get working. Better to find the real thing. But finding an engine room big enough to work in, and not have it look like something that was driving the *Queen Mary*, was a problem.

For weeks I roamed the waterfront, looking. Long Beach, San Pedro, San Diego. Marinas, large and small. I saw hundreds of vessels, inspected dozens of engine rooms. I couldn't find anything suitable.

I was making my second tour of all the places I'd already been, just in case I'd somehow overlooked something. If I didn't find it this time, I'd start working my way up the Coast toward Nome, Alaska. It turned out I had overlooked something. A sadly neglected boat, tucked away at an obscure wharf in San Pedro. Zombie gray paint, blistered and peeling. Soot, salt, and grime. Square, old-fashioned lines. But somehow it seemed right. I wanted to see inside.

We went aboard. I traveled with a small group—an assistant, a still photographer, a location manager who arranged for me to see whatever I wanted. The inside surprised us all. This was no ordinary boat. She had been converted to a Coast Guard cutter during the war and had never been reconverted. Yet, in spite of the rust, the electric cables sagging from every bulkhead and corridor, the torn-out fixtures, the scabrous layers of paint that covered everything, underneath there was a lady. You could feel it. It was hard to explain, but I felt comfortable on board. It all seemed familiar, as though I'd been there before. *Déjà vu.* We wandered through the corridors, the staterooms, the main salon. I had the still man take photos of everything. Perhaps, I thought, I could use some of this. Spruce it up and maybe supplement the set we were building at the studio.

Then we came to the engine room. Perfect. A maze of intricate-looking machinery. Ample space in which to work. Plenty of interesting angles. The scale was right, not overpowering. It was the only area that had been kept up. Not only was it clean, it also was in working order. I knew I had found what I was looking for.

At our next production meeting at the Goldwyn Studios I made my report. "Howard," I said, handing him the processed stills of the boat, "take a look at this. It'll work great for us. I can even make use of some of the other areas, besides the engine room. These stills cover everything."

He started looking through them, one by one, picture by picture. As he progressed through the stack his pace became slower and slower, his concentration more intense. When he got through the complete lot of them he looked up at me. He looked quizzical. Then he started through the pictures again, slowly. He was about halfway though when he said, "I can't believe it. I just can't believe it." Without taking his eyes from the pictures he asked, "Where in the world did you find it?"

"San Pedro," I said, puzzled.

A smile was spreading across his face. "Do you know what this is? Do you know what you've found?" he asked, the smile widening. "This is the *Oceania*. This is my old yacht!"

Out of all the places I'd searched, all the boats I'd seen, I'd come up with that particular one. I was as flabbergasted as he was.

He wanted to know all about it, and I gave him as much information as I had. For him, it was like finding a long-lost friend. Then I began to realize where my feelings of *déjà vu* had come from. Howard had subconsciously patterned the action we invented to fit the floor plan of his old yacht. The layout of our set on the stage was the same as the one in the *Oceania*. No wonder I felt comfortable when I was aboard her. I knew where everything was.

The main focus of our attention, though, was the engine room. The action there involved a high-pressure steam pipe that had to burst. Howard studied the photos. "No. No. This won't do," he finally announced. "We can't use this engine room at all." After all my weeks of searching and coming up with this prize, I wanted to know why. It seemed perfectly fine to me. "This is a diesel engine," he answered. I shook my head in perplexed acknowledgment. I mean, all yachts have diesel engines, don't they?

"What about it?" I asked. "What's wrong with it?"

"Well, a diesel wouldn't have a high-pressure steam line," he replied, as though this was the most obvious observation in the world. It wasn't obvious to me, though. By me, an engine is an engine.

"Why can't we just stick a special-effects steam pipe in among all that machinery, where we need it?" I suggested. Then, hoping to capitalize on the Felton theory, I said, "Who's to know?"

"Everybody!" he replied, just a little exasperated at my blatant ignorance. "No, this yacht won't do." And then he continued, disastrously, "And neither will the one we have in the picture." We all sat bolt upright. "What we need is a steam yacht."

A steam yacht! I wasn't sure that I heard right. Once more our Stage 22 boat was on the point of foundering.

"But Howard," I said, incredulously, "there hasn't been a steam yacht in existence since 1916." This seemed to be something he hadn't contemplated. He became pensive. I pressed on, desperately trying to reverse the "abandon ship" command. "To me that engine room is just a tangle of pipes. I couldn't tell if it was run by diesel, steam, or spaghetti sauce."

Howard held up a photo for me to see. "Just look at all those valves and rockers," he said, using a finger as a pointer. "It's a diesel, and there's no mistaking it or hiding it. It's a diesel, and it has to be steam."

In the end he compromised. We wouldn't have to find a steam yacht, just an engine room with a steam engine. Howard's old yacht was out. We'd keep the yacht that was in the picture. We could all climb out of the lifeboats again.

There was a nice nostalgic aftermath, though. Nowhere in the picture was the name of the yacht either seen or referred to. Howard asked us to call it the *Oceania*.

Shooting began on February 1, 1951 . At our last meeting with Hughes, before production began, he drew me aside.

"Now, Dick," he said with great sincerity and intensity, "I want you to understand something. I want it perfect. I don't care how long it takes, or how many times you have to do something over, I want it perfect." It sounded like the answer to a director's prayer. Make it perfect. Who could ask for anything more? Putting Hughes's mandate into practice was not the joy I'd assumed it would be. After all, when is anything perfect? How do you know when you've achieved it? Maybe Michelangelo would know. He threw a hammer at the *Pietà* to mar it when it was finished because he thought he had blasphemed. He believed he had created something perfect and that that was a privilege reserved only for God. Not being Michelangelo, I was in constant danger of unwittingly committing blasphemy. I was striving for perfection. In the process I tortured myself and the actors. When something was good, would doing it over a few dozen more times make it any better? If you squeezed blood from a stone, would squeezing even more give you maybe orange juice? Where I used to be able to say, with great authority, "Good! That's a print," I was now tormented by agonizing doubts and painful indecision. If I didn't achieve perfection, would my God throw a hammer at me?

The atmosphere on the set was pleasant, relaxed, even jovial.

The actors were cooperative, which was helpful. Since they were all under contract to the studio, the original crew had been recalled. They filled me in on the local gossip. Lots of stories, too, about the previous director, John Farrow. The prop man asked me if I'd like to sample some John Farrow scotch. This got a big laugh from everyone in earshot. Farrow, they told me, had set himself up as a connoisseur of scotch and women. Apparently, at lunchtime, there was a daily sampling of both in his portable office on the stage. It didn't take much persuasion from the prop men to have one of these ladies pee into a jar, which was then added to the contents of one of his choice bottles. They kept a close watch on the liquid level, which dropped day by day. There was no reaction at all from the great connoisseur. Farrow scotch became famous, if not popular, on the set.

No one was having a better time during the additional shooting than Vincent Price. The character he was playing, Cardigan, was a comedic ham actor, a "legit" type whose manner and dialogue were flamboyantly Shakespearean, in the worst sense of the word. Vinny relished the role. It was also Hughes's pet character, and we gave it a heavy buildup in the new writing.

One scene in particular was a Hughes favorite. Cardigan rounds up a boarding party of Mexican soldiers to rescue Mitchum from the yacht, and piles them into a boat, overloading it until the gunwales are awash. They push off from shore, Cardigan standing in the prow in a *Washington Crossing the Delaware* pose. Naturally, a few yards out from shore, the boat sinks, going straight down. It was a direct steal from Buster Keaton's *The Navigator*.

It was not an easy shot to make. A lot of bulky rigging had to be placed under the boat to get it to sink on cue, and in exactly the same place each time we did it.

I knew precisely what the shot should look like. After the boat reached a certain point, it had to sink fairly slowly, the water coming up to the chins of the smallest seated soldiers. After our first rehearsal I knew we were in trouble. The special-effects people had put so much rigging under the boat it couldn't sink deep enough. The water came only chest high on the shortest men. I couldn't understand it. Here we were in the biggest tank in all of filmdom and it wasn't big enough to sink an oversize rowboat. Special effects assured me that they couldn't make their rigging any smaller. Well, what about making the tank deeper? I asked. This got a patronizing chuckle from the studio production people. Did I know what I was asking? they wondered. Why, this tank was solid, reinforced concrete. Anyhow, even if it was possible, which it certainly wasn't, production would be held up for weeks digging a big enough hole, then sealing and waterproofing it, and letting it dry. They shrugged the whole thing off. This tank was big enough for every other movie ever made in Hollywood. Why wasn't it big enough for me? I would just have to make the best of it. I was not amused.

I got Bob Fellows on the phone and asked him what to do. "Go ahead and shoot it," was his advice. The next night Fellows, Felton, and I ran the film I had shot. I expected it to be lousy. I wasn't disappointed. It wasn't right; it wasn't funny; it was far from perfect. "Christ," I moaned. "What will Howard say?" He would be running this film alone, either later that night or the following day. "I think he'll love it," Earl said, a malicious grin crossing his face. "You may even get a raise."

The phone rang shortly after I got home from work the following evening. It was a poor connection, full of static. The voice sounded faint and muffled. "Let me talk to Dick Fleischer, please," it said.

"Speaking."

"Dick? This is Howard."

In all the time we'd been working together never once did Hughes ever call me direct, or, for that matter, even speak to me over the phone. I knew who this was. "All right, Earl," I said wearily. "What do you want?"

"Hello?" said the voice. "This is Howard."

I was tired, and nervous, and in no mood to play. "All right, you son-of-a-bitch," I said. "Very funny. End of joke."

"Hello? Is Mr. Fleischer there?" the voice sounded genuinely confused. "This is Howard Hughes." It hit me then. There was no mistaking that Texas accent. I mumbled an awkward apology, which he didn't seem to hear.

"The boat sinking with Cardigan. That wasn't how we discussed it," he went on. "The water doesn't come up to their chins. It isn't funny the way it is." I agreed, of course, and explained what the problems were. "I understand," he said, "but it's just no good the way it is, so you do whatever is necessary to make it work." I assured him I would.

After my conversation with Hughes, I phoned Fellows and gave him a rundown. His reaction was, "I knew he'd say that." I asked him to arrange a meeting of department heads on the set, first thing in the morning.

The five-day week hadn't even been thought of at that time.

The following day was a Saturday, a regular working day. When I walked on the stage everyone I'd asked for was already assembled. "Gentlemen," I addressed them, "I've seen the dailies and it looks like we're going to have to dig a big hole in this tank." I perceived a ripple of annoyance go through them. Hadn't they already given me, in great detail, all the reasons why this couldn't be done? I listened with infinite patience while they ran through their routine yet again. When they ran out of steam I raised my shoulders, held my outstretched palms toward them, and, repeating the Bob Fellows refrain, said, "Howard wants it."

We studied each other for a moment. I could read their minds. Was I being a headstrong bastard, or was I telling the truth? There was absolutely no way for them to check. They were wracked with doubt, and it was a pleasure to watch. Finally, the question I was waiting for was asked. "When do you need it?" They'd had their fun. Now it was my turn. "First thing Monday morning," I said, and walked away.

The effect was approximately that of a stun bomb dropped by a SWAT team. It was a lie, of course. I could have shot other sequences for at least two weeks, but here was a golden opportunity, a once-in-a-lifetime chance, to push around the people who had been pushing me around for years. This was great sport. I would show no mercy.

I went about my business of directing, but kept an eye on this uneasy group, who had now been joined by other studio executives. Usually they were staring into the tank, with their hands behind their backs. Occasionally there'd be a brief gathering around a runner who was bearing a communiqué. By lunchtime, reports began to filter back to me. They were having a hell of a time. The hole, they figured, would be as large as a ten-foot-deep, Olympic-size swimming pool. The job had to be done nonstop over the weekend, starting when I finished work. They had been calling contractors and pool builders for estimates. What with overtime, double time, triple time, golden hours, and quadruple golden hours, there was just no way to get an estimate. If we have to give an estimate, they were told by the few willing even to consider doing it, we don't want the job.

I began getting inquiries. Did I have to have this thing by Monday morning? "Howard wants it," I'd answer. "If you can talk him out of it, go right ahead. Be my guest." Howard couldn't have cared less, I knew, but I wanted to see how far I could go. There seemed to be no apparent limit.

They capitulated and hired a contractor who was about to become very rich. I was asked to give them one big break. Would I please quit early so that they could get started? This was the final irony. I had always been ruthlessly made to work up to the last second. Now they were pleading with me to stop. I graciously gave my consent.

I stayed around long enough to see the commencement of the work. The tank was emptied. A crane lowered a huge bulldozer to the bottom. Its engine roaring, the dozer smashed its steel-pronged scoop onto the concrete. With a great clashing of gears it lurched forward. All the steel prongs on its mighty maw bent backward. It was ruined. When I left, the crane was hoisting the broken bulldozer out of the tank.

By midmorning on Monday, Vincent Price and his waterlogged Federales sank in their boat exactly as planned. Everything worked perfectly. The water came up to the precise place on the precise chin. There was no question about it. It looked funny. When I said, "Print," there was a small cheer, with scattered applause. Everyone looked pleased; even the formerly disgruntled studio executives seemed gruntled. There was a great sense of accomplishment, as though the Panama Canal had been built overnight. The biggest tank in Hollywood was now even bigger.

A week later I received an extraordinary communication from Howard Hughes. He would occasionally send out short memos, but this was seven pages long. It contained minutely detailed notes about the entire end sequence, some of which had already been shot. It was a fascinating document, not because of the information it contained, but because of the insight it afforded into his mind: the absorption with trivial details; the indecisiveness that plagued him in some instances contrasting with a firm mind-set in others; the cool philosophy about killing. I found these excerpts particularly illuminating:

2/28/51

NOTES FROM MR. HUGHES
HIS KIND OF WOMAN

My original conception of the scene at the wharf was that the boats were up on a beach. Then they either push them down on the sand, or maybe there is a rough wooden ramp into the water that they push the boats down.

I originally pictured this where he said, "Heave ho, my

lads." They push this boat down into the water. Then they start loading the people in and continue to push as the people keep jumping in it.

I am not at all sure that it would be any funnier to have the boat sink away from the dock and it might be a whole lot more difficult to accomplish the physical shooting so, if you want to do it at the dock, it is all right with me. But I don't think the boat should tip over. I don't like the scene of Cardigan with arms flailing and losing his balance.

Another way to do it would be for them all to get in the boat, and have the boat settle right down. I think having them take off in the boat is even better because it is funnier. Once he is in the boat, he has the chance to assume the great gesture and then, if it just goes right down, it would be funnier. If it is moving, however, you are going to have the wake around him.

Everybody goes down in the boat simultaneously and nobody holds his gun above water as I feel that would destroy the comedy. We should definitely go ahead and wet the guns and ammunition and not worry about that.

The water should come just to the very chin of the short ones when they elevate their chins to the maximum. It should be very smooth water so that the water can come just exactly level with the elevated chins of the short people.

I think it would be more dramatic if the boat they finally go in is one of those whaling boats. It would give you the time element because a motor boat would get to the yacht so damn fast and they would have to talk over the engine. Also, I think it is much more magnificent for him to be at the helm of a rowboat.

I think, if the first one is a small motor boat, that is the one that sinks. Then they get back on the dock, and there could be one of these big whaling boats with about three oars on each side on the dock, or it might be better if it were in the water.

The next point I have to make is that I feel there is more suspense in any kind of picture, or dramatization, if we don't have a lot of harmless shooting where nobody gets hit.

I have noticed that in RKO's picture *Gunga Din*, all those pictures like *Beau Geste*, all the battle pictures fighting the

Arabs, and all their Indian pictures like *Fort Apache*, it seems to me like all the shooting just makes a hell of a noise. I thought, if we could play this thing for less shooting, and more killing when somebody does shoot, it might carry a little more suspense and also wouldn't be as noisy and heterogeneous.

. . . Mitchum runs forward through the *Oceania* hallway on the starboard side into the smoking room, just forward of the engine room casing, onto the port deck and then moves forward on the port deck, the distance required to cover the galley and the dining room.

Then, at this point, the exchange takes place between Mitchum and Cardigan.

After the Musketeer business with Cardigan, we will take Mitchum all the way aft on the port deck (we will not take him up above by a ladder on the port deck). We will take him all the way aft and around the aft end of the deck house and up the ladder at this point.

Mitchum puts the revolver and the box of ammunition down on top of the same engine room casing that he uses for cover. He takes his gun, pulls the clip out, and to his right puts his gun down on the corner of the engine room housing, skylight, ventilator setup. He reaches in his pocket or, if he has been holding the box of ammunition in his hands, he puts the box of ammunition down in the same place, takes the cover off, and pulls out a few shells ready to load them.

This suffocating minutiae continues endlessly until, at the end of page seven, he concludes:

I don't want to show at any time the gangsters as cowardly, inefficient, folding up, weakening, running for cover, or anything that will lessen the menace existing to our people aboard. I don't want victory to appear in sight at any time.

Thus from small bridges do large yachts grow.

Two days later another communication arrived from Hughes. If the long memo was extraordinary, this was certainly bizarre. Hughes had invented, during our story sessions, a new character, an evil German doctor. After Mitchum is captured by the heavies, the doctor proposes giving him a mind-destroying injection. This particular scene fascinated Howard so much that he insisted on writing the doctor's big speech. Perhaps it was pride of authorship that prompted it, but to ensure that this speech was properly delivered by the actor, he recorded it himself on an acetate record. He made four takes of the following dialogue, each take being preceded by his announcing, "Third paragraph of doctor's speech."

But in overdose quantities, this drug is very damaging. For example, an injection of, oh . . . let us say, seven or eight cubic centimeters . . . then certain brain tissues are destroyed. The patient never regains his memory. Death usually follows within a year.

I listened to this recording with a mixture of embarrassment and hilarity. Howard Hughes, with his Texas drawl, doing a highly melodramatic but amateur reading in what he believed to be a heavy German accent. It came out sounding like a Swede imitating a Chinese dialect.

Accompanying the acetate was a memo. He had picked out specific line readings from each of the four takes that he liked best and thought they should be used. The second sentence in the third take was a better reading than the one in the fourth take, he instructed, and the third sentence in the first take was better than the one in the second take. It was the typical, overly complex, tortuously involved Hughes approach. The whole thing was an exercise in futility. Even if he had done it well, there was no possible way to use any of it. Howard Hughes sitting down in a recording studio, and seriously devoting himself to making these appalling dramatic readings, was an image I could not shake from my mind.

Eventually, as it must to all films, the shooting came to an end. It had taken two months. After another month of editing, I found I had ended up with eight reels of new material, about an hour and twenty minutes of additional movie. This was almost as long as the original picture. The last half of the last reel had grown even larger than the yacht.

As soon as Hughes knew we were ready to run the film for him, we were called to Goldwyn Studios. He was really anxious to see it. We arrived at the office about midnight. For once Howard didn't keep us waiting. He didn't even have his brown paper bag with him. We went directly to his private projection room, which was almost opposite the office door on the other side of the dingy hallway. None of us had ever seen this projection room before. It was stylistically the same as the office: barren. On the right, as you entered, the screen. In front of it, about twenty feet back, six decrepit theater seats. On the wall to the left of the screen and a little in front of the theater seats, a small desk; a worn leather chair behind it, a battered gooseneck lamp on it.

Howard seated himself at the desk and put on a set of aviators' earphones, the kind that have outsize rubber cups for the ears. There was a primitive intercom on the desk so he could contact the projectionist. He flipped the switch. "Charlie," he said, "I'm not getting enough gain on these things." He listened for a moment while Charlie apparently turned up the sound level. "That's it," Howard said with a laugh. "Now we're operating on the same wavelength." He was in high good humor. "We're ready for takeoff whenever you are."

An hour and twenty minutes later, we landed. The lights came back up, Howard took off the earphones. He turned toward me, beaming. "I can't tell you," he said, "how pleased I am with what you've done. It's far better than I ever hoped it could be. Far better." I took my first breath in eighty minutes and looked at my colleagues. They were smiling as smugly as I was. Howard went on rhapsodizing. We went on lapping it up like thirsty tigers. "I really think that what we've got is great," he went on, "but I've got one problem with it: I don't like the actor who plays the chief heavy, the part of Ferraro."

Knowing Hughes, we should have expected the unexpected. But we didn't. "I don't think he's that great either, Howard," I said, "but it's the same actor who plays Ferraro in the original picture. I had to use him."

"Well," he said, "he annoys me. I don't like him at all. Now, I don't want you to feel bad, because it isn't your fault, but I think we should replace him."

"Ferraro's in practically every scene I shot," I said as the full implication of what he was saying dawned on me. "We'd have to redo almost everything."

"That's right. That's what we'll have to do."

"But what about all those scenes he's in earlier in the picture, the parts I didn't shoot? We can't have two different actors playing the same role."

"Redo those, too."

"Those, too?" I repeated stupidly.

"Yes, we'll get another actor and redo everything he's in all the way through the picture." I felt like a boxer who had raised his arms in a victory handclasp only to be hit in the solar plexus. Suddenly I was hanging on the ropes. But Howard was continuing, pacing back and forth in front of the screen.

"Now, since we're going to replace him, let's get the best heavy in town. We'll start an exhaustive search. I want you to interview everybody. Call all the agents." We sat there slackjawed. Then, in typical Hughes fashion, he started to expand on the idea. After we had interviewed every possibility, we were to select the five best candidates. Howard wanted stills of them. But not just your plain, garden-variety stills. Far from it.

"I want them tested in a scene from the picture, but not with a movie camera," he explained. "Use a high-speed still camera and shoot it as though you were actually doing the scene. Nothing posed. Shoot them in action, dialogue and all. Use the real actors who would be in the scene, not doubles or anything like that. Use the real set and have the lighting done by our regular movie cameraman, not by the still man. The people and the set should look exactly as they will in the picture." What he was talking about meant that hundreds upon hundreds of stills would have to be taken. He thanked us all once again for the great job we'd done and bade us farewell. We stumbled, dazed, into the night.

We did as we were told: called all the agents; interviewed everybody; selected five prospects; made hundreds and hundreds of stills and sent them to Howard. Then, as usual, we waited. After six weeks we got further orders. He liked three of the actors and wanted to do more tests of them. This time the tests were to be made with a movie camera. The selected scene was to be shot exactly as though it would be used in the finished picture. It may have been a streak of sadism on Hughes's part, but the scene he had chosen for all of these tests involved Mitchum getting beaten up. It was an ordeal for Bob. I found him to be a man of infinite patience, with bruises to match.

The final choice turned out to be Robert J. Wilke, an actor of no great renown. But he had a lot going for him. Big, rugged. A face mean enough to give a Cossack pause. He was also a first-rate actor.

We started over.

■ ■ ■

I was walking from my mobile office on the stage in Culver City, on the way to the set. We were more than three quarters through the reshoot. Wilke was doing an excellent job. Everything seemed fine and dandy. A large, distinguished-looking man, early thirties, was walking toward me. "Mr. Fleischer?" he asked rhetorically.

"Yes."

"I was sent over here to see you."

"Oh?"

"My name is Raymond Burr." The name was unfamiliar to me. He could have been a process server for all I knew.

"Oh?" There was an awkward pause while I waited for him to go on.

"I'm supposed to talk to you about the part of Ferraro," said this Raymond Burr, whoever he might be.

"The part of Ferraro!" I said with a chuckle. "It looks like you're just a little late. That was cast weeks ago. Bob Wilke is playing it."

"I know that," he said. There was another awkward pause while he watched me knit my eyebrows together. "Didn't anyone tell you about this?"

"About what?"

"I'm replacing Bob Wilke."

"You're *what?*" I asked, my voice rising in disbelief to become a squeak. "Who told you that?"

"Mr. Hughes," he replied almost apologetically.

"Please, Mr. Burr, Raymond," I stuttered. "Please wait here for a few minutes. Sit down. I've got to make a phone call. I'll be right back."

I stumbled to my office, grabbed the phone, and called Fellows at the studio in Hollywood. "Bob," I shouted, "what the hell is going on? Did you know about this Raymond Burr?"

"Yes Howard called me early this morning."

"Then it's true? He's going to replace Wilke?"

"Yes, I'm afraid so."

"But what happened? I thought Wilke was doing a great job. So did Howard."

"He did, but he saw Raymond Burr in some movie the other night and he liked him so much he decided to put him in the picture."

Just like that. After all the searching and interviewing and selecting and testing. After all the weeks of retakes and reshooting. No consultation, no asking, no nothing. None of it meant anything.

Raymond Burr, picked almost at random, was going to play the part.

We started over.

Vincent Price threw a party on the stage. He was celebrating his first year on the picture.

Mitchum took to drink. Who could blame him? This picture was finally getting to him. The happy hour became an established institution in his dressing room. It started at five o'clock and you could forget about working with him after that. He began stashing vodka in water glasses at strategic places all over the set. Whenever there was a delay of some sort, there was always a glass at hand. I didn't catch on for quite a while. It often puzzled me how he could start a scene sober and finish it drunk. His sense of humor remained as wicked as ever. If he spotted obviously out-of-town visitors on the stage, he delighted in sitting on a short stool, smoking a cigarette, and reading a newspaper, with his trousers dropped down around his ankles. We had no trouble at all in getting rid of visiting firemen.

Inevitably, late one day, we came to the evil German doctor's sequence. It was the last scene we were scheduled to shoot. When it was completed, the picture would be finished. Over. All of us were more than anxious to get it over with. If I could just get the opening shot that afternoon, I could wrap up the whole picture the following day. The action was simple enough. Two heavies drag the struggling Mitchum into the salon of the yacht. That's all I needed. No more, no less, no dialogue. But it was four in the afternoon. We wouldn't be ready to shoot before a quarter to six. If this were a normal situation I wouldn't hesitate to go for it. But this was not a normal situation. There was the happy hour to contend with. What the hell, I figured, I'll have a little chat with Mitchum.

I made a quick assessment when I entered his dressing room. He looked fine. Bright-eyed, sharp, pleasant. Alone. That was a very good sign. No suspect glasses of water in sight. "Bob," I said, "I think I can finish the picture tomorrow."

"You can? Great!" he responded. "That's the best goddamn news I've heard in a year."

"There's only one thing that would prevent it."

"What's that?"

"Well," I said, rather tentatively, "I've got to get the first setup today."

He glanced at his watch. "It's still early. How much of the scene do you want to do?"

"Not much," I answered. "Just the very opening. You know, where the two guys drag you in. It won't take any time to shoot. Hell, you've done this scene so many times in the tests you don't even have to rehearse it."

"Sure. That's a cinch. What's the problem?"

"Time," I said. "It's going to take about an hour and a half to light the set, and that'll push us past five o'clock."

"That's okay with me. I don't mind."

"Well, Bob, I know you don't, er, well, you know, like to work after five," I said as diplomatically as possible, putting a heavy emphasis on "like."

A small smile crossed his face. The point had not been lost on him. "No. No. I want to do it," he protested.

"You sure?"

"Absolutely."

"Terrific," I said and left to spread the good news among the crew.

The possibility of finishing the next day spurred everyone on. We were ready to shoot shortly after five. Mitchum was sent for.

Disaster.

Bob was drunk.

My heart sank into my stomach. My instinct was to call a wrap and go home. But that would be a humiliation for Mitchum. It could send him into a fury. I'd come this far without getting into any scraps with Mitchum. Why risk it now when we were so close to finishing? Besides, I felt it wasn't a good idea to make an enemy of the first star I'd ever worked with. Word gets around very fast in Hollywood.

Better, I thought, to try to get this simple shot. After all, he had two stuntmen to hold him up. It seemed the wiser and safer course.

"All right," I said, "let's try it." Bob went outside the door of the salon for his entrance. The two stuntmen held him by each arm. A fragile, very elderly gentleman with a wonderful German accent was playing the evil doctor. I stood him about twenty feet from the door, in front of a heavy, round, green, felt-covered poker table. The camera rolled and I called, "Action!"

Mitchum and the two stuntmen struggled through the door. Once inside, Bob gave a mighty and totally unexpected shove. It caught the stuntmen by surprise. They were sent stumbling across the room, landing in a heap in front of the old doctor. Bob stood there panting, crouched with clenched fists, in a fighting position. I didn't like the look of that at all. "Cut! Cut! Cut!" I yelled. "What's going on?" I asked the stuntmen. "You have to hold on to him. He's not supposed to win this fight."

"Sorry, boss," they said, dusting themselves off. They laughed and looked a little sheepish.

We tried it again. Bob put much more violence into the action this time. The stuntmen went flying.

The situation became clear. Mitchum was in a drunken, macho mood. He was proving to all of us that he was stronger and tougher than any two stuntmen. I wanted to call the whole thing off, but how could I? Tell him he was too drunk and nasty to work? With the temper he was in, it just, somehow, didn't seem the right approach. Not if I was interested in surviving. Discretion, I was always taught, was the better part of valor. I decided to try that first. I talked to Bob privately.

"You're using too much strength, Bob. You're too strong for them," I said, figuring that flattery might get me somewhere. "Give the guys a break. Fake it a little."

"I am faking it! They're not holding me hard enough. It's not my goddamn fault," he responded in anger.

"Well, try to fake it a little more, for Christ's sake." In spite of myself there was an anger rising in me, too. "If you don't I'm going to wrap it up before somebody gets hurt."

"Okay. Okay," he said impatiently as he walked behind the set. I called, "Action."

If there was any faking before, there was certainly none at all this time. Not from him and not from the stuntmen, who felt challenged. It was turning into a real brawl. I started yelling, "Cut! Goddamn it. Cut!" It was about as effective as using a squirt gun to douse a warehouse fire. It ended when the stuntmen got thrown into the heavy poker table, which toppled over onto the terrified doctor.

The whole scene was frozen in a tableau. The crew stared in shocked silence. The only sound was Mitchum's labored breathing. He stood in the center of the set fuming, like a grenade with its pin pulled. I may have appeared calm on the outside, but inside I was boiling.

"Bob," I said quietly, slowly, and clearly, "I don't know if you're trying to make a complete fool of yourself, or of me, but you have succeeded in doing both."

The grenade went off. "That does it!" he screamed. "That does it! I'm not taking any more of this shit! I've had it with you and this fucking picture and with this whole goddamn thing!" and he went on a rampage.

He started with the lighting equipment. He smashed every lamp on the set. Every piece of furniture, he completely demolished. Chairs, tables, sideboards, pictures were reduced to rubble. His rage was complete. The shouted threats and invective never stopped. At any moment I expected him to turn his violence on me. I stood my ground, inwardly quaking. He found a piece of pipe and bashed out every window. He kicked down every door. He put his foot through every wall. He totally and completely destroyed the set and all that was in it. Me next, I thought. Me next.

When there was nothing left of the set to smash he stormed around the outer reaches of the stage, screaming insults at me. If a chair or a piece of equipment came within reach, it went sailing. There was nothing I could do except stand there and watch and hope the fury would finally drain out of him. It didn't. It went on and on. He was sick and tired, he shouted, of being taken advantage of. Everybody was riding his coattails to fame and he would have no more of it. Stinking directors riding on his back to make a name for themselves. Unknown actors trying to find glory by working with him. Burr and I were fags, anyhow, he raged. And fuck Howard Hughes, too.

Eventually he went to his dressing room. The door slammed shut with the sound of an explosion.

My insides were all churned up. I felt like vomiting. On my way to my office I passed my assistant. "Wrap it up," I said quietly.

"What about the set?" he asked.

"Get it fixed," I replied.

The two stuntmen followed me into my little office. "Boss," they said, "we want you to know we were ready. If he made a move toward you we would have killed him." I believed them and nodded my thanks.

Ray Burr was waiting outside the office door. We had become close friends during the filming. It must have been a friendship Mitchum somehow resented. Ray put his arm around my shoulders and silently walked me to the stage door. He then phoned my wife. "Mickey," he said to her, "you've got a sick guy coming home. Make him a big brandy and give him some tender, loving care."

I didn't sleep that night. I tossed. I turned. I analyzed. The more I analyzed, the angrier I got. By morning I was in the grip of a cold indignation. I couldn't wait to get to the studio. There was going to be a shoot-out at the O.K. Corral, and I was ready for it.

I got to the studio early. Everything was well rehearsed in my mind.

You're a bully, I would say, threatening and intimidating me the way you did. And you're totally unreliable. You let me believe you'd be in shape to do the scene, and you let me down. Besides that, you're a coward, fighting with stuntmen who are paid not to fight back. In other words, Bob, you're an unreliable, cowardly bully.

I would wring an apology out of him.

When I got to the dressing room I didn't bother to knock. I flung the door open.

The makeup table was directly opposite the door. Bob was sitting at it facing the mirror, his back to me. Shotgun Britton, his makeup man, hovered over him. Mitchum looked into the mirror. My reflection glared back at him. Slowly he raised both his hands and covered his face. "O my God," he said. Then he slid out of the chair onto the floor and rolled under the couch that was on his left. He disappeared completely.

"Shotgun," I said to the makeup man, "get out, will you?" He scurried out. I closed the door behind him and addressed the couch. "Bob," I said, "come out."

Bob's right arm appeared. He was lying on his stomach. The arm made a waving motion, as though it were swimming the breast-stroke. "Go away, please," he said, his voice muffled by the couch.

"Come out, Bob."

"I can't," he said. "I'm too ashamed. I can't face you. Please, go away."

"Come on out. I've got something to say to you. I'm not leaving until I do." He crawled out and stood up. I suddenly realized what a big man he was.

"Don't say anything," he said, holding out his hands as though to fend me off. "I feel bad enough about yesterday."

I started into my prepared speech anyhow. "I want you to know that you're a bully and a—" but Bob interrupted.

"Look," he said, "I'm sorry about what happened. I apologize. What more can I say?"

I felt like a full-rigged sailing vessel that had run into a sudden calm. The wind had definitely gone out of my sails. There wasn't much left for me to say.

"Bob," I said, "you're a son-of-a-bitch."

"I know."

We shook hands and finished the picture.

Shortly after the finish of shooting, Fellows and I were summoned to Bungalow 19 at the Beverly Hills Hotel. Howard had called us there to give final instructions about the editing. After the constant delays, restarts, and leisurely pace, he was now in a great rush to get the picture into the theaters.

Would we work on the editing seven days a week and as many nights as we could stand? he asked us. Damn the overtime charges for the editing crew, full steam ahead. If we did this for him we would all get a fine bonus. I wondered what it could be. What would this movie mogul, this manufacturer of oil drills and airplanes, this owner of Trans World Airlines, consider an irresistible reward?

It turned out to be a two-week vacation with pay. John D. Rockefeller was famous for giving dime tips, too.

Naturally, we agreed. It was an offer we would in no way refuse. The sooner we were rid of this picture, the better.

As we were taking our leave, Howard said, "I'm afraid you won't be seeing much of me anymore." We asked him why not. A big and highly mischievous grin took over his face. "Well, there's a little airplane down in Long Beach I've got to look after," he replied.

After all these years he was still preoccupied with the *Spruce Goose*. With anyone else you might feel like throwing your hands up in despair. But not with Howard. Not with that daredevil look and those smiling eyes. You had to like him.

It was the last time I ever saw Howard Hughes.

He may have physically been gone, but the dark secrecy, the cloak-and-dagger atmosphere, the almost byzantine machinations remained. It pervaded our previews.

In ordinary circumstances when you have a sneak preview you know in what theater you'll be running the picture. You might even advertise it. Usually it's not that big a secret.

We had four sneak previews of *His Kind of Woman*. The CIA couldn't have run a more covert operation.

There were four of us in the privileged preview group. Besides Fellows and me, there was the editor and the head of the Editorial Department. None of us ever had the foggiest idea where we would be previewing.

Preview nights we would dine at Lucy's Restaurant, across the street from the studio, at 6:15 P.M. At precisely 7:15 P.M. a limousine would pick us up at the curb in front of the restaurant. We'd pile in, and close and lock the doors. If I'd worn a cape, I'm sure I would have hidden my face in it. The limo would pull away. After we were in motion, the head of Editorial would produce a sealed envelope from an inside jacket pocket. It was then that we'd learn the breathtaking news of our destination. Pasadena, perhaps. Or even Glendale. No secret had ever been better kept. Not even the Manhattan Project.

The previews all went moderately well. Audiences were quite receptive. After every running, though, we invariably heard the same rumor. Howard Hughes had been in the audience.

It could have been true. Then again, it probably wasn't. Certainly it was undeniably typical of him. I could just imagine him sitting in the dark, cloaked in anonymity, enjoying the secrecy and the crafty deception. Still, it was only conjecture.

We never did find out, one way or the other.

His Kind of Woman was released in 1952. It lost $850,000, precisely the amount spent on making the new sequences.

The Narrow Margin also came out the same year. It was one of the biggest sleepers in RKO's history.

There were more than two thousand employees at RKO when Hughes took over in 1948. When I left, in 1952, there were fewer than five hundred.

VI

Howard Hughes kept his word. When *His Kind of Woman* was finally wrapped up, he approved a loan-out deal from RKO so that I could go to work for Stanley Kramer and direct *The Happy Time*, the picture I was longing to do. By that time Kramer had entered into one of the strangest alliances known to Hollywood. Harry Cohn, the tyrannical head of Columbia Pictures, had contracted Kramer's company to make thirty films in five years. Kramer was to have complete autonomy over what he produced. Cohn was an archconservative, and Kramer a socially conscious liberal, but it wasn't the differences between the two men that made people wonder; it was the one, big similarity. They were both fiercely independent. Like most well-publicized Hollywood marriages, no one expected it to last. It didn't.

The honeymoon was still on, however, when I joined the Kramer outfit, and I was glad to be there. Even though I was relieved to be out from under the RKO contract, I nonetheless had to sign another long-term contract, with the Kramer Company. Working under a long-term contract was *de rigueur* at that time. I had no trepidation about signing because Stanley was one of my closest friends and I knew him for what he was—a completely ethical, creative, sensitive producer. The thought of forcing someone to make a picture he didn't want to do would just never enter his mind.

The thing that did give me pause, though, was Harry Cohn. As unlikely as it seemed at the moment, I could contemplate a time when the Cohn-Kramer marriage might prematurely dissolve. As in any divorce case, someone must get custody of the children, or in this case, the personal service contracts. I didn't want to see my contract being assigned to Columbia and the tender mercy of Harry Cohn. After all my struggling, I'd be right back where I started, under the yoke of a major studio and a major monster. I insisted on and got a nonassignable contract.

I was probably the happiest director in town when I made the move up Gower Gulch to Columbia Studios from RKO to join Kramer and Foreman. I was even able to get Earl Felton hired to write the script. Now I was working with my three best friends. While I may have been happy and content, much of Hollywood was not. The Communist witch-hunt and the blacklist were in full cry, and uneasy lay many a head. Some of the people I knew at RKO were already in trouble. It was all quite frightening and alarming. I knew, however, there was no likelihood that this McCarthy business could ever touch me. I was not given to making political statements. The only organization I'd ever joined was the AAA. I never attended meetings of any sort, not even of my kids' nursery school.

Even guilt by association didn't worry me. The only one who could possibly cause me some concern, in that regard, would be my closest of close friends, Carl Foreman. I always considered myself a liberal, but Carl was *liberal*. Still, in all the years we'd been bosom companions, he never gave me reason to believe he was more than just that. We seldom talked politics. He was active in liberal causes but never proselytized, never asked me to join anything. My friendship with Carl gave me no qualms at all. I was merely an apolitical, appalled observer of the panic in the streets of Hollywood.

The casting on the picture was going extremely well. Kramer had lined up Charles Boyer for one of the leads. He may have been past his zenith as a star, but he couldn't have been more perfect for the role. Louis Jourdan was ideal for the charming, profligate brother. The centerpiece of the movie was the young boy on the cusp of adolescence, Bibi. This part went to Bobby Driscoll, who had just completed *Song of the South* for Disney.

The only leading role left to cast was the always tipsy Uncle Louis. This part had been played in the stage version, on Broadway, by Kurt Kasznar, and he was brilliant. We desperately wanted Kasznar for the film, but he was, rightfully, demanding a lot of money, more than Kramer wanted to pay. Stanley had a fine eye for casting and came up with a great alternative, an idol of his, Zero Mostel, one of Broadway's great entertainers.

Mostel had been before the Un-American Activities Committee, and jobs for him had evaporated like a morning mist on a hot summer's day. Stanley tracked him down to an address in Westwood, on Little Santa Monica Boulevard, and we paid him a visit.

It was heartbreaking. He was living in a one-room garret. Outside of a large rumple-sheeted mattress on the floor and a couple of rickety stools and chairs, there was virtually no furniture. A card table held a small hot plate and the usual dishes and cooking equipment a bachelor collects. Even though the room was barren of furniture, it had a cluttered, chaotic look because of the dozens of oil paintings he had been working on. They were large canvases, covered with vivid colors and dark, dramatic compositions, and were scattered everywhere. The air reeked with the heavy smell of oil paint and banana oil. Zero himself looked like an elephantine, bohemian artist. Shoeless, with baggy, soiled sweatpants and loose pajama tops enclosing a blubbery body, he was pathetically appealing. It was the face, though, that got to you. Even in the best of times that face wore a mournful look. Now you could read despair in it as well.

We knew immediately he was our man. He would be as good as Kasznar, maybe better. He was, in fact, the one and only possible replacement we could think of. Stanley handed him the script and told him about the part and that we wanted him in the picture. I had to fight back tears as I watched him react. As an actor he had been trained to show his emotions, not hide them, and show them he did. A look of gratitude, happiness, and love for us flooded his face. The deal was set then and there. Kramer could have picked him up for a bargain, but, bless his heart, he didn't. He offered him the same price as he had Kasznar. Kramer and I were delighted with the way things turned out. We not only had a great Uncle Louis, but also we felt that we'd done a good deed about which we could both be proud.

Zero never got to play in the picture. When the contract came to Harry Cohn's attention, he killed it. No Commie was going to be in one of his movies. Kramer fought to keep Mostel, but it was hopeless. Cohn held the purse strings, and he would pull them shut if Kramer insisted on Mostel. So much for autonomy. Stanley and I were sick about it, not just because we were losing a wonderful actor but also because of the disappointment and hurt we had inadvertently inflicted on someone we both admired. Our kind of good deed he could have lived without. It was my first direct contact with the blacklist, and I was shaken.

Kurt Kasznar got the money he demanded, and he was superb in the movie.

A few weeks before we were to commence photography on the picture, the Screen Directors' Guild, as it was called at that time, presented a controversial issue for its members to decide. We were being asked to vote on whether, as a requirement of membership, everyone had to sign a loyalty oath stating he was not now, or had ever been, a member of the Communist Party. The thinking behind it, I suppose, was that this would be a great way to root out Communists, because no Communist would ever sign such an oath. Anyone who refused to sign was, ergo, a Communist. The fact that the Communist Party was not yet outlawed in this country made no difference to the drafters of the proposal.

Everyone I knew in the Guild was outraged. Why did we have to swear we were not Party members unless we were all under some sort of suspicion? Why, as loyal Americans, was it necessary to swear to our loyalty unless someone thought that we were not? There was no doubt, among those I talked to, that our integrity was being questioned. I received many phone calls from my friends in the guild urging me to vote against the odious loyalty oath.

It was a secret ballot that came through the mail, and it had all the usual safeguards, envelopes within envelopes, that go with such a ballot. I voted against the loyalty oath, as I knew all my friends would also do, and mailed it back.

The results of the voting were announced in the trade papers *Daily Variety* and *The Hollywood Reporter*. Their headlines proclaimed that the loyalty oath had won by an overwhelming majority. Of about fifteen hundred guild members, only some 12 voted against it.

The Hollywood Reporter went well beyond merely reporting the news. It had somehow invaded the sanctity of the secret ballot and published, on the front page for all to see, the names of those unpatriotic scoundrels who voted against the loyalty oath. There stood my name, in a list of people I did not know. Not one of my friends who had urged me to vote "no" was on the list.

My reaction was pure fear and panic. All I could see was my promising career in ashes, my life in ruins. Blacklist, here I come. I cursed myself for jeopardizing so much by voting for what I believed in.

Two weeks passed, and the devastating revelation of my treasonable act seemed to be arousing not the slightest reaction. Nobody mentioned it to me. Nobody seemed to care. My fluttery stomach was calming down, and I had stopped jumping when someone knocked on my office door.

Then I got called to the office of one of Harry Cohn's henchmen. He came right to the point. "We've got a report that you fought the non-Communist oath." It wasn't a question, it was a flat statement.

"Fought it?" I answered. "I never fought it, I just voted against it."

"Why?" he asked.

I couldn't contain myself. "Why?" I burst out, my fear and nervousness disappearing. "Because it's goddamn stupid, that's why, and I don't like it and I don't like being questioned this way. What the hell is this, the Un-American Activities Committee, or something?"

"Okay, okay," he said, trying to calm me. "I know how you feel, but I had to ask you those questions. Just write a letter to the Kramer Company saying you're not a Communist and that'll be the end of it. Okay?"

"Why should I?" I said, still steaming.

"You want to direct *The Happy Time?*"

"Of course I do."

"Then I'd advise you to write the letter," he said pleasantly.

I left his office and went to see Kramer to tell him about this persecution. Stanley shrugged it off. Apparently he'd been through this a few times before. "Don't get your bowels in an uproar," he advised. "Just write the goddamn letter and forget it. Fuck 'em."

I took Kramer's advice and wrote the letter. In it I tried not to grovel too much and to preserve some shred of dignity with a hint of indignation. It was humiliating and I hated myself for doing it, but fighting it would have been just plain stupid.

The making of *The Happy Time* was an unadulterated delight, and we were all pleased with the result. In the 1950s Radio City Music Hall was to movies what the Palace Theater used to be to vaudeville. To play the Palace was to achieve the pinnacle of success. To play the Music Hall was something to be proud of. *The Happy Time* played the Music Hall.

In *The Good Earth*, a movie about life in old China, Luise Rainer played a superstitious peasant woman. When she gave birth to a boy child she was so terrified that the gods would be jealous and take him from her, she wrapped him in a blanket to hide his face, looked up to the heavens, and said, "It's only a poor, pockmarked girl child." I should have done that with my Kramer deal. The gods were certainly jealous of it.

Immediately following *The Happy Time* Kramer put me to work developing another human comedy, *Full of Life*. It never went into production because everything started to come unglued at the Kramer Company.

My wife, Mickey, and I had a permanent Saturday night bowling date with Carl and Estelle Foreman, and my writer friend from Yale, Herbie Baker, and his wife, Camille. Dinner at Dominic's first, then bowling at Art Linkletter's alleys on Beverly Boulevard a block away. Usually we said our good nights after the last game and went home. One night, however, Carl said, "Why don't we go back to Dom's for some coffee? I've got something to tell you."

We settled around one of Dom's beat-up tables and Carl gave us the news. "I've been summoned to appear before the House Un-American Activities Committee."

We all reacted with shock. "But why, Carl?" I asked. "Why did they call you?"

"Because I'm a Communist."

We sat for a minute digesting the implications of what he had said. Carl watched us ruefully, then said, "It's like telling your parents you've got cancer."

"I wanted you to hear it from me first," he went on. "It's going to be a rough time for me, and I don't want any of it to rub off on you. It might be a good idea if we went our separate ways."

It was typical of Carl—concerned for his friends, understanding of their problems. We wouldn't even consider his suggestion. The idea of walking away from Carl and Estelle and their little daughter, Katie, was simply out of the question. We told him, and we meant it, that we were their friends and that they could count on us.

A great rift developed between Kramer and Foreman. You could feel the enmity growing. They tried to hide it, keep it from becoming public, but that was hopeless. Everyone knew what was going on. It was particularly difficult and awkward for me. They were both my best friends. At work the situation became an embarrassment. Felton and I would have a story conference with Kramer then, later, Foreman would come into my office and have another story conference with Felton and me. The two conferences wouldn't jibe creatively, and we didn't know whom to listen to.

I told Stanley about what was happening. He sympathized and told me to keep meeting with Carl, but to follow his, Stanley's, instructions. The situation was being resolved, he said. He was going to buy Carl out, and Carl would leave the company. But I was still faced with a dilemma. They were both my best friends, and I didn't want to lose either of them. How could I go on seeing them both socially and not alienate one of them? Stanley, being Stanley, said there was no reason for me to lose either of them as a friend. He promised he would never talk to me about Carl. I told this to Carl, and he made the same pledge about Stanley. They both kept their word and I kept my friends. Up to a point.

The committee appearance took place in Hollywood and was not televised, but broadcast on radio. Estelle accompanied Carl to the hearing. They dropped Katie off at our place in the morning, knowing she'd be in good hands while Carl testified. Katie played with our two young sons, Bruce and Mark, while our ears were riveted to the set. Carl handled the interrogation well. He seemed relaxed, calm, collected, very sure of himself. All of Movieland was listening, wanting to know if he'd name names.

The interrogator finally got around to the crucial question: "Would you tell this committee, Mr. Foreman, what people you have worked with in the motion picture industry?"

There was a pause before he answered, then he listed as many unreproachable star names he could think of and ended up with, "Gary Cooper, Adolphe Menjou, and Richard Fleischer."

I phoned Carl at home later in the afternoon. "You were great," I said. "You handled the whole thing beautifully."

"Thank you."

"But why, for God's sake, did you mention my name before the committee?"

"Why, I was doing you a big favor."

"What kind of favor is that?"

"Well, I wanted to protect you, because of our relationship. So I linked your name with the biggest reactionaries I could think of."

"You put me in great company, pal. The reactionaries know I'm not one of them, and now the liberals won't speak to me after this."

"You'll survive."

Shortly after the hearing, Carl left the Kramer Company, having been bought out by Stanley. Then a strange thing happened: The Foremans stopped seeing us. Whereas before, we talked to each other by phone just about every day and were together two or three evenings a week, now there was nothing—no calls, no dates. Our messages weren't returned.

This had been going on for more than a month, when I came home from work one evening and found Mickey in tears. She had taken our younger son, Mark, for his regular visit to the pediatrician. When she walked into the tiny anteroom, there was Estelle Foreman, waiting for Katie to come out of the doctor's office. Mickey was surprised and delighted to see her. "Why, Estelle, hello!" she said, holding out her arms in greeting. Estelle turned her back to her. "Estelle!" Mickey repeated, shocked. Estelle wouldn't turn around. Then Katie came out of the office and they left, walking right past Mickey without a word. She had cut Mickey dead.

A few weeks later we learned that the Foremans had left the country for good and had taken up residence in London. What happened still remains a mystery. After all those years of friendship and camaraderie, the bowling, the dinners, the working, and the vacations together, what happened?

The only thing we could think of was that someone, for whatever reason, had bad-mouthed us. Someone had said something to the Foremans to make them feel we were disloyal to them or treacherous. The thing that hurt the most, though, was that they never spoke to us about it, never gave us a chance to confirm or deny anything. Whatever it was that turned them against us they had accepted at face value, they believed it without question. Still, when you think about it, even that is understandable. To believe unfounded rumors as gospel, to accept malicious gossip as truth was the temper of the times. The House Un-American Activities Committee had done its job well.

Many years later I came to live in London while I directed three pictures in a row there. Mickey and I were in a theater one night, walking down a flight of stairs, when a program dropped on my head from above. I looked up. It was Carl, a big grin on his face. "Hey, Fleischer," he called down to me, "you're getting a little thin on top."

By that time Carl had remarried. His new wife, Eve, was a beautiful, charming girl. They invited us over to their house for lunch, and our friendship resumed. It was never like it was before, nowhere near, but it did resume. One night, at a dinner party, Mickey said to Carl, "Would you mind telling me what the feud was all about?" All Carl would say was, "I don't want to talk about it."

We were just about ready to commence photography on *Full of Life* when my worst fears came true. (It's only a poor, pockmarked girl child.) The Cohn-Kramer relationship fell apart like a rotten roast, and Harry Cohn took over all the Kramer contracts—all, that is, except mine.

Cohn didn't want any of the people he'd inherited, but he was stuck with their commitments. The only way he could wriggle out of that would be to give those unfortunates the worst possible picture assignments, films so far beneath their stature that they would quit rather than make them. There was a lot of anguish and anger involved, and those who could afford to, quit. The others had to suffer their degradation and somehow cope with it. I, at least, was spared all that. Stanley made a modest settlement of my contract and I was, for the first time in my life, out of work.

VII

Finding myself suddenly out of a job, after eleven years of continuous employment, was a little scary. Those long-term contracts, with their false sense of security, had left me emotionally unprepared. I hadn't been able to put aside much of a nest egg in all that time because my salaries were always minimum. The picture for Stanley Kramer was done under loan-out from RKO, and I was paid my regular contract salary, which, for that option period, came to $750 a week. The next film would have been done under a new and considerably better deal, at least three or four times better, but that had self-destructed. Offers of new jobs weren't exactly flooding in, and I was getting nervous about supporting my wife and two small boys.

Ever since *Bwana Devil* hit the screen, in 1953, and became a huge money-maker, 3-D movies had become the hot item in town. They became even hotter when *House of Wax* followed a month later, and it, too, started melting house records. The selection of the director for *House of Wax* caused a great deal of merriment in Hollywood. Warner Brothers Studios were producing the film, and Jack Warner, its monster-mogul, had two directors under consideration for the job, Raoul Walsh and André de Toth, both one-eyed directors. Jack Warner, apparently, was the only person beyond a kindergarten education who didn't know two eyes were necessary to see anything in three dimensions. Walsh and de Toth together couldn't see 3-D. The idea of putting a one-eyed director in charge of a 3-D movie was simply flabbergasting. De Toth got the job, and the picture was a howling success. Maybe Jack Warner knew something we didn't know.

When I got an offer to do a picture for MGM, it looked mighty attractive to me. The money and the screenplay weren't great, but it was employment and it was 3-D, a guarantee of success. The auspices under which the movie was to be made were certainly favorable, since Arthur Loew, Jr., a very young and very funny young man-about-town, was the producer. Arthur was the scion of the Loew's movie theater chain family, and the family also held the controlling interest in MGM. In fact, every sign posted around the studio bore the legend "Loew's, Inc." on it.* The film, called *Arena*, was a rodeo story. The idea of bucking broncos and Brahma bulls charging right into the audience in 3-D sounded exciting.

I managed to avoid having to sign a contract for more than just the one picture and reported to MGM. They gave me a quick course in 3-D photographic technique, and we were off to Tucson, Arizona, to shoot a real live rodeo.

By a great piece of good fortune the big Tucson Annual Rodeo was about to be held, and the idea was that I would photograph the real rodeo with all its crowds, color, and contests. Once we knew what cowboy was going to ride what horse or bull, we'd pay him to wear the same costume as one of our actors. Arthur Loew had contracted for the entire rodeo, cowboys, horses, and bulls, to remain behind when the rodeo was finished so that I could shoot close-up stuff with our actors in their midst.

The villain of the story was a big, vicious, man-killing Brahma bull. He was the leitmotiv of doom and disaster. When you saw him you knew, for sure, someone was going to get killed. All cowboys trembled if they were unfortunate enough to drew this monster for the Brahma bull ride. Naturally, at the climax of the story, our hero has to ride this terrible beast.

Since the selection, or casting, of that particular bull was vital to the success of the movie, I arrived in Tucson a couple of days early so I could make a choice from all the bulls that were going to be used in the rodeo. There were about seventy-five Brahmas penned in a large corral, and a tall ladder was set up outside the fence so I could look them over.

They were a mean-looking bunch, tough and battle-scarred. Almost any one of them was right for the part. But I was looking for that "special" bull, one that would, so to speak, stand out from the herd. I wanted one that looked like no other and would be instantly recognizable on the screen. I wanted the epitome of all Brahma bulls—arrogant, statuesque, and perfect. As I looked them over I

* Arthur pointed that out to me one day and said, "That's why they can't fire me. It'd be too expensive to change all the signs."

realized they all had the same flaw: There wasn't one pair of horns in the bunch that wasn't broken. They had been in too many rodeos, butted too many cowboys, and bucked into too many stadium fences. Then my eye came to rest on the bull of my dreams.

Huge, by far the biggest in the corral, he towered menacingly over the others. His coat was jet black. No other bull was jet black. A large white diamond marking emblazoned his massive forehead. He was the only one with such a marking. And best of all, he had an enormous pair of unbroken, perfect horns. This animal was unique. No other bull looked even remotely like him. We had our villain, all two tons of him. His name was Number 48.

The first day of shooting, Number 48 got to do his stuff. We dressed the cowboy who was to ride him in our picture outfit. I placed the 3-D cameras in strategic spots around the arena and warned the camera operators to be on the alert because this would be a wild ride. If the rider stayed on the bull for more than three seconds we'd be lucky. We got ready. I wished the cowboy luck, and the doors to the chute flew open. Number 48 minced out.

He pranced a few steps forward, came to a dead halt, and looked around. The tensed-up rider froze, waiting for the fireworks to begin. No fireworks. Slowly the cowboy straightened up and looked around, too. The cowboy kicked the bull with his heels to try to get it to move. Nobody in that crowd of rodeo fans had ever seen a Brahma bull being kicked to get it to move. Jeering could be heard from the stands. The cowboy sat on Number 48 for about ten seconds, then slid off and walked disgustedly away amid an ovation of wild hoots and applause from the audience. I knew then why Number 48 had unbroken horns: He never did anything with them.

I was leaning against the fence with my head in my arms when there was a tap on my shoulder. It was Arthur. "What was that?" he asked.

"I don't know, Arthur, he sure looked mean."

"Yeah. I think you picked a Ferdinand. He's just another pretty Hollywood face with no talent. Now what are we going to do?"

"I'm not ready to give up yet. He's so perfect. I'll talk to the wrangler and see what he can come up with."

The wrangler had a suggestion. "When he's in the chute, just as we open the gate, I'll give him a shot in the balls with an electric cattle prod. That should send him out right lively."

We told the rodeo officials what we were up to and asked them to take Number 48 out of competition and just let us use him unofficially between other rides so we could still use the crowds and the background. They agreed.

The next day we tried the wrangler's suggestion and zapped poor old Number 48 just as the gate opened. He jumped around some. Nothing spectacular, maybe six inches off the ground. The rider looked like he was sitting in a rocking chair. I yelled at him to make it look good and fall off. He obliged. The following day we added a few firecracker noisemakers to the zapping plus whoops and hollers from nearby cowboys and some thwacking of his backside with their hats. The jumping improved somewhat. Day by day, with careful selection of low angles, and judicious undercranking of the cameras to make him appear to be moving faster than he really was, we slowly built up a sequence that started to look pretty good. It was the magic of movies. What I needed to punch it up and make it really work would be some big, head close-ups of Number 48. They were absolutely vital. With fake foam around his mouth, his snout dripping glycerine, and a few other tricks I had up my sleeve, I would make him into the Godzilla of bulls.

The day after the rodeo ended I got everything in readiness for shooting the critically important close-ups of Number 48. He had his own private pen because we didn't want him to get into any arguments with other bulls and maybe get gored, or break a horn. The cowboys dubbed it "The Star Dressing Room," and the crew had tacked up a big star and a fancy plaque with his name on the gate.

Because everyone was so amused by what was going on, I thought we'd make a little ceremony out of this event. We all gathered around the special pen and I called out, "Welcome to Stardom, Great 48." Then, with a sweeping gesture of my arm, I commanded, "Open the gate!"

We all stood back and the gate swung open. There stood our magnificent beast in all his glory. He gave us a glowering look, took three steps forward, staggered, and dropped dead.

No one moved. All we could do was stare in disbelief at the lifeless mountain of beef that was now the late, great 48. Our bull was history. Out of all the bulls I had to choose from I had picked the only one that would, at the most crucial moment, keel over and die.

Arthur Loew had missed the whole thing. Now he came running up to me. "What in God's name happened?" he asked breathlessly. "Stage fright," I replied.

It was a terrible, awful moment. We were, as the expression

goes, in deep shit. All eyes were turned toward me. How was I going to get out of this one? I did the only thing I could think of at the moment. I went over and sat on the bull's side and rested my chin in my hands. Everyone wandered away to leave me with my thoughts.

What with the rodeo over and the crowds gone, it would have been impossible to reshoot all that had been done. There was no alternative but to find another bull and try to fix it up to look like the late, great 48. Once again the tall ladder was set up outside the big corral, and I selected a successor to our star.

This one was no Ferdinand. He was a mean and ornery bastard who'd just as soon gore you with one of his broken horns as look at you. He wasn't jet black but a sort of dust gray. I thought we might just get away with that. Naturally, he had no large, white diamond emblazoned on his forehead. Only our ex-star had that.

I called our painter over and pointed out the bull I'd selected. "Do you think you can paint a white diamond on his forehead?" I asked. "I dunno," he answered dubiously, "I never painted a bull before." I said we'd give it a try.

The only possible way to do such a thing would be to get the bull in a chute. This is where rodeo riders mount their animals, just before they're released into the arena, by dropping down onto them from a straddle position above them. More cowboys get seriously injured in the chute than anywhere else. There's almost no room for the bull to move around in there, but a powerful beast like a Brahma bull makes its own room.

The cowboys wrangled our bull into the chute, and he didn't like it one little bit. He started banging and smashing his body and head in all directions. The painter took one look and said, "I'm not getting near that son-of-a-bitch." His solution was to tie a paint brush to the end of a three-foot stick. Painting anything with a three-foot brush handle, even if it's absolutely stationary, isn't going to produce a very satisfactory result, but our painter tried. Within a matter of seconds we had a bull whose face, neck, and shoulders were painted completely white, as well as any bystanders in the vicinity. I told the painter to forget it and see if he could somehow wash the paint off.

Next, I conferred with the prop man. "What about those broken horns?" I asked. "Can you do anything about them?" "I dunno, boss," was his reply. "I never did nothing like that on a bull before, but I'll try." We spent several hours after that twisting Dixie cups into horn tips, dipping them in plaster of Paris, and then trying to stick them on the broken ends of the bull's horns.

We tried everything to see if we could get one of the Dixie cups on the bull. It was a dangerous thing to do because the instant the bull got a hint of anyone approaching he'd go into a fit, smashing his head back and forth. Those flailing horns could punch a hole right through you. This was the kind of game the cowboys loved. They tried sneaking up on him, showing the same kind of reckless bravery as a toreador. Once in a while a falsie would actually get put in place, to cheers and cries of "olé" from the cowboys, but one vicious shake from that massive head and it went flying. We thought of trying to put his head in some kind of vise, but the wrangler vetoed the idea. "I don't know how you'd get his head into such a thing," he said, "and if you did he'd thrash around so much he'd break his neck in no time."

Toward the end of the day the wrangler took me aside. "I've got an idea that maybe would work," he said.

"I'll try anything. What's your idea?"

"Well," he said, and spat out a long stream of tobacco juice, "if your prop man can rig up a pair of fake horns, maybe we can hook them onto the broken ones and cover them up."

"It sounds possible," I said. "But how do you propose to get them on him?"

"We'll let him cool off now and give him a good feed," he explained. "Then tomorrow morning, a little before we go to work, we'll give him a good shot of Bourbon. That'll gentle him down enough for us to slip those horns on him."

"Sounds good to me," I said. "Let's give it a try."

The next morning I walked into the arena bright and early. The cowboys were all smiles. The wrangler ambled over to me. "Well, boss," he drawled, "we done it. You got yourself one handsome bull in the chute." I rushed over to take a look. He was right. There was the bull, a little befuddled-looking but still feisty, wearing a spectacular pair of perfect horns, a duplicate of the late, great 48's. "Better get shootin' fast," the wrangler advised. "That booze is wearin' off and if he gets crazed he'll bust those horns before he gets out of the chute."

I whipped the crew into action and we got the camera placed and barricaded in record time. I just needed one 3-D camera, aimed directly at the chute's gate, to get the full impact of the furious beast rushing right into the lens and into the audience's lap.

"Okay, we're ready!" I yelled to the wrangler. The cowboy who was to ride the bull lowered himself gingerly onto its back and gave a quick nod. The wrangler gave me the "ready" signal. "Roll it!" I screamed. "Rolling!" the camera assistant confirmed. I took a deep breath. "Action!" I shouted, my heart beating a lot faster than normal.

The gate to the chute flew open and out he came like a runaway express train. This was one mad bull. The booze had worn off. His eyes were bloodshot and filled with murder. He didn't need fake foam and glycerine—the real thing covered his nose and mouth. Best of all, he was coming right at the camera as though he'd been aimed at it. My God, I said to myself, this is incredible, this is fabulous, this is terrific. He took a couple of huge strides toward us, then took his first buck, a monumental leap into the air, all four hooves off the ground. He seemed to hang there, about three feet off the ground, for a full second, then came down with an earth-shuddering impact.

That's when the horns fell off.

A few days later Arthur Loew got a phone call from Joe Cohen, the studio manager in Hollywood. "I got a bill here for $500 for a bull," he said. "Why would Metro buy a bull?"

"Metro didn't buy a bull," Arthur answered. "That's for the bull's funeral."

"What do you mean, 'funeral'?"

"Well, the bull we were using in the picture died of a heart attack."

"How do you know it was a heart attack? Was there an autopsy?"

"No, there wasn't any autopsy. Why should there be an autopsy?"

"Because maybe it was something he ate."

This was too much for Arthur. "Listen, Joe," he replied, "bulls eat hay. They don't eat in delicatessens like you," and hung up.

We muddled through with the rest of the shooting in Tucson. The new bull didn't have the horns, the size, the color, or the white diamond on his forehead, but he gave us plenty of wild action. We did some fancy cutting when we put the picture together, and no one seemed to notice that two completely different bulls were playing the lead heavy. One of the main reasons no one noticed, other than the cutting, was that practically no one ever saw the movie. By the time the picture was released, the 3-D craze was over. It stopped like somebody had pulled a switch. *Arena* played in only one theater in 3-D, the Rialto, in New York. It was projected normal, or flat, everywhere else before it disappeared into the sunset.

VIII

Shortly after finishing *Arena* I was sitting at home, wondering, as all directors do, if I'd ever get another job. Doing *The Happy Time* for Kramer had been a nice step forward toward the goal of getting a big picture with real stars. Doing *Arena* was half a step back. I was mulling this over when the phone rang. It was my agent, Ray Stark. "I just got a very strange call," Ray said.

"Really? Who from?"

"Walt Disney."

"Yeah? What did he want?"

"He wants to see you."

"*Me?* He wants to see *me?*" I was incredulous. "You've got to be kidding."

"No, he wants to see you at ten tomorrow morning at his office. Can you be there?"

I was perplexed. "Well, what does he want to see me about?"

"He didn't say. Just that he'd like you to come to his office. How about it?"

"Well, I guess so," I replied a bit tentatively. "I'll be there. Are you sure he wants to see *me?*"

"That's what he said."

At my parents' house "Disney" was a dirty word. If you said it at dinner you were sent away from the table. My father, Max Fleischer, let alone being a full-fledged, authentic genius, was the nicest, sweetest, kindest, funniest, most tolerant man who ever lived. But mention "Disney" in his presence and his whole personality changed. An internal, seething anger would grip him. He was a man not at all given to profanity, but invariably you'd hear him mutter, "That son-of-a-bitch." There was good and ample reason for this, but still, knowing my father, I was always taken aback by the vehemence of his reaction to that name.

There was a Max Fleischer long before there was a Walt Disney. He was a world celebrity, loved and admired by moviegoers everywhere for the brilliance, the artistry, and the fun of his animated cartoons. He was to the public then what Disney is to the public now. They knew the name and recognized the face.

He was quite a guy. In 1909, when he was in his teens and living in Brooklyn, New York, he was so in love with cartooning that he went to the *Brooklyn Daily Eagle* and offered them $2 a week to let him just sit in the Art Department and watch. They countered by offering him $2 a week to help deliver papers to newsstands from a horse-drawn wagon. Four years later he was a staff artist on the paper and the youngest comic strip artist in the country.

At that time, animated cartoons existed as more of a curiosity than anything else, but the public seemed fascinated by them. As more and more cartoonists became interested in this new magic of animation, movie audiences began seeing various cartoon series called *Colonel Heezaliar*, *Krazy Kat*, and *Felix the Cat*. They were called animated cartoons by virtue of the fact that they moved, but the movement was merely a series of jerks and jumps, with none of the fluidity and grace we are accustomed to now. Audiences liked them anyhow, but found them hard to watch for too long.

My father worked as an animator on the *Colonel Heezaliar* series, and finally decided, in 1915, to do something about the jerky quality of the pictures. With some money that my mother had saved up from her household allowance (they met when he was twelve; my mother attended his bar mitzvah), he took a year off and invented and built a machine that would give cartoons smoother and more lifelike action. He called it the Rotoscope.

To demonstrate its capabilities, though, he had to make his own cartoon. He had to draw every frame of film by himself and photograph each one separately. At the end of the year he had drawn and photographed twenty-four hundred frames and had a movie that was three minutes long. He still hadn't seen what he'd created, however, since he had no way of projecting the film. It wasn't until he adapted a camera with an electric light bulb behind the eyepiece and projected the images onto a four-inch-square piece of cardboard that he saw his cartoon for the first time. It was perfect. The action was smooth and lifelike. Cartoons would never look the same again. The Rotoscope would revolutionize the budding animation industry.

By further experimentation with the Rotoscope, Max found that he could combine live action with animated cartoons in the same frame. This was what he'd been waiting for. He devised a cartoon series called *Out of the Inkwell*, which would open with him sitting in front of a drawing board. Dipping his pen into an inkwell, he'd draw KoKo the Clown, the character he'd created for the three-minute experimental film, and, lo and behold, it would come to life, jump off the drawing board, and crawl all over him. Together, Max and KoKo would have all sorts of adventures in real-life settings, and at the end KoKo would dive back into the inkwell and my father would screw the top of the bottle into place. The cartoons were utterly and completely charming, original, and funny. There was nothing like them, nor could there be, since Max held the patents. They were an instantaneous sensation. KoKo became a star and Max rocketed to fame. Moviegoing was much more of a passion in those days than it is even now, and soon there wasn't a moviegoer in the world who didn't recognize the short, rotund figure and the round face with the tiny mustache of Max Fleischer. And Walt Disney wasn't even on the horizon.

When Walt Disney entered the business, in 1921, it was as an imitator of my father. His first, unsuccessful series was a direct steal from *Out of the Inkwell*. Each film started with Walt sitting in front of a drawing board. My father considered him a young upstart, and it was the beginning of a long and bitter enmity.

In that same year Max entered into an association with Paramount Pictures as an independent producer. It was this association, and decisions of Adolph Zukor, the president of Paramount, that ultimately led to the overtaking and eclipsing of the Fleischer popularity by Disney.

With the advent of sound in motion pictures, in 1928, my father and Disney became each other's main competitor. Disney won the first round with a sound cartoon introducing Mickey Mouse. It was, indeed, a historic first. Max had wanted to make the first sound cartoon, but Adolph Zukor didn't think it was such a great idea and vetoed it.

The Fleischer-Disney fight was on in earnest, and Max hit back with a flurry of smashes. First he converted his immensely popular but silent creation of the sing-along Bouncing Ball Cartoons to sound. Next he created Betty Boop, the first "talking" cartoon. The Disney shorts may have been the first "sound" cartoons because they had music and sound effects. Mickey and the other characters, however, didn't speak. They squeaked or grunted or made strangling sounds. Betty Boop not only talked but also sang and Boop-oop-a-dooped her way into movie audiences' hearts. Then he brought the spinach-loving Popeye to the screen. The battle between the two men was now pretty equal.

Color came in. In spite of Max's pleadings, Zukor couldn't see it for cartoons. Disney was first again, and Max had to counterpunch. It isn't easy to win a fight when the guy in your corner keeps tying one of your hands behind your back.

Then came *Snow White and the Seven Dwarfs*, and it was a staggering blow. Max had wanted to make the first full-length feature animated cartoon. Adolph Zukor didn't think it would work and turned the idea down flat.

The phenomenal success of *Snow White* became apparent even to Zukor, and he gave his belated blessings to the feature Max had wanted to make, *Gulliver's Travels*. This was to be an enormous undertaking. The office space at 1600 Broadway, in Manhattan, was patently going to be too small. Much larger quarters had to be found, but the kind of space needed in New York City would be prohibitively expensive. Max had always dreamed of building his own studio that would be ideally suited to the making of animated cartoons. Now he began to give it serious consideration, particularly when the city fathers of Miami, Florida, where we had a vacation home for several years, made him an attractive offer of tax breaks and other advantages if he'd build his studio there. Besides the construction involved, it would mean relocating the entire studio staff and their families to Miami, and it would be costly. Still, Max felt, the long-term advantages far outweighed the disadvantages, and he decided to go ahead with it.

Then he made a fatal and tragic error that eventually destroyed him, his studio, and his dreams. He borrowed the money to carry out the entire project from Paramount Pictures.

Construction started in Miami, in March 1938, and in less than a year there stood a single-story concrete structure four city blocks square. It contained the latest in everything pertaining to animated cartoon production, including state-of-the-art sound equipment, and was the first fully air-conditioned building in the state of Florida.

The two hundred or so artists employed by Fleischer Studios weren't nearly enough to produce *Gulliver's Travels* and all the other Betty Boops and Popeyes that still had to be made. Seven hundred fifty were needed. During the construction of the Florida studio, schools were set up in New York and Miami to train the additional artists.

It was an ambitious, bold, and courageous project.

Gulliver's Travels opened on December 22, 1939, and broke house records everywhere it played. It was an out-and-out hit, so much so that Paramount immediately ordered a second feature. Things were looking good, and the future was bright and promising for Fleischer Studios. The major annoyance, as usual, was Walt Disney. The Disney Studios were stealing away the Fleischer animators. The lure of Hollywood and more money siphoned off many artists. There was a joke making the rounds that the studio had been built over part of the old slave underground railway and that there was a hole in one of the offices that led into a tunnel that came up in the Disney Studios in California. My father was not amused. He had spent years and a fortune training and employing those people, and he cursed Disney for raiding his staff.

Mr. Bug Goes to Town, the second feature, was released in 1942. Like Disney's second feature, *Pinocchio*, it was a financial failure. The difference between the two failures was that Disney owed money to the banks while my father owed a great deal of money to Paramount. He had negotiated a ten-year loan with them, and there were still five years to go. Without warning or notice, with no advance indication of any kind, Paramount called the note. There was no way my father could meet it, and almost immediately Paramount took over the studio, lock, stock, and barrel. The vast bulk of the employees were fired, and the remainder were brought back to New York. The name of the studio was changed to Famous Studios.

My father's career was over. The real villains in the piece were Paramount and Adolph Zukor, but my father couldn't hide his bitterness toward Walt Disney. Max could have been, and by his lights, should have been the winner of the contest between the two master animators. At every crucial moment, though, Disney had snatched away the prize and the recognition that went with it. I'm sure my father never saw the Disney name without thinking, "There, but for the grace of Adolph Zukor . . ."

Years later, immediately after the Rotoscope patents expired, Disney started making films, such as *Song of the South*, that combined live action with animated cartoons. The world had forgotten that Max Fleischer had invented the process, and the genius of Disney was frequently given both the praise and the credit for bringing this magic to the screen. Walt did nothing to dispel this impression. My father developed an ulcer.

I was uncomfortable driving onto the Disney lot in Burbank. This was enemy territory. Mickey Mouse Lane, Donald Duck Walk. I was more uncomfortable as I walked past showcases filled with prizes and awards outside Disney's office, and wondered what this was all about. Why had he called my agent and told him he'd like to meet with me? When I announced myself to his secretary, there was no waiting. I was shown in at once.

There he was, standing behind his desk, smiling warmly, my father's nemesis. We shook hands. A Fleischer shaking hands with a Disney? I felt it was a minor historic moment, but I didn't mention it and neither did he. Card Walker and Bill Walsh, two of the company's top executives, were also there, and Disney introduced me to them, too.

We all sat and I waited expectantly for Disney to get to the point of this exercise. I didn't have to wait long. He pointed to the wall opposite his desk. "You familiar with that story?" he asked.

I looked where he indicated. On the wall, obviously temporarily tacked up, was a large watercolor painting, vividly rendered in dramatic colors, of a strange-looking craft entangled in the tentacles of a giant squid. Below it was the legend, in baroque lettering, *Twenty Thousand Leagues Under the Sea*. "Of course," I said. "Who isn't familiar with it? I don't think there's anyone who hasn't read that book."

"That's right," he agreed. "That's why we're going to make a movie of it."

"Sounds terrific. Animated, of course."

"No, this'll be an all-live-action feature. And it'll be, by far, the most expensive picture we've ever made, about four and a half million." I gave a low whistle. In the early 1950s that was as big as they came. *Snow White* was considered enormously expensive, and that cost $1.7 million. "We're negotiating for James Mason to play Captain Nemo and Kirk Douglas for Ned Land," he continued, mentioning two of the biggest stars of the period.

"They should be great." I was genuinely impressed.

"And we want you to direct it."

"Me?" I wasn't sure I'd heard right.

Walt nodded and smiled broadly at my reaction. I shook my head in disbelief. The big picture with the big stars, the thing I'd dreamed of, was being dropped in my lap by, of all people, Walt Disney.

"I'm overwhelmed," I said. "Certainly I want to direct it. But why me? Why do you want *me* to do it?"

A big grin covered his face. "We saw your picture *The Happy Time.*" I remembered then that Bobby Driscoll, who'd played the lead in it, also starred in Disney's *Song of the South.* "Well," Walt continued, "anybody who can make an actor out of Bobby Driscoll has got to be a great director."

All of us burst into laughter. Walt got up from his desk and walked over to me. "How about it? Are you coming to work for us?"

I got up, too, and studied him and the others in the room for a moment, trying to get a clue from their faces. Then I said, "You do know who I am, don't you?"

Walt chuckled. "Yes, we know. That doesn't make any difference."

"That's wonderful, because more than anything in the world I want to do this picture. But I can't accept it without talking it over with my father first. I'm afraid he might think I'm disloyal, or something. If he did, I just couldn't do it."

"I understand," Walt said as he walked me to the door of his office. "You're absolutely right. You talk to your father tonight and call me tomorrow morning."

I phoned my father in New York as soon as I got home, told him the whole story, and held my breath. "Of course you should do that picture," he reassured me. "You didn't have to call me. You go right ahead and take the job."

"You sure?"

"Absolutely. And you tell Walt one thing from me."

"What's that?"

"You tell Walt that I said he's got great taste in directors."

I felt an odd, *Alice in Wonderland* feeling when I started to work on the Disney lot. It was as though I belonged, but didn't belong. Animation studios were my natural habitat, but my father was always the boss, not Walt Disney; I was surrounded by strangers, yet I knew many ex-Fleischer employees there, such as Dick Huemer and Ted Sears, for my entire life; I was making a live-action movie in a place completely devoted to making cartoons; I liked Walt Disney, but felt guilty about it. Everything seemed slightly out of joint.

It was interesting to compare how the two men ran their studios. They both insisted that everyone, without exception, call them by their first name, and they were both strongly anti-union. Those were the biggest, perhaps the only, similarities. At Fleischer Studios everyone loved Max. He was a father figure and the whole place was one big, warm family. Not so at Disney. Much to my surprise, I learned that the employees didn't like Walt and lived in terror of him. What they disliked most was his habit of prowling the corridors and, without warning, randomly opening doors to see if the artists were working. He opened the door to my office a few times, I think by mistake, apologized, and withdrew.

There was a general feeling of nervousness and insecurity about the place, which was attributed to the frequent mass firings that seemed to take place capriciously. I took the "capricious" theory with a grain of salt until Walt confirmed it one day. "You know," he said to me, "every once in a while I just fire everybody, then I hire them back in a couple of weeks. That way they don't get too complacent. It keeps them on their toes."

There was another conversation I had with Walt that I thought was quite revealing. For a while he didn't want me to do the underwater sequences in the picture. Since it didn't involve actors, only stunt doubles, he felt this work could be done just as well by a second-unit director. My argument was that those scenes were the very heart, the essence, of the movie and they required as much skill, care, and talent to direct as anything we had to do with actors. How could the director of *Twenty Thousand Leagues Under the Sea* not direct what the picture was all about?

We were walking down the studio street having this discussion when he put his arm around my shoulder and said, "Would you like to be as successful in your job as I am in mine?"

"Yes, I certainly would."

"Well, then, why don't you do as I do? Let somebody else do all the work and you take all the credit."

There was a mean, penny-pinching attitude about Walt that wasn't too pleasant. The one who got hurt the worst by this was Harper Goff. Walt had taken him off his job of designing Disneyland and started him developing production design for *Twenty Thousand Leagues* two years before I arrived on the scene.

Harper, a blond, chubby pixie with an endearing, infectious, childlike laugh, was an unbelievably talented man. He had conceived, designed, and planned the *Nautilus* down to its last rivet and had set the design for the entire film. He was, without question, the art director/production designer of the picture. The only trouble was that Goff was not a member of the IATSE union that represented those positions and, therefore, couldn't get screen credit for the magnificent job he was doing. If he joined the union he'd be able to get the credit, but he would also get a substantial salary increase, since the union minimum was well above what Disney was paying. Walt made it clear that it wouldn't be wise for Goff to join the union, since he had no intention of continuing to pay that salary once the picture was finished. Goff liked the security of working for Disney, so he took the hint and didn't join.

To satisfy the IATSE requirement, Walt hired a union art director, John Meehan, so he'd only have to pay the union salary for just the one picture.

Meehan followed Goff's drawings exactly and won an Academy Award.

In general, though, I found Walt to be genial and friendly. Only once during the entire production did I ever see him lose his temper. It had been his idea to use a trained seal as Nemo's pet on the submarine. This was the famous "Disney touch," since the seal doesn't exist in the Jules Verne book. He got hold of Harper Goff and told him to design a large gold medallion in the shape of the letter "N" that the seal would wear around his neck on a broad ribbon. Almost a year later, when we were ready to shoot the first scene with the seal, Walt came on the set. There was no medallion on the seal. Harper had forgotten all about it. With the hundred thousand complex details he had to handle on the film, it was no wonder. Still, Walt was unforgiving and blasted him up one side and down the other. If he hadn't been irreplaceable he would have been fired on the spot. Harper ran off the set like a scalded cat and twenty minutes later was back with a medallion on a wide ribbon. Walt approved it and the incident was never mentioned again.

Talking about what a lousy sailor he was, Jack Benny once said of a popular singing group of the time, "I have to take a Dramamine just to listen to The Yacht Club Boys." Benny and I were in the same boat. When I was a kid, my mother used to take me and my sister, Ruth, to Europe every summer. We always took a slow boat over, fifteen days, and I'd be sick for fifteen days.

There was not much joy in my search for the underwater picture locations. Freddy Zendar, our water expert, taught me to use the Aqua-Lung in the pool at the Ambassador Hotel, in Los Angeles, which wasn't too bad. But once I got out on, and under, the deep blue, things were different. I threw up a lot. Once I even got seasick underwater and threw up into the Aqua-Lung mouthpiece, which, if it wasn't so messy, could be called a neat trick. Zendar thought the best place to look for underwater locations were the

Bahama Islands, and over a period of about three weeks I managed to vomit on most of them.

We settled on a fantastically beautiful reef on the western tip of New Providence Island, where Nassau is located, at a spot called Lyford Cay. All of our underwater sequences would be shot there.

We were having dinner and celebrating our decision to shoot at Lyford Cay when our Bahamas expert and guide, Howard Lightbourn, said to me, "You know, there's a real old guy lives here in Nassau who made the first movie version of *Twenty Thousand Leagues* forty years ago." I was surprised. I didn't even know there was an earlier movie. "He's a friend of mine. Name's John Williamson. He'd love to meet you." "Great," I said. "How about tomorrow?"

J. E. Williamson turned out to be a thoroughly delightful old gentleman. Tall and thin, with hawklike features and a shock of pure white hair, he wore a rumpled white suit and a Panama hat and looked like an ancient southern plantation owner. He had, indeed, made the first *Twenty Thousand Leagues* forty years ago, and, yes, it was a huge success when it opened. The whole thing felt a little weird. We spoke of the same problems facing me that he faced so many years earlier: working underwater; the *Nautilus* submarine; the fight with the giant squid; the underwater burial sequence.

Finally he said to me, "I understand you've been all over the islands looking for underwater locations."

"That's right."

"And where did you decide to do them?"

"Well, we found a beautiful reef right here, just off the tip of the island, called Lyford Cay."

"Why," Williamson exclaimed in astonishment, "that's exactly where I shot my picture!"

I'd had not only the whole Caribbean, but the entire globe to choose from, and yet I'd picked the exact spot that he had chosen for the original film four decades earlier. Williamson and I embraced like long-lost brothers.

The sea, as Freddy Zendar used to say, is only there to defeat you. We started the picture underwater on January 11, 1954, at Lyford Cay, and the sea did its best to prove him right. The biggest problem turned out to be the silt on the sea floor. Almost anything could disturb it, and then it would billow up into an obscuring cloud and would take forever to settle back down and be clear enough for photography. Just the flick of a swimmer's swim fin too close to the bottom, or the changing of the tide, could wreak havoc. Sometimes we had as many as thirty-three men underwater shivering patiently until their air ran out, waiting for the silt to settle.

To compound the problem, the actor-divers worked in heavy, self-contained suits with lead-weighted boots. They couldn't swim in those outfits, so they walked from where they dropped off our barge to the shooting location. By the time they arrived at the appointed spot all we could see through the camera was a complete white-out.

I was worried sick about the situation. Here I was with a crew of water experts, technicians, divers, generators, compressors, over twenty tons of equipment, a fleet of boats and barges, hundreds of compressed air tanks, and I was getting almost nothing on film.

We tried putting heavy hemp carpetlike runners on the sea floor so the divers could walk on them and not directly on the bottom. It helped a lot. For places that were too distant to walk, Zendar devised a system of transporting the nonswimming divers by towing them underwater out to the location on ropes dangling from the bottom of a lifeboat. When they got to the right spot, they'd let go and drift down to the set and land on preset hemp carpets. Standing by the camera and watching those strangely suited, helmeted figures float down from the surface in slow motion had a surreal beauty of its own. Jules Verne would have loved it.

We started making headway once we got the silt settled, but still nothing was easy. Almost every dive had its special problems, some more than others. One of the major sequences we had to shoot was a shark attack on the two divers representing Kirk Douglas and Peter Lorre. We informed the local fishermen that there would be a healthy bounty paid for anyone bringing in a live eight-foot, or larger, shark.

It took a couple of weeks before we got one, an eight-footer. Since there's no way to work in the water with a live shark, the plan was to kill it and hook it up to a cable system so it could be pulled down through the water, like a dive bomber, and go just where we aimed it.

Killing a shark is no easy matter. They seem to be almost impossible to kill. A few months earlier I'd seen some fishermen cut open a shark, trying to salvage a fish they'd just caught but that the shark swallowed while they were reeling it in. They thought it would still be in its stomach. The stomach was empty, but the shark was still alive and dangerous. They tried killing it, but it just

wouldn't die. Finally, they cut its heart out and left it on the pier.
When I left, about fifteen minutes later, it was still beating.

Everyone on the crew had a suggestion about how to kill a
shark. The consensus was that first you had to whack it very hard
several times, between the eyes, with a ball peen hammer. That was
supposed to kill its brain. Then the shark had to be left out on the
deck of our barge, in the hot sun, for one full day. That should do
it, all the experts agreed.

There was one doubter in our midst, our guide, Howard Lightbourn. He'd been on another movie, he told me, where they had
done the same thing. Just before they were going to start filming
with the shark, they moved it to the water's edge. Howard thought
he could get some great gag photos, so he had his girlfriend take
pictures of him with his head in its mouth. Then he stuck his foot in
its jaws. Finally, with an expression of fierce pain on his face, he put
his hand in the shark's mouth. That's when it came alive.

Howard could feel the jaws tighten on his hand. Then the shark
gave a little jump. Then another. Each jump brought it closer to the
water. By this time Lightbourn was hollering and yelling. No one,
including his girlfriend, thought he was serious. Good old Howard,
hamming it up as usual. The shark kept jumping, pulling Howard
with him, until almost half of it was in the water. If it ever got
completely in the water it would head for the depths, and good-bye,
Howard. Pretty soon his screaming became convincing enough to
bring the others over. By that time it was a real struggle to keep the
shark from taking off. Several divers wrestled with it in the water,
trying to get it back onshore, still with Lightbourn's hand firmly
clamped in its jaws. Eventually they had to cut off the shark's head
before they could release his hand.

We went ahead with our plan and bashed the shark on the
forehead with a ball peen hammer, then left him out of the water
and directly in the bright Bahamas sun for a full day. The following
morning we were about to put the shark in the water and hook it to
the cable rig, when Lightbourn's story flashed through my mind.
"Wait a minute," I said. "I know we're all satisfied that this shark is
genuinely dead, but just for the hell of it, why don't we wire its
mouth shut?"

I thought this suggestion would be greeted with small signs of
exasperation from some of the crew. Not at all. They were experienced water men and they had boundless respect for sharks. "That's
a good idea," Freddy Zendar said. "Why didn't I think of that? I'll
go get some piano wire. It won't take a minute."

The cable rig worked perfectly, and we got some excellent long shots of the shark diving down directly at our actors. The shark looked very much alive in the scene because pulling it through the water gave movement to its body and tail. You couldn't tell that its mouth was wired shut unless you got up very close. Watching it gave me the inspiration for a terrific camera angle I hadn't thought of before. I signaled for everyone to get out of the water and back to the barge for a conference.

"Why can't we," I said, when we were all gathered on the deck, "tie a camera to the shark's back and get a shot directly over its head as it attacks the actors? It should be a sensational point of view." Till Gabbani, our underwater cameraman, enthusiastically agreed. It needed almost no preparation to do. All that was necessary would be to rope the small camera to the shark's back with a slipknot. In that case, if there was an emergency, he could free the camera by simply pulling the loose end of the rope.

We got back into the water, and Gabbani tied the camera onto the shark's back. I took a ride down the cable, straddling the shark and looking through the camera. It was a real thrill. At the last moment, Gabbani decided to shoot the scene the way I did the test run because he could see that I had to keep adjusting the camera to keep the shot in view.

Gabbani mounted the shark, turned on the camera, and I signaled for action. The shark went down the cable like a dream. I got the thumbs-up signal from Gabbani that he'd gotten the shot; then he gave me the hand signal for "one more." I got everything back to starting positions and, once again, signaled action.

About halfway down the cable something strange seemed to be happening. The shark's head wasn't aimed at the actors as it was supposed to be. In fact, the whole shark was at an angle. I glanced at the divers who were controlling the cable. They were pulling with all their might. I looked back up at the shark. Gabbani was no longer looking through the camera but hanging onto it. The shark had stopped moving downward. Suddenly all the cables attached to the shark snapped. It was now free-floating. Gabbani was working frantically on the rope holding the camera to the shark. Then it happened. The shark started to swim.

It made a couple of lazy circles around the set, with Gabbani on its back still working feverishly on the rope. Then, as it revived more and more, it became agitated. It made an attacking pass at the two actors, who scrambled like never before, made a sweep at

Zendar, then disappeared at high speed into deep water, with Gabbani still clinging to its back.

All the divers with Aqua-Lungs were galvanized into action and took off after the shark and Gabbani. I was petrified. What could have happened to Gabbani? Why didn't he let go of the rope? Or did he somehow get entangled in it and couldn't let go? During the time it was actually happening I was screaming at him to let go, but in an Aqua-Lung all you can do is scream silently.

About two minutes later I could see the swimmers returning, two of them supporting Gabbani. He had the camera in his hands.

When we got back on the deck of the barge, Gabbani told me what had happened. When he had gotten halfway down the cable, the shark stopped, and Gabbani almost fell off, so he grabbed the camera for support. He'd thought, at first, that the cable had jammed. What had happened, in fact, was that the shark had started to revive and was pulling away from the cable. The two divers who were pulling the shark down through the water also thought the cable was stuck, so they pulled harder. This caused all the wires attached to the shark to break.

When Gabbani realized the shark was reviving and starting to swim, he pulled on the slipknot rope. It wouldn't slip. He started tugging at it frantically. Nothing happened. It never entered his mind to abandon the camera. He was determined to save the camera, no matter what, so he just hung on, tugging on the slipknot. When the shark reached deep water, it dived for the bottom. It was during that dive that Gabbani ruptured both eardrums and the knot finally came loose.

Gabbani saved the camera and the film from the first take over the shark's head. It turned out to be a hell of a shot.

Unfortunately, I wasn't finished with all the scenes I'd planned with the shark. I still needed it. The entire crew had gathered to hear Gabbani's story, so I made an announcement. I offered a substantial bonus to anyone who could find the shark and bring it back. It wouldn't be dangerous, I pointed out, since its mouth was still wired shut. They were all gung ho, and all the Aqua-Lung swimmers jumped into the water and took off in all directions.

The U.S. Navy had sent two frogmen to act as official observers of our operation, since it was certainly one of the largest of its kind ever attempted. The frogmen joined the shark hunt, too. They swam out into deep water. The shark could have been anywhere by this time, but they went toward the area where it was last seen. They scouted around but didn't see anything. One of them had an underwater still camera and started taking picture of some odd-looking fish swimming nearby. His partner watched this for a while, became bored, and turned around to continue his scanning of the sea. And there it was! About thirty feet away was the shark, just lying there in the water, not moving, its tail to him.

He couldn't believe his luck. Not only would he get the bonus, but he'd be a big hero into the bargain. He figured all he had to do was to get the shark aimed toward the barge and sort of herd, or doze, it in that general direction. He swam over to the side of the shark's head, opposite its left eye, and flailed his arms up and down. The shark slowly turned its head to the right but didn't move. Now the frogman swam back and gave its tail a healthy twitch. Lethargically the shark moved forward. Then he went back and waved his arms by its left eye again. This time the shark moved too far to the right, so the frogman swam over to the other side and waved his arms in front of its right eye. Then back he went and shook the tail some more.

Suddenly he felt a tap on his shoulder. It was his partner. The partner put his hand to his face mask, in front of his mouth, and with his finger made an up-and-down zigzag motion. Then he wagged his finger in front of his face in a "no-no" gesture. The mouth was not wired. It was the wrong shark.

I was sitting on the barge, waiting for some news of the search, when the two frogmen exploded out of the water like beach balls and landed on the deck. They were prostrate with laughter, and it took them almost five minutes to tell me what happened.

We never did find the shark.

We were into the last few weeks of shooting, in Nassau, when *Life* magazine sent Mary Leatherbee, their entertainment editor, and a still photographer to cover our moviemaking. They got all the material they needed for a good story, but Leatherbee still wasn't satisfied. What they needed, she felt, was an exciting episode, like an underwater emergency. As far as we were concerned, that was the last thing we were looking for. Zendar was a fanatic about water safety and so far we hadn't had a single situation where a diver had to be taken out of the water in a hurry.

On their last day with us, since nothing untoward had happened during their stay, we agreed to stage an emergency for them. Almost as soon as we got in the water for our first shot of the day, we had an emergency, the real thing. One of the actor/divers tore his suit on a piece of coral. Zendar and the safetymen went into action, and they had that diver out of the water, with his helmet off and breathing fresh air, in less than two minutes.

We had no sooner dealt with that situation when a second emergency occurred. *Life* magazine was running in luck. But this was an odd accident. Nobody, not even Zendar, could have anticipated it.

There were two kinds of divers on the picture: safetymen, and those we were photographing, called actor/divers. The safetymen wore Aqua-Lungs and could swim freely and unencumbered. The actor/divers were a different matter. They had to wear what appeared to be a version of the traditional deep-sea divers' outfit, with lead-weighted, heavy boots and a brass helmet. The difference between these outfits and the conventional ones was that we couldn't have an air hose leading from the helmet to the surface. Our divers had to be self-supporting and completely independent.

No diving gear like this had ever been built, so Harper Goff and Fred Zendar designed and engineered a new model. The basis was the Aqua-Lung, with the mouthpiece inside the brass helmet. There were two problems, however, that had to be solved. One was the mouthpiece. Since it was to be inside the helmet, what would happen if it accidentally dropped out of the diver's mouth? He couldn't use his hands to pop it back in again. The solution was to support the mouthpiece on a rigid tube so it would always be in the same position. In that way a diver could deliberately let go of the mouthpiece and then regain it simply by leaning his head forward.

The other problem had to do with exhaled air. The diver would be getting oxygen through the Aqua-Lung, but his exhalations went directly into the suit. It wouldn't take long before the suit had so much carbon dioxide it would blow up like a balloon. That could result in a calamity, because the carbon dioxide-filled suit could rocket up to the surface, where the lack of water pressure would cause it to burst. That in itself wouldn't hurt the diver, but because of the heavy boots and the brass helmet, the diver would sink to the bottom like a stone. It is an event known among deep-sea divers as a *fusca*.

There was a simple solution to that problem, too. Goff and Zendar had a valve installed in the back of the helmet that would vent the exhaled air. Whenever a diver felt himself getting too buoyant, all he had to do was hit the back of his head against a plunger. The plunger opened the valve and—*voilà*—the air escaped.

One of the divers, Shorty, had been having a minor problem with the plunger. It was a little stiff, and the back of his head was getting bruised from hitting it against it. He was too macho to mention it to anyone, so he found his own solution. He would wear a woolen sailor's cap, and that would cushion the impact. This particular day was the first time he'd tried it.

It seemed to work fine. Then he began to notice something disquieting. Each time Shorty hit the plunger with his head it pushed the cap a little farther down on his forehead. There was no way to fix this. He couldn't get his hands inside the helmet. It wasn't long before the cap, slowly but surely, slipped down over his eyes. Now he was completely blind.

Shorty did the only thing he could do: raise one arm with a clenched fist. This was one of our well-rehearsed underwater signals that meant, "I've got a problem. Not serious." The actor-diver closest to him tried to look through his face plate, but it was too dark and he couldn't see anything. The divers had learned early on that if you put your helmet against someone else's helmet, and let go of the mouthpiece, you could carry on a perfectly clear conversation. He did this and said, "What's the matter, Shorty?"

Shorty let go of his mouthpiece to answer. "My cap," he said, "is covering . . ." As he spoke, the cap slipped farther down and covered his mouth. Now he was not only blind but also he couldn't get the mouthpiece back into his mouth to breathe. Once again, he did the only thing he could do. He raised both arms with clenched fists. This meant, "Get me out! Quick!" The safetymen went back into action, and Shorty was breathing fresh air in just about one minute.

The *Life* story turned out great. We got the cover and an eight-page picture spread. The only sour note in it for me was that throughout the piece the credit for directing the movie was given to someone called Robert Fleischer. The name of one of the divers who had an emergency was Eddie Czynski. They got that right.

For such a big picture, we had a very small cast. Not counting Esmarelda, the seal, about 99 percent of the film was carried by just four actors: James Mason, Kirk Douglas, Paul Lukas, and Peter Lorre. They all had reputations for being temperamental and difficult, and I wondered how we were going to get along for several months trapped in the cramped confines of the *Nautilus* submarine. As it turned out, the most temperamental of the bunch was Esmarelda, the seal.

Esmarelda's dressing room was a tank filled with water just outside the stage door. When we needed Esmarelda in a scene, her trainer would lure her onto the set by feeding her herring along the way. The actors she had to play her scenes with filled their pockets with herring not only to keep her interested, but as a reward for playing the scene. Sometimes the set smelled like the Fulton Fish Market. It always amused me to see the distinguished James Mason reach into his pocket, after a shot, for a herring and feed it to the seal, saying, "Well done, Esmarelda. You played that very nicely, indeed."

But Esmarelda was temperamental. When she got bored with whatever we were doing, she would just leave, even in the middle of a scene. Off she'd go, flip-flopping across the stage floor, barking all the way to her dressing room. Nothing could persuade her to remain another minute—not more herring, or promises of a nicer dressing room, or having her own makeup man, nothing. And she wouldn't come back until she felt like it.

The lack of temperament among the actors was a welcome surprise. I'd been surprised earlier when I met Mason and Douglas for the first time, long before shooting began. I had always visualized James Mason as a short, thin fellow and Kirk Douglas as tall and brawny. The opposite was true. James was well built and about six feet tall, but Kirk, while brawny, was not much taller than I was, about five-foot-seven. My false impressions must have come from their personalities. James, being quite introverted, had the feeling of being smaller than Kirk, who was an expansive extrovert.

Maybe it was the Disney influence, but Kirk was on his best behavior during the filming. There were none of the tantrums and overheated arguments I'd witnessed when I visited the set of *Champion*, which he'd starred in for Stanley Kramer a few years earlier. There it was all *sturm und drang*. Here it was all good cheer and fellowship.

He may have kept his temperament in check, but he was difficult to work with. During the first few days I had problems blocking, working out the placement and movement of the actors, of any scene he was in. This was very disquieting to me because ordinarily I block scenes quickly and easily. I would stage the scene, rehearse it until I was satisfied, and get ready to turn it over to the cameraman for lighting, when Kirk would say, "I can't do the scene. I just don't feel comfortable."

For me, one of the prime requisites of my work is to make the actors feel comfortable and natural while doing a scene. A scene just won't work if an actor feels awkward about anything—saying a line, making a move, doing a piece of business. The actor must feel that the way he's doing it is the only way it can be done. So when Kirk would say "I don't feel comfortable," I would want to know why. He never had a specific answer; it was always vague. "I don't know why," he'd say. "It just doesn't feel right. It's awkward."

Naturally, I'd start fooling around with the staging, moving people into different positions, until suddenly Kirk would say, "That's it! That's much better. I can do the scene now." What had I done? What miracle had I wrought? I wasn't sure. I was just happy to get Kirk feeling "comfortable" so we could get on with the work. I didn't have this problem with the other actors if he wasn't in the scene. It was only with him, and it puzzled me.

Then I had a revelation. Suddenly it dawned on me what was happening. Kirk couldn't get "comfortable" unless he was in the center of the picture, facing the camera, with everyone else facing him. In the theater it's called "upstaging," and that's what he was doing. I couldn't believe it, not from Kirk Douglas. This was something a stage ham actor, inexperienced in moviemaking, might try. Upstaging simply doesn't exist in movies because the camera can always change its point of view, while a theater audience can't. In a movie, if an actor happens to have his back to the camera for an important line, or when you want to see his face, you make a separate shot of him. This is called "coverage." No more upstaging. Yet there it was. Kirk knew very well what he was doing but didn't want to come out and say so. Not in front of the professionals he was working with. He manipulated me into figuring it out for myself. Kirk was certainly experienced enough to know there was no sensible reason for doing what he was doing, but it fed his ego. It was an ego that needed lots of nourishment.

As soon as I realized what was going on I started staging his scenes with everyone else facing him and saved myself a lot of time and grief. He was really hooked on the upstaging concept, so much so that it was difficult to get him to turn his back to the camera at all. There was one scene, however, where there was no way out. He *had* to play with his back to the camera. He struggled against it, tried every which way of playing the scene, but it was clear that the only right way was the way I'd staged it, with his back to the camera. I insisted on it and he knew I was right. Suddenly, after a final discussion, he brightened appreciably and said, "Yeah! Of course! That's the way to play it. I can do a *lot* with my back."

It's every director's hope, or should be, that actors will bring some suggestions to him for every scene he has to play—some piece of business that illuminates his character; a fresh insight into a line reading; a meaningful mannerism. I've always thought of it as a tray full of jewels that an actor brings to the director and says, "Here. These are my offerings. Choose what you want."

Kirk didn't bring a tray full of jewels, he brought a whole marketplace full of trinkets. Sometimes there was a gem or two, but there was also an awful lot of junk jewelry. The difficult part was that he wouldn't rest until he'd shown you every last piece he had to offer. "Does this have any value?" he'd ask, and try the scene with his shirt off. "Does this have any value?" and he'd do the scene while chinning himself on a doorframe. "Does this have any value?" and he'd juggle some seashells. There was absolutely no way to short-circuit this routine. If you didn't allow him to demonstrate everything, he'd show exasperation and indicate strongly that you not only didn't recognize a creative contribution when you saw one but were stifling the artist as well. It made directing the scenes time-consuming because everything had to be discussed and analyzed before being rejected.

It was an actor's insecurity carried to an extreme, a supreme procrastination before actually having to get down to work and do the scene. It was just damn difficult getting Kirk "comfortable" in a scene. "Does this have any value?" became a byword throughout the company. Kirk was unaware of it, but the crew thought the whole thing was terribly funny. Every time I made eye contact with any of them during these discussions, they'd roll their eyes up toward the ceiling.

We were still in the first few weeks of shooting in the studio. Kirk and I were standing in the middle of the set discussing one of his myriad suggestions when a voice interrupted us. "Excuse me, Dick," it said. Kirk and I were startled. No one interrupts a conversation between a director and a star. We looked up. It was the second camera assistant, a rather lowly position on the camera crew. I gave him one of those "How dare you" looks, but it didn't faze him. "I'm sorry," he said, "but this is something I have to know," and he held up a small square of glass for me to see. I recognized it as a lens filter. "Does this have any value?" he asked.

Then I looked past him. The entire crew had formed a grinning semicircle, arms crossed, watching us. This was daredevil stuff on their part. They were testing Kirk, challenging him. Would he react like a shit and throw a tantrum, or could he take a kidding?

I looked at Kirk. There was a flash of white fury in his eyes as he stared at the camera assistant. He definitely didn't like being made fun of. Then he, too, became aware of the others around us and began to realize that he was being put on the spot. His face turned red. There was a long and very uncertain moment while he made up his mind. Then he laughed. It was very loud and long and, I thought, just a touch theatrical. But it convinced the crew and they laughed and applauded. It didn't stop him from saying, "Does this have any value?" but from then on it was usually accompanied by a small joke or a wisecrack. When the picture was finished Kirk gave me a gift, a gold money clip. On it was engraved, "Does this have any value?"

We were shooting on the set of the *Abraham Lincoln*, a full-scale replica of a post-Civil War U.S. warship complete with firing cannons. Harper Goff came up to me in the morning and said, "Well, today's the big day."

"Why's that?"

"The bankers."

"What bankers?"

"Didn't you know? Today's the day the bankers are running all the film you've shot so far."

I didn't understand this at all. "I don't get it, Harper," I said. "Why are they doing that?"

"Because Walt's run out of money. He needs a big loan from the banks to finish the picture. So he's showing them all of your film this afternoon, to impress them. If they're not impressed, we won't have to come to work tomorrow."

Making the picture must have strained the financial capacity of the studio to its limit. The budget apparently didn't allow for contingencies. And we had a contingency. A whopper. When we returned to the studio from our Caribbean locations, the first sequence I had to work on was the fight with the giant squid. It was a total disaster.

Everything that could be wrong with a sequence was wrong with this one. It was poorly conceived and badly executed, and we were all to blame. The fight was written to take place on a calm sea at sunset. Big mistake. The deck of the *Nautilus* was built in the studio tank, but not built on rockers. Big mistake. The giant squid was worked entirely by wires and mostly stuffed with kapok. Very big mistake.

I did everything I knew to make the sequence work, but the film I shot was horribly embarrassing. Compared to us, a Keystone Kops comedy would look like an Ingmar Bergman film.

The flat, calm sea added nothing to the sequence except phoniness. The cloudless sky backing looked exactly like what it was, a studio backing. Lighting the set for day not only exposed every wire that was used to manipulate the squid but also showed every flaw in its construction, and there were many. The deck of the *Nautilus* looked like a concrete slab. With all the sailors and the huge squid, it should have canted a little, or rocked. It didn't. Then there was the squid itself. The stuff it was made with started to deteriorate. Big hunks of the tentacles would drop off when the sailors were wrestling with it. Sometimes whole tentacles would come off, and we'd have to stop and glue them back on. Worst of all was the kapok stuffing. It absorbed water like a sponge and became so heavy the wires used to control the squid would constantly snap. After less than a week of shooting, the giant squid lay on the deck of the submarine like a giant blob, completely immobile, bloated, and obscene-looking.

That's when Walt came to me and said, "What you're shooting is a joke. Why don't you abandon this sequence for a while? Start shooting the dramatic scenes and give us a chance to rebuild the squid and try to figure this thing out." I couldn't have been happier to walk away from that mess.

My old friend Earl Felton had written the screenplay, and Walt had kept him on for the entire shoot, in case I needed him for rewriting. I needed him now. He screened the miserable film I'd shot and came up with a suggestion. It should, he said, be a night scene in a big storm with crashing waves and howling winds blowing spray over everything. Right away it sounded exciting. The darkness and the spray would cover up the wires, he went on, and we should see the squid mostly in flashes of vivid lightning. The deck of the *Nautilus* should be canted over by the weight of the squid. Sailors slipping and falling and fighting the waves and wind. Nemo and Co. fighting the elements as well as the monster.

Clearly, this was the way to go. This was the answer. If they could build a better squid, we'd be in business. I kissed Earl's foot and ran off to see Walt. I found him walking down the studio street and told him the new concept. He hardly took a moment to think about it. "You're right," he said. "That's the way to do it. Tell Earl to write it. And don't worry about the squid. I've taken some of the geniuses working on the Disneyland project and put them on it. They'll come up with something."

It was a wise decision, but it was heavily responsible for putting us in the financial crisis we now faced. It meant acquiring dozens of wind machines, water cannons, huge dump tanks, and wavemakers; reconstructing the deck of the *Nautilus* so it listed to starboard; and redesigning and building a new and improved squid. The new squid would have twenty-foot tentacles filled not with kapok but with pneumatic tubes, spring steel, and air pumps. The body would be filled with foam and a mass of electrical wiring. It would be able to raise itself several feet out of the water and move in any direction; it would move its eyes, and it would have a beak that could not only retract or project, but snap, too. The whole squid would now weigh almost a ton and would need fifty puppeteers in the stage rafters to operate it. Just the squid would cost $200,000. Then there were several additional weeks of shooting time plus all the extra people needed to operate all the new machinery. It was an expensive decision.

All of this was a contingency no one had planned for. And now the bankers were looking at the film.

Harper stuck around the set all day. He was too nervous to work in his office. It was one of the days when the full-scale warship, the USS *Abraham Lincoln*, was firing its cannons at what it thought was a sea monster. There were quite a few invited visitors that day, watching the fun. The cannons made a fearful noise and a lot of smoke. To keep himself occupied and his mind off the fateful screening that was under way, Harper would sidle up unobtrusively to the visitors watching the filming, with a cannon ball cradled in his arms. When the cannons would fire, the visitors would flinch, and Harper would drop the cannon ball at their feet. The screaming of the women was something to hear. But they all had wonderful stories to take home to Idaho, or wherever they came from, about the near-miss they had on the set of *Twenty Thousand Leagues Under the Sea*.

Late in the day Harper left the set to check on the result of the screening. He'd had a runner spying on the projection room door to tell him when they came out. He returned about a half hour later, all smiles, and whispered in my ear, "They gave him a million dollars to finish the picture. They loved it."

When we finally got around to shooting the giant squid fight it went extremely well, except for one incident that came close to being a tragedy. James Mason has been thrown into the raging sea by the squid, and Kirk Douglas has to dive in and rescue him. When I rehearsed it with some stuntmen to get a camera lineup, we found that the swimmer who was towing the unconscious Nemo couldn't get back to the sub against all the wind, churning water, and currents we were manufacturing. It was decided to pull Kirk toward the boat with a cable and, to keep the two men in a straight line and not be swept off course, also to attach a cable to James Mason that would be slowly paid out.

We got the mechanics and the timing worked out with the stunt doubles, then hooked up the actors and prepared to shoot the scene. We didn't rehearse this action with the actors. They had watched the doubles, knew what to do, and didn't want to wear themselves out rehearsing.

Once all the machinery got going, the wind machines, the dump tanks, the generator motors, and the water pumps, it was sheer bedlam. The noise was completely and totally deafening. The cameras started, and I gave the signal for action. Kirk started to swim on his back toward the *Nautilus* with one hand holding Mason, also on his back, by the collar. Most of the time they were covered by the waves and the spray, which made it looked realistic as hell. The action was wonderful, terrific. But it seemed to be taking longer to reach the boat than it did in the rehearsals. Much longer. Kirk was swimming like mad in a one-arm backstroke. Now Mason started to flail his arms. Since I hadn't seen the actors rehearse this scene, I thought this was Mason acting. It wasn't. It was Mason drowning.

Slowly, very slowly, they gained the deck, the sailors rushed over to help Nemo, and I cut the cameras. By the time I got from the camera platform to the boat, they were giving Mason artificial respiration and pumping the water out of him. I think I stopped breathing until I saw James start to move and cough. He was shaken, but he came around quickly and I found out what had happened.

The underwater cable attached to Mason had semijammed so that it was difficult to pull. The crew pulling on Kirk's cable didn't know that, so they kept on pulling. Kirk couldn't tell, in all the noise and turmoil of the water, whether he was making progress toward the boat; he just assumed he was and kept a tight grip on Mason's collar. The result of this was that the tension on Mason's wire was actually pulling him under the surface. Kirk realized he was having a tough time holding on to Mason, but since he hadn't rehearsed the action, he thought that was the way it was supposed to be. He kept a death grip on the collar. He didn't want to let go and ruin the scene. James, meanwhile, was drowning.

It was the last shot I had to make in that sequence. It was damn near Mason's last shot, period.

▪ ▪ ▪

Twenty Thousand Leagues was a box office hit and garnered four Academy nominations and two Academy Awards. Reviews ranged from excellent to raves, although one London paper said, if memory serves, "The most surprising thing about this Disney film is how unexciting it is." Well, you can't win 'em all.

With a success like that I expected my career to rocket. It helped, but the rocket didn't really ignite. The problem lay in the fact that everyone was bedazzled by the Walt Disney mystique. It was a common belief, even in Hollywood, that Walt was responsible for *everything* in the films he made. It was naive, but people thought he actually wrote the scripts and drew the pictures for his cartoons. There was the impression that he totally produced and directed everything that came out of his studio. It was a Disney picture, and no one ever associated another name with it. ("Let somebody else do all the work and you take all the credit.") It wasn't until years later, when the film began to be considered a classic and people became more aware of the true filmmaking process, that I began to get some recognition for it. "Oh, yeah! Did you direct that? That's one of my all-time favorite movies. Gee!"

Near the end of December 1955, my mother and father came to California to celebrate their golden wedding anniversary with me and my family. There was an item about it in Army Arched's column in *Daily Variety*. The following day I got a call from Walt. "I see your father's in town," he said. "I think we should meet. Why don't you bring him over to the studio? I'll round up some of his boys and we'll have lunch." I was touched by this gesture, and so was my father.

On January 4, 1956, the two great animators met. This time the Fleischer/Disney handshake was truly important. Walt was a charming, flattering host. My father seemed to be enjoying himself, but in Walt's presence he seemed somehow diminished, and my heart broke for him. I had the feeling that Goliath had defeated David.

We took a tour of the studio and had lunch in the commissary. Many of my father's ex-employees, his boys, were there, and there were plenty of "in" jokes and fond reminiscences. There is a historic picture of the event, with everyone's signature on it. On the bottom of the picture there is a large handdrawn scroll bearing this legend:

Inkwell Reunion
or
What Cartoons Can do to Cartoonists.
Jan. 4 1956

Shortly before he died, in 1972, at age eighty-nine, my father was hospitalized at the Motion Picture Country House and Hospital in Woodland Hills, California. He was suffering from hardening of the arteries of the brain and had all but lost the ability to speak. My sister Ruth came out from New York to visit and we were sitting around his bed in his room. There was a pile of magazines on a nightstand, and Ruth riffled through them and came across an issue of *Life* magazine that had a picture of Walt Disney's face on the cover.

"Look, Pop," she said, handing him the magazine. "It's your old friend."

My father studied the picture of Walt for a moment, then pointed to it with his finger and started to move his lips as if to speak. My sister bent over and put her ear close to his mouth to catch what he was saying. Then she burst into laughter.

"What is it, Ruth?" I asked. "What did he say?"

"He said, 'Son-of-a-bitch.' "

IX

The jungle telegraph was working in Hollywood. It wasn't exactly working overtime on my behalf, but they were telling it on the drums that *Twenty Thousand Leagues Under the Sea* was something special. It didn't make me the Flavor of the Week, but it did garner some attention. Dore Schary, the head of production at MGM and under whom I'd made *Arena*, sent me a knockout script that would star Spencer Tracy and would be called *Bad Day at Black Rock*. I had just finished photography on the Disney picture and still had several months of postproduction left and was wondering how I could also manage to do the Schary picture. Walt resolved my dilemma for me. I met him in the studio street one day, on my way to lunch. "I understand you've got an offer from Metro," he said. "That's right," I answered. "How did you know?" "Well, I just got a phone call from Europe from my friend Spencer Tracy," Walt explained. "He wanted to know what I thought of you." I gave him a quizzical look. Walt smiled and said, "I gave him a pretty good report. But," he went on, "you know there's no way you can do that picture. You've got to stay here and finish this one." It was frustrating, but it was true.

Shortly after I did the final wrap-up on *Twenty Thousand Leagues* and was truly free (read, "out of work"), an offer came from Twentieth Century-Fox. After his triumphant production at Columbia of *From Here to Eternity*, Buddy Adler had joined Fox as a producer and was about to make his first picture there. It was called *Violent Saturday*, and he wanted me to direct it. Adler was the new fair-haired boy, the screenplay showed promise, and Fox was the place I wanted to be. I accepted the offer and the inevitable long-term contract that went with it. For the next fifteen years I worked mostly for Fox.

My first surprise, on joining the studio, was to find that my old friend and mentor-tormentor Sid Rogell was now studio manager. We immediately went out and inspected the property. He didn't have the life-and-death power he once possessed, but the iron fist could still deliver a mighty blow. It was a great comfort having him around. He filled me in on how things were run at Fox, who had clout, who to beware of. Darryl Zanuck was the *capo de tutti capo*, the supreme boss. When I asked Sid what kind of executive system the studio had, he replied, "Planetary."

The influence of Zanuck was pervasive. You could feel it in the air. In the commissary was a huge Art Deco mural, the centerpiece of which was the face of Darryl Zanuck wearing an expression that was a mixture of Clive of India and Genghis Khan. Even while you ate, his influence poured over your food.

Zanuck ran the studio with a grip of iron and a will of steel. No one worked with him, they worked for him. It was a one-man operation right down the line.

Production meetings with DZ were illuminating but scary. As demonstrations of absolute, monolithic power they were classic. As theatrical performances they were as formalized as a Kabuki play.

Armed with notepads, a troupe of us—producer, director, head of casting, head of production, and others of that ilk—would file into Zanuck's office, a largish room with a huge desk cluttered with mementos. Several chairs were scattered about haphazardly. Everyone would find one and wait—which wasn't long.

From an adjoining room, Darryl would burst in, trailing a cloud of cigar smoke. There seemed to be an electromagnetic force field around him. You could actually feel it.

With a brusque, "Hi, boys," he would seat himself behind the desk, grab a handful of notes, and launch into the first of a series of topics he wanted to discuss. "Discuss" may not be the appropriate word. "Mandate" is probably closer.

As he warmed to the subject and the creative juices started flowing, he would suddenly rise. This was the cue for an odd bit of choreography. Anyone seated near the door leading to the adjoining room would immediately move his chair away from it so there was a clear passage between the two rooms. From what we could glimpse through the doorway, the other room seemed to be filled with big-game hunting trophies.

At this point the meeting would take on a distinctly bizarre aspect. Zanuck would walk briskly into the other room. A few moments later he'd come literally charging out through the connecting door, a miniature polo mallet in his hand, and commence pacing between the two rooms with furious energy. He spoke in rapid-fire, staccato bursts, the little polo mallet swinging violently in time with the driving tempo of his legs.

Back and forth between the two rooms he'd march, taking the exact same number of steps each time, turning sharply and marching back, like a mechanical bear in a shooting gallery. He kept disappearing into the other room. You couldn't see him, but you could still hear him as he continued speaking. There was a certain element of comical danger present, too. If you got in his way you would surely get trampled underfoot or bashed with the mallet. Maybe both.

His dialogue—monologue, really—was stream-of-consciousness and schizophrenic. He asked and answered his own questions and talked himself into and out of various ideas. It sounded something like this: "Now for the part of the Peeping Tom . . . how about that guy with the funny face . . . you know . . . Noonan. . . . That's his name, Tommy Noonan . . . great face. . . . But can he act? . . . Yeah, he can act. . . . And what a face! [Zanuck bursts into laughter.] That guy kills me. Just thinking about that face makes me laugh. . . . I'm just not sure about him as an actor. . . . Yeah, he could do it. . . . He'd be terrific, absolutely terrific . . . and a great actor, too. . . . I want him for that part . . . nobody else could play it the way he will. He's perfect. . . . That's it— Noonan plays that part!"

So the meeting would continue. The dialogue, and the mad pacing, would go on uninterrupted by any of us until, finally and abruptly, he'd say, "That's it, boys," and disappear into the other room for good.

We'd pick up our notes and silently file out. End of meeting. We had all enjoyed the democratic freedom to agree enthusiastically with our master's voice.

However many movies were in production at the same time, nothing escaped Zanuck's scrupulous attention. Every Monday morning, producers with a production in front of the cameras would get a well-organized, detailed memo from DZ. The week's dailies would be reviewed and analyzed, director and actors would be praised or criticized, upcoming dangers would be signposted. Nothing was overlooked. Nothing was ambiguous. The memos were marvels of insight, clarity, and comprehension.

The main thing about the memos, however, was there was no

argument, no appeal. This was the last appeal. Just shut up and do it.

Once photography was finished on a film, Zanuck maintained a hands-off policy about the editing. Hands off, that is, until he'd screened the version of the picture that the producer and the director felt was the best they could do.

Those screenings could be traumatic.

There was an ironclad rule that when the screening was finished no one could speak before he did. The sooner he spoke after the end of the picture, the better he had liked it. Conversely, the longer he took, the worse his reaction.

Those moments before he spoke were like drops of water in the Chinese water torture. It was tolerable if not too many drops hit you on the forehead. But just wait a while. After Charles Brackett and I ran *The Girl in the Red Velvet Swing* for Zanuck, we sat in agonizing, sweating silence for a full twenty minutes before he got up and left without ever saying a word. No "Good," no "Bad," no "You're fired," no nothing. He left behind two human wrecks who could barely drag themselves to Romanoff's to get drunk.

On the other hand, the first time Richard Zanuck and I showed him *Compulsion,* he was on his feet, shouting, "Great! Terrific!" before the last frame was off the screen. Naturally, young Zanuck and I went to Romanoff's and got drunk.

It was always part of the Zanuck mystique that he was a genius film editor. He was, indeed, a genius film editor. Up to a point.

He had the uncanny knack, after seeing a film for the first time, of immediately putting his finger on exactly what was wrong with it. Invariably he was right. Without hesitation he would order new scenes written and put into production. Virtually every movie made at Fox went back to the sound stages for additional scenes. The improvement to the film was usually remarkable. That's when the trouble would start.

As soon as the new scenes were edited into the movie he'd start screening it. The first few times his editing suggestions were right on. They worked. The problem was that Zanuck was a busy and impatient man. His boredom threshold was very low. Familiarity breeds impatience. After a few runnings he'd feel the picture was getting slow. More and more scenes would get cut out. Soon the cuts would become brutal. Motivational scenes would be dropped. The plot would fall to pieces. Arguing with Zanuck would bring down a torrent of wrath and harden his position. Producers and directors suffered in anguish but in silence.

There was, I discovered, a simple way around the problem. It seemed obvious to me that Zanuck didn't like being challenged on the spot. All I did was wait two or three days, then either phone or go see him. "Darryl," I'd say, "I've been giving your suggestion a lot of thought. I haven't slept nights worrying about it. I hate to say it, but I just think it would be very harmful to the picture."

That's all there was to it. Darryl would say, "Okay, leave it in." It worked every time. I've often wondered how many others had found this Rosetta stone.

X

For years Earl Felton had been nurturing a very funny story treatment he had written about a movie company, on location in Mexico in the early 1900s, being captured by Pancho Villa. The hero of the piece was a laconic American soldier of fortune, Villa's right-hand man, who falls in love with the movie company's leading lady. He rescues her from Villa, takes her back to Hollywood, and becomes, by accident, a movie star himself. A perfect role for someone like Robert Mitchum.

A young producer, Robert L. Jacks, read it, liked it, and set it up for production with United Artists. Then he got Robert Mitchum to agree to star in the film and asked me to direct it. I couldn't have been happier. From the moment I'd read it a few years earlier, I'd wanted to make it. Now I was going to get my chance.

I didn't expect it to be an easy picture to make, because there really isn't such a thing. They are all hard. It's just that some are harder than others. A lot harder. And I had heard rumors about pictures that were fun to make, but I hadn't run into one so far. *Horse Opera*, however, looked like it would be about as easy and as pleasant a picture to make as you could hope for. All the elements were right: Jacks was a good guy; Mitchum was a lot of laughs; the story was a lighthearted, satirical adventure; the whole thing would be shot in picturesque, romantic Mexico. What's not to like? Maybe this could be the fun one.

There was just one problem that worried me. I couldn't ride constant herd over Felton while he was developing the screenplay because I had to do another picture at Fox first. (*The Girl in the Red Velvet Swing*, starring, in her first American movie, a young English beauty named Joan Collins.) In spite of his lifeless legs and his total reliance on a crutch and cane to get around, Felton was much given to self-indulgences and debaucheries. I feared the worst. Still, with such a good screen treatment, of his own devising, how could it go wrong?

Six months later *The Girl in the Red Velvet Swing* had swung her last swing and I asked for the script of *Horse Opera*. I shouldn't have asked. It was little more than a half-completed script about a gunrunner who supplies munitions to both sides in the Mexican Revolution. No movie company, no leading lady, no Villa, no Hollywood, no anything I could recognize. It was like the kind of plastic surgery some government witnesses receive to disguise their identity. Even the name was changed. *Horse Opera* was now called *Bandido*. Earl had obviously mounted his horse when I left and ridden off in every direction except the one in which the signpost pointed. Whatever it was, it was not the story I had contracted to direct. I told Robert L. Jacks that I wasn't going to direct the picture.

When a star is involved and the director walks off the picture because he hates the script, everyone becomes hysterical. They fear that the star is liable to become spooked and they could lose him, too.

Jacks informed United Artists of my decision, and they did not take kindly to it. They wanted Mitchum, and they didn't want me to scare him off. I had a contract and they would hold me to it. Walk off and get sued, buddy.

I could have walked and maybe I would have won a lawsuit. But what if I lost? Litigation at this stage of my career was something I really didn't need. So I said, okay, you've got me, but the script has to be rewritten. Sure, fine, they said, as long as you start shooting in six weeks. Mitchum's got other commitments, you know, and this picture has to start on schedule, okay? It was not okay, but go fight City Hall.

There wasn't enough time to resurrect the original script of *Horse Opera* and start from scratch. We had to rewrite the existing screenplay and try to make some sense out of it. This meant taking care of all the usual preproduction chores and still keeping Felton's battered nose to the grindstone. When I went to scout locations in Mexico I schlepped Felton along. Earl loved Mexico, and this turn of events delighted him, although he whined a lot about how hard I was working him.

He stopped complaining once we got to Mexico, and I managed to fall down a long flight of slippery stone steps in an Aztec ruin and broke a rib. It really didn't hurt much except, as they say, when I laughed, and then the pain was excruciating. Felton, of course, instantly dedicated himself to making me laugh. It was his revenge for my working him so hard. By the time I got to the local doctor for X rays Earl was lying in front of the doctor's door waving his crutch in the air and pitifully shouting, "Don't go in there, *señor*. This man is a butcher. Look what he did to me!"

My resentment about being forced into a picture I didn't want to make gradually subsided as the script began to take some sort of decent shape. Since I was now resigned to doing the film, I figured I'd make the best of it and try to enjoy myself. After all, except for the story, the original, attractive elements were still in place. Anyhow, when rape is inevitable . . .

We started shooting the picture in Mexico like so many other Hollywood productions, half-cocked. The script was far from finished, but enough pages were completed so we could work for about two weeks before we ran out. The hope was that Felton would keep supplying us with enough new pages so the company wouldn't catch up to him. Eventually, since he was not exactly speedy Gonzales, the company did catch up, and from then on we were neck and neck with disaster.

For a star, Mitchum had a surprisingly modest retinue. Outside of a personal secretary, Riva Fredericks, who stayed in Hollywood most of the time, he was accompanied by his makeup man, Layne (Shotgun) Britton, and a fellow named Fred, whose last name I never did catch. Fred was a lot of things for Bob: bodyguard, stand-in, gofer, drinking companion, you name it. His main value, though, was as Bob's stunt double. He wasn't the best stunt double I've ever seen, but from even a short distance away he looked a lot like Bob in both face and physique. Little did I realize the problems this modest little retinue would create.

A half hour's drive directly east of Cuernavaca, where we were living, lay the village of Tepitzlan, which was our location site. Spectacular as it was, in a bowl of towering mountains, even more spectacular was the enormous cathedral that Cortés had built there. Why he would build such a vast structure for the handful of Indians who lived around there was a mystery. But there it was, a romantically ruined huge, white hulk still in pretty good shape even though it was hundreds of years old, abandoned, and had been used as a fortress during the Revolution. It was perfect for our movie.

After we'd been working in Tepitzlan a while I learned there was a fabulous tiny hotel tucked away only a couple of hundred yards up the mountainside. It was called the Posada del Tepizteco and had been built as a secret hideout for a famous gangster. If it wasn't pointed out to you it would be impossible to find, since the exterior was designed to blend into the crumbling, whitewashed adobe houses around it. Once inside the thick wooden gates it was another story. Whoever the thug was who built it, he was a thug with good taste. It had been turned into a *posada* with apparently no change at all, and it was a gem.

As soon as I got a look at this place, I moved in. Compared to the wooden firetrap hotel in Cuernavaca where we were staying, with its sleazy *cantina* and food even the roaches ignored, this was like finding the Kohinoor in a dung heap. Mitchum wasn't interested in staying there. He preferred the high life of grungy Cuernavaca and the raucous company of Fred and Felton.

We had been warned that Tepitzlan had a reputation for violence, but we paid little attention until one day when traffic had to be stopped for a few minutes on the highway while we were working nearby. A bus driver got impatient and blew his horn. The cop in charge of traffic control went over and shot him.

One morning we arrived at the cathedral to find it blocked by a large group of villagers armed with rifles and machetes. They looked like one of those Diego Rivera murals where the exploited Indians have taken up primitive arms against the ruthless capitalists. We had been working inside the building for the past couple of weeks, but now the villagers were determined not to let us in. The reason, we learned, was based on a rumor that we were going to buy the cathedral and move it to Mexico City. They weren't about to let that happen. It took the local *jefe* of police, armed with a shotgun and a very mean look on his face, to convince them otherwise.

They left, and I suppose it was all very colorful and romantic and Mexican, but somehow it loses something when the machetes and rifles are meant for you. We weren't certain that they might not change their minds and come charging into the cathedral intent on making gringo enchiladas. What with the shooting incident and now this threat of violence, we were all unnerved. This location wasn't turning out to be a pleasure cruise at all.

Midway through our stay some of the star-struck *dolce vita* of Mexico City threw a party for Mitchum and the company. Just about everyone made the trip over the mountains, one Saturday night, to attend. I was too tired, too disinterested, and had too much work to do even to think about going. The *posada* was good enough for me. The next day, however, I heard all about it.

There was a large crowd at the party, and while our movie

people knew hardly anyone, they were toasted and feted and had a good time. It was a well-behaved affair and there were no incidents worth mentioning. A little after 2:00 A.M. Mitchum, unaccountably sober, grew tired of the whole thing and quietly left, along with Felton and all the other movie people—all, that is, except Fred, Mitchum's double, bodyguard, and pal. Fred was having too good a time and wanted to stay. He would find his own way back to Cuernavaca.

Shortly after the group left, some sort of ruckus started and fists flew. Fred was in the middle of it, whether to participate or to break it up has never been clear. What was clear, once the dust settled, was that a pretty *señorita* had been at the receiving end of a haymaker and lay unconscious on the floor. She was taken to the hospital, where she remained in a coma. The *señorita*, it turned out, was the mistress of a high-ranking officer of the Mexican Secret Police.

Wisely, Fred and everyone else involved in the dust-up took it on the lam and disappeared. There was one unfortunate difference between Fred and the others, however. Since Fred was Mitchum's double and looked so much like him, the rumor immediately started that it was Bob who had delivered the blow.

Late Sunday afternoon Mitchum moved into the Posada del Tepizteco. The well-hidden gangster's hideaway suddenly looked very attractive to him. Besides, word had come down that the high-ranking officer was out to "get" him. Bob didn't know exactly what that meant, but presumed the worst.

That night at the *posada* was a long one. Bob refused to go to bed and wouldn't let me go either. I had to sit next to him on the big sofa in the living room. He was sure, he told me, that they were going to kill him. I wasn't any too comfortable sitting there next to him. A fat lot of good I would have been if an assassin had burst in, guns blazing. But Bob didn't want to be alone and needed someone to keep him company. What he really needed was a bodyguard, but the bodyguard was not only responsible for this terrible mess but also was off somewhere, hiding in the Mexican boondocks.

There was no word from Fred for the next few days. We knew he didn't have much money with him, he never did, and true-blue Bob was concerned about his friend. But there were other things to be concerned about. The *señorita* was still unconscious, and there was talk of arresting Mitchum and deporting all the U.S. citizens in the company. We would be sent back to the border by train, in chains.

When at last the *señorita* regained consciousness she cleared up the confusion about Fred and Mitchum and the heat was taken off Bob and the rest of us. But they were beating the bushes for Fred. We were all preoccupied and apprehensive about it. If the Secret Police caught up with him we were sure he'd be found mysteriously dead. Ah, you know, *señor*, these *bandidos*. They probably wanted his shoes.

Every few days we'd get a frantic, cryptic call from him. He was still alive, still on the run, but he wouldn't tell us where he was calling from. He was afraid the line might be tapped. Finally a rescue plan was conceived. We'd hire a private plane to fly him out of the country. The plane would be standing by in a remote field on a specific day. Riva, Bob's secretary, would arrange everything. The next time Fred checked in we gave him the information about where and when he should meet the plane. Could he make it? He'd sure as hell try, he said.

The rescue went off like a cheap movie melodrama. It was almost dusk, the plane was waiting in a dusty field about sixty miles from Cuernavaca. One of our company cars with Riva Fredericks and some trusted office staff stood nearby. A filthy wreck of a taxi jounced and bounced its way across the open fields, leaving a plume of oily smoke behind it. The plane started its engine and the propeller kicked over. The taxi skidded to a stop next to it and a furtive, unshaven, unkempt figure dashed out of the taxi and into the plane. Riva handed him a packet of money, kissed him, and slammed the door shut. The propeller raced, and the plane trundled down the field and took off. Good-bye, Fred, and thanks for the memories.

There was a collective sigh of relief from the whole company when Fred disappeared into the wild blue yonder. We only had a week to go before finishing in Tepitzlan and moving south to our next location, Taxco. The Secret Police were no longer after Mitchum, no one was deporting us in chains, and the locals weren't threatening us with guns and machetes. We looked forward to settling down and to start enjoying ourselves. I sent for Mickey to come down from Los Angeles. For sure, we weren't having any fun yet, but things were bound to improve from now on.

A few days before we were scheduled to leave for Taxco my driver called me aside. He seemed nervous. "Excuse me, Señor Fleischer," he said, "but I must speak to you."

"Of course, Francisco," I said. "What is it?"

"It's about Señor Shotgun," he said.

I wondered why a driver would want to talk to me about Mitchum's makeup man. "Oh?" I asked. "What about him?"

Francisco seemed to be having trouble putting his answer into words. "Well, *señor*, it's like this. The drivers and some of the Mexican crew have taken up a . . . how do you say? . . . a collection for him."

"Really, Francisco? What for?"

"To have him killed, *señor*."

"To do *what?*"

"They are going to have him assassinated, *señor*," he explained. "With the money they have hired an expert from Mexico City. On the first day we work in Iguala he will be on a rooftop and will shoot Señor Shotgun. I thought you should know about this." Although the company would be housed in Taxco, the location was actually in Iguala, a dozen miles to the south.

"Thank you for warning me, Francisco," I said, "but tell me, why do they want to kill him?"

"They do not like him, Señor Fleischer," he replied. "He yells at everyone and insults them, and he calls them bad names. They are very angry, *señor*."

I thought the crew's reaction to Shotgun's behavior was a trifle extreme, but knowing the dignity and pride they possessed it was almost understandable. Shotgun was certainly a character and, no matter what your nationality, he took a lot of getting used to. If there was such a thing as the Ugly American, then he was the Ugly Texan. Everything about him was loud, from his flashy, atrociously color-uncoordinated clothes to his high-speed, unintelligible speech. There was not only an impossibly thick Texas accent to cope with, but also he had his own patois of made-up words and completely *non sequitur* sentences. We seldom had a clue as to what he was saying, much less talking about.

He had a very bad habit of calling all Mexicans "Mezkins." Maybe it was his horrible Texas accent and he couldn't pronounce it any other way, or maybe he thought it was a funny and friendly way of endearing himself to the natives. The natives were not amused. More than anything else, I think it was being called Mezkins that infuriated the crew. He probably never realized how offensive the Mezkins found his loud voice and his violent gestures whenever he had to deal with them. They, like us gringos, could hardly understand a word he said, but they must have assumed, by the nature of his delivery, that it was all insults.

I told Mitchum, Riva, and the staff what I had learned. We

knew we couldn't possibly take a chance with Shotgun and that we had to spirit him out of the country quickly before anyone knew what we were up to. We didn't want someone deciding to move up his appointment with the *pistolero*.

At dawn the next morning a weeping, bewildered Shotgun was bundled into a car and whisked away to another lonely field, where the rescue plane waited. The *Bandido* airlift was back in business.

We finished shooting in Iguala just before lunch on December 8, 1955. The date sticks in my memory, since it was my birthday. No rooftop sniper had appeared, and nobody in the company had gotten picked off. The police hadn't shot anyone, there hadn't been a native uprising, no one had been arrested or deported, and we hadn't flown anyone out of the country for two weeks. Things were looking up.

The plan was to drive to our next location, Acapulco, as soon as we finished work. Glamorous Acapulco, with its terrific beaches and wild nightclubs. We could hardly wait to get there. If you can't have fun in Acapulco, then you'd better forget it, pal. You're not going to have fun anywhere.

Mickey and I and our cameraman, Ernest Laszlo, got into the car and were handed box lunches to eat on the way. About fifteen minutes after we got started we opened them up. I took one look at mine and threw the whole thing, box and all, out the window. Mickey and Ernie were shocked. "Why did you do that?" Mickey asked.

"Because it consists entirely of bacon, lettuce, and tomato sandwiches."

"What's wrong with that? They look delicious."

"Eating a tomato in Mexico," I explained, "is the same as signing your own death warrant. Eat one and you're guaranteed to get the *turistas*, Montezuma's Revenge, and the Aztec two-step all at the same time. Take my advice and throw it out the window."

"I will not!" Mickey said with some annoyance. "You're just a chauvinist, saying things like that. No wonder the Mexicans get angry with some Americans. Well, I'm starving and I'm going to eat mine." She took a big bite out of her sandwich and Laszlo did the same with his.

"You'll be sorry, the both of you."

"It's delicious," she said, her mouth full of bacon, lettuce, and tomato.

We had planned to have dinner that night at the famous La

Perla restaurant, where the floor show consisted of death-defying divers leaping off a high cliff into the sea. It was to be the start of our long-delayed "Fiesta Time in Old Mexico." But it had been a big day, what with working from the crack of dawn, and the long, hot drive to Acapulco, so we decided instead on a quick meal at the hotel and to get to bed early.

When I was ready to turn in, around midnight, I wanted to ensure that I got a good night's sleep. I had just placed a large sleeping pill on my tongue and taken a mouthful of mineral water in the bathroom when I heard Mickey call from the bedroom, "Diiiick!" It sounded strangely weak. I had to swallow the water and gulp down the sleeping pill to answer. "Yes," I said, "what is it?" "I'm dying," came the reply.

It was the attack of the killer tomatoes, and she was violently sick the rest of the night. I phoned the company doctor, but he pretended to be down with the flu and couldn't come. The hotel said they'd send up a local doctor, but he never arrived. In the meantime, the sleeping pill kicked in and I was left groggy, hardly able to stand, fighting off sleep, but still trying to rush Mickey back and forth between the bedroom and the bathroom. She was doing the Aztec two-step while I was doing the last tango in glamorous Acapulco. Fred Astaire and Ginger Rogers we were not. If only she had called me one second earlier, I wouldn't have swallowed that damn pill.

Early the next morning the company doctor showed up, miraculously cured of the flu. He took over and I went downstairs to be driven to the location. The car was waiting with Ernie Laszlo inside. Compared to him, Mickey looked radiantly healthy. He was limp and green. I begged him to go back to bed, but he refused. He would be all right, he assured me, once we got going.

The location was a dense, weirdly beautiful mangrove swamp east of the airport, about a forty-five-minute trip. We drove there with Ernie's head out the window, throwing up the entire way. I pleaded with him to go back to the hotel, but each time he vomited he said he was feeling better and would insist on staying.

At the swamp we transferred into tiny canoes that took us through twisting, narrow, root-clogged waterways for about a half mile to where we had our camera set up on a small island. The swamp was made up of thousands of small islands formed by mangrove roots and organic decay. Ernie's retchings echoed spookily through the gloomy, moss-hung trees. The setting was very Edgar

Allan Poe, with me repeating my refrain of "Go home, Ernie," and him quothing, "Nevermore."

Shortly after we arrived at our spot and were lining up the first shot, Ernie came to me and whispered in my ear that a paddler was going to take him in a canoe to a nearby island. Diarrhea had reared its ugly tail.

Ten minutes later he was back, doubled over in pain. "You won't believe what happened to me," he gasped. "I went behind a bush, took off my pants, and squatted down . . . and some kind of terrible insect bit me on the ball." "Ernie," I said, "*go home!*" He did.

He was out for a week. We had a standby Mexican cameraman who took over, so work didn't stop. After four days of agony and contemplation of suicide, Mickey decided she'd had enough. In spite of dire warnings from the doctor, she was going home, and that was that. "You're under treatment," he warned. "If you do this, you're going to die." "I'm going to die in Los Angeles," Mickey insisted. I tried urging her to stay. She'd be feeling better soon. We could see some of the things we'd planned on seeing—the divers at La Perla, for instance. "To hell with the divers at La Perla," she said and booked herself on a flight to L.A. and, like the others, fled Mexico.

We finished the picture at the Churabusco Studios in Mexico City, two days before Christmas. The following morning we were all flying back to Los Angeles on a chartered Mexicana Airlines flight. Ernie Laszlo and I celebrated that night. We had a leisurely dinner at the best restaurant we could find and then went to the jai alai games. On the way back to the hotel we reminisced about our various adventures during production and how lucky we were that nothing totally catastrophic had happened. Just before we entered the lobby of the hotel I told Ernie that the thing I was happiest about was the fact that Mitchum had stayed out of trouble.

The minute we stepped into the lobby it was clear that I had spoken too soon. Almost everyone in the company was there, talking in subdued little groups. There was a blanket of gloom over everything. Earl Felton was near the door. He looked pale and worried as he came swinging over to me. "What is it, Earl?" I asked. "What the hell is the matter?"

"Mitchum's been arrested."

"You're kidding! What for?"

"Possession of marijuana."

"Christ! Do you know where he's being held?"

"Yeah. He's being held here in his room, incommunicado. John

Burch is the only one they let in there." Burch was our production manager and in charge of all the money. It made sense.

"In his room, here in the hotel? Who arrested him?"

"The Secret Police." That made sense, too.

"Well, why did they bring him here? Why didn't they lock him up?"

"They're waiting for some big guy from the Secret Police to show up." *That* made a lot of sense. Then Earl told me the whole story.

He and Mitchum were being driven to dinner in Bob's car when they were pulled over by an unmarked sedan. Four beefy, swarthy types got out, flashed their badges, and told Bob's driver to open the trunk. It was stuffed full with marijuana. The driver nearly passed out. Obviously, it was a plant. Mitchum was arrested (but not Earl or the driver), and they were going to take him to prison. Earl, being something of an expert on Mexican jails, knew if that happened we might not see Mitchum again for months. There would be no way to spring him loose in the foreseeable future. So he begged, pleaded, and cajoled them into not doing that, but to take Mitchum back to his room at the hotel until something could be worked out. That may or may not have been what the cops had in mind all along, but that is what they did.

We stood around in the lobby fretting about what we should do. If Mitchum got locked up, could we just go off and leave him in the morning, or should we stick around and somehow try to help? It was a tough decision. After all, I hadn't even done my Christmas shopping. While we were debating our options the big guy from the Secret Police suddenly appeared, surrounded by bodyguards, and strode across the lobby to the elevators.

He left, two hours later, $10,000 richer. He had exacted a suitable punishment on the scoundrel who beat up his mistress. So it wasn't the right guy. But he looked like him, didn't he? Mitchum was practically Fred's double, wasn't he? And what about the humiliation he suffered when he found that the true culprit, surely with Mitchum's help, had skipped the country? Somebody had to pay for that, didn't he? So, okay. What's fair is fair, right?

Nobody was late for the plane the next morning. We gathered in a small waiting room. There was plenty of tension and no conversation. We just wanted to get on that plane. Outside the waiting room door an uncommonly large group of soldiers with rifles lounged, regarding us with stone-faced stares. To board the plane, about one hundred feet away, we had to walk right past them. They seemed to be paying particular attention to Mitchum. I was expecting to hear, at any moment, a voice saying to Bob, "One moment, *señor*!" It was a very tense, uncomfortable walk.

When we felt the wheels leave the runway there were cheers, applause, laughter, and handshaking. The tequila flowed, and I was so relaxed that when lunch was served I found that I had eaten halfway through a tomato salad without realizing it. Before the flight was over, Montezuma was knocking on my door.

The flight itself was uneventful except for the last two hours. Los Angeles International Airport was socked in with fog, and we had to circle. An hour and a half later we were still circling, until the pilot announced we were being diverted to Burbank. We hopped over the Santa Monica Mountains to the Burbank side and groped through the fog there for the airport. He couldn't find it. He kept dipping down attempting to get under the cloud level, then zooming up to get above it, trying to find a landmark.

The pilot finally committed himself and we broke out of the fog about one hundred feet above Ventura Boulevard, which he seemed to be using as a road map. When Ventura Boulevard swung to the right, we swung to the right; when it went to the left, so did we. He was obviously following a major boulevard and hoping for the best. Everyone in the plane was glued to the windows, except Gilbert Roland, a Mexican-American star who lived in L.A. He had his eyes shut tight with a scotch in one hand and a rosary in the other.

The plane was sinking lower and lower. The flaps came down. The wheels came down. We all strained to see the airport, but there wasn't any. What we did see directly in front of us, however, was the roof of a huge Sears, Roebuck warehouse. The pilot saw it at the same time we did. The flaps and the wheels went up and so did the plane, right to the top of the fogbank. The pilot got on the intercom. "Ladies and gentlemen," he announced in a voice that would brook no interference, "we are going to land at Los Angeles International Airport." And so we did.

The *Bandido* airlift was finally over.

Bandido turned out to be quite a good, commercially successful picture. It has, however, absolutely nothing to do with the picture I started out to make. I still think *Horse Opera* could make a hell of a movie. Maybe, someday, I'll get to do it. It would surely be a pleasant, easy picture to make. You know, sort of a lark. And Mexico's a great place to shoot, so romantic and colorful. We'd have a ball. Just one laugh after another. It would be fiesta time! Cha-cha-cha!

XI

Following an unhappy writing stint with Cubby Broccoli, producer of the James Bond movies, Earl Felton remarked, "Well, I've learned one thing: Never work for a producer named after a vegetable." We, who are not producers, all have our pet theorems about them. Mine is, never work for a producer who is also the star. I know. I worked for Kirk Douglas when he produced and starred in *The Vikings*.

We had gotten along so well during the making of *Twenty Thousand Leagues* that when he offered me the job, I leapt at it. I could see no reason why working on this film wouldn't be just as enjoyable as the last. Sure, he was difficult. And yes, his "Does this have any value?" and his upstaging habits were annoying, but he was, after all, a star. A *real* star. And real stars must be forgiven most things because they are enormously talented.

There was a screenplay Dale Wasserman had adapted from Edison Marshall's book *The Vikings*. (At that time the script was titled, for obvious reasons, *The Viking*, but regained its plural later, when Tony Curtis joined the cast.)

It wasn't a good screenplay, but the subject matter was fresh and exciting. It promised to be great fun—a roistering, rowdy, swashbuckler; plenty of action, adventure, sex, and violence; and it all took place in a romantic, time-shrouded period of history that hadn't been done to death in a hundred other movies.

Right from the beginning Kirk and I saw the picture the same way. We aimed for two goals: quality and authenticity. And we wanted a superior screenplay. Kirk hired an English writer, and we all went to work.

You couldn't ask for a better producer, during the preproduction period, than Kirk. He was knowledgeable, creative, and pas-

sionately involved. There was no penny-pinching or cutting corners. Most importantly, I had his confidence and trust. It seemed
too good to be true.

With his enthusiastic endorsement I hired a professor from
UCLA who was a Viking period expert. The chief curator of the
Viking Museum in Oslo also became a consultant. I scoured the
fjords of Norway and the coast of France looking for locations. The
Viking Ship Museum in Oslo had the remains of three ships. I went
there with the art director (Harper Goff again, from *Twenty Thousand Leagues*) and got the blueprints. A shipyard near Bergen was
contracted to build the three ships to the exact blueprint specifications. Because of the strange twisting motion of these ships at sea
(which is why they are also called "snake" ships) they had to be built
of oak. Any other wood shatters under the stress of the twisting
motion, sending the boat to the bottom. But oak no longer existed
in Scandinavia. It had to be imported at great expense from the
United States.

I spent days in the Rare Books section of the British Museum
library in London searching for anything that could be used in the
picture; customs, superstitions, mores, dress, jewelry, anything.

We hired dozens of bearded men in Norway and Denmark who
were members of rowing clubs and engaged trainers to teach them
to row and maneuver boats in unison. When winter came we supplied them with sunlamps so they would have healthy tans when we
started shooting the following spring.

Harper Goff commenced building an entire Viking village in
Hardanger Fjord.

Housing in the fjords was a major problem. What with a huge
crew and dozens of Vikings there would be about 150 people to take
care of. Transportation was another headache, since we had several
locations scattered many miles apart throughout the Hardanger
area. The solution was to hire two dormitory ships. In that way we
would not only be able to house everyone but also would be able to
sail during the night to our next location. (One of the ships, the
Brand VI, was Barbara Hutton's old yacht. It was so big that the
garage area became the main dining room for the entire company.)

Almost every department needed its own ship. There would be
a special-effects ship, a wardrobe ship, a prop ship, and an electrical
supplies ship. And there were other boats needed to carry water,
fuel, mail, and supplies. Including the three Viking ships we assembled a flotilla that rivaled the Spanish Armada.

Logistically, the film was going to be a brute, with locations and heavy construction not only in Norway, but also at Fort Lalatte in Brittany and the Geiselgasteig Studios in Munich.

Early in 1957 Kirk left for Munich to start work with Stanley Kubrick on *Paths of Glory*. I carried on in L.A. with the picture's preparation. The script was coming along beautifully. Kirk and the rest of us thought the writer was doing a wonderful job. We were particularly impressed with the style of the dialogue he had devised. It verged on blank verse and gave the story a mystical, poetical feeling that seemed perfect for the period. By avoiding modern vernacular and sidestepping the usual Hollywood-historical "Yonder lies the castle of my father" tradition, the tone was raised from comic book to semiclassic.

In early spring I left for Norway to commence final preparations before shooting. However, Kirk asked me to travel via Munich so we could meet. The first night there I had dinner with Kirk, Kubrick, James Harris (Kubrick's partner), and Calder Willingham, one of the cowriters of the *Paths of Glory* screenplay. That's when I first found out that it really was too good to be true.

They had all read the *Vikings* script. Their opinions were unanimous: The dialogue stank. Kubrick said that no actor could speak those lines, and they all agreed, including Kirk. I was dumbfounded.

I argued my position throughout dinner that they were dead wrong, all of them. It was pointless, however. As far as Kirk was concerned it was a *fait accompli*. I hadn't actually realized that was so until he told me that Calder Willingham was going to rewrite the dialogue. You know, get rid of the mystical crap, make it more colloquial. Good-bye semiclassic, hello comic book.

It was a humiliating position to be in. I was fighting against Kubrick, Harris, and Willingham and had lost long before I even began. Kirk had long since been won over to their side, which meant he had more confidence in their judgment than he did in his director's. Our relationship was eroding and we hadn't even started the picture.

I left Munich for Bergen, Norway, very depressed. After a year's painstaking preparation I would be starting the picture without a script.

The plan was to shoot preproduction stuff for ten days: scenics, a major battle at sea, the burning of the Viking funeral ship. At the end of that time Kirk would arrive on the location with the actors and deliver the first batch of new pages. Meanwhile I would be shooting blind.

My spirits were lifted momentarily when I landed in Bergen and the stewardess asked me to deplane first. Harper Goff was there with fifty fierce-looking, bearded, and costumed Vikings lined up in a double row from the plane's door to the tiny terminal, swords raised to form a canopy and singing a Norse war song. The bewildered passengers burst into applause.

The two weeks before preproduction shooting started were mostly taken up with solving the problems caused by our slavish devotion to the blueprint specifications for the three Viking ships. The first problem we ran into was anthropological. The oarholes in the sides of the ships were too close together. Our Vikings couldn't row without banging their oars into the backs of the rowers in front of them. Their arms were too long. The original Vikings obviously must have been short, squat guys with arms to match. We had to plug up every other oarhole.

The keels were too shallow. Under sail it was impossible to keep the three ships in formation because they skidded sideways. We built detachable keels that could be put on for sailing or taken off for rowing. (The ships, incidentally, were not designed to tack.)

The rudders weren't deep enough. The boats couldn't be turned around in less than a full mile, which meant it took forever to bring them back into position. We added an extension to the bottoms of the rudders.

The sails were made of heavy canvas. It would take a full gale to fill them with enough wind to move the boats. We replaced them with nylon sails and installed wind machines on the decks to fill them up. Hidden diesel engines (with wake suppressors) actually powered the boats.

One thing we learned for sure: When the Vikings built their boats, they didn't have movie work in mind at all.

The weather for the first day of preproduction shooting was fabulous: cloudless, sunny, and hot. We worked with our shirts off. At the end of the day one of the Vikings came up to me and said, "Well, how did you like our summer?" But he was wrong. Summer lasted for a good two weeks.

The scenic stuff was spectacular: 150 miles of zigzagging, emerald green, forested cliffs rising 3,000 feet out of sapphire blue water; wide, roaring waterfalls that sparkled like diamonds; the Viking ships bathed in brilliant sunlight and sailing with savage dignity through the wide, majestic canyons.*

---

* I was astonished to read in Kirk's book *The Ragman's Son* that those scenes were never used because the weather turned bad after we shot them and he decided to

The last thing I was going to photograph at the end of the preproduction shooting, the day before Kirk and the actors were scheduled to arrive on the location, was the long shot of the burning Viking ship for the burial at sea sequence. We had planned to do it as a miniature shot—that is, burn a rowboat rigged out as a Viking ship instead of using our full-scale and very expensive ship. The theory was that out on the open sea, where there was nothing to compare it with, you couldn't tell how big or how small it really was.

A few days before we got to the shot I asked to see the miniature ship. It looked exactly like what it was: a rowboat trying to look like a Viking ship. I called a meeting with Harper Goff, the special-effects people, the stuntmen, and Freddy Zendar, our water and safety specialist. Was there a way to use the real Viking ship? I asked. The most effective thing we'd see burning would be the sail. Why couldn't we burn one of the heavy canvas sails that we now had no use for anyhow? And could we rig gas jets around the inside of the gunwales so we would have the illusion that the entire boat was aflame? And would it be safe? Special-effects people would have to be on board to operate the controls.

The answers to all my questions were positive. Everyone thought it was a great idea. There was no question that this was the way to go. My two biggest concerns were that no one get hurt and that we didn't sink the Viking ship. Zendar reassured me on all counts. Stuntmen would be mixed in with the special-effects people not only to protect them but also to help control the fire in the unlikely case that it got out of hand. In addition, a large pump would be installed on board. As soon as I gave the signal that we'd gotten the shot the intake hose would be dropped over the side and the pump started. And just for double protection there'd be a fast emergency boat, with an extra pump and fire fighters, stationed next to the camera boat. In case of trouble they'd dash right out and help. I decided to take the gamble and go with the real ship.

It was ten-thirty at night, in the Land of the Midnight Sun, before the sun got low enough to look like a sunset shot, which was what I was after. The camera was set up on a seagoing tug for steadiness, the emergency boat alongside. Three hundred yards away the Viking ship drifted. The sea was calm, the sun was in the

have everything redone in bad weather. His memory is faulty on this point. Every frame of film shot in good weather is in the film.

right place, and my heart was in my mouth. I signaled for them to light the fires.

A dozen tiny, silhouetted figures scurried around the deck of the Viking ship with torches, lighting the gas jets and the gasoline-soaked sail, then ducked for cover, hiding themselves from the camera. I called "Roll it!" and we started filming.

It was perfect. The flames grew larger and larger. The ship appeared to be engulfed in fire. There was a majesty and a grandeur about it that could only come from the real thing. It was a thrilling sight. I felt justified in taking the chance. I knew I was right.

The problem with shooting such a scene is that you don't know exactly when to stop. It might look terrific now, but in a couple of seconds it might look even better. Wait and see. Then wait some more. Wouldn't it be terrible if you cut just before something wonderful happened?

Then something did happen, only it wasn't so wonderful. I noticed a change in the quality of the fire. The flames were getting redder, the smoke blacker. This wasn't gas and canvas burning, this was wood! The Viking ship was on fire! For real!

Frantically I ordered three long blasts on the tug's deep-throated steam horn, the signal that the shot was over and to put out the fire. My assistant got on the walkie-talkie and relayed the order. Nothing happened. The fire roared on. Three more blasts and still nothing happened. Three more! Maybe they hadn't heard the whistle. Or the walkie-talkie wasn't working. Or maybe they'd all been barbecued and the Viking ship would sink in flames! Without that ship there would be no picture. There would be no insurance because what we were doing was unauthorized. It wasn't just the ship going up in flames, but my career, too!

Finally we saw some figures running around on the deck. Thank God for that, I thought. We could see them huddled around the area of the pump. A minute went by. Two minutes. Nothing was happening, and the flames were still roaring away. Then something truly frightening happened: They took off their jackets and started beating the flames with them! The goddamn pump wouldn't start!

I hadn't thought about the emergency boat with the backup pump. I'd been too engrossed in what was happening. Where the hell was it? I looked around. There it was, still moored alongside us. "What the hell are you waiting for?" I screamed at them. There was no reply, only dumb stares. My French assistant yelled at them in French. They still stared at us. Someone tried German. Nothing.

Danish. Nothing. Finally the tug captain called out in Norwegian. The boat took off like a shot.

We watched the emergency boat speed toward the Viking ship and pull alongside. I expected to see a stream of water squirt from it onto the fire, but that didn't happen. Instead, the crew boarded the Viking ship, took off their jackets, and started beating the flames with them. This is ridiculous, I thought. What in God's name is going on? I yelled to the tug captain to make for the ship and told everyone to grab a bucket or anything that would hold water. We were halfway there when suddenly a great stream of water erupted from a hose on the Viking ship. In seconds the fire was out.

When we got alongside I saw that no one was hurt and I assessed the damage. The mast was charred and the gunwales a bit scorched here and there, but that was all. Easily reparable. I breathed a mighty sigh of relief, maybe the first real breath I'd taken since the whole thing started, and asked what had happened. It was a comedy of errors.

They never heard the walkie-talkie. The heat of the fire interfered with the radio reception. And they didn't hear the tug whistle either, because of the roar of the gas flames. When it got too hot for comfort, they turned off the gas jets, but the wooden mast and gunwales were burning on their own. The pump, like all pumps everywhere, wouldn't start. That was when they started beating the flames out with their jackets.

The emergency boat was so anxious to do a good and efficient job that they threw their pump's intake hose over the side while they were still under way. The propeller promptly cut it off. They arrived at the fire with a pump that worked, but no hose. They joined the others beating at the flames with their jackets. The fire was almost out of hand when the big pump finally came to life.

The burning funeral ship is a memorable shot in the movie. It should be. It was almost my funeral.

The following day Kirk arrived with the actors and the first batch of script pages from Calder Willingham. A cablegram for Kirk also arrived that same day. It was from the English writer whose script Willingham was redoing. It read, simply: MENE, MENE, TEKEL, UPHARSIN. Puzzled looks all around. Nobody knew what it meant except me. It was a quote from the Bible and were the words that appeared on the wall at Belshazzar's feast. Daniel interpreted them to mean that God had judged and doomed Belshazzar's kingdom. It was the writing on the wall. As we were about to sit down at our Belshazzar's feast, I didn't think it was a good idea to take on the role of Daniel and enlighten them by interpreting the cablegram.

It had been three years since I'd last directed Kirk. I wondered if he had changed. He hadn't. The first thing I had to do with him was a scene in which he, Ernest Borgnine, and James Donald are poring over a map on a round table. Not a very complicated shot. I remembered my lesson from the past and put Kirk in the middle and the other two actors on either side of him. There wasn't anything more to the scene than them standing there discussing some sort of strategy.

It felt dull and visually flat to me, so during the rehearsal I started to circle the table slowly, looking for an interesting angle. As I moved, Kirk moved, trying to stay in the center of what he thought was my frame. When Kirk moved, the others moved, trying to keep their positions. I kept walking and they kept shuffling around the table. Then I reversed direction and started walking the other way. They did, too. Then I quickly walked to the exact opposite side from where I was, so that I was right behind them. Consternation among the actors! They all started to scramble around the table so they could be facing me. Kirk blew up. "Where the hell is the camera in this scene?" he wanted to know. "Why, I don't know yet, Kirk," I replied, trying to look a little surprised that he'd ask. "Does it matter?"

After the first few days of First Unit shooting the weather turned bad. In the next eight weeks we had exactly one day of sunshine. All that rain, fog, and gloom, however, actually helped the picture's mood. But not Kirk's. The foul weather was slowing us up. We were losing ground every day and Kirk was getting nastier with every minute lost.

There was an unreasonableness about his temper flare-ups that I found highly disturbing. Like blowing up at me for not having new, rewritten pages in my script when he had neglected to provide me with them. Arguments would erupt when Kirk would accuse me of being confused about the story when I'd suddenly be confronted with changes that were made in his script but not in mine. These were not mere contretemps but full-blown diatribes laced with the kind of heavy sarcasm even a backward child would recognize.

There were a few light moments during our stay in Norway. The two big dormitory ships were always good for a laugh. One had a Danish captain, the other Norwegian, and there was great rivalry between them. The two ships would park side by side. When we had to weigh anchor and move to the next location it was a matter of pride as to who would get under way first. The captains were trying to treat these huge, lumbering craft like hot rods. We never got away from any location without the two ships colliding amid cheers and jeers from the passengers. By the time we were finished with them their sides were masses of bumps, dents, scrapes, and giant dings. The owners must have been thrilled when they got them back.

On the Fourth of July the English camera crew challenged the Americans to a game of cricket. They had brought a cricket ball and bat with them. There was a tiny island in the fjord close to the ships, and that's where the historic event was held at sunset, about 11:00 P.M. Everyone showed up in hip boots and thick turtleneck sweaters. The Americans went to bat first, and the game ended in less than three minutes when the propman hit the ball into the fjord. The Americans had won again. There was a grand victory celebration the next night.

One of the results of my research at the British Museum was the discovery of a fascinating Viking custom, the "Running of the Oars." When the ships approached their village after a long sea voyage, the rowers would hold the oars out, parallel with the water, and the other Vikings would run on them, stepping from oar to oar, from the stern to the bow.

It's not an easy thing to do. Our stuntmen practiced for a couple of weeks before they became any good at it and they still kept falling into the water a lot. The day we shot that sequence I had the camera set up on shore, the three ships coming down the fjord right at us, the Vikings running on the oars. It was a stirring and moving sight, a direct, authentic glimpse into the ancient past, something no one in the whole world had seen for more than a thousand years!

I felt a tap on my shoulder. It was Kirk. He seemed as excited as I was. "I can do that!" he said.

"Come on, Kirk, those guys have been practicing for weeks."

"If I can do it could you get close enough so that you can see that it's really me doing it?"

"Of course. I'll put the camera in a boat. We'll be right on top of you."

"Great! I'll get changed." He started to run off.

"Kirk!" I called after him. "That water's awfully cold."

"Never mind. Just get the camera out there." He was as excited as a kid.

I had my misgivings, but we got out on the water with the camera and I called "Action!" Kirk ran the oars as though he'd done it all his life. He was far better than any of the stuntmen. I was impressed.

He did it twice, perfectly. On the third take an oar broke and he fell into the frigid water. I knew I shouldn't have let him try it, I thought. The Viking outfit was heavy enough without it being soaked in water. And what if he got hypothermia, or a cramp from the cold? It flashed through my mind that if he drowned it would be even worse than losing the Viking ship.

Kirk swam frantically toward us. Everyone reached out to grab him, but he ignored our hands and gripped the side of the boat. "Did you get it?" he yelled at us. "Did you see me fall in?" "Yes," I yelled back at him. "We got it." "You didn't cut the camera when I hit the water, did you?" "No," I assured him, "we got it all." "Great!" he said. "That should be a terrific shot!" and with that he pushed off and swam back through the icy waters to the Viking ship.

Again, I was impressed. Not so much by his physical prowess but by his unbounded, boyish enthusiasm for moviemaking. He was more concerned with getting a good shot than he was for his personal comfort, safety, or anything else. In spite of all the aggravation and *tsuris* he was giving me, I had to admire him.

Toward the end of our Norwegian location shooting, Kirk was becoming aware that morale wasn't too great among the cast and crew, although he was probably unaware that he was the primary cause of most of it. In any event, he thought it would be a good idea if he gave a big party for the crew and have the actors put on a slapstick variety show. It would have an all-star cast: Kirk Douglas, Tony Curtis, Janet Leigh, Ernie Borgnine.

There was a small stage at one end of the dining room on the *Brand VI*. The carpenters built a set on it, the electricians lit it, the wardrobe department made costumes, and the ship's chef baked some whipped cream pies.

The show played like gangbusters. The American and the British crews loved it. The Danes and the Norwegians didn't understand all of what little dialogue there was, but they roared with laughter at everything anyhow. The finale of the show was the time-honored sketch called, "Stand-in!" The big, pampered movie star (Kirk) does his bit until something dangerous has to be done, like getting punched or hit on the head. Then the director (me) calls "Cut! Stand-in!" The star steps out and the stand-in (Tony Curtis) takes his place and gets socked or kicked by the heavy (Ernie Borgnine) while the star is drinking champagne and smooching with the leading lady (Janet Leigh). The climax of the skit occurs when the heavy throws a pie, the stand-in ducks, and the star gets it full in the face.

The sketch was a howling success, but there was a twist at the end. The chef didn't make just a few pies, he'd made dozens, and they were hidden all over the set. As soon as the first pie hit, everyone on the stage found a pie and let fly at Kirk. It was the pie-throwing fest of all time. Dozens of pies, each one a bull's-eye. Kirk finally took refuge in a large, covered, wicker basket that was part of the act. Every time he opened the lid to see if he could come out, wham! Another three pies in the face. Were the actors trying to tell him something?

The show seemed to raise everyone's spirits somewhat, but it didn't do a thing for the weather. It remained miserable, and we were losing more and more time because of it. There were still two weeks of work scheduled for Norway (but would probably take longer) when Kirk called for a night production meeting to be held in the dining room. The weather was killing us, he explained. We had to leave this location as soon as possible. Was there anything that was still to be shot here that could be done on a sound stage in Munich instead? We went through the script shot by shot. When we finished we found that we had no work left in Norway at all! One way or another, by "cheating" and by changing some exteriors into interiors, everything could be done on a sound stage. We could wrap up and sail away in the morning.

We were all elated. The fjords were staggeringly beautiful, but we'd had it with the hard living conditions, the cold, the rain, and the fog. But there was one sobering thought that somewhat dampened our spirits: the Norwegian and Danish Vikings. How were we going to break it to them that they were finished, when they were planning on at least two more weeks of work? It could be unpleasant. There might be trouble.

We were still sitting around our conference table pondering what to do about this problem when we were suddenly interrupted by the arrival of a rather hostile deputation from the neighboring dormitory ship that housed all the Vikings. They had a list of demands: more money, shorter working days, television sets in each cabin. If they didn't get what they were asking for, they'd leave. Kirk said, "You're not getting it. Leave. And have a nice trip home." The deputation was stupefied. They couldn't believe what they'd heard and left in confusion.

A finer example of bad timing would be hard to find. We opened a couple of bottles of champagne after they left. But Kirk wasn't all that happy about what had just happened. In fact, he was hurt and furious. He felt that they'd been well treated and cared for, that their contracts had been scrupulously respected. Beyond that, he felt that the big bash and show he'd given them had forged some sort of familial bonding. He was truly shocked that they would try this coercion, this extortion, on him. The fact that a moment before we were about to pull the rug out from under them I don't believe ever entered his mind. Still, our action was forced on us. It wasn't a matter of choice. Theirs was just plain strong-arm stuff. They'd thought they had us over a barrel.

The deputation came back to our ship a little later, wanting to talk to Kirk, but he refused to meet with them. They were willing to withdraw their demands, keep the status quo. No way. Kirk had assumed the role of the injured man of the highest moral and ethical principles. It was half sham and half real. An interesting dichotomy.

There was no race between the two captains, the next morning, as to who would get away first. The *Brand VI* weighed anchor and slowly backed into the center of the fjord. The Vikings lined the rail of their ship and watched unbelievingly as we slid past them. Some of them called out, "Don't go!" I saw tears glistening on more than one beard. We waved mournfully at each other. The Norway location was over.

The Fort Lalatte location in French Brittany was great. The weather was sunny and dry, the work was exciting, we lived in comfortable hotels in the nearby resort of Dinard, and the food was three-star. My family had visited me in Norway for a while. My daughter, Jane, being five, was a little too young to understand what was going on, but my two boys, Bruce and Mark, who were twelve and nine, respectively, were completely swept away with the whole romance of the Vikings. The crew, of course, pampered them to pieces. The wardrobe people made complete Viking outfits for them, horned helmets and all, the prop department constructed swords they could handle, and the stuntmen engaged them in fights to the death.

My wife, Mickey, and the kids had left the Scandinavian location for a driving tour of Europe. It was planned so that they would meet me in Dinard. As soon as they arrived, the boys donned their Viking outfits and came to the location with me every day.

The most spectacular action of the picture took place in and around Fort Lalatte (standing in for an impregnable castle on the coast of England). However, one of the most memorable moments of the entire location took place directly in front of the hotel en-

trance in Dinard. A large group of us had gathered there, as we did
early every morning, to wait for the cars and buses to take us to the
location. My kids were, as usual, dressed in their Viking outfits.
Suddenly Mark, the nine-year-old, drew his sword with a flourish,
turned to Kirk, who was standing next to him, and said loudly and
with tremendous intensity, "Odin must have sent you! Where is
Morgana?"

It was Kirk's first line of a very dramatic confrontational scene
that he had played with Tony Curtis in Norway. Mark had witnessed it, had identified with Kirk, and was now challenging him to
play the scene with him, even though Mark was playing Kirk's part.
Kirk stared down at him, off-balance for a moment. The crowd fell
silent and watched them. Mark's big, black eyes had locked onto
Kirk's and never wavered. Kirk glared back and then, with the same
dramatic energy as Mark's, answered him with Tony's line, "In
Aella's Castle." To which Mark responded with anger, "You dare to
come back here just to tell me this?"

It was a fairly long scene, and they played it out to its finish.
Kirk performed with sincerity and integrity without the slightest
hint of condescension. It was actor to actor, professional to professional. When it was over Kirk held out his hand, and they shook.
The watching crowd gave them both a warm round of applause. In
spite of his rough, domineering, insensitive treatment of me and the
others, I had to like him for what he had just done.

Munich followed Brittany as our final location. It was a relief to
get there and be able to work under the roofs of the Geiselgasteig
Studios after all those months of battling Kirk and the weather. But
while it may have been more comfortable working on a sound stage,
it wasn't much easier. Right from the beginning it was a difficult
picture to make. When you expected clear sailing, you ran into a
fogbank. As a matter of fact, one of the first things we shot in the
studio was a sequence with Tony Curtis in a fogbank. He's in a
small boat at sea (on rockers, on a stage) at night, in the fog.
Borgnine, who has been chasing him in his large Viking ship, runs
aground and falls overboard. Tony pulls him from the sea and takes
him captive, but to do so he must knock him out. We'd rehearsed it,
worked out the action, filled the stage with fog, and gotten all ready
to shoot when Tony said, "I refuse to hit him!"

"Why not?" I asked, exasperated.

"Because it would be bad for my image."

"What image? What are you talking about?"

"My fans. They wouldn't like it if I hit an old man."

"Why, he's been chasing you with a whole pack of Vikings. If he caught you he'd kill you. Your fans will love it if you hit him."

"No, I can't do it. I won't hit an old man."

Borgnine spoke up in a deep-chested growl. "Awww, c'mon, Tony. You can hit me. Honest, I won't mind."

It took a half hour of persuasion before we reached a compromise. He'd hit Ernie, but the blow had to be hidden from the camera. I had to stop everything and reblock the action to make it work. I hope Tony's fans appreciated it.

Another scene that should have been easy but wasn't was the "wolf pit" sequence. While Tony and some others watch, Borgnine is to be thrown into a pit of wild, ravenous wolves. I talked to an animal trainer about how to do this. He told me the only way it was possible was for him (the trainer) to double for Ernie and work with German police dogs. He'd get about a dozen and clip them to look to look like mangy, wild wolves. But would they really act wild? I asked. *Ach, ja*, he assured me. He'd put them through a training program. For anyone but him even to get near them would be *unmöglich*, impossible. They would *verrückt*, mad, go. I explained that the main shot I was after was shooting down into the pit, over the backs of Borgnine, Curtis, and the others, and seeing the wolves leaping, snarling, showing their teeth, trying to get at them. *Ach, ja*, it would be no problem. Just be sure, he cautioned, that the pit enough deep was.

We not only gave the animal trainer plenty of time to get the police dogs prepared, we also went well beyond that. We had an exact reproduction made of the wolf pit we'd be working with so the dogs could be trained in it and wouldn't suddenly find themselves in strange surroundings when we started shooting. The day before we were scheduled to do the sequence I asked the trainer to give me a demonstration.

The training pit, like the set, was about six feet deep, with a three-foot wall around its edge. I looked over the wall. Twelve mad, rabid, ferocious wolves flew up to get at me. Their saliva-flecked jaws seemed only inches from my face; the barking was deafening. They scared the hell out of me. I involuntarily drew back. "Great!" I told the trainer. "Just make sure they're like this tomorrow." *Ach, ja*, until tomorrow they would no more food get. They would *sehr*, very, wild be. I was a little worried that the pit enough deep wasn't.

The next morning I lined up and rehearsed the shot over the actors' backs into the wolf pit, but without the dogs. I didn't want them to get used to the actors (and vice versa) or wear them down with many repetitions. When we were ready to shoot, before the dogs were to put into the pit through a door in the bottom, I made a little speech to the cast and crew. No one was to touch or even go near the dogs. And no one was *ever* to enter the pit while the dogs were there. When we needed a shot from inside the pit looking up toward the actors, the camera and crew would have to be in a covered barricade.

When you came down to it, the shot itself couldn't have been simpler or easier. The actors would look over the edge of the wall into the pit, the dogs would jump at them, and that was it. The actual shooting time would be ten, maybe fifteen seconds. The only way this shot could be screwed up was if a dog jumped over the top. It was extremely unlikely, but I had a couple of dog handlers standing by anyhow, just in case. I'd seen enough the previous day to make me doubly cautious.

The actors took their positions one or two steps back from the wall so they couldn't be seen by the dogs. On "Action" they would step forward and the fun would begin. The last adjustments were made to the lights, and I called for the dogs to be brought in. In the bottom of the pit the door opened and the wolves slunk in, mean and vicious-looking.

The camera rolled, I called "Action!" The actors stepped forward. The dogs stood there. They appeared bewildered. They didn't even look up. Some of them sat down.

I called to the actors. "Make a noise!" I told them. "Attract their attention." They did their best. They clapped their hands, waved their arms. Some said, "Here, boy!" and made kissing sounds. Some of the dogs looked up. I cut the camera.

Part of the scene called for Frank Thring, who played the evil king, Aella, to dangle a piece of raw meat over the pit to drive the wolves into an even greater frenzy. We had a basket filled with pieces of raw meat on the set. I asked Thring to try dangling a piece on the next take. That should stir up the hungry beasts.

We tried it. Nothing happened. He couldn't get their attention. I told Thring to drop the piece of meat in among them; maybe they'd start salivating and figure out that there was more where that came from. No such luck. Some of them sniffed at it, then wandered off, disinterested.

I talked to Ach Ja, the trainer, but *ach, nein*, he had no suggestions. The American propman came to me. How about letting him cover the floor of the pit with a wire mesh? Put a light electrical charge in it. You know, just enough to get the dogs angry. He'd done it before and it really worked. I was getting desperate. Not only was I losing time, but I also didn't know how to get the shot. I asked him how long it would take to rig what he had suggested. Fifteen minutes, he replied, give or take a half hour. I told him to go ahead. The trainer took the dogs out of the pit, the propman went to work, and the rest of us had coffee.

Forty-five minutes later the actors were once again in position, the dogs were in the pit. The camera rolled and we threw the switch. The dogs did not go mad with anger. Instead they started to prance around in a sort of dainty minuet, delicately lifting their paws in a most refined manner. I called a halt to the proceedings and had the wire mesh disconnected.

My old writer pal Earl Felton, a rascal if there ever was one, used to tell me about the cruel sport he'd had as a kid when he'd smuggle a cat into a movie theater, give it a swipe under the tail with some turpentine, and then watch it go scorching down the aisle and claw its way up the screen. I'd always look askance at him when he told me this story, but now it came to mind and sounded pretty good to me. If it did that to cats, why not to dogs? It was worth a try.

I told the propman what I wanted to do. He thought it was a great idea and got two poles about fifteen feet long for himself and his assistant. He wrapped one of the ends in rags saturated with turpentine. The two of them leaned over the wall surrounding the pit with their long sticks, trying to get under the dogs' tails. Trying to hit a bull's-eye with the end of a fifteen-foot pole is like trying to pin the tail on a donkey with St. Vitus' dance. The dogs got swabbed on their necks, their bellies, their paws, everywhere but ground zero.

By now the wild wolves had become thoroughly bored. Some were wandering around disconsolately; most were sitting or lying down. None of them minded the occasional, refreshing dab of turpentine that wavered their way. The propman was much more agitated than the dogs. He turned to me and said, "This isn't going to work. I know a better way," and he and his assistant put down the poles and left the set.

A few moments later the door in the bottom of the pit opened and the two prop men appeared, each with a handful of rags and a can of turpentine. "Are you crazy?" I yelled down at them. "Get the hell out of there!"

They looked up at me and smiled. "Don't worry about us. Just get ready to roll the camera," they called back. Then they started lifting tails and swabbing. They walked blithely through the whole pack, lifting and swabbing. No more sloppy aiming. A hole-in-one every time!

The dogs liked it. They licked the turpentine off their bottoms and off of some of their friends' bottoms, too. Then they lay back down to continue their naps. I called off the propmen.

The animal trainer came over to me. I looked daggers at him. "Herr Fleischer, *ist nicht der* fault from the dogs. Ist from *der* lights," he informed me. *"Ist zu heiss*, too hot. *Ist machen* sleepy, the dogs." I looked up at the lights. They *were* big and hot. I looked at the dogs. They surely were wilted. I looked at my watch: lunchtime. I told Jack Cardiff, the cameraman, to kill the lights and told my assistant to call lunch, but leave the dogs in the pit and get an air-conditioning unit to cool them down. Maybe they'd be livelier in an hour.

When we came back from lunch the dogs were a lot peppier, but we still had no solution as to how to get them riled up. We dangled some more red meat, we fired blank cartridges, we even showed them the studio cat. The dogs couldn't have cared less.

Someone, probably one of the trainers, had left some old clothes on the set during lunch: a big, floppy, beat-up peasant hat; a dirty, loose-fitting blouse; a heavy walking stick. Tony Curtis found them and, just for laughs, put on the hat and blouse, then leaned over the pit, waving the walking stick in his hand, and said, "Hi, fellas!" to the dogs.

As soon as the dogs got sight of him in that outfit they went wild! Pandemonium in the pit! They were leaping, barking, snapping, lips rolled back, teeth bared. If they could have gotten to Tony they would have torn him to shreds. He backed away in terror. The dogs still kept up their vicious excitement for another thirty seconds. Whoever owned that outfit was someone those dogs would dearly love to get their teeth into.

We all looked at each other. Could this be the answer? When the dogs had quieted down I asked Tony to try it again. Once more the dogs went into a frenzy. I got the actors into position and worked out a routine with Tony. The plan was to have all the actors in position except for Tony, who would be dressed in the peasant outfit. We'd roll the camera and, when it was up to speed, he'd lean over the pit making wild gestures. Once the dogs started leaping and jumping, he'd whip off the hat and blouse, drop the stick, and play the scene in his Viking character before the dogs calmed down.

In fifteen seconds the scene was in the can, and we went on to the next setup. Tony did the quick-change act for the rest of the sequence. It looked like sheer lunacy, but it worked. The most difficult thing now was for the actors to keep a straight face while we were shooting.

But all of these various problems are to be expected on a film of this size and complexity. What you don't need are problems brought on by unreasonableness, ego, and short temper, which Kirk supplied in ample quantities. Story conferences and discussions on the set were marked with his great impatience and a resulting loss of temper. If he didn't immediately see the significance of one of my suggestions or ideas, it would be dismissed out-of-hand with a humiliating outburst. On the other hand, he demanded that his suggestions, no matter how many or how subtle, be given the fullest, most respectful consideration and patient analysis.

Even simple scenes with him became surreal nightmares. There was one pretty ridiculous, but quite typical, incident with Kirk. We were doing a scene between him and Ernie Borgnine. They were seated at a small table, across from each other. Ernie, in a long speech, was explaining something to Kirk. He had all the dialogue, Kirk had none. Ernie spoke, Kirk listened. That's all there was to it. Simplicity itself.

I did an angle over Kirk's shoulder onto Ernie. Then I moved in for a close-up of Ernie. What with getting the readings, shadings, and nuances exactly right it took close to two hours before I was ready to make a shot over Ernie's shoulder of Kirk listening. Actually, I only needed a few seconds of this, since Kirk did absolutely nothing except sit there with his elbows on the table, his arms crossed, listening. But, since he hadn't had his face in the camera for a little while, and since he was the star, I didn't want him to feel slighted. I ran his shot for the entire length of the speech, about a minute. It was *noblesse oblige* on my part; *droit du seigneur* on his.

A full minute of Kirk intently listening to Ernie was boring but completely satisfactory. I had more than enough of what I needed for editing purposes. When it was over I said, "Cut! That's a print. Thank you very much," and started to walk away.

"Just a minute!" Kirk said. I stopped and looked at him. "Were you completely satisfied with that take?" he asked.

"Yes, I was. I wouldn't have printed it if I wasn't."

He stared at me. "Don't you think it could be better?"

"Better? How better? I thought it was just fine."

"Well, did you notice how I was sitting there, with my right arm crossed over my left? Like this?"

"Of course I noticed. What about it?"

"Would it be better if I had my left arm crossed over my right? Like this?"

I thought he was joking. "As far as I'm concerned it wouldn't make any difference at all."

His temper flared. "It's *got* to make a difference!" I was wrong. He wasn't joking. "One has *got* to be better than the other. Which one do you think is better?"

"The one you're more comfortable doing."

"It's not a matter of comfort! Which one is better?"

"The one we shot!"

"I like the other way better!"

"Okay! Do it that way! I'll shoot it again!"

"I don't want to shoot it that way!"

"Why not?"

"It doesn't feel comfortable!"

"What the fuck do you want from me?"

"Forget it!" he shouted, getting up from the table and walking away. "Forget the whole fucking thing!"

If it hadn't been for Kirk, it would have been a wonderful picture to make. Of course, without Kirk there wouldn't have been any picture. In the long run, it was worth putting up with his browbeating and petty tyrannies, since the picture turned out to be a great critical and financial success and did both of us a lot of good. Probably he was unaware of the despotic nature of some of his actions. But there's no doubt about one thing: He's difficult to work with. Apparently Kirk doesn't think so. He says that people who think he's difficult are untalented sons-of-bitches. Maybe so.

A year after the release of *The Vikings* there was a private screening at Twentieth Century-Fox of a film I was very proud of, *Compulsion*. A lot of important movie people attended, including Kirk. He was seated just two seats away from me. When the picture finished he came over and offered his congratulations. I was still nursing the wounds and bruises of having worked with him, so I almost flinched when he put his arm around my shoulders. "You know," he said with a laugh, "you're the only director who ever survived two pictures with me!"

His choice of words was apt. Certainly he was accurate about one thing: You don't make pictures with Kirk, you survive them.

The Narrow Margin. From left, Charles McGraw, Don Haggerty, Marie Windsor, Don Beddoe. *Still courtesy of the Academy of Motion Picture Arts and Sciences.* © *1952 RKO Pictures, Inc., All Rights Reserved.*

John Wayne.
Photofest

Howard Hughes in 1947.
Photofest

His Kind of Woman. Robert Mitchum menaced by Raymond Burr aboard our "ghost" yacht. *Still courtesy of the Academy of Motion Picture Arts and Sciences.* © 1951 RKO Pictures, Inc., All Rights Reserved.

Vincent Price at the end of Howard Hughes's favorite scene in *His Kind of Woman*. *Still courtesy of the Academy of Motion Picture Arts and Sciences.* © 1951 RKO Pictures, Inc., All Rights Reserved.

The author (left) and writer Earl Felton chat with Charles Boyer on the set of *The Happy Time*. *From the author's collection*

Captain Queeg (Stanley Kramer, right) and a mutinous scoundrel (writer Earl Felton), sailing to Catalina. *From the author's collection*

Arena. From left, the distraught director and the late, great 48.
*The Richard Fleischer Collection/Archives of Performing Arts/University of
Southern California*

The two master animators, Walt Disney (left) and Max Fleischer,
study the plan for the newly completed Disneyland.
©The Walt Disney Company

Twenty Thousand Leagues Under the Sea. The author, on the right,
directing underwater in the Bahamas. Cinematographer Til Gabbini
is behind the Disney designed camera. © *The Walt Disney Company*

Twenty Thousand Leagues Under the Sea. The *Nautilus* attacked by the
new and improved giant squid. © *The Walt Disney Company*

Bandido. Robert Mitchum (left) and Gilbert Roland. *Photofest*

The Vikings. Kirk Douglas playing the scene with Tony Curtis that he later played with my young son Mark. *Photofest*

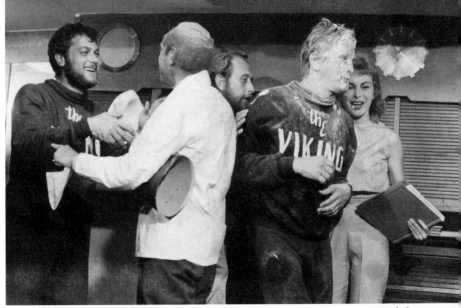

The Vikings. Aboard the *Brand VI.* A pie in the face is always good for a laugh. From left, Tony Curtis, the author (back to the camera), Per Buchoj, Kirk Douglas, and Janet Leigh. *From the author's collection*

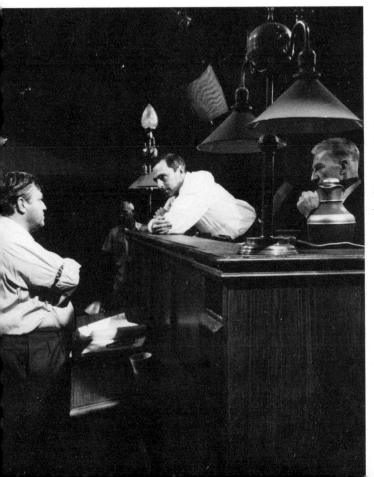

Compulsion. The author directing Orson Welles. *"Compulsion" © 1959 Twentieth Century Fox Film Corporation. All Rights Reserved.*

E. G. Marshall, seated on left, and others had to keep their eyes closed while Orson Welles addressed them during this courtroom sequence in *Compulsion*. *Still courtesy of the Academy of Motion Picture Arts and Sciences. "Compulsion" © 1959 Twentieth Century Fox Film Corporation. All Rights Reserved.*

Crack in the Mirror. Juliette Greco emotes in a French courtroom. Brad Dillman peers over her left shoulder. *Still courtesy of the Academy of Motion Picture Arts and Sciences. "Crack in the Mirror" © 1960 Twentieth Century Fox Film Corporation. All Rights Reserved.*

Head of Twentieth Century-Fox, Darryl F. Zanuck with constant companion. *From the collection of Richard D. Zanuck*

Conference on the set of *Barabbas*. From left, Jacopo Tecchio, the author, Anthony Quinn, and screenplay writer/poet Christopher Fry (*The Lady's Not For Burning; A Phoenix Too Frequent*). *From the author's collection*

Silvana Mangano, wife of Dino De Laurentiis. *Photofest*

The playwright Brendan Behan.
UPI photo/The Bettmann Archive

Raquel Welch and Stephen Boyd
aboard miniaturized sub in
*Fantastic Voyage. Still courtesy of the
Academy of Motion Picture Arts and
Sciences. "Fantastic Voyage" © 1966
Twentieth Century Fox Film Corporation.
All Rights Reserved.*

The author meeting the Queen of England at the Royal World Premier of *Doctor Dolittle* in London, while Arthur Jacobs, the film's producer, looks on. *From the author's collection*

The Fleischers arrive at the Odeon Theater for the Paris premier of *Doctor Dolittle*. *From the author's collection*

Doctor Dolittle. (The French Premier at the Odeon Theater, Paris) First row: sixth from left, Dick Zanuck, Lili Zanuck, Rachel Roberts, and Rex Harrison. Second row: second from left, Leslie Briscusse, Evie Briscusse, Mickey Fleischer, the author, and, ninth from left, Andre Hakim, Helen Gurley Brown, and David Brown. *From the author's collection*

Rex Harrison and the author mingle with some of the "extras"
during the *Doctor Dolittle* location filming in Castle Combe, England.

Rex Harrison and his wife Rachel Roberts enjoy a relaxed moment
with some of the actors in the cast of *Doctor Dolittle*, Polynesia the
Parrot, Chee-Chee the Chimp, and Sophie the Seal.

Japanese film director
Akira Kurosawa.
UPI/Bettmann

Charlton Heston feeds Edward G. Robinson in a scene from *Soylent Green*. *Still courtesy of the Academy of Motion Picture Arts and Sciences.* © *1973 Turner Entertainment Co., All Rights Reserved.*

Mr. Majestyk. Mug shot of Charles Bronson.
Photofest

Glenda Jackson as Sarah Bernhardt in *The Incredible Sarah*.
Still courtesy of the Academy of Motion Picture Arts and Sciences. The Reader's Digest Association, Inc.

Crossed Swords (aka *The Prince and the Pauper*). From left: David Hemmings, Raquel Welch, Charlton Heston, Rex Harrison, Mark Lester, George C. Scott, Ernest Borgnine, and Oliver Reed.
From the author's collection

Laurence Olivier and
Neil Diamond in *The
Jazz Singer*. *Still courtesy of
the Academy of Motion Picture
Arts and Sciences.*

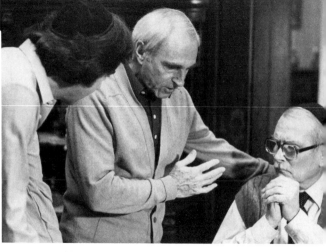

The author directing
Neil Diamond, on left,
and Laurence Olivier
during filming of *The
Jazz Singer*. *From the
author's collection*

Max Fleischer poses
with his creation
Betty Boop.
From the author's collection

XII

Nepotism begins at home. In Hollywood studios it is endemic. When I worked at Metro making *Arena* there was a group of young writers and producers whose famous surnames were followed by a "Jr." We called them "The Sons of the Pioneers."

The placing of relatives in important jobs may not always be fair, but sometimes it works out very well, as it did with Arthur Loew, Jr. And as it did at Fox with Richard Zanuck. Dick had come up through the ranks at the studio, from messenger, to publicist, to budding producer. In the normal order of things, when Darryl left the studio to form his own company and become an independent producer in Paris, Dick should have been the obvious heir apparent. But he was far too young and almost totally inexperienced. Instead, Buddy Adler took over. Dick, even then, would have done a better job.

For his maiden voyage as a producer for Darryl F. Zanuck Productions, in 1959, Dick decided to make the Meyer Levin best-seller *Compulsion*. I had only a nodding acquaintance with young Zanuck at that time, but my reputation was glimmering at Fox, and he offered me the screenplay. It was the best I'd ever read. It was the true story of society's first thrill killing, a completely motiveless crime done by two young, homosexual men, with genius IQ's, from extremely rich Chicago families. Their names were Leopold and Loeb. The families brought in the most famous lawyer in the world, Clarence Darrow, to save them from the gallows. When I learned that Orson Welles had already been cast as Darrow, my tongue was hanging out. I would kill to do this movie.

The first time I actually met Orson was in his dressing room the morning of the first day of shooting on *Compulsion*. He did his own makeup and was in the process of applying a false bridge to his nose.

Outside of a circus, I had never seen such a fat man. "Huge," "obese," and "enormous" are thin words to describe the impact of that first impression. "Grotesque" and "monstrous" come more easily to mind. "Awe-inspiring," too. I wondered how his thin ankles could take the weight. They couldn't, of course, and his biggest worry on any picture was the danger of turning an ankle on one of the cables that always litter a stage floor. It was something that happened to him frequently.

When I questioned the necessity of the false nose he was so painstakingly attaching to his face he said, "My nose is just a button. It doesn't look like anything. Do you know I've only appeared once in my life with my own nose?" "No," I said, "I hadn't realized that." "Larry Olivier does the same thing," he went on, "always wears a false nose, even though he doesn't need one. We talked about it once and decided that the real reason we do it is because we both need something to hide behind." His Falstaffian laugh rattled the mirror.

Normally you meet all the actors long before you start working with them. This was not possible with Orson. He had all sorts of tax problems that severely limited not only the time he could spend making the picture but of even staying in the country. What with the state of California breathing down his neck for back taxes and the necessity of staying out of the United States for a certain number of days each year to avoid the federal tax, we ended up with exactly ten days in which he was available for all we had to do with him. Since the entire last third of the picture was all Orson, the time was extremely tight. And there was no leeway, no cushion. He had, in fact, driven up from Mexico that very morning and was booked out on a freighter to China that sailed the night of our last day's work with him. During the one weekend he had during the shooting schedule he went to Mexico on Friday night and drove back to the studio Monday morning. Also, typical of Orson, while he was in Mexico he had arranged to shoot some scenes for *Don Quixote*, a film he had been working on, in dribs and drabs, for about fifteen years. He never did finish that picture because most of his key actors eventually died.

All actors use one of two schools of acting. They either use what is called the "Method," or, well, there is no formal name for the other school of acting. Method actors need deep inner inspiration, soul-searching, intellectualizing, and sometimes turn out to be Marlon Brando. The other kind of actor relies on technical skills and personality. Both styles have masterful practitioners who can come up with memorable performances. Sometimes, however, when one actor is Method and the other is not, problems can arise. A story is told about Jackie Coogan rehearsing for a television drama when he was all grown up and no longer playing The Kid to Charlie Chaplin's Tramp. Coogan, who was not Method, had to play most of his scenes with an actor who was. The actor wouldn't look at him but kept staring down at his shoes while he wrestled with some inner emotion. Coogan wanted eye contact with the Method actor, talked to him about it, but wasn't getting it. The actor said it would spoil his concentration. When they started shooting the show live, in front of an audience, the actor went into his usual routine of looking down at his shoes. This time, though, Coogan's shoes came into his field of vision. On one shoe he had written the word "Fuck" and on the other, "You."

I took the earliest opportunity I could, that first day of shooting, to find out what style Orson used. It turned out that he loathed the Method.

I got an impression of his impatience with the Method when we were rehearsing a scene in which Orson walks down a hallway surrounded by a large group of eager reporters. At a certain point he stops to answer a question and the reporters stop with him. It was a tricky scene to stage because I wanted to have the reporters who were between him and the camera stop in exactly the right spots so that we could glimpse Orson between them. I didn't want him to be too clearly visible, as though a "hole" had been opened up for the camera, but I didn't want him totally covered, either.

I rehearsed the scene several times and it all went perfectly except for the reporter with the most critical stopping position. Each time he would end up completely blocking Orson's face. After about the sixth try I said to the young actor, "What is it? Why can't you hit the mark? You always take one step too many." "I know," he replied in torment. "I'm sorry. I just can't help it." "Why not?" I asked. "Is someone pushing you off the mark, or don't you see it, or what?" "No, no, it isn't that. It's just that I have this uncontrollable urge to take that extra step." That's when Orson spoke up. "Well, fight it, boy!" his voice boomed out. "*Fight* it!"

A director is usually as much an actor as the actor he is directing. We all like to enhance the mystique of our job. Directing isn't easy. It's tough, grueling work that must be supported by a mixture of experience, technique, intuition, and inspiration. A little embellishment, however, never hurts. Add a flourish here, some razzle-dazzle there, and, depending on how good an actor (or how big a ham) you are, it impresses the people you're working with. It was obvious from the start that this wouldn't work with Orson. There was no fooling him about the mystique of directing. He knew what you were going to do as soon as you started to do it.

It was a challenge working with Orson. Since he knew as much about directing as I did, and was a bona fide genius in the bargain, I thought more than twice about how I was going to handle every scene he was in. If he found my work pedestrian I would be in trouble: He would walk all over me and start taking over the direction. It was a case of inspiration or death. I must have passed the test. Not once, during the entire time I filmed with him, did he ever make a directorial suggestion. He was the actor, I was the director, and that was that. We developed a wonderful working relationship based on mutual respect.

But as an actor he did have his idiosyncrasies, some charming, some annoying, some strange, indeed. He had problems remembering lines. You could see him go blank in the middle of a speech. He wouldn't quit and admit it, but would stumble around until he found the lines again. When the shot was finished I'd say, "Once more, please. Let's go again." Invariably Orson would say, "Why? What was wrong with that one?" To which I would have to reply, "I think I detected a stumble, a little bit of 'reaching' for the lines." "Of course you did!" he would respond, a shade too ingenuously. "That was deliberate. I thought that was what you wanted. You said you wanted it to sound realistic. That's what I was trying to do." "Orson," I would say, "that was just a little too realistic. It sounded like you'd forgotten the lines." "Well," he'd say, even more ingenuously, "we can't have that," and we'd do it again. It was a little game we played several times a day.

On the other hand, he had an uncanny ability with dialogue memory when it came to his playing a scene to an offstage actor. It is standard practice when making a close-up of an actor who has dialogue to place the other actor behind the lens, right next to the camera. In this way the actor being photographed not only has eye contact but also gets all his cuing and timing right. (Without fail, the actor not being photographed will forget his lines.) But this was not standard practice with Orson. He didn't want anyone next to the camera on the side where he was supposed to look. In fact, he wanted no one in his eye line clear to the stage wall. And he didn't want to hear the other actor's dialogue. He would stare at the place where the actor was supposed to be and play the entire scene just as though the actor were there. He would react to the nonexistent dialogue, respond with his own, interrupt, overlap, laugh, grow angry, whatever, exactly as though there were someone there speaking to him. His memory and his timing were uncanny.

One of the things most actors value highly is eye contact. It is essential to them that they can look directly at another actor and have that look returned. Not so with Orson. Eye contact bothered him, which is probably why he would sometimes stumble on speeches and why he insisted on playing lines to an off-camera actor the way he did.

Not being able to look people in the eye when you speak to them is a not too uncommon psychological problem. It afflicts many people in all walks of life. It is rare, however, for an actor to have this difficulty, particularly an actor of Welles's stature. I never suspected that he had this problem until we came to the courtroom sequence.

The Clarence Darrow summation is one of the longest, if not *the* longest, single, uninterrupted speech in movie history. It runs for eighteen minutes. It was far too long and complex in its staging to shoot it in one long take. A movie camera holds only ten minutes of film, anyhow. It had to be broken up into bits and pieces, most of which, by movie standards, were quite long unto themselves.

A great deal of the speech is delivered to the courtroom spectators, and Orson had no trouble with that. Some of it, though, had to be spoken directly to that wonderful actor E. G. Marshall, who played the district attorney (and started him on a long and successful career of playing the title role in the television series *Mr. District Attorney*). Orson had big trouble with that. He just couldn't get through those speeches.

Finally he said to E.G. "Would you do me a big favor? Would you keep your eyes closed when I talk to you?" Not only did he want E.G.'s eyes closed, but those of all the assistant DA's sitting next to him as well. It was certainly the strangest request any of us had ever heard from an actor. E.G. understood and agreed to do it, and it was all right with me, since the camera was over E.G.'s and the others' backs. During one of the rehearsals curiosity got the better of me. I had to see what the scene looked like from Orson's point of view, so I walked around to a position behind him where I could see E.G. and company. There they were, all lined up, listening intently, with their eyes closed. It was a ludicrous but memorable sight. It seemed to me that the image he was facing would have been more distracting than having them looking at him, but no, Orson breezed through the speeches without any trouble at all.

Between setups Orson and I sometimes would sit around swapping stories and experiences. I gathered a good deal of insight into his personality and feelings from these chats by some of his small comments and throwaway lines. Once, while we were sitting together, the still photographer came over to show him some photos he had taken of him and for which he needed his okay before turning them over to the publicity department. Orson drew himself up as though he were a king addressing a scullery knave. "How dare you interrupt me," he said imperiously, "while I'm talking to the director? Your pictures aren't worth looking at, anyhow. You attach too much importance to them, as though they were works of art. Well, there's no art to taking snapshots. Anybody can do it. All you need is a camera, and if you take enough pictures one of them is liable to turn out all right by sheer chance. Now leave us alone," and he dismissed him with a wave of his hand. "Good God, Orson," I said, "you treated that poor guy as though you were royalty." "I *am* royalty!" he answered.

Therein lay the tragedy of Orson Welles, the once but not future king. His royal line ascended through the Mercury Theatre, through radio, and into his first motion picture, *Citizen Kane*, which was rightfully acclaimed as a work of genius and possibly the best movie ever made. He was the acknowledged and revered king of moviemakers. But once you've made the best picture ever made, where do you go from there? Orson peaked too early. He shot his bolt on his first picture. The rest of his career was doomed to a downhill slide, a fall from grace. The magnificent achievement of *Citizen Kane* and its disappointing aftermath must have been like a worm constantly and painfully eating away at his insides. Now he was like a king in exile who still considered himself king.

Orson was his own worst enemy. His reputation for extravagant excess, his profligate, sky's-the-limit way with studio funds, and his totally undisciplined approach to time were the grease on the skids. Studios became very wary. No one trusted him with the responsibilities that go with directing a film.

Working with him, I was aware of all that. And I was aware, too, that he must have felt a great jealousy of me as a director. Directing was what he treasured most, but as time went by it was firmly denied him. During one of our chats we talked about his desire to direct. "You know," he said, "I still get offers to direct. They send me the worst, the most impossible, the most ridiculous pieces of crap you've ever read. They say to themselves, 'Welles is a genius. Maybe he can do something with this mess. And we can get him cheap, too.' They're so bad that even I wouldn't do them." At least he had no illusions. He covered his jealousy of me pretty well, but it did peek through once.

We were working on a set that was a revamp from another picture. To save a buck here and there studios tried to use sets that were already standing. A little paint, some different trim, and if it suited the style and action of the picture you were making, you had a set for almost no cost. This particular set worked fine for me except that it had no wall on the right-hand side. That was acceptable because the way I had planned to shoot I didn't need that side of the set and could easily avoid getting it in the frame.

I blocked out the scene with Orson and the other actors and then said to him, "When you make your exit you walk straight back from here and go out that door on your left." He thought about it for a moment than made one of the few arbitrary demands of the entire filming. "I think I should exit to the right," he said.

"I'm sorry, Orson, you can't."

"Why not?"

"Well, you may have noticed that there is no wall on the right-hand side."

He looked and thought for a moment. Then the jealousy and the challenge came out. "Do you know what I would do if I were directing this picture?"

"No, I don't. What would you do?"

"I'd wait until they built me a wall."

"That," I said, "is why I am directing this picture and you are not."

He was momentarily taken aback. Then he bowed as deeply as his mammoth frame would allow in a gesture of *noblesse oblige*, or perhaps it was *touché*, and said, "I shall exit to the left."

Every once in a while—for his own self-esteem, I suppose—Orson felt the need to demonstrate to the world at large that even though he was a king deposed, he was still a monarch in his own sphere. To keep the royalty franchise from lapsing he had to do something operatic, something bravura whenever the opportunity presented itself. It presented itself one day on the courtroom set.

I called the crew together to watch a blocking rehearsal of Orson interrogating our young leading lady, Diane Varsi. Everyone had just gotten into position, Varsi in the witness chair, Orson standing close to her, the crew gathered in a tight group to observe, when the unit publicity man walked onto the stage. Orson got sight of him, a tall, blond fellow in his thirties, with a puffy face. He was a tasty dish to set before the king.

"What are you trying to do, ruin me, you incompetent nitwit?" Orson roared at him in his overpowering, Shakespearean voice. Pavarotti would sound like a pip-squeak next to that voice. The publicity man looked as though he'd just been hit in the face with a pie. "I told you to cancel my appointment with Hedda Hopper last night," Orson bellowed, "but you were incapable of following a simple order and now you've placed me in a terrible position. I don't know whether she'll ever speak to me again and you are entirely to blame." "But . . . but I did call her," the publicity man stammered. "I told her you weren't—" A tidal wave of sound from Orson smothered the rest of his reply. "An hour later! You called her an hour later! It should have been done immediately. Have you no comprehension of urgency or priority? Didn't this seem important to you? What you did was totally irresponsible, inefficient, and lazy! Did you have the sense to send her flowers?" The publicity man's face turned red with embarrassment. His lower lip and chin started to quiver. His eyes filled with tears. "I didn't know you wanted me to send—" Again a tsunami crashed down on him. "You didn't know? You didn't know?" Orson was in high gear now, his body quivering with rage, his eyes blazing. "Can't you think for yourself, you witless oaf, or has your calling destroyed your brain? Are you so unqualified that you have to be told how to do your job? An ape could be trained to do it better. All you're doing is keeping a monkey out of work." The publicity man finally managed to call out in some anger, tears running down his face, "You're not a very nice person, Mr. Welles!"

That really did it. "Don't you tell me what kind of person I am," Orson shouted, all stops out on the mighty Wurlitzer, the words pouring out in a relentless torrent. "Look to yourself, you nincompoop. You are an irresponsible and unreliable fool whose inadequacy is equaled only by his ineptness. You are a member of an overpaid and undertalented profession, and I want you to leave this stage and never show your face around me again. Now at the time of this meeting, you had a deep attachment for another boy?" Without missing a beat or taking a breath, he had turned to Diane Varsi on the witness stand, dropped his voice until it was barely above a whisper, and had started the scene. You could read the confusion in Varsi's eyes, but only for a moment. She picked up the cue. "Yes, sir," she answered quietly. And they continued right through to the end of the scene, playing it flawlessly.

It was a tour de force for Orson, a display of dazzling virtuosity. He had shown us a flash of royal purple. The whole thing, from start to finish, was a bravura performance. He had captured us, manipulated us, and finally entertained us, if you can call the spectacle of a Christian being eaten by the king of beasts entertaining. When he reached his last line, "No further questions," he knew he had us in the palm of his hand. He turned and sailed off to his dressing room like a mighty dreadnought under full steam and never looked back. Curtain.

During another one of our little *tête-à-têtes* Orson made what turned out to be a prophetic remark. "You know," he said laughingly, "you're being very lucky with me on this picture." "Really?" I asked. "How come?" "You've only got me for a short time," he explained. "If I'm on a picture too long I get bored. Then I can cause problems." As it happened, my next picture, *Crack in the Mirror*, also had Orson in it. This time he had a long schedule. The problems he predicted didn't amount to much, but what did come out was a more obvious indication of his jealousy of me as a director.

We were shooting in the Studios Boulogne in Paris, and on Saturday evenings, after work, the company would have a few drinks on the set. It was a pleasant end-of-the-week ritual. At one of these soirees Orson came over to me. He wasn't drunk, but you could tell he'd had a few drinks. "You think you did a great job on that picture, don't you?" he asked rhetorically, making an obvious reference to *Compulsion*. "Well," he went on, "you're taking a lot of credit for very little. All you've got is one outstanding performance that made you and the whole picture look good."

"Orson," I said, "I want to tell you something. I think it's one hell of a fine picture and I'm proud of it. I've never been proud of a picture before, but I am of this one. And I'll tell you something else. I'm not going to let you spoil it for me."

We stared at each other, then he said quietly, "You're right. You're absolutely right. I shouldn't have said that. I'm sorry. I apologize." Then he turned on his heel and walked away.

I never doubted that he meant the apology, but the idea of his not directing still rankled. We never had an outright confrontation about it during that picture, but he began to challenge me in a different way. He became increasingly difficult to direct as the filming went on. The slight penchant he'd shown during *Compulsion* for arbitrariness became pronounced. If I asked him to move from one position to another, he'd find a reason to insist on going in the opposite direction. If I asked him to sit, he'd find a reason to stand. Arguing about it in front of the cast and crew was just what he wanted. If the producer, Darryl Zanuck, happened to be on the set, you could count on Orson making an issue of some insignificant point. It was his chance to show that he knew more about directing than I did and that I was the one being arbitrary. In any event, arguing against the power of the Wellesian voice was like trying to shout down a hurricane.

The solution, I found, was ridiculously easy, but it worked. I appealed to his mastery of technique. Taking him aside, I'd talk to him privately, confidentially. "Orson," I'd say, "I've got a problem and I don't know what to do about it. I'm really stuck." Orson would become immediately interested. The director stuck? Good.

"What's the problem?"

"Well," I'd lie, "I'd like to get you from the chair where you're sitting over to that table over there, but I just don't know how. I can't find a motivation for your making the move. I don't know what to do."

"Why, that's no problem. I can do that."

"You can?" I would exclaim with mock surprise. "But how are you going to motivate it?"

"Just watch me on the next rehearsal."

We'd do the next rehearsal and Orson would make the move. As soon as I'd say "Cut!" he'd look over to me. I'd give him a big smile and make a surreptitious circle with my thumb and forefinger. He'd give me a small wink in return. I used this gimmick, with infinite variations, over and over, and he never tumbled. Eventually he got bored with this game, too, and ended up just doing what I asked him to do without any arguments.

But that was all in the future. Now I was facing the long summation speech in *Compulsion*, an extremely complicated sequence to plan and to shoot. Because of the time limitation imposed by Orson's tax problems I had to do the speech wildly out of continuity. Any other way would have taken weeks, and I had all of four days. What it entailed was setting up the cameras (three of them) in one direction and then shooting every part of the speech that happened to take place in that direction. When you'd done all that, you pointed the cameras in another direction and picked up all the pieces that took place in *that* direction, and so on until you'd done a complete 360 degrees.

It's a very efficient way to work, but in this kind of sequence, very tricky. I'd blocked out the entire staging of the speech with Orson and we had given it tremendous variations. This meant we had to know precisely when and where his tempo would be racing or contemplative, when the volume and temper of his voice would be shouted or whispered, and we had to know his timing and speed of movement when he entered or exited a shot so he didn't leave one angle slow and enter the following angle fast. When you shoot in continuity you can keep track of things like that. This way it was like throwing a large jigsaw puzzle into the air and planning it so all the pieces would fall in exactly the right place, with all of them fitted together perfectly.

The last part of the speech I'd decided to do in one long, three-minute piece. Each time there was an opportunity to shoot it, Orson would shy away from it. "No, no," he'd say, "I'm not ready for it. I can't do it now. Let's do something else." It became his *bête noire*. Each time I suggested doing that shot he reacted like a horse to a rattlesnake, rearing up with panic in his eyes. Finally I asked him what the trouble was. "Stage fright!" was his reply. "I'm scared to death of that scene. Please, let's do it the last thing."

The next-to-last day of shooting with Orson on the picture I had completed the entire summation speech except for that three-minute endpiece. "Orson," I said, "this is it. The moment of truth has arrived. There's no way out. You've got to do it." "All right," he said, "but I've got a proposition to make to you." I asked him what it was. "What I'd like to do is this," he explained. "We'll rehearse the scene until you're satisfied that it's technically perfect. I won't attempt to give a performance, I'll just walk through it mechanically for the camera and the lighting. When you feel it's so well rehearsed that there can't be a technical error, then I'd like you and the crew to leave me completely alone on the set. I want to rehearse by myself until I feel I'm ready. I don't know how long that'll take, maybe an hour, maybe two, whatever it takes. I'll let the assistant director know when I'm ready, then he can ask you and the crew to come back. What I want to do is give a performance for my director. That's why I don't want you to see any of it beforehand. If you don't like it, I'll do it over any way you want, as many times as you want. How about it?"

The idea of Orson Welles wanting to give a performance just for me was irresistibly touching and flattering. I agreed. It was one of the most complex shots of the picture, the three cameras tracking simultaneously, getting interesting angles and compositions without getting in each other's way, starting and ending their moves on precise words. For Orson it was much more daunting. He had to run the whole gamut of acting, from a thundering outrage against the courtroom spectators who wanted the boys to hang, to a muted, tortured appeal to the judge not only for compassion but also to allow the power of love to influence his decision. No wonder Orson was nervous about doing it. It was a fine line to negotiate between sincerity and histrionics, a delicate balance between passionate conviction and maudlin bathos.

I rehearsed the scene until we were blue in the face. If Orson came up with the kind of performance we were both hoping for, it would be a one-time thing, not reproducible. To have it ruined by a technical mishap would be tragic. Then I cleared the stage and went to my office, leaving Orson alone.

An hour and a half later I got a call from my assistant. Orson was ready. I came on the stage and Orson gestured to a chair. It was my reserved seat for his performance. I asked him if he wanted another technical rehearsal with the crew. "No," he said. "Let's do it." And do it he did. Everything we had worked on and planned was there. He had perfected every nuance of thought and emotion. It was deeply moving. It was Orson Welles at his best. There was spontaneous and prolonged applause from the crew when I quietly said, "Cut. Print." I stood up and applauded, too. Orson came over and embraced me.

There was an odd aftermath to this episode, however. Somehow or other a rumor started around town that what I have described didn't happen that way at all. The story went that Orson and I didn't get along and that when it came time to do the summation speech he banned me from the set. I wasn't, it would seem, there at all.

Orson's last day on the picture was relaxed. We knew he'd be finished on schedule, so the pressure was off. We all breathed a sigh of relief. He was booked on a slow boat to China that sailed at midnight from Long Beach. There was some technical work for him to do before leaving, and it was scheduled to be done after we'd finished photography and had seen the previous day's dailies.

As is usual with every film, some of the sound tracks needed replacing. There's always an occasional line of dialogue that isn't clearly recorded, or an extraneous noise covers an important word, or the sensitive sound recording equipment picks up a camera hum that the ear doesn't catch. When you work with three cameras in close proximity to each other, as we had done, you're almost certain to run into some problems. The process to correct these dialogue flaws used to be called "looping". (It is now called ADR, for auto-mated dialogue replacement.) Each bit of film with a defective sound track was made into a loop and projected endlessly on a movie screen. The actor was then recorded as he synchronized his voice to the picture.

After we'd wrapped the day's work, before we screened the dai-lies or did the looping, the entire company gathered in the lobby of the studio's Main Theater for a send-off party for Orson. There were drinks and hors d'oeuvres, and Orson was mingling with the crew, being warm and friendly. He was in high good spirits, and his hearty laugh boomed out frequently. The only one who hadn't yet shown up was our producer, Dick Zanuck. He'd said he'd be there, but he was late. Very late.

It was almost time to wrap the party and go into the theater and see the dailies when he showed up looking pale and shaken. He looked furtively around the crowd until he saw me waving at him and scurried over.

"My God," he said to me, "do we have a problem." I asked him what it was. "The sheriff has just garnisheed Orson's entire salary for the picture," he explained.

"Holy shit! You mean he's not going to get paid?"

"Not a penny. I don't know what to do. If I tell him now he may blow up and not do the looping."

"I don't think you've got any choice. You've got to tell him. He's leaving the country in a few hours. Maybe there's something he can still do about it. If you don't give him time to contact his lawyer, or something, he might be able to sue you."

"Yeah. I guess I better tell him. Wish me luck," and he was off to give Orson the news.

Five minutes later, Dick was back. "What happened?" I asked.

"Nothing," he answered with a laugh of relief. "He took it just fine. He said he was expecting it to happen, and he sort of brushed the whole thing off. He doesn't even want to call his lawyer." Dick poured himself a stiff drink. "He says he's ready to do the looping right after he sees the dailies."

"I don't believe it. Something's going to happen. I can feel it in my bones."

Except for the producer, I make it a rule to limit severely those who are permitted to see dailies: the cameraman and his operator, the editor and his assistant. That's it, no one else, not even the actors. Especially not even the actors. To let an actor see himself in dailies is to invite disaster. This time I made an exception. Since it was Orson's last day and what we would be screening was the three-minute speech he had been so worried about, I invited him to the running. I had no apprehension about this set of dailies. I knew they were good.

None of us was prepared for the blast that greeted us when the lights came up after we'd run the film. Orson had been sitting alone near the front of the theater, the rest of us about ten rows back in a little group. He rose from his seat looking like an Old Testament version of God in all His wrath. "That is the worst film I have ever seen in my life," he declaimed. "It is a disgrace. You should all be ashamed of yourselves for being associated with it!" There seemed to be small black clouds, with little flashes of forked lightning, roiling about his brow as he stepped into the aisle and started to pace. His voice supplied the necessary thunder. "It is a total disaster from beginning to end. I am shocked and dismayed by what I've seen," he roared. We sat there immobile, hypnotized. He took off on me. How could I, he demanded to know, select such poor angles? Didn't I know better than to show him in a chest-size figure that made him look like a character in a Punch and Judy show? Couldn't I see that the American flag behind him in the rear of the courtroom distracted from his speech?

He went on roaring and raving, pacing up and down the aisle. When he got through with me he started on the cameraman. Bill Mellor was one of the industry's finest cinematographers, the favorite of George Stevens, and doing a superb job for us. He was sitting next to me on my left and I heard him grunt in anger and could feel him start to rise from his seat. Without looking at him I jammed my left elbow into his arm and pushed him back down. I didn't want to see Orson's blood staining the cream-colored walls. Orson went on nonstop, hardly pausing for breath, heaping acid invective and vile criticism on our heads until he finally stormed out of the theater.

None of us moved. We just sat there until Mellor said, "If you hadn't stopped me I would have killed him." Dick Zanuck cleared his throat and found his voice. "He's full of shit. The film's terrific. It was that goddamn sheriff that brought this on." The editor stood up. "He's out of his mind," he said. "That's the best thing I've ever seen him do."

We all wondered what would happen next. We were supposed to go directly to the looping room and do Orson's loops. From the way he left we couldn't tell if he intended showing up there or not. The looping room was in the basement of the theater. We went down there and waited. No Orson. After about twenty minutes

Dick said to me, "Come on. Let's see if we can find him. Maybe we can talk him into working tonight."

We looked every place we could think of on the lot, but there was no sign of him. The security guards hadn't seen him. We made the rounds again, but it was fruitless. So we returned to the looping room to tell them they could all go home. Orson was there, waiting for us.

He was still in a cold fury, but he started to work. Some actors are wonderful loopers. They can synchronize their voices to the lip action on the screen perfectly. Other actors are hopeless. That night Orson was hopeless. He'd do one rehearsal and one take. If it came close to fitting, okay. If not, too bad.

The last scene he had to do was the very end of the three-minute courtroom speech. Camera hum had almost ruined the final twenty seconds. Orson turned to me and said, "I refuse to loop this scene. This is a matter for the Screen Actors' Guild." And with that he left and never came back. He got on a boat and went to China.

I could never understand Orson's reasoning about that. Here was an obviously flawed sound track of the most important part of his most important scene. Yet he was willing to harm the picture as well as himself by walking away from the opportunity to make it right. For all his brilliance, his genius, his intellect, he was at this moment an immature, unreasonable juvenile, cutting off his fake nose to spite what? Himself? Me? The movie business that wouldn't let him direct? It didn't make sense to me then and it doesn't make sense to me now. But maybe, just maybe, it's the basic genetic, tragic flaw that brought this movie giant down.

The editor, Bill Reynolds, did an unbelievable job on the faulty track. He found words, and even pieces of words, from other Welles sound tracks in the picture and fitted them painstakingly, vibration by vibration, into Orson's lips. No one has ever noticed that not one syllable he says during the last twenty seconds of that speech was actually spoken by him while the shot was being made. When Reynolds first showed me what he'd down with that track I said, "Congratulations, Bill. You've just fucked Orson Welles."

Six weeks later, a letter addressed to me arrived from China. It was from Orson. It was an apology for his behavior that last day on the picture and asked my understanding and forgiveness. It was, he said, the goddamn sheriff what done it.

XIII

I believe it was Tom Stoppard who said, "Nothing recedes like success." Twice I had succeeded in making outstanding films, and instead of reaping the rewards and acclaim that usually follow, I ended up in the limbo of suspension. It was a punishment imposed not because of a heady claim of self-importance, or some newfound, arrogant unreasonableness, but because of a dogged determination to march forward instead of backward. The irony was that the people who would benefit most from my success, the people who held my contract, were the ones who were blocking my path. After *The Narrow Margin*, RKO wanted me to go back to the ooze I'd clawed my way out of, and I had rebelled. Now, after *Compulsion*, a film that had brought me great critical acclaim and a Directors' Guild nomination, Fox was treating me like a hack. They could think of nothing better for me to do than make a flawed John Wayne movie, and again I said no.

The basic problem, of course, was the infamous studio system and its long-term contract inducement. The tantalizing lure of security was the bait in the trap. It always sounded great. A contract! No more worry about where the next job was coming from. A guaranteed income.

It was at best a mirage, at worst a fraud. The price, if you had a scrap of talent, or self-confidence, was too high. You paid with your artistic freedom and the control of your career. Security was pure illusion. No one knows better than the studios that contracts are made to be broken—by them, not by you. Their out, on most contracts, was the six-month option. Every six months they had the option of dropping the contract and kicking you out. Very few of us, with that kind of contract, felt comfortable about buying a house. A contract with longer option periods was usually just as bad, sometimes worse. There was a producer at RKO who was a leftover from the Dore Schary regime. Schary had given him a three-year, no-option deal, and when Schary left, the studio was stuck with a producer it didn't want. It is standard practice in the industry that when a regime leaves a studio, everything even remotely connected with it goes, too. Projects, pending deals, friends, relatives, secretaries, everything goes. But this guy had a three-year contract.

Management watched him like a hawk, waiting for him to do something that could be called a breach of contract and bounce him. But he knew the game, too, and checked into his office at nine every morning and left at six every night. He had nothing to do except read, do the crosswords, and twiddle his thumbs. It was driving him mad, but he had neither fame nor fortune and couldn't afford to quit, even though being out of circulation was hurting his career. Studios, however, have their ways. I was in Sid Rogell's office when he made a phone call to a top executive at another studio. "Why don't you offer this guy a job?" he suggested. "He'd be an idiot if he didn't accept and ask us to release him from his contract. Then you can change your mind about hiring him and we'll be rid of the son-of-a-bitch." The producer was a friend of mine, and I warned him about the trap. He rode out his contract, and when he finished his three years he was a forgotten man. Contracts were a fact of life. If you wanted to work for a major studio, and there was almost no other choice, you worked under contract.

I was in the doghouse at Fox. My erstwhile friend Buddy Adler wouldn't talk to me, and Charlie Feldman was in a proper fury. The whole *North to Alaska* episode had had a greater emotional effect on me than I'd realized. To be on suspension after the high expectations I'd built up for myself after *Compulsion* was devastating. What hurt more than anything else, I think, was the high-handed manner in which I had been treated. I was angry, frustrated, disillusioned, and just plain fed up. I was desperate to find a way out of my situation, but there just didn't seem to be any.

Until the phone call came from Paris. After Darryl Zanuck had abruptly resigned and left Fox, he opened an office on the Rue de la Boétie, in Paris, under the banner of DFZ Productions. He was now in business as an independent producer, releasing his films exclusively through Fox. He had already made one film, *The Roots of Heaven*, and was now going to make another. That's why I got the phone call. It was an inquiry from DFZ Productions wanting to know if I'd be interested in doing a film for them in Paris. What a question. It wasn't a question, it was manna from heaven. If it worked out it would be the solution to all my problems. Working for the Zanuck company was not only permissible, it also would get me out from under the direct control of the Gang of Two, Adler and Feldman. And working in Europe sounded great. I needed a complete change to get the bitter taste of Hollywood out of my mouth. What better place than Paris to do that? Besides, I was tremendously flattered that Darryl Zanuck wanted me to direct a film for him. That phone call did wonders for my bruised ego, and twenty-four hours later I was high above the dark Atlantic, on my way to the Continent. There was a slight tug of apprehension as I wondered about the script before falling asleep on the plane. I knew nothing at all about it and was going on blind faith that it would be good. But, I reassured myself, if Darryl Zanuck wanted to make it, how bad could it be?

I was met at Orly, that summer morning in 1959, by John Shepridge, one of Zanuck's—well, I don't know what you'd call him. He was a combination companion, procurer, and dog walker. He also met airplanes and ran general errands. What he was, though, was charming, a dapper man in his early fifties and handsome in a debauched way. He looked like the picture of Dorian Gray about halfway through its cycle. His Continental charm as well as his accent came from being Hungarian. Naturally, everyone called him Goulash.

Shepridge got me set up at the George V, then whisked me off to the Berkeley for lunch. I was expecting to meet Zanuck, but he explained that Darryl was in the South of France. I was to read the script, which Shepridge gave me at lunch, then meet with Zanuck the next day at the Hôtel du Cap in Antibes. I wondered what would happen if I didn't like the script. Back to Hollywood on the next plane, I supposed.

The script was terrible. It was something called *The Ballad of the Red Rocks* and concerned an Israeli prostitute to be played by Juliette Greco, Zanuck's current obsession.

I reread the script trying my best to like it even just a little, looking for some redeeming feature, some aspect that would make me feel better about it. Nothing worked. Late in the afternoon I decided to phone Shepridge to tell him what I thought.

He didn't seem at all surprised. What did surprise him, however, was my asking him to book me back to L.A. the next day.

"You can't do that! You're going to the South of France."

"What's the point? I don't want to direct this picture."

"That doesn't matter. Darryl said you should go to the Hôtel du Cap, so I think you should. He's expecting you to be there. Do you have something against the South of France? It's not so bad, you know." I had to agree with him.

"So go."

"Okay."

"Oh, and one other thing: Don't bring up the subject of the picture until he does."

"If you say so." Curious, I thought.

The Hôtel du Cap is probably the most grand, most luxurious, and most exclusive establishment on the Côte d'Azur, an area awash with grand, luxurious, and exclusive establishments. A chauffeured limousine had met me at the Nice airport, and I arrived at the hotel in the style befitting a big-time movie director.

My accommodations were elegant. Everything white. Wicker furniture, walls, ceiling, and drapes, all white. It was seductive as hell, and I kept wishing I could like the damn script. There was a message waiting for me. Could I please join Darryl at his cabana for a swim before lunch?

Darryl greeted me effusively with his rabbit-toothed smile. In his swim trunks he looked small, bony, and wiry. The ever-present cigar was clamped in his brown-stained teeth, a strand of saliva-soaked tobacco hanging from the gray mustache. There was always a piece of wet tobacco hanging from some part of his face. He not only smoked cigars, he also chewed the ends. When he took the cigar out of his mouth about an inch of dripping, loose tobacco strands would be dangling from it. If he scratched an ear or an eye or his forehead with the cigar hand, a piece of the slimy end would usually lodge in that general vicinity.

There were two other people at the cabana. One was André Hakim, a short, pudgy, baby-faced gentleman of Lebanese extraction. A jolly, friendly fellow, he was the head of the Twentieth Century-Fox office in London, which, therefore, made him the head of the entire TC-F operation in Europe. He was also Zanuck's son-in-law.

The other person was Juliette Greco.

Juliette was a cabaret singer and was considered a celebrity in France. Her popularity stemmed from the days following the end of World War II when she and a small group of entertainers opened a cellar club and called themselves The Existentialists. The name attracted an intellectual crowd. The cult philosopher Jean-Paul Sartre became a regular. It was a time of great shortages in France, particularly in women's clothes. Because they were more available and a lot cheaper, Juliette began wearing men's clothes, which worked very well on her boyish figure. It started a fad, and women could be seen dressed like Juliette all over Paris. With her trend-setting clothes, her association with Sartre and existentialism, and her attractive singing voice, Juliette became the darling of the Latin Quarter and eventually a popular entertainer all over Europe.

Now she made a striking figure, petite, with a good body and a passionate Corsican temperament to go with it. Puffy-lidded, jet black eyes hovered over the most distinctive and disturbing feature of her face, the nose. Juliette, it seems, had had a series of nose jobs in the past to whittle it down until there was hardly any nose left at all—just a fleshy little blob with no bridge to support it. Apparently she'd had one job too many.

It was a beautifully hot day and, after introductions and a welcoming drink, Darryl urged me to go for a swim. He loaned me some trunks, I changed in the cabana, and soon I was floating around in the Mediterranean with André Hakim.

The water was bathtub warm. Hakim and I were luxuriating in it. He seemed to be enjoying it especially. "Isn't it great?" he said to me as he drifted in the water, basking in the hot sun. "I can't get over how warm the water is."

Because it really was so warm I thought I'd make a small joke. "Oh, I don't know," I said nonchalantly, "I find it a little cool."

He turned his head toward me, his eyes widening ever so slightly. "Do you think so?"

"Yes," I said, continuing the obviously silly routine I'd begun. "I think it's actually a little chilly."

"Really?" he said, a note of concern creeping into his voice.

"Yes, really." I floated on my back, not looking at him. "In fact, this water is freezing."

"I don't feel well." There was panic in his voice. I turned and looked at him. Hakim was no longer floating. He was treading water, his face had turned blue, and he was vibrating with a terrible chill. I became alarmed.

"André! What is it? What's the matter?"

"It's the cold water," he said, making his way to the shore. "I can't stand it. I'm freezing to death. I've got to get out."

And get out he did, blue, shivering, and shaking. I wanted to stay longer in the warm sea, but he was unsteady and needed help walking the few steps to the cabana.

I stood there marveling as I watched him bundle up in a huge terry cloth beach robe. In less than a minute the power of suggestion had changed him from a warm and happy *bon vivant* to a sick and quivering mass. I couldn't believe it. This chicken-brained twerp was the head of Twentieth Century-Fox in Europe?

"I'll think of it all tomorrow at Tara. . . . After all, tomorrow is another day." For the better part of a week Scarlett O'Hara and I shared the same philosophy. Darryl, Juliette, and I were tripping the light fantastic all over the Riviera. Swimming and sunning during the day. Dining and casinoing during the night. Not a word was said about the script, which was all right with me.

It was at the end of a lazy lunch at Eden Roc, the hotel's restaurant, that the subject finally surfaced. Like the Loch Ness monster.

Darryl was lighting one of those immense stogies when he said, between puffs, "Now, about the script." Better start packing, I thought. Got to get back to Tara. "Well, Darryl—" I began, but he interrupted me with a wave of his hand. "Don't tell me about the script," he said. "I know you don't like it. No point in discussing it." He groped under the table for something. It wouldn't have surprised me if he came up with a gun.

What he came up with was a script. "Here," he said, handing it to me. "I just got this. You read it right away. If you like it, we'll make it."

Vintage Zanuck. Movie mogul time. Wham, bam, thank you, ma'am. It would have taken six months to get a decision like that in Hollywood.

An hour and a half later I walked down to the cabana, the script of *Crack in the Mirror* tucked under my arm. Juliette was sunbathing, Darryl in animated conversation with a biggish man who was lounging in a deck chair. I couldn't see his face. Zanuck broke off his conversation and rushed toward me. He yanked the cigar out of his mouth. A strand of wet tobacco fell on his cheek. "Well," he said impatiently, "what do you think?"

"I like it. It's good. I think it could make a helluva picture."

Darryl was genuinely excited. He grabbed my arm and pulled me toward Juliette. "Did you hear that, Juliette?" he called to her. "He likes it! I knew he would! He thinks it could be great!"

Moses coming down off the mountain with the tablets couldn't have been greeted more reverently. It was a bit confusing. I knew I was a good director, but not that good.

Zanuck was yanking my arm again, this time in the direction of the man in the deck chair. "Say hello to the guy who brought me this script. You know him. He's an old friend of yours."

The figure rose from the chair and extended his hand, a wry smile on his face. An old friend, indeed.

"Hi, Dick," said Charlie Feldman.

I couldn't help being amused by the irony. The man who had driven me into leaving Hollywood and fleeing to Europe was now responsible for my staying there.

He had brought the script of *Crack in the Mirror* to Zanuck because he was finding it impossible to sell it to anyone who would make it into a movie. It had nothing to do with the story, or the quality of the screenplay, but of the reputation of his client, the man who wrote it and wanted to direct it, Jules Dassin. The Hollywood blacklist was supposed to be long gone, dead, and buried, but it obviously wasn't. No one would touch Dassin, even after *Rififi*. They not only wouldn't let him direct it, they also wouldn't buy his script. (That is why, when he wanted to make *Never on Sunday* a year later, all he could scrape together for financing was $150,000.) I don't know if Zanuck would have bought the script from Feldman if I wasn't there at that moment, but the timing was perfect. As a tribute to the lasting power of the blacklist, Dassin's name couldn't remain on the script. Zanuck replaced it with his own *nom de plume*, Mark Canfield, a name he used when he wrote the screenplays of the *Rin Tin Tin* movies in the early twenties.

Preproduction got under way immediately, and I made my first important discovery about Darryl Zanuck. He didn't know how to produce a picture. He knew how to run a major studio, all right. As head of a studio he handled six or eight productions simultaneously and was on top of everything and everyone. Doing a single picture at a time, however, seemed to daunt him. He just didn't know where to begin.

When Zanuck gave up running the studio and went to Paris to become an independent producer, circumstances changed him. His whole modus operandi was different. He was no longer riding herd over a bunch of movies. Now he had to get down to the technical realities of producing just one at a time. Surprisingly, he knew very little about that aspect of filmmaking. His wide scope of domination was now severely limited. The movie mogul had shrunk a bit. He still wielded plenty of power, but it wasn't the same.

Something else had changed him, too.

Juliette Greco.

He was head over heels in love with her. "Infatuation" is too shallow, and pale, a word. This was a man possessed. His life completely and totally revolved around her. Zanuck dedicated himself to pleasing her, to making her happy, to making her love him. It did not seem to be a mutual undertaking.

For her part, as far as I could see, it was just plain taking. She took the gifts, the clothes, the jewels he showered on her. She must have given something in return. All I ever observed was an almost dangerously apparent distaste for him.

If Darryl was aware of this, it either didn't show or it didn't matter. The slavish devotion, and the expensive baubles, never let up. What Juliette wanted, Juliette got, including the most expensive bauble of all: a movie.

There aren't many people in the world who can give their girl-friend a movie as a gift. Darryl Zanuck was one of the few. If that's what Juliette wanted, if that's what would keep him from losing her, that's what she would get. She wanted a movie career. Darryl would do his damndest to give it to her. She wanted to be a star, Darryl would make her one.

Once I became aware of this, pieces started falling in place for me. Some of the puzzling things of the past few weeks began making sense.

It seems pathetic when you think about it, but Zanuck was trying mightily to impress Juliette. He had obviously promised her a string of movies, with the best of everything attached to them—the best screenplays, directors, productions. He wanted desperately to make good on his promise.

He came up with a screenplay that he felt was a great vehicle for her, overlooking the fact that it was a lousy story. All he saw was a starring role for Juliette Greco and was blinded to all else.

He came up with me as the director. Darryl was apparently much taken with my work on *Compulsion*. When he entered the picture in the Cannes Film Festival and the three leading actors in it tied for the Best Actor Award, that clinched it for him. Fleischer directs the picture!

Zanuck then set about convincing Juliette that I was better than William Wyler and George Stevens put together. He didn't have to convince her, he *wanted* to convince her, to impress her that he was getting her the very best.

Now that he'd set me up in such a lofty position, it must have been a real rocker to learn that I hated the script. He would lose face with Juliette. She might start to doubt that he was as powerful and influential as he'd led her to believe. He had to keep me from leaving, and find another screenplay in a hurry.

Which is why he kept me hanging around in Antibes. Which is

why he was so overjoyed when I liked *Crack in the Mirror*. Which is
why, whenever I said something about the picture, it was as though
the pope were issuing a papal bull. Darryl would grab Juliette's arm
and shake it while saying with great reverence, "Listen, dear, listen!
He's saying something *important!*"

Filming went well, with one source of irritation. Ordinarily it would
have been major, but I held my temper, bit my tongue, and tried to
tolerate it. I was determined to keep it minor.

Darryl never came on the set while I was shooting, except for
those scenes involving Juliette. He wouldn't be there for the rehearsals with her, just for the actual shooting. Someone must have
been keeping him informed, because he always showed up just as I
was starting to make takes. This didn't bother me.

He'd pull a director's chair up as close to the set as he could get
without actually being in the shot. With his cigar smoking away
he'd lean forward, elbows on knees, chin resting on fists, a picture
of intense concentration. This didn't bother me.

I'd shoot the scene, and as soon as it was over, even before I
could say, "Cut," he'd call out, "That was great, Juliette! You were
wonderful!" *This* bothered me.

This is strictly a no-no. A great breach of form, etiquette, and
behavior on a set. It is tantamount to cutting a scene before the
director does. Nobody, but nobody, speaks at the end of a scene
before the director says, "Cut." I couldn't believe that Darryl didn't
know that. He'd been in the business far too long not to know
better. I had to put it down to his total absorption with Juliette. He
wasn't even aware that anyone else, much less the director, was
around. It was sadly juvenile, but he wanted to show her how much
he loved, admired, and approved of everything she did.

The crew never got used to it. Every time he'd speak before I
called, "Cut," they'd jump with surprise and look to me for my
reaction. They were expecting an explosion. They didn't get it.

It was irritating as hell having him do that, but it was a delicate
and tricky situation. How could I possibly blow up at Darryl
Zanuck? I had too much respect for him to embarrass him in front
of the crew, or, for that matter, even in private. And I felt sorry for
him, too, playing a lovesick adolescent in public. There was no
malice in what he was doing. There was no thought, on his part, of
undercutting my authority. There was just no thought, period.

The only way I felt I could play it was by showing tolerance
tinged with humor. I would usually have to say, deprecatingly,

something like, "Well . . . I think we can do it better. Let's try it again, shall we?" The crew would chuckle knowingly.

We all learned to accept this thoughtless habit, annoying as it was. Where it really started to bother me and the actors was during the love scenes, and we had many of them. Zanuck showed no sensitivity at all. He'd try to get as close to the actors as the camera. Closer, even. His cigar smoke would drift into the shot. I had to split my concentration between the actors and Darryl because he'd get so involved with the scene his shoulder, or a piece of his head, would threaten to encroach on the lens. I'd have to reach over gently and pull him back. It was voyeurism, pure and simple. Well, maybe not so pure.

Darryl's behavior was becoming a gross intrusion on the intimacy of the actor-director relationship. With him in the way, no one was doing his best work. Everyone was self-conscious and uncomfortable. I knew the time had come when I had to do something about it.

Late one afternoon I stopped by Juliette's dressing room to discuss the situation. It didn't take much discussing. She was as annoyed with Darryl's pushy presence as I was. I would, I told her, have a chat with him about the situation and try my best not to offend him. "No," she said in her sexy French accent, "let me take care of it. I'll talk to him tonight. I know what to do."

The next morning Darryl showed up in my office before work started, something he'd never done before. He sat down on the sofa and started talking in a desultory manner. Up to now I'd never seen him ill at ease, or at a loss for something to say. But there he was, both.

It appeared to take a bit of effort, but at last he said, "Is everything all right? Is there anything I can do for you? Make things easier?"

Juliette appeared to have done her job. Obviously Darryl was giving me a prime opening, letting me bring up the subject rather than the much more painful other way around. I took the lead he was offering. "Now that you mention it," I said, "there is something I've been wanting to talk to you about," and I launched into the problem as diplomatically, as gently, as I knew how.

He listened quietly. There was no sign of offense being taken on his part. No umbrage. He heard me out, then stood for a moment contemplatively, nodding his head. "Yes," he said. "I see what you mean. I didn't realize. You're right. I'll watch that from now on."

I thanked him and told him how difficult it was for me to have to tell him what I did. "No, no," he said. "I wish you'd mentioned it sooner." We shook hands and he left. I felt very relieved it had gone so well.

Ten minutes later my door flew open. There was Darryl, livid, trembling with rage. Behind him, in the hallway, stood Juliette, looking wide-eyed and scared. "I want to talk to both of you in my office! Right now!" he said fiercely through clenched teeth and stormed off down the corridor. Juliette and I looked at each other, puzzled. She put out her hands and shrugged in typical Gallic fashion. Then we followed him down the hall.

We walked into his room and he slammed the door behind us. "Never," he stormed, his teeth clamped halfway through his cigar, "never have I been treated this way! You two have been conspiring behind my back. Plotting and scheming to keep me off the set. It's an outrage! An absolute outrage!" He was ranting, saliva dribbling from the corner of his mouth.

"But Darryl," Juliette pleaded, "tell us what's wrong. What did we do? What are you talking about?"

He yanked the cigar out of his mouth, wet tobacco pieces flying, and pointed it at her accusingly. "After I left Dick's office I went in to see you," he shouted, "and you told me the same thing he did. You don't want me on the goddamn set!"

It hit me then. Juliette hadn't told him after all. From Darryl's misleading behavior I'd assumed she had. As they say, assumption is the father of all fuck-ups.

"It's just a coincidence," she cried, waving her hand, trying to dismiss the whole thing as trivial.

"I thought so, too, at first," he shot back, "until I got out in the hallway and realized you both used the same words. *The same words!*"

Juliette feigned great impatience with him. "Well, of course," she answered, "how many different ways are there to tell you about a situation like that? You have to use the same words! So we did! So what?"

"I ought to fire both of you. I would if it wasn't in the middle of the goddamn picture," he went on. And on.

Slowly Juliette calmed him. She knew the right buttons to press. He simmered down, but still simmered. Since we were now committed to it I backed up Juliette's coincidence theory, and apologized for any hurt I may have caused to his feelings. It was the last thing I wanted to have happen, I told him. Which it was.

Eventually I went down to the set and started the day's work. I was shaken by this insight into the Zanuck personality. It was surprising to me that this enormous ego was so fragile, that he was so defensive of it. His response to the situation was vastly out of proportion to its gravity.

On the other hand, when you think of his psychological conditioning for all those years as an unchallenged, undisputed studio boss, it's understandable. For anyone to offer any criticism of him, no matter how unimportant, was unthinkable. It was totally inimical to his persona. He had to reject it, violently.

Juliette worked her magic. Darryl cooled off and mended his ways. The storm passed. But not completely. A vestige was left behind in Zanuck's mind.

Photography was finished on *Crack in the Mirror*, we were several weeks into postproduction at Studios Boulogne, and a major crisis was looming for Darryl. He needed another picture for Juliette Greco to do, and he didn't have one.

She was making impatient noises, and he was getting nervous. The situation was becoming crucial, and he let everyone know it. A picture for Juliette must be found, and he was dedicating himself to finding it.

Out of desperation, and to all our dismay, he resurrected *The Ballad of the Red Rocks*. In spite of the fact that there was no discernible enthusiasm from anyone, he forged ahead with the project. Juliette had to be kept happy, no matter what. Even if he actually had to make this piece of dreck.

He asked me if I'd direct it, but I made my feelings clear. I still disliked the story. Two writers were being brought from London to do a rewrite, he told me, and would I wait to see the result before making a final decision? Since I had nothing to lose, I agreed. Why not?

Still, I was surprised that he asked me to do the picture. After the "conspiracy" incident I felt a slightly cooler, more impersonal attitude from him. Most likely it was Juliette who wanted me on the show. Whatever Juliette wants, Juliette gets.

The English writers arrived, dived into the project, and were churning out pages of rewrite. The improvement was not discernible. All of us were pretty depressed. Not Darryl, though. He seemed in good spirits, and never missed an opportunity to tell Juliette what a great job the writers were doing.

It was about six weeks after the rewrite started and we were having our coffee after lunch at the Cadron Bleu, an excellent restaurant just down the street from the studio. It was the usual group. Zanuck; Julien Derode, the production manager; Christian Ferry, the assistant director; and I lunched there together every day.

Zanuck lit up his cigar and said, "I want to ask all of you something and I want you to answer separately." We all looked toward him expectantly. "Do you think we should make this picture?" he asked.

Darryl Zanuck asking an opinion? This was highly unusual. He turned toward Derode. "No!" Julien said firmly. Zanuck looked at Ferry. "No!" said Christian. Then it was my turn. "No!" I said, loud and clear.

He looked at us for a moment, then reached into his jacket and took out an envelope. From it he took a piece of paper and held it up for us to read. On it was written in large block letters, "I DO NOT WANT TO MAKE THIS PICTURE!"

We all started to laugh, Darryl harder than anyone. It was as though a great weight had been lifted from him. He was thoroughly and completely enjoying the moment. "It's a piece of shit," he said between gasps for air. "I never wanted to do the goddamn thing." This was greeted with another gale of laughter from all of us.

At this precise moment, in the midst of the hilarity, Ed Leggewie, Zanuck's office manager, entered the restaurant. He came over to the table. When the laughter subsided somewhat, he got Zanuck's attention. "What is it, Ed? What do you want?" Darryl said, wiping his eyes.

"I just came to tell you that the writers have finished the script and want to know what to do with it."

"Tell them," Darryl replied, "to shove it up their ass!"

My opinion of Zanuck went up quite a few points at that moment. He'd finally decided to stop humiliating himself, I believed, for the sake of keeping Juliette happy. That idea was almost instantly dispelled. "I've got another story," he told us, "a much better one." No wonder he'd shown such bravado in discarding the other one. "I want to do a story about a small group of people bringing a big truck from Ireland to Africa. It'll be an *African Queen*, but with a truck." Then he dropped the real bombshell. "The script will be written by Irwin Shaw."

I was impressed. One of America's best-known writers was going to write the script? A combination of Irwin Shaw and *African Queen*? Zanuck turned toward me. "How about it? You interested?"

"You bet! It sounds good to me."

It turned out that there really wasn't a full-fledged story in existence. It was merely an idea. Zanuck and I went to work, developing it in quite some detail, giving it a beginning, a middle, and an end. One thing we definitely decided on was that the major part of the story should be the trek across Africa with the truck, the *African Queen* part.

When the outline of the story was sufficiently developed, Darryl sent me off to meet with Irwin Shaw at his home in Klosters, Switzerland. Shaw was quite a guy. A square, solid block of muscle, with a sharp beak of a nose.

He kept to a strict routine: Write in the morning, ski in the afternoon, drink all night. He told me that he didn't have much skiing technique. He did it by sheer brute strength. His skiing reflected his personality.

That visit was the first of many to Klosters. I looked for excuses to get back there. Irwin and I held numerous story conferences, and it seemed to be coming along nicely. Each time I emphasized the importance of the trek across Africa. It had to be the bulk of the story.

He never showed me any pages. That wasn't his style, he said. The first time Zanuck or I would see what he'd written would be when he finished the screenplay. This is always a dangerous procedure, but Zanuck had so much confidence in Shaw he was willing to accept it.

It was, of course, a mistake.

About three months after Shaw started to work, the screenplay arrived in Paris. I read my copy immediately. Everything was pretty much as we'd discussed: An Irish lad and his Corsican (what else?) wife buy a truck in Dublin. They have to take along one of his relatives (comedy). They put the truck and themselves on a freighter to Africa. The sea voyage (romance). Sighting the coast of Africa from the ship. The End.

THE END! I looked around for more pages. There weren't any. They sight the coast of Africa, the people and the truck are still on the ship, and it's The End? Impossible! After all our discussions, meetings, and conferences, it's The End? Just when the adventure, the trek, the *African Queen* part are supposed to start, it's The End?

I called Zanuck. He had just finished reading it, too, and was as dumbfounded as I was. He asked me to come to his office, and we placed a call to Klosters. Shaw had left for the United States. I couldn't blame him.

This time, and rightfully so, Zanuck was in a proper fury. Shaw couldn't have spent more than a couple of weeks writing the script. He'd paid Shaw, his friend, an enormous fee, and what had he done? He'd followed that good old homespun adage of take the money and run.

Time was getting short. If we wanted to get the picture into production during the summer, we just couldn't waste any more of it with another writer who would have to start over. The only sensible plan of action left open to us was to put Mark Canfield, the author of all those wonderful *Rin Tin Tin* movies, back to work. Zanuck/Canfield would do the rewrite while I scouted locations and got the wheels of production into motion.

You'd think, if you were going to make a picture simply to put your girlfriend to work, you'd pick something easy to do. Something not too complicated, with not a lot of distant locations. Something fairly inexpensive and confined. Like *Crack in the Mirror*, for instance.

This movie, aptly titled *The Big Gamble*, was going to be anything but uncomplicated, inexpensive, and confined. It was to be shot in Paris, Dublin, London, the Provence district of France, and Côte d'Ivoire on the West Coast of Africa. A tramp freighter had to be hired for shooting in Ireland, then sent to Africa for various scenes on board while at sea and for the unloading of the truck. It was not going to be easy.

XIV

Ireland has never been counted among the world's wealthier nations. In 1960 it must have been a hot contender for last place on the World's Poorest list. I got my first impression of Irish poverty on the way into Dublin from the airport. This was the first stop on my far-flung search for locations for *The Big Gamble*. There was roadwork being done, and some of the laborers were using rocks to drive nails into wooden planks. The Public Works Department couldn't afford to provide hammers.

While conditions in Ireland may have been primitive, the people were anything but. Everyone an eccentric. Every one a lover of the intellect. Every one endowed with an impish humor, which was used as a buffer against a dour and gritty environment. That, and staggering amounts of whiskey and Guinness.

As I stepped out of the hotel my first night there, a twelve-year-old newsboy confronted me, urging me to buy one of his papers. I didn't want a newspaper, but one look at him and I couldn't resist. He was a street urchin in every conceivable sense. Barefoot, with filthy, ragged clothes, disheveled red hair, and a pug-nosed, dirty face that had the map of Ireland written all over it. I dug into my pocket and came up with a fistful of small change. "Here," I said, calling him over and holding open my coin-filled hand, "I'll take a paper, but I don't understand the money. You do it."

He didn't hesitate. Poking around in the coins, he picked out the exact amount and gave me a paper. "Good for you," I said. "I know the money, all right. I just wanted to see what you would do." With that, I poured the rest of the coins into his hand. "This," I said, "is for being honest."

It didn't come to much money, five shillings at the most, but his blue eyes widened and his face lit up with an open-mouthed smile.

"T'anks, mister," he said in awed tones, obviously overwhelmed with this remarkable windfall. Then he turned and ran off down the street. I was the patronizing American spreading largess among the unwashed peasantry and feeling rather smug about it, too.

The next evening I left the hotel with several of my colleagues. As I came out the door I saw my newsboy, and he saw me. "There he is!" he started shouting and pointing. About eight other newsboys came running to him. It was clear they had been waiting for me. This, I thought, is going to cost me dearly.

"There he is!" my lad continued to shout as the others gathered around him. "That's him! The crazy American millionaire!" Then, instead of rushing at me with outstretched hands, as I expected, they literally fell about, laughing. They screamed with laughter and held their sides and stamped their bare feet as they pointed me out to the passersby. They weren't there to exploit the situation. They were there to have a good laugh at the lunatic who gives money away. It was humiliating, but it was insightful.

I got another insight a few days later. Not feeling too well with an upset stomach, I stopped in at a chemist's—pharmacist's—shop not far from the hotel. A young, rosy-cheeked girl in a white smock was behind the counter. I asked for a bottle of Entero-Viaform, which was a popular prescription cure in the 1960s. The young lady said "Yes, sar," and disappeared through a curtained doorway at the rear of the tiny shop.

A minute or two later Barry Fitzgerald came bustling out through the curtain. If it wasn't Barry Fitzgerald it was someone who was trying hard to be just like him. He wore a rumpled, stained, open white smock over a well-worn, slightly frayed tweed vest and trousers. "Whell, now," he said, coming toward me, "are ya the gentleman wantin' the Entero-Viaform?" I said that I was.

"Ah, yes," he said. "I'm afraid I can't give it to ya. It's on the pyson list, ya know."

"The pyson list?" I asked. "What's that?"

"The pyson list," he replied. "Like arsenic and stuff like that. It's ridiculous, of course, but it's on the list."

"That's strange," I said. "I've been taking it for years without any problem, and I really need it now."

He gave this some thought for a moment. "Would it be too much trouble for ya to get a doctor's prescription?" he inquired politely.

"Yes, it would," I answered. "You see, I'd have to go back to the hotel and call a doctor. Then he'd have to come over and examine me and then he'd prescribe Entero-Viaform and charge me a nice fee and then I'd have to come back here."

"Ah, yes," the chemist said, nodding his head in understanding. "I see what ya mean." A small, devilish smile crossed his face, and the skin beside his eyes creased in conspiratorial humor. Then he made three statements that, to me at least, encompass a great deal of Irish philosophy and logic.

"Whell," he said with a chuckle, "it's only the law, ya know." He started toward the curtained doorway, then stopped and turned back. "Anyhow, who'd be the wiser?" he half-whispered. Again he moved toward the curtain and again he came back. "Besides," he said, topping it all off, "it'd be good for international relations." He'd covered all the bases and I got my Entero-Viaform.

The reason for my being in Dublin was not for location scouting alone, but also to do some casting. That part had gone quite well. How could it not when you had the Abbey Players and the Gate Theater to chose from? Hilton Edwards was running the Gate. Orson Welles idolized him and claimed that he'd learned what he knew about acting from Edwards during the years they'd worked together at the Gate. The reason Orson didn't end up at the Abbey, he'd told me, was that one of the requirements there was that you had to learn to speak and act in Gaelic. This Orson refused to do, and the Abbey's loss was the Gate's gain. Since I'd worked with Orson on my last two films, Hilton and I had much in common.

We were lunching one day, Hilton and I, in the staid and proper dining room of the Shelbourne Hotel, where I was staying. Edwards told me that his colleague and principal actor of the Gate, Micheál MacLiammóir, would be joining us. He did, and I wasn't prepared for him at all.

He breezed through the dining room, wearing a full-flowing opera cape; carrying a huge, gold-topped cane; and wearing a large black fedora hat pulled well over one eye, à la John Barrymore. He swooped down on our table like a great bat. After the waiters divested him of his props, I got a close-up look at him. I was startled but tried not to show it. Under a green velvet smoking jacket there was an extremely wide-collared, madly flowing white silk blouse with an extravagantly full black bow tie. He was an Oscar Wilde version of Little Lord Fauntleroy.

Most alarming of all were his face and head. On top was a wavy, black, shoulder-length wig. There was no attempt to disguise what it so obviously was, since it didn't fit him at all. It was nicely askew, and you could easily see right under the hairline.

Heavy, theatrical eye shadow and thick mascara adorned his large, expressive eyes. Two large, round red spots on his cheeks made him look like an escaped chorus girl from *Blossom Time*. His whole face was plastered in pancake makeup, best described by something that Goodman Ace once said to me about the appearance of Tallulah Bankhead. "She wore," he said, "seven layers of pancake, with syrup in between."

His whole aspect was so outlandish I couldn't possibly ignore or overlook it. Some comment was in order, I felt, or else I'd surely be insulting him or be considered an insensitive lout. This getup had to be intended for some theatrical event, I reasoned, so I pursued that concept.

"What time do you have to get back to the theater?" I asked.

"Oh, no special time," he replied airily.

"Don't you have a performance this afternoon?" I went on.

"Not today."

"Oh. A rehearsal, then?"

MacLiammóir looked puzzled. "No, we're not rehearsing anything at the moment."

"Oh."

I covered my face with the menu while I tried to extricate my foot from my mouth. This was his everyday appearance. He *always* looked like this. Once again I was trapped by the Irish character. I realized then that I was the only one in the room taking any notice whatsoever of this flamboyant eccentric. No one stared, the diners didn't even look up. The captains, waiters, and busboys greeted him with affectionate recognition and took care of his needs no differently than they did anyone else's. Eccentricity is a way of life in Hibernia. He was one of them, and God bless him who lives his life as he damn well pleases.

Although the casting may have been going well, I was having some difficulty with the location search. I couldn't find a pub. Not that there aren't enough pubs in Dublin to fill a book the size of the Manhattan telephone directory. I just couldn't find one I liked. Over a two-day period I saw dozens, but they lacked character and color. Some were drab, some were dreary, all were dirt-poor and depressing-looking.

At the end of a wearisome day of pub-crawling I called my staff together at the Shelbourne. Obviously, I told them, we're missing something. There's got to be an interesting, colorful pub in this town. We just don't know where to look. See if you can find a real pub expert, someone who knows every place there is. There must be somebody like that around.

The next morning, as I stepped off the elevator into the lobby, Julien Derode, our production manager, greeted me, his face wreathed in smiles. "We found your pub expert. We were very lucky, but we got him. He's the very best there is," he said, pointing proudly to a tubby figure seated in one of the lobby armchairs.

I walked over to where he was pointing, and the figure rose to meet me. Pub expert, indeed. I found myself shaking the hand of Brendan Behan.

The last time I saw Behan was at Wyndham's Theater in London. I hadn't met him, but I saw him. There was no way of avoiding it. It was during a performance of his play *The Hostage*. He was seated in a box just to the right of the stage and making a spectacle of himself. He was gloriously drunk and shouting a mixture of ribald advice and insulting criticism at the actors on the stage. The actors, being a spunky and spirited bunch, were giving back as good as they got. It was hilarious. The audience loved it and got into the spirit of the thing, shouting abuse at both parties. Behan turned his attention to the audience, showering them with profanity. The place was in an uproar. Apparently this was something that happened several times a week. It was one of the best nights I've ever experienced in the theater.

Now, there he was before me, the eccentrics' eccentric, the embodiment of all the wonderful madness that is Ireland's. Looking like a retired, overweight prizefighter with his bloated face, much-broken nose, and missing front teeth, he wore a cheap suit two sizes too large for him. Derode was right about our being lucky. Behan had, that very morning, been released from the hospital, where he'd been "drying out." He had come, in fact, directly from the hospital to the hotel.

We chatted for a few minutes while I described what I was looking for and he told me about his health. His liver was shot and he had diabetes. The hospital had detoxified him, kept him "dry" for some time, and discharged him with a warning that if he drank, he would die. "One drink," he told me, "and I'm gone." I inquired if he really felt up to doing what I was asking, visiting pub after pub for most of the day. Wouldn't the temptation to drink be too great? I didn't want to be responsible for the death of Ireland's greatest living playwright, I told him.

Behan laughed delightedly at that and assured me he was taking the doctor's advice seriously. He would stay strictly with fruit juice, he promised. Not only that, he had brought along insurance in the form of a friend, a gray-haired, military-looking gentleman with a huge, curled mustache and whom he introduced as the captain. The captain would keep an eye on him and see that, no matter what, he didn't touch alcohol. We had a car and driver standing by and hit the first of his recommended pubs about three minutes after opening time. It was already half filled with customers, all of whom gave him a boisterous greeting. Brendan waved his right arm at them in response. This brought a laugh and a query from one of them. "What's happened to y'r hand, Brendan?" he asked.

I noticed then, for the first time, that he'd tucked his right hand up into the loose sleeve of his jacket so it wasn't visible. "I don't know," he answered. "It's gone. Left it somewhere." This started the patrons speculating as to what could have happened to it, but Brendan paid no further attention to them. He used the "missing hand" gag for the rest of the day, and it always got the same reaction.

True to his word, Brendan ordered a fruit juice in every pub we visited. The captain, however, had a whiskey. After the third pub the captain was having trouble walking, and Brendan had to assist him. After the fourth, we both had to assist him. After the fifth pub, Brendan's insurance lapsed. The captain was too drunk to stand up and finally fell asleep in the car.

Riding in the car seemed to bring out something in Brendan. Something wild and wonderful. In the pubs he was quiet and reserved. Everyone knew him and were obviously tremendously pleased to see him. He'd converse softly but briefly with his friends, then settle down contentedly at a table with his fruit juice while I looked around.

Once in the car, his entire demeanor changed. He became a fountain of poetry, limericks, anecdotes, blasphemy, jokes, history, literature, and song. Totally stream-of-consciousness and nonstop, it flowed and gushed from him in English, French, and Gaelic. It was a display that would have put the fountains of the Villa d'Este to shame. I was enthralled.

We came close to hitting an old woman at an intersection. She raised her cane and shook it angrily at us and told us to look where we were going. Brendan rolled down his window and stuck his head out. "Aw, shut up, you old bitch," he yelled at her furiously. "What are you complainin' about? You'll be dead soon enough, anyhow!"

On a busy corner on Grafton Street about six old crones in

black dresses and shawls were queued up waiting for a bus. Brendan shouted for us to stop the car. We all thought something was wrong, but he leapt out of the car before it came to a halt and joined the old biddies. They gathered around him, cackling like the witches in *Macbeth*, kissing him and patting him and asking after his health.

With his arms akimbo, Brendan launched into some sort of Irish song and jig. The crones, who were now joined by several more who appeared from nowhere, formed a circle around him, clapping their hands in tempo as he sang a bawdy anti-British song at the top of his lungs and whose verses ended up with the stirring words, "and we'll wrap our balls in the English flag!" The crones shrieked with laughter every time he came to that part.

By the time he finished, a sizable crowd had gathered and gave him a rousing cheer as he came back to the car. The crones waved and shouted their blessings on him until we were out of sight.

We were passing through one of the more depressed areas of Dublin, on a street lined on both sides with identical tall, decaying red brick, Georgian buildings, when he pointed out what he referred to as his ancestral home. We stopped to look at this famous site. It was a tenement, just like all the others on the street. In fact, it was a tenement when the Behans lived there, before Brendan was born, during the time of the Troubles.

That was a truly terrifying period, he told me, particularly because of the almost constant artillery shelling of the neighborhood. Sometimes the family couldn't get out of the house for days, and they became desperate for food and supplies.

What they'd had to do, he said, was wait for a break in the bombardment, then dash madly out to any nearby building that had been hit, blindly grab the first thing they could lift, then run back home. "One time," he related, "when they were practically starving there was a lull in the shelling. My father ran across the street to a shop that had just been wrecked. He was scared to death, so he grabbed the first two boxes he saw and ran like hell, thinkin' that any minute he'd be killed. When he got home he found he'd brought back, at the risk of life and limb, twelve wigs and six pairs of ballet shoes." The shop, it seems, had been a theatrical supply house.

"It wasn't too bad," he added. "My uncle brought back two pairs of skis."

By the time we reached the last pub, we were all feeling a bit tired. The captain had recovered sufficiently to rejoin us for a refreshing pint of Guinness. Brendan settled into a booth and ordered his fruit juice, and I sat alongside him. "You know," he said to me, "I've been invited to do a speaking tour of Canada and then do an appearance in Los Angeles. Do you think I should go?"

"Don't you want to?"

"Oh, yes, I do."

"Then what's the problem?"

"Well, do you think I'll be lionized?"

"Without question. Of course you'll be lionized."

"Will they make me drink, do you think?"

"They'll certainly be offering you drinks, but no one can force you. You can always refuse."

He shook his head doubtfully. "I'm afraid if I go on this trip, I'll die." He was completely and touchingly sincere.

"Then don't go, Brendan," I urged. "Please, don't go."

He sat there thinking for a moment, then looked at me and said, "What do they charge for a room at the Cedars of Lebanon Hospital in Los Angeles?"

That question really came out of left field. I was so startled that I laughed. How did he even know the name of a hospital there? I wondered. It was an indication of how deeply concerned he was about his health. I told him what I thought the going rate was, and he brightened considerably. "Well, now," he said. "That's not as bad as I thought. Maybe I'll go after all."

Then he changed the subject. "Tell me, if I wrote a screenplay for you, would you direct it?"

I was thunderstruck. Brendan Behan writing a screenplay for me? It took me a minute to recover. "Would I direct it? It would be one of the greatest honors of my life to do anything you wrote."

"Okay. What do you want it to be about?"

Again I was stunned. "Brendan, I'm not interested in doing a picture about what I think. You're a great, innovative writer. I want to do a film about what *you* think. I want your ideas."

"Ah, yes, I see. Then that's what I'll do. I promise you." He held out his hand, and we shook on it. I couldn't believe he was serious, but it didn't matter to me. I was too flattered to care.

We were leaving for London in a couple of hours, so we returned to the Shelbourne to pick up our luggage and check out. A wide, wooden veranda, with old-fashioned rocking chairs, lined the front of the hotel. As we walked up the broad steps to the entrance, Brendan scurried away from us and sat in one of the chairs, folded his hands in his lap, and started rocking. I came over to see if he was all right.

He paid no attention to me but started a conversation with the empty chair next to him on his left. "Good mornin', Father O'Herlihy," he said. "It's a fine day, now, isn't it?" He then got up and sat in the chair he'd addressed, crossed his hands in his lap, and started rocking. "Yes, it is, Father Flanagan," he responded to the chair he'd just left. "In fact, it's better than we deserve here in East Orange, New Jersey."

I stared at him in delighted wonderment. There had been a very small item in the morning newspaper about some crazy, funny thing that had happened to two priests in East Orange, New Jersey. It had caught my eye and I read it with some amusement. So, apparently, had Brendan. Now here he was doing an entire sketch about the two priests, playing both parts, hopping from one chair to the other.

His antics stopped a small group of bewildered, gaping tourists, but Brendan went right on for my benefit. The dialogue and the situation he was improvising were screamingly funny. It was a display of dazzling, creative brilliance, and I knew I was privileged to be in the presence of an extraordinary human being.

We said good-bye in the lobby. "Brendan," I said, "this has been the most memorable day I've ever spent. I'll never forget it." He embraced me in a big bear hug. "Me, too," he said. "Me, too. And I won't forget about the screenplay, either." Then he left with the captain.

About an hour later we checked into the airport. At that time there was a small, fenced-in area outside the departure gate where visitors could watch passengers board their plane. As I passed by this area I heard my name being called. Surely, I thought, it was meant for somebody else with the same name, but I looked around anyhow. There, behind the fence, waving and laughing, were Brendan and the captain. I went over to them. "What are you doing here, Brendan?" I asked, amazed. "We said good-bye at the hotel."

"I know," he answered, delighted that he had surprised me, "but I just wanted to see you off." We shook hands again. "Have a safe flight and God bless you," he said.

I walked out to the plane and climbed the portable gangway. When I got to the top I looked back. Brendan was still there, waving a crumpled white handkerchief. I waved back and entered the cabin. There was an empty seat on the side facing the terminal. I took it and looked out the window. Brendan could no longer see me, but there he was, still waving the handkerchief.

Ten minutes later the plane started to move. Brendan was still there, waving. A few moments later we were rushing down the runway for takeoff. My window still faced the terminal and I could see the now almost deserted visitors' area. Brendan was still there, waving his white crumpled handkerchief. I watched him until he was lost to view.

I had a large lump in my throat most of the way to Paris.

About a year later I was in my apartment on Via Monte Giordano, in Rome, when a small package arrived in the mail. On opening it I found a book and an accompanying letter. The book was a copy of *Borstal Boy*, by Brendan Behan. The letter was from someone I didn't know but whose name was familiar: Michael Todd, Jr.

The book, the letter stated, had been purchased for film production by Todd, Jr. The screenplay was to be written by the author. Brendan, the letter went on, was insisting that I direct the movie. He would hear of no one else. Would I please read the book and let them know if I was interested?

To say that I was touched would be a monumental understatement. After a year of great activity for him, at the very peak of his mad, brilliant career, he hadn't forgotten our brief encounter. And he hadn't forgotten his promise. He still intended to write a screenplay for me.

I didn't have to read the book to know that I'd want to do it, but I did. It was as good as I'd hoped it would be. I sent a letter to Michael Todd, Jr., telling him how much I loved it and how happy I'd be to direct the screenplay.

I never received a reply. There were financing problems, I learned subsequently, and the project was abandoned.

Behan died in 1964, having literally drunk himself to death. I couldn't claim to be a close, longtime friend of his. I wasn't a pal or a confidant. The time that I knew him was measured in hours, not years. Still, I felt a strong sense of loss. I thought of the wonderful plays and books he'd written in the short, fiery forty-one years he lived. And I thought of the wonderful plays and books and, yes, even screenplays he had in him that the world would now never see. This immensely talented, madcap, ribald Dublin wit had gone and had taken all that great promise with him.

Commenting on the death of Behan in the London newspaper, the *Daily Telegraph*, Alan Brien wrote:

I remember visiting him in hospital in London some years ago when the obituaries were already in type. "Brendan," I said, "do you never think about death?" He heaved his bulk about in silence under the covers like a beached whale.

Then he burst out—"Think about death? Begod, man I'd rather be dead than think about death."

It was one of the most courageous and honest remarks ever made by a dangerously sick man. I would like to remember it as his epitaph.

XV

After scouting the Irish locations for *The Big Gamble*, I proceeded on to the Camargue in the South of France, and to Côte d'Ivoire on the West Coast of Africa. After sizing up the various problems I had run into I knew I would need help. There was simply too much to do in too many distant locations. With Zanuck's okay I sent for Elmo Williams to come over from Hollywood to direct the Second Unit. He would do some of the time-consuming elements, those that didn't involve actors.

I had an association with Elmo Williams from the time I first came to Hollywood in 1945. He was, without question, an absolutely brilliant film editor. We'd worked together on several films over the years. I recommended him to Stanley Kramer and he won the Academy Award for *High Noon*. He was my editor on *Twenty Thousand Leagues Under the Sea* and got an Academy Award nomination. He did a fabulous job for me on *The Vikings*. He came to us with impeccable qualifications as an editor.

He was, however, not going to be the editor. Second Unit directing was his job.

True to the Peter Principle, Elmo wasn't content being a first-rate editor. He, like everyone else in the world, wanted to direct. The problem was that Elmo wasn't suited for it. He was charming, great company, fun to be with. Sensitive and comprehending when it came to art. Got along extremely well with people. He had a lot of the attributes for directing, but he lacked just one: the knack of handling actors, of getting them to appear natural and relaxed.

However, I'd let Elmo direct the Second Unit on a couple of big pictures—*Twenty Thousand Leagues* and *The Vikings*—and the results were surprisingly good. His lack of directing ability was painfully apparent when you looked at the raw film he shot. It was always quite terrible. But Elmo, with his extraordinary talent as an editor, knew precisely what pieces he was going to use before he shot them. When he got through putting it all together, it looked fine. Until then, though, you had to have faith.

I wanted Elmo to do this film because he was a great technician and efficient as hell. I knew I could rely on him to get everything we needed in the way of coverage, without shooting a lot of unnecessary angles and film.

Among other things, he would do the unloading of the truck from the freighter in Africa. It was a tough and dangerous sequence because the spot chosen, the tiny port of Sassandra, was one of a kind. It had a pier, but large ships, like our freighter, couldn't get to it. A wicked reef kept them several hundred yards at sea. Huge canoes, manned by twenty native paddlers, would go out to meet the ships beyond the reef. The sea was always wild and turbulent out there. That's where cargo was unloaded into the heaving canoes.

It was hair-raising to watch, much less to perform. Huge crates of cargo would be lowered over the side by the ship's crane. The rolling of the ship had to be coordinated with the pitching of the canoe. If it was mistimed, the load would either crush the paddlers or go right through the canoe. Our truck would exactly fill the width of a canoe, with hardly an inch to spare.

And that wasn't all. Once the cargo was somehow loaded onto the canoe, the paddlers would then have to shoot through the gigantic waves created by the reef, like a surfboard. That area was nothing less than a maelstrom. If a boat capsized in it, there'd be no hope for anyone aboard.

It was going to make a fantastic sequence for the movie. That's why I wanted Elmo to photograph it while I was working elsewhere with the actors.

The only item left to resolve before photography commenced on the film was that of the public relations position. Normally this isn't too much of a problem, but Darryl considered it extremely important, and with reason. On both of his last two films, *Roots of Heaven* and *Crack in the Mirror*, the PR man had gotten much too friendly with Juliette. Much too. He didn't want that to happen again. But who to get? Zanuck agonized over this question.

Then a miracle happened. Zanuck found the perfect solution to his problem. He happily reported to me and the production staff that he had been introduced to a French World War II flying ace who had shot down four German Messerschmitts on the last day of the Battle of France. Not only that, but in doing so he had been wounded where no man should ever be wounded.

Zanuck was apparently thunderstruck. He had produced, at Twentieth Century-Fox, Hemingway's *The Sun Also Rises*, and here was a real-life Jake Barnes. And the news got even better. This gentleman just happened to be in public relations! A little down on his luck at the moment. Looking for a job, in fact.

What a piece of news this was. A publicist, a French war hero, and most important of all, a man who was not a man. Darryl could stop worrying. He had found a eunuch to guard his queen.

We started shooting the picture on some interior sets at the Studios Boulogne. Zanuck began to exhibit some pretty weird behavior. If his actions on the set of *Crack in the Mirror* were annoying, they now became ridiculous. He didn't appear on the shooting stage just for Juliette's scenes. He was present all the time, for everyone's scenes, including the rehearsals.

Whereas formerly he used to sit on the edge of the set, just out of camera range, now he did something I'd never seen or heard of before or since. He moved his chair right onto the set.

This was no accidental encroachment. This was deliberate. He'd sit there, smoking his cigar, script open in his hands, following the dialogue, never looking up. If the actors had to move from one place to another, they had to go around him. Or he'd hike his chair over a couple of inches to let an actor pass. Sometimes, when I was directing, I'd step back and bump into him. The actors were quite bewildered.

He'd stay there, ensconced on the set, even after I'd say, "All right, let's try a take." The assistant director would call out, "Quiet!" Bells would ring loudly. A hush would settle over everything. Still he'd sit there.

We'd wait. Neither I, nor anyone else, would say a word. We'd just wait. At last he'd look up and say, with seemingly ingenuous surprise, "Oh, are you ready?" I'd indicate that we were. Then he'd get up and sit down just outside the sightlines while an assistant would snatch his chair off the set.

Everyone came to me, cast and crew, asking what was going on. I said I didn't know. But I did.

It was, in short, a festering by-product of the "conspiracy" episode. This was Zanuck's way of ostentatiously reinstating himself as the boss. Nobody was going to try to get him off any stage and get away with it. The once-powerful mogul was making a pitiful attempt to salvage some authority. It was a ludicrous and infantile method.

Clearly, too, he was trying to get me to quit. Since, because of Juliette, he couldn't fire me, he wanted me to fire myself. I wasn't about to do that because I wanted the continuity and stability this job provided.

After I signed on to do the first picture for Zanuck I realized that I was feeling happier than I had for a long time in Hollywood. I was being treated with deference and respect by Zanuck, instead of being mugged by Adler and Feldman. And then there was the freedom I'd rarely experienced before. Until this time, I'd been under contract for virtually my entire career. Now, since my Fox contract was not binding in Europe, I was a free agent. I could accept or reject jobs without punishment. It was a novel feeling, and I liked it. But it was a little scary, too. I felt like a canary that's been let out of its cage but still missed the security of the iron bars.

Since there weren't many American directors residing abroad, and there seemed to be plenty of opportunities for work, I decided to bring my family over and try living in Europe for a while. I was confident I was doing the right thing until the first night after Mickey and the three kids arrived in Paris. I went in to kiss my six-year-old daughter, Jane, good night. She was crying and I asked her what was the matter. Looking at me with tear-filled eyes, she said, "Why didn't you leave me where I was happy?" Suddenly I wasn't so confident anymore.

Uprooting Mickey, the two boys, and Jane from home and transplanting them to Europe worked better than I thought possible. They fell in love with Paris. But Jane's words haunted me. As strangers in a strange land, the last thing I wanted was to have them feel insecure in any way. Walking off a picture, with the resultant probability of a lawsuit, and being out of work, job-hunting in a foreign country, was not the best possible move I could make at this time. Besides, it is never good policy to gain a reputation, deserved or not, of being too temperamental, or too unstable, to remain with a picture all the way through. Zanuck may not have been what he once was, but he still was powerful and dangerous enough to do me some real damage if he wanted to. Darryl could spread a vengeful rumor as well as the next man. Better to roll with the punches than become a beat-up martyr.

So I tried to cope as best I could with Zanuck and find humorous ways of dealing with the situation. Sometimes, sitting there in the middle of the set when I was ready to shoot, he'd innocently ask, "Am I in the way?" I'd usually answer, "Oh, no, Darryl. Not if you put on a wig and some makeup."

I kept my temper, ignored the provocations, and didn't quit. We kept up this rotten game for the rest of the picture.

He grew more irritable day by day, more given to caviling and captious criticism. By the time we finished our studio work in Paris and moved to the Provence district of France, things were heating up nicely. Elmo Williams had preceded us there with his Second Unit to shoot some river crossing scenes with the truck. Zanuck complained constantly about his work. He was shooting too many angles, too much film. The action was lousy. None of this was true except the part about the action. It didn't look too great but, as I patiently explained to Darryl, Elmo's stuff never looked like much until he cut it together. You had to have faith. There was a great deal of skepticism on Darryl's part, and he was beginning to talk about getting rid of him.

I had chosen this location as I do all locations—as close as possible to the best hotel and best restaurant in the area. The company, therefore, settled in at the Oustaù de Baumanière, in Les Baux, one of the five best hotel/restaurants in all of France. Almost immediately there was trouble.

Darryl was jealous of my accommodations. All the suites at the Baumanière were exactly alike but he was convinced that my quarters were better than his. He blamed my assistant director, Christian Ferry, for this outrage and was determined to fire him. I knew nothing about this at the time or I would have invited Darryl's inspection of my rooms, or would have switched with him. The only difference between the two suites was that mine was on the second floor, directly above his. Ferry kept his job because our production manager, Julien Derode, threatened to leave if Ferry was fired for such a ridiculous reason. And if Derode left, the entire French crew would leave with him. Zanuck was becoming as testy as a fighting bull who had just been worked over by a picador.

After a couple of weeks of our working together, Elmo moved his unit to the Côte d'Ivoire and commenced shooting truck runbys prior to tackling the big freighter sequence. True to form, his film continued to look terrible.

On Sunday mornings Zanuck and I would run all the previous week's dailies at a movie theater in Arles. We'd also see Elmo's film that had arrived from Africa. Each week, after the screening, he'd say to me, "Well, your alleged cutter friend has done it again." Zanuck always referred to him as "your alleged cutter friend." "His stuff stinks. I'm going to get rid of him."

"But Darryl," I would hasten to assure him, "when it's cut together it'll look fine. This is the way his film always looks, but it comes out great when he gets through working on it. Believe me."

"If he doesn't do better next week, I'm going to fire him," he'd say and walk off, chewing on a wet cigar.

So it went. Each week Darryl would threaten to fire Elmo, and each week I'd save his job.

When we landed in Abidjan, Côte d'Ivoire, to commence the African sequences, Elmo greeted us at the airport. Riding to the hotel with him in the car, he was exuberant. He'd just finished shooting the scenes of the transfer of the truck from the freighter to the canoe, and he was ecstatic. The sea was rough, the action terrific, the danger real. Altogether, it would be a spectacular sequence in the movie.

He couldn't wait to show me the stills that had been taken of the action. As soon as I got to my room at the hotel he handed me a packet of eight-by-ten photographs and we started to go through them.

The pictures were spectacular, all right, but after I'd seen the first half dozen or so, I became increasingly concerned. "Elmo, I see that everyone in these pictures is wearing a white pith helmet."

"That's right."

"Did they wear them just for these still pictures?"

"No, they wear them all the time."

"Everyone?"

"Sure. Everyone."

I was becoming more alarmed by the moment. "Even the canoe paddlers?"

"Oh, yes. Everybody wears them."

"And that's the way you photographed them for the movie?" I asked, already knowing the worst.

"Of course. Why? What's wrong with that?" I told him what's wrong with that.

Darryl's favorite scene in the screenplay was the moment when the comedic brother-in-law, David Wayne, appears on deck when the boat arrives in Africa. Outfitted like a great white hunter, *he is the only one wearing a white pith helmet*, and an oversize one at that.

He stands out like a diamond in a goat's behind, and the white pith helmet becomes the target of fun and ridicule.

Under his African tan I could see the color drain from Elmo's face. "Oh my God, I forgot about that." He looked at me plaintively. "What are we going to do?"

A good question. This was a king-size, world-class error. There was no way to patch it up by doing a few shots over, here and there. The entire action sequence, two weeks' tough and dangerous work, was involved. The only way to fix it was to do it all over. This, certainly, would be the end of Elmo when Zanuck heard about it. I didn't want to see that happen. Elmo was my longtime good friend and I knew how much this would hurt him both personally and professionally. Besides, I didn't want to give Darryl the satisfaction of finally firing him.

I considered the situation for a few moments and came to a conclusion.

"Elmo, has anyone besides you and the still man seen these pictures?"

"I wouldn't think so. He just gave them to me this morning."

"Good. Get your hands on every still you can from that sequence and burn it. I don't want anyone to see them, ever."

"Okay. But why?"

"Because I'm going to reshoot the sequence and, if I can work it right, no one will ever realize what I'm doing."

My plan was risky, for me as well as Elmo, but quite feasible. Reshooting a sequence without the producer's permission was not exactly a desirable thing to do, but it was the only way I could think of to protect my friend.

There were two elements that made me feel fairly confident. One was that before we left France we had not received any film from Elmo of the truck/freighter sequence. The only ones who knew that it was actually being shot were the people in the production department who were getting report sheets from the African location. Most producers read these reports avidly. I was counting on Zanuck not reading them. He was more preoccupied keeping track of Juliette close at hand than to paying much attention to what was going on some three thousand miles away.

The other element was that I had to do many camera setups with the actors that were similar to those already shot by Elmo. Since none of my First Unit crew knew what had previously been photographed, I could go ahead and restage everything without raising any eyebrows. The only ones who could blow the whistle on the whole operation were Derode and Ferry. I told them what I was doing and why. Neither of them held much affection for Zanuck at this point, and they agreed to look the other way.

It was, purely and simply, a cover-up.

It worked perfectly. Except, of course, that the sea became dead calm for the shooting. All of the excitement was gone. The maelstrom reef looked as dangerous as a boat ride in the lake in Central Park.

What also helped keep the whole business from being uncovered was another drama that was simultaneously taking place. The company was headquartered in Abidjan, but the truck/freighter location was in the tiny port of Sassandra, 150 miles away. The only way to get there by land was via a dirt track through the jungle, a grinding, bone-jolting car trip of about eight hours. Once you arrived, living quarters were virtually nonexistent. Three primitive beach cabins that could accommodate six people was it. Everything else made those three cabins look like the Plaza Athenée in Paris.

Luckily Sassandra had an airstrip, if it could be dignified with such a name. It was, in fact, a short, narrow, pockmarked strip of dirt on top of a nearby mountain. This so-called airstrip ended with a six-hundred-foot sheer cliffside drop to the shiny boulders and crashing surf below. The only airplane of any size that could handle this situation was a French-made curiosity, a twelve-passenger, four-motor aircraft. The engines looked tiny enough to have come from a model airplane kit, with propellers that were three-foot-long toothpicks.

Since there were about sixty people in the company, the only practical solution was to keep the French crew, who comprised 80 percent of the group, in native hovels in Sassandra. The remainder, the Americans, would have to take the one-hour flight each way every day from Abidjan. The French crew were delighted. They hated that airplane and wanted no part of it. They wouldn't have traded places with us for anything.

Juliette didn't want any part of it either, so it was decided that she and her makeup, hairdresser, and wardrobe ladies would occupy the three cabins in Sassandra. Darryl wanted to join her but she wouldn't hear of it. There was no room, she said, she wanted to be alone, he would be in the way. She won. Darryl stayed in Abidjan and made the daily commute with the rest of us. Juliette stayed in Sassandra.

There was someone else staying in Sassandra, too, and Zanuck was not at all happy about it: the public relations man. He and Juliette had become close friends in Paris and now he had chosen to stay with the French crew. Physical disability or not, he was a lot closer to her than Darryl could tolerate, and he was jealous. He tried to bring him back to Abidjan, but Juliette squashed that. He was doing a story about her, she said, living in the jungle in the most primitive conditions. He had to be there for the atmosphere. Darryl pleaded with her daily to let him stay, too, or to send the PR man back. She refused to do either. He wanted to replace him with an American publicist. She said he was chauvinistic. Darryl was in torment. He wasn't too concerned with what I was shooting.

As it must to all cover-ups, there was an uncovering. It was my freightergate. Someone had tipped off Darryl, and he confronted me in a fury cold enough to frost our relations for the remainder of the picture. I admitted all and waited for the ax to fall. It didn't. To replace me on a distant location when we were within a month of finishing photography was not a good idea. Even someone blinded with anger could see that.

The ax didn't fall on Elmo, either. By this time he'd been felled by something else. He had contracted some sort of tropical fever and was confined to his bed, about as sick as a human being is allowed to be. I would stop by and visit him after work each day and he'd put on a brave face, but as Will Rogers once observed, it was the hope of dying that kept him alive. Not even Darryl had the heart to fire him under these circumstances.

Eventually Elmo recovered and continued with his Second Unit, while the rest of us moved to London and then back to Paris to finish the picture. Zanuck barely spoke to me for the remaining months of postproduction. We were cordial to each other but not friendly. On the last day of my work on the film I left for Rome with my family, to start preparing *Barabbas* for Dino De Laurentiis. Darryl and I didn't say good-bye to each other.

There is a nicely ironic postscript to this story.

After I left Paris, Zanuck became more suspicious than ever about Juliette. Whoever the informer was in the company, he was still doing his job. Darryl hired a private detective to keep her under surveillance and to make a report.

The report was an eye-opener. Among other things it revealed that the PR man Juliette had become so friendly with, the man who was not a man, apparently was not the man Darryl had described to us. He was not a World War II flying ace who had shot down four

Messerschmitts on the last day of the Battle of France. And, it would seem, he had not been grievously wounded where a man should never be wounded. No Jake Barnes, he.

The Darryl Zanuck-Juliette Greco relationship was over.

Now Darryl was left virtually alone. The once busy Paris office was almost deserted, since no movies were being made or planned. Friends seemed to have drifted away. Juliette, the main motivation of his life, was gone. And then, to top it off, he came down with a mild stroke and a severe case of shingles, an agonizingly painful skin disease that is accompanied by neuralgia, with eruptions sometimes extending halfway around the body.

Sick and forlorn in a foreign land, far from home, Darryl Zanuck became the central figure of a Greek tragedy. A colossus of the movie industry, a mogul among moguls brought to his knees by a fatal flaw: an unreasoning obsession for an unresponsive, unappreciative girl.

Elmo Williams didn't return to Hollywood when the picture was over, but stayed on in Paris. He was moved by Darryl's distressing situation and took to visiting him in his dark apartment at 44 Rue du Bac. There was no ulterior motive. He just felt terribly sorry for him. Elmo gave him friendship and companionship when he needed it most, and Zanuck appreciated it.

Sometime during his slow recovery period Zanuck came across a book he liked. It was an enormously difficult and complex story, and Darryl asked Elmo to work with him to try to whip it into shape for a major movie project.

The Brasserie Lipp was just a few streets from the apartment, and it became their office. They'd meet there at the same table each day for lunch, then stay for the rest of the afternoon translating the book into a workable motion picture format.

By the time Zanuck regained his health, *The Longest Day* was well on its way to becoming a movie.

It saved the Hollywood studio from financial disaster and restored Darryl Zanuck to his former stature in the industry. Elmo Williams became chief of the London office of Twentieth Century-Fox and head of Fox film production in Europe.

It is passing strange when you think on it. I was Darryl Zanuck's fair-haired boy when we started, and we ended up not speaking to each other. And the guy whose job I saved, time after time, even at the risk of my own, ended up in a position of power and influence.

A few years later, when things went sour for me in Europe and I desperately needed a job, I looked toward Elmo. Zanuck may have had something to do with it, but when I needed him, Elmo, alas, turned his back.

E Finita la commedia.

XVI

Just at the moment when things had reached their nadir between Zanuck and me, right after we'd returned to Paris to finish *The Big Gamble*, Providence descended from heaven and kissed me on the brow. Dino De Laurentiis showed up and offered me a job.

A couple of years earlier Dino had pursued me in Hollywood to direct *War and Peace*, but it didn't work out. Now here he was in Paris offering me a huge biblical epic based on Nobel Prize winner Pär F. Lagerkvist's novel *Barabbas*. Christopher Fry would write the screenplay, and it would be shot in Rome. As soon as I finished my chores on *The Big Gamble*, Dino wanted me to report for work immediately on *Barabbas*. I could already feel the warm Italian sun melting the Zanuck ice from my bones. Even if I had loved Darryl, I would have gladly jilted him for this assignment.

My family was something less than ecstatic about having to leave Paris. It hadn't been easy for them to become adjusted to Parisian sophistication after the barbecue and jeans life-style of California. Uprooted from their native home and friends, they had to put down new roots in foreign soil. There were plenty of tears.

Now, a year later, there were more tears. Why did they have to leave Paris? They loved Paris. It was their home. Their friends were here. Wait, I told them. Rome is beautiful, too. You'll see, you'll love it. Honest.

There was a World War I song that went, "How're you gonna keep them down on the farm after they've seen Paree?" We weren't exactly down on the farm, but we had seen Paree—and Rome, at first glance, was something of a letdown. I mentioned this to my Roman assistant, a jolly, chubby, hyperthyroidal young intellectual with the wonderful name of Guido Guiderini. "Ah, but you don't understand!" he effused, his arms making graceful circles in the air.

"Paris is a common whore! She lies there naked on the bed, her legs spread apart. Nothing is hidden. A vulgar display of the obvious. But Rome! Rome is a mysterious seductress. Her beauties, her charms are hidden. Slowly, tantalizingly, she reveals them to you until you are overwhelmed, intoxicated by her." Guido may have been a bit operatic, but he was right. When we left Rome four years later, everyone was crying again.

There are some beautiful slums in Rome, like Trastevere and Campo dei Fiori, slums with style and character. However, the mysterious seductress kept her charms well hidden when it came to the location of the De Laurentiis studio. It was in a dreary, industrial slum on the Via della Vasca Navale and consisted of a decrepit, bilious-green, two-story wooden building that contained the offices, and close by, three decaying stages.

There was one fascinating element to the whole setup, however. The second-floor hallway, in the back of the building, had a row of windows that overlooked a Gypsy encampment. It was virtually impossible to walk down that hallway without stopping to gaze out the windows and study the home life of the Gypsies. It was like watching an ant colony in a glass-sided box.*

As you entered the small lobby of the office building you were confronted with a profile view of the De Laurentiis logo, a two-foot-long bronze statue of a magnificent lion. It stood on a waist-high pedestal dead center in the room. Arrogantly displayed under its raised tail was a splendid pair of very shiny balls. There was a superstition (probably promulgated by Dino) that rubbing these burnished testicles brought good luck. Absolutely nobody passed by them without giving them a rub, so they were always highly polished.†

There aren't many people in the world who are immediately recognized by their first name alone, but Dino is one of them. Even

*The head Gypsy was completely legless. His body rested on a sort of enlarged skateboard and he propelled himself by pushing the ground with his hands. I thought he'd make a colorful extra as a beggar in the crowd scenes in ancient Jerusalem, so I offered him 10,000 lire a day (about $16, which was pretty good money then), with a two-week guarantee. He turned me down. "I make 20,000 lire a day as a real beggar in Rome," he said. "Why should I be a fake beggar for half as much?" Eventually the lure of stardom overwhelmed him and he showed up for work anyhow.
† The lion with the shiny balls followed Dino when he moved to New York years later, and then on to Hollywood where their efficacy, but not their luster, finally dimmed, probably from too much rubbing.

in the fifties all you had to say was "Dino" and everyone knew whom you meant. He seems, somehow, to have been born a legend.

An impeccably tailored bundle of raw energy and volatile emotions, he is not only a legend, but also a character. The impact of meeting him for the first time is something akin to sticking your finger into an electric light socket. Short, dark, high forehead, steely black eyes with bushy eyebrows that sweep up satanically at the ends. The word "gravelly" was invented to describe his voice, which he uses to bark out short, staccato, exclamatory sentences. His personality is the same as his speech: curt, abrupt, brusque.

And then there is his smile. It can be open and winning, even disarming. But it can be something else, too. He can give you a smile with his lips only, the rest of his face immobile. It is like looking into the face of icy Death. I know. He did it to me once.

Dino's English was impossibly bad. The only way I could tell that he was trying to speak English instead of Italian was when he talked a little slower. We had to have a translator present at every meeting. It took a while to get used to his vehement manner of speaking; in fact, it was quite frightening at first. I'd come into his office and present him with a suggestion or an idea. The translator would do his job and Dino would go into what seemed to be an apoplectic fit. He would yell and shout, pound the desk with his fists and elbows, jump to his feet and gesticulate accusingly at me, his voice filled with deep emotion. Shit, I would think, I've done it now. He thinks I'm an idiot. I'm fired for sure. Dino would drop back down into his chair, breathing heavily, and nod curtly to the translator, who would turn to me and say, "He loves it."

Over the years his command of the language has changed considerably for the better, but not his pronunciation. English still sounds like a totally unknown, undecipherable, foreign tongue when he speaks it. His comprehension is excellent, except when he conveniently doesn't want it to be. Then he'll say, "I no understand" and revert to hyperspeed Italian. This usually happens in any money discussion that's not going in his favor. His grasp of the language suddenly evaporates.

His use of primitive sentence structure still amuses me. I know he has a sophisticated knowledge of grammar, but he still will say, "I like!" or "I no like!" I've observed him in meetings when an agent and a producer are pitching a project. Dino will listen for a while, then suddenly interrupt with, "I like! We do!"

Story conferences with Dino sometimes had their moments. We were discussing the final shot of *Barabbas*, with a confused Barabbas finding himself crucified and not really understanding why. Christopher Fry had written a moving, poetic final speech for him as he dies on the cross. Dino was much taken with it. Jumping to his feet behind his desk, he reenacted the scene with great passion. He flung out his arms, looked up toward heaven, and read his version of the final speech in Italian. The translator broke up in gales of laughter. "What's so funny?" I asked. "What did he say?" "Hey, God!" he translated, "What the fuck is going on?"

His blunt, almost crude manner can be disconcerting, particularly to young actresses. Over the more than thirty years I've known him I've introduced him to hundreds of actresses for casting purposes. I don't think I've seen a single interview last more than thirty seconds. They're in and out before they know it. Frequently they burst into tears once they're outside. But in the thirty seconds they were in his office, they were given a very thorough anatomical examination by his X-ray eyes. As soon as the girl was out the door he'd usually say to me, "No tits. Next!"

The abrupt treatment, however, wasn't just reserved for actresses. The actors got it, too. Not long ago I brought an actor to his office for his approval. The actor stood before Dino's desk for a couple of minutes while Dino finished a phone conversation. When he hung up he stared at the actor for several seconds. Finally the actor said, "Do you mind if I sit down, Mr. De Laurentiis?" Dino responded with unaccustomed graciousness. "Sure. Sit down," he said, motioning to a chair next to the actor. The actor sat down and Dino said to him, "What's your name?" I was impressed. Dino must really like this guy to take this much time and interest. "Fred," said the actor. "Good-bye, Fred!" said Dino.

Dino has always been a master at business dealings and negotiations, although they always seem to be conducted in a free-wheeling, emotional, and intuitive manner. He was certainly a charter member of the club that made offers you couldn't refuse. If Dino wanted someone, or something, he would get what he wanted by offering a deal that was too attractive to turn down. Reality would set in later. There was a popular saying that Dino considered a signed, sealed, and delivered contract merely the start of serious negotiations.

Whatever his faults, flaws, and deficiencies, Dino was and is, above all else, a consummate salesman and an unsurpassed showman. And a manipulator. I got my first taste of all three when we started casting *Barabbas*.

The name of one of France's leading, most respected actresses,

Jeanne Moreau, came up as a possibility to play an important female role. She was not only a fine actress but a star as well. I was highly enthusiastic and so was Dino. "We bring her to Rome," he said. "You make screen tests. Not for acting. For clothes, for makeup, for hair. And we invite newspapers. They love Moreau. They go crazy to see her. We get big publicity. It no cost nothing!"

He was right. We brought Moreau to the De Laurentiis Studio and the press went mad. There were about thirty reporters and photographers on the stage where I was to make the tests, milling around, crowding in on her, elbowing each other out of the way. It was almost impossible for me to reach her to introduce myself. Dino stood by, watching with enormous satisfaction. After almost an hour I got my assistant directors to clear the mob back, and I proceeded with the tests. She was wonderful. Even though the tests were purely mechanical, she became the character in the script the moment the camera turned. Even under those conditions her spiritual beauty shone through. Obviously she was ideal for the part. I was thrilled with the idea of working with this great actress.

Moreau returned to her home in St. Paul de Vence, in France, and we reaped the benefit of her brief visit. Front-page photo coverage, long articles about the picture and the genius of Dino De Laurentiis for managing this casting coup.

A week later Dino called me into his office. "We no use Moreau!" he announced.

"Why not?"

"I got better idea. Much better."

"Who?"

"We use Silvana!"

Click! The whole thing suddenly fell into place. Silvana Mangano, a great Italian beauty and movie star, was Dino's wife. I could never prove it, but I just can't imagine that the idea of using Silvana for that part had not already been set in his mind. He just couldn't resist the publicity opportunity that had presented itself. I had no qualms at all about using Silvana in the film. She was ideal, too. If she'd been suggested first I wouldn't have hesitated a moment in saying yes. But what rankled was the realization that we'd all been sold, exploited, and manipulated.

Yul Brynner was another case. Dino wanted him to play Barabbas (and so did I), but Brynner wasn't interested. That didn't daunt Dino. He made arrangements for me to meet a reluctant Yul Brynner in Paris and try to talk him into it. It looked hopeless to me, but off I went. I spent most of a day in hot discussion with Brynner, and by the time I left he had agreed to play the part. We shook hands and he said how much he was now looking forward to working with me. I phoned Dino in Rome and he shouted, "Bravo, Deek, bravo."

Several days later Dino called me into his office.

"We no use Yul Brynner!"

"Why not?"

"He crazy. He want a fortune. He think he really king of Siam."

"Damn! That's too bad."

"How you like Tony Quinn?"

"He'd be terrific."

"Bravo, Deek! I like. We use!"

A few weeks later a letter arrived from Yul Brynner. He was upset to learn that the reason for his not being in the picture was because I didn't like him.

Click! Again I couldn't prove it, but the only logical source of that misinformation must have been Dino. After the hype and selling he'd previously given Brynner it made him look better if the blame could be switched to me on a personal basis, rather than on Dino's reluctance to come up with the money.

Thirteen miles south of Rome runs an imaginary border that separates the more affluent North from the poverty-stricken South of Italy. The government created this boundary to help lure industry to the southern region, called the Mezzogiorno, by offering cheap land and huge tax breaks. Dino bought several hundred acres of grassland in the South, smack up against the line. It was here that he planned to build a huge, state-of-the-art movie studio.* In late 1960, when I reported for work, it was still just hundreds of acres of grassland.

Early one morning, soon after I started work on the film, I was taken out to see this barren emptiness. The production designer, Mario Chiari, and a small troupe of his assistants came with me. We looked over the rolling fields that stretched to the horizon, then Chiari turned to me and said, "Now where do you want us to put ancient Jerusalem?" I gulped and waved my arm in a vague direction. "Well, over there, I guess." "Okay," he said. "And where do you want the Praetorium?" A knot formed in my stomach. I'd studied the model of the entire city that Chiari had built in the studio, but this was no model. This was just *empty fields*! Once I made a

---

* Eventually he did build the studio. Officially it was the Dino De Laurentiis Studios, but everyone insisted on calling it Dinocittà.

decision, four hundred workers would labor for four months building this set. If I made a wrong decision now, it would be a disaster later. "How about over there, by that rock?" I said. "Okay," Chiari replied, "this will be the southwest corner," and he had one of his assistants drive a stake into the ground at the spot I'd pointed out.

So it went for several hours while we laid out the positions of buildings, streets, and squares to hold how many people? Three hundred? Five hundred? With horses? Chariots? You want a hill here? Okay, how high? We finally got through it, all one hundred multistoried buildings of it. I was wrung out, a little sick from nervous tension, but glad it was over. Then Chiari came back to me from driving in the last stake. "Okay," he said, "now where do you want ancient Rome?"

It's always a good idea to start shooting a picture when you can, with some of the easier scenes so the company has a chance to break in, get used to working together, solve the inevitable organizational problems. We began filming on one of our biggest, most difficult, and most complicated sequences: the spectacles and gladiatorial combats in the two-thousand-year-old arena in Verona, which was doubling for the Colisseum in Rome. Talk about "with a cast of thousands"—our first day's shooting broke a world record for the number of costumed extras, 9,115.

Knowing the reputation of the Italians for being something less than highly organized, I had my doubts about their ability to do the hairdressing, wardrobe, makeup, props, and God knows what else, for more than 9,000 extras, 300 gladiator-stuntmen, and an entire circus with lions, elephants, and bears, and have them on the set and ready to go by 9:00 A.M.

I was wrong. They did it. Commencing at 4:00 A.M., a fleet of seventy-five buses went to nearby towns and outlying districts of Verona and shuttled the previously hired thousands of extras to the arena, where they went through a production line and came out looking like Roman citizens of two millennia ago, perfect in every detail. Much to my surprise, by nine-thirty in the morning I was ready to line up with the actors. I called for Tony Quinn to come on the set. At nine forty-five I called for him again, and again at ten. By ten-thirty I was frantic. The extras were getting restless, the lions were sleeping in the sun, the excitement was draining away. Where the hell was Tony?

The answer, when I finally got someone to admit it, was dismaying but somehow not altogether unexpected. They had left his specially designed gladiator sandals in Rome! Now they were working like mad trying to mock up a temporary pair so we could at least get through the day. We got the first shot before lunch, which, any way you look at it, was something of a miracle. It seems the Italians (if this crew was at all representative) are extremely efficient down to *almost* the last detail.

Trying to use the huge crowd to its best advantage, I decided to jump out of continuity and shoot the end of the gladiatorial battle between Quinn and our chief villain, Jack Palance, where Tony is victorious and the crowd calls for Palance's death. Nine thousand people screaming, with their thumbs down! What a shot! The result was unexpected. When the crowd saw Tony, in response to their thumbs-down gesture, kill Palance, they cheered, got up, and started to leave the arena. All nine thousand of them. They thought the show was over! It took an hour to get them stopped and headed back to their seats.

On the second day of shooting we were working closer to the crowd and I could scrutinize it. I was looking for good character faces I could feature in various reaction shots. There were some excellent types, but one face truly stood out, that of an eighteen-year-old girl of stunning beauty. She was gorgeous. A knockout. I pointed her out to my assistant and told him I wanted her in every close shot I could possibly use her in. And I asked him to find out who she was and where she came from. It turned out she was the daughter of an officer at the U.S. military base in Vicenza.

It wasn't too long before Jack Palance also spotted her. And it wasn't too much longer that she moved in with him. Her name was Sharon Tate.

Before the picture was over there was another example of the crew's near-perfect efficiency. We were in Sicily, near the top of Mount Etna, with five hundred extras dressed as Roman slaves. Getting five hundred extras, plus the crew and tons of equipment, up there was no easy task. We had to shoot the sequence on a Sunday, since that was the only day we could get that many people from Catania, a two-hour, twisty, mountain drive from the top.

When we got there, the weather was terrible. Heavy overcast, with black clouds covering the black volcanic cinder surface. There was no definition between the sky and the ground. It was black on black with not enough light even to get an exposure. I had no choice but to wait it out. If the weather didn't break, and it sure didn't look like it would, it would be a very expensive shooting day down the drain, and we'd have to wait another week to try it again.

All I needed was one shot, but it was quite a shot. It would start on a long line of slaves snaking back to the horizon (if you could see the horizon), moving slowly toward the camera. We pan past the line and end up close on Tony Quinn and Vittorio Gassman, who are going to be chained together at the ankles. The camera tracks past them and zooms in on a white-hot, fiery, charcoal brazier and we see a pair of tongs pluck a rivet from the charcoal and then see it used to link the two loose ankle chains together.

I rehearsed the shot until it was mechanically perfect. If the sun ever did break through I wanted to be able to shoot it without any foul-ups. The only part I hadn't rehearsed was the actual riveting of the chains. I decided we should try that, too, even though we had a professional blacksmith to do the job when it came time to shoot. That was when we made a terrible discovery. They had forgotten to bring the charcoal!

Two propmen took off in a car at breakneck speed down the treacherous mountain road back to Catania. It was Sunday, every-thing would be closed, but they'd do their best. I called lunch.

Lunch came and went. I rehearsed some more, our eyes scan-ning the mountain road, looking for some sign of the car. We watched the sky, too. No break there. It was as solid as ever. I was dying.

It was approaching the time of day when, clouds or not, it would be too late to shoot, when someone shouted, "Here they come!" Sure enough, it was our car racing up the mountain. I looked at the sky. Unbelievably, a hole was opening up, there was a small patch of blue. The company was galvanized into action. The slaves ran to their starting positions. The car screeched to a skidding halt in front of us and the two propmen leaped out with a bag of charcoal. They dumped it into the brazier and two other propmen blasted away at it with blowtorches. The hole in the sky grew and sunlight flooded through it, lighting exactly the area we were using for the scene. I called, "Action!" The shot went perfectly. As I called, "Cut!" the hole in the clouds closed up and we were in near-total darkness.

Everyone was applauding and laughing, but I was in a fury. I let the prop department feel my wrath, blasting them up one side and down the other. The company stopped and stared at me. They looked surprised and offended. My assistant director came over to me. "Signor Fleischer, why are you so angry?"

"How can you ask me a question like that?"

"Well, how many shots were you going to make?"

"Just the one."

"Did you get it, *signor*?"

"Yes, I did."

"Was it satisfactory?"

"Yes."

He held his hands close to his shoulders, his palms up, a look of mock bewilderment on his face. "Well, then?"

Working with Italian crews has a certain charm. There's a preference for improvisation rather than complete preparedness that adds a quality of *commedia dell'arte*. And then there's temperament. Almost every crew member, sometime during production, will have his operatic "moment." A few come to mind: the production designer breaking down and bursting into tears when construction wasn't going as he wanted; my first assistant director chasing the head carpenter all over the stage with a hammer; the soundman asking the cameraman if he would adjust a light so the microphone wouldn't cast a shadow on the set, and the cameraman leaping at him in a blind fury, trying to strangle him; things like that.

And then there's a relaxed attitude that can be beguiling. The head of the crew came to me one day, looking very embarrassed. "Signor Fleischer," he said, "I'm terribly sorry but our union says that tomorrow we must go on strike for one hour."

"What hour will that be?"

"Whatever hour you choose, *signor*. Whenever it will be convenient for you."

"Really? Any hour I choose? How about lunchtime?"

"That will be fine. Tomorrow we strike for one hour during lunch."

Barabbas had its world premiere on Monday, June 4, 1962, at the Odeon Haymarket, in London. It was also the premiere of the theater itself. There was a glamorous, celebrity-studded dinner afterward at Quaglino's. Seated at my table were John Davis (chairman and managing director of the Rank Organization), Mike Frankovich (head of European production for Columbia Pictures), Sam Goldwyn, Dino, the Right Honorable Ernest Marples, M.P., Lord and Lady Morrison of Lambeth, and Tony Quinn. Scattered around the room were, among others, the Duchess of Argyll, Lord Balfour, the Duke and Duchess of Bedford, Paul Getty, Nubar Gulbenkian, Harold Lloyd, Sir Michael Redgrave, Peter Sellers, and David Susskind.

The opening of *Barabbas* also marked the end of my nineteen-month job for the Dino De Laurentiis Cinematografica. Since it was a biblical epic, it was only fitting that there be an elaborate Last

Supper. But Dino wasn't ready to let me go. He had another project in mind, called *Zackary*, the story of an American spy living in Japan just prior to Pearl Harbor. It was an interesting and unusual yarn based on reality. I signed a one-year contract, commencing August 15, 1962, to do the picture. My family was simply delighted. To them, Paris now seemed like a summer romance compared to their true love, Rome. The mysterious seductress had worked her wiles on them.

Work did not go well on *Zackary*. Dino seemed to have a staff of truly terrible Italian hack writers under contract. He gave them a crack at the story, with ghastly results. Then he got a great idea. He'd heard of a famous Japanese screenwriter (famous in Japan, that is) and thought it would be a fine idea to have him write the script. He brought him to Rome, set him up with a suite at the Excelsior Hotel, and told him to do his stuff.

About four weeks later I inquired as to how he was getting along, so a meeting was set up for me to go to his hotel apartment and review what he was doing. I arrived with an interpreter who spoke English, but not Japanese, to find the writer sitting cross-legged in the center of the huge, completely empty living room. All the fancy furniture, lamps, and carpets had been removed. Next to him were a large inkpot, several paint brushes, and a large, rolled-up scroll of paper. We did the customary bowing and smiling, then he took the paper scroll to one corner of the room and started to unroll it. It went clear across to the opposite corner and was covered with large, brush-painted Japanese characters. This was the script. We stood there admiring his handiwork. It would have made wonderful wallpaper. I hadn't the foggiest idea what it meant and there was no way he could explain it to me, since he spoke no English or Italian. After about five minutes of staring at the scroll the interpreter and I bowed and smiled our way out the door.

I don't know what Dino was expecting, but when I reported my experience to him, he threw up his hands in exasperation and said, "I fix! I fix!" Apparently he then found an Italian who knew Japanese, because shortly after that I received a page-and-a-half translation of what had been written on the scroll. It was pure gibberish. The writer was sent back to Japan and the picture was abandoned.

Dino was unflagging, and we started work on Upton Sinclair's *Lanny Budd*, followed by *Don Camillo*, *Salvatore Giuliano*, and *The Dark Angel*, each, in its turn, abandoned.

With four months of my contract gone we finally hit on a project that looked like it would see the light of day, *Sacco and Vanzetti*.

The fact that Dino took my suggestion and hired Edward Anhalt, one of Hollywood's most professional and respected writers, to work on the screenplay in Rome gave me reason to hope for the best.

"Hope," as the saying goes, "deceives more men than cunning can," and it surely deceived me. Anhalt finished the screenplay in three months, then left for California. The project languished. Nothing was moving ahead. There was no talk of preproduction.

Then something ominous happened. My paychecks stopped coming. At first I thought it was some bookkeeping slipup. After a few weeks I realized it was no slipup. Dino was on an extended trip to New York and there was no one else to talk to about it. I put the De Laurentiis corporation on notice that my contract was being breached, but on the advice of my agent and an Italian lawyer, I continued to report for work every day. After five weeks I stopped. The De Laurentiis dream was ending with a whimper. But not quite. On July 1 I sent them a legal notice that I was suing them for default of the contract.

Five days later, on July 6, I answered the door to my apartment. A small, shabby man stood there smelling like a process server. "Signor Fleischer?" he asked. "*Si, sono Io,*" I replied. He pulled a long envelope from an inside pocket, handed it to me, tipped his hat, and left. It was, indeed, a summons. I was being sued, it informed me, for default of contract for failure to report for work! Not only that, but there were damages resulting from my nonperformance. The amount? One million dollars!

The De Laurentiis dream was truly over, not with a whimper, but a bang.

There was a lot of hand-wringing going on in my home. In 1963, being sued for a million dollars was staggering. Even today it's no laughing matter. My Italian lawyer was very confident about the merits of our case, but Mickey and I were more than a little apprehensive. I was, after all, a foreigner suing Italy's most important producer. What if we drew a Fascist, or just plain anti-American, judge? There were still plenty of them around. It didn't make for restful sleeping, especially when you didn't have a million to your name.*

* Several years later, after returning to California, the case was about to come to trial in Rome. A judgment there would be valid in the United States. The idea of an unfriendly judge still plagued me. I offered to drop my case against Dino if he'd do the same with me, and that's the way it was settled.

The agony of our situation was relieved substantially when Providence once more intervened, this time in the form of a gentleman by the name of Philip Yordan. I'd known him casually in Hollywood and now he sought me out in Rome. Yordan, a tall, balding writer, smoked huge, Zanuck-type cigars; wore glasses that looked like the bottoms of a couple of Coke bottles; and behaved like the spring in an overwound, cheap alarm clock. Actually, he was no mean writer, with a list of credits as long as your arm, some of them quite distinguished, such as *Anna Lucasta, Broken Lance, The Harder They Fall,* and *God's Little Acre.*

He could never be described as an attractive man, but he had a string of several young, beautiful wives to his credit and boasted a child by each one. I once asked him why he got married so often. "I'll tell ya," he explained. "Once they start askin', 'Who am I?' I get rid of 'em."

At the time we met in Rome, Yordan was closely associated with Samuel Bronston Productions, which was making big spectacle films in Madrid. He particularly wanted me to make one for them because of their past experience with other directors. They all had spent far too much money. Yordan wanted me because I was able to handle very big productions and knew how to cut budgetary corners without harming the quality of the picture. It was to be an epic about the Sepoy rebellion called *The Nightrunners of Bengal.* The offer (and it was a good one) couldn't have come at a more opportune time. I agreed to work for the Bronston company.

O! I am Fortune's fool.

It was a very peculiar company, the Bronston company. The money they spent was prodigious, but there was no lack of it because they had found themselves a "pigeon." Perhaps "angel" would be a kinder word. Pierre S. Du Pont.

This worthy gentleman had signed open-end completion guarantees for all the pictures. He committed himself to making up any shortfall of money for financing the films and/or supplying the funds to complete the movie if it ran over budget. Open the wine! Bring on the flamenco dancers! Spend the money! It was fiesta time in old Madrid!

They had made one successful epic, *El Cid,* which did so well they built a large studio, with a huge back lot, on the outskirts of Madrid. Then they embarked on making more extravaganzas: *55 Days at Peking* and *The Fall of the Roman Empire,* both miserable failures. At the time of my arrival they were shooting *Circus World,* with John Wayne (also headed for disaster at the box office). Every picture ran well over budget, and Du Pont was there to pick up the tab. It seemed like these turkeys were laying golden eggs. One of the reasons I signed with Bronston was that Du Pont had given his usual completion guarantee for *The Nightrunners of Bengal.* My salary, at least, would be protected.

Yordan was in an enviable position. Even though he performed as a producer for the company, he wasn't one at all. He had his own company, United States Pictures, which had contracted to supply screenplays to the Bronston company. His staff of writers, recruited mostly from the Hollywood blacklist, were paid as little as possible. His rationale was that since they couldn't work anywhere else, they should be grateful for being able to work at all. He was the only wheel in town. The writers felt the same way. They would have starved without him, and they appreciated the work. The word was that Yordan sold these inexpensive screenplays to Bronston Productions for a healthy profit.

I went about my job of preparing the picture, trying to save money wherever I could. The resistance from everyone was considerable, even nasty. The art directors, Colesanti and Moore, went into a positive snit when I restrained them from building large portions of sets I knew I'd never photograph. The propmakers sulked when I stopped them from making hundreds of props I didn't need. And so it went, right down the line. Everyone was used to wallowing in unlimited funds. Economy and discipline were anathema. Nobody liked me except Sam Bronston's right-hand man, an obese *bon vivant* and Russian ex-patriot, Mike Washinsky. He liked the good things in life and seemed to have them in abundance.

The budget I came up with was millions of dollars lower than anyone expected. I turned it in to Washinsky, and he was delighted. It was just what he'd hoped for. Then he said something I didn't understand at all. "Don't talk about this budget to anyone. This isn't going to be the official budget. You'll get a new budget next week. It'll be quite different than this, a lot higher. But I don't want you to question it, just accept it. Hokay?" and he slapped me on the back in conspitorial fellowship. "If you say so, Mike," I answered.

Then I began hearing stories about Washinsky. He had, it was said, a percentage not of the profits of the picture, which would be normal, but of the *budget* of the picture, which would not. No wonder they wanted to beef up the budget. I would make the picture for the original price I turned in, but the surplus would be skimmed off.

I learned that on the previous picture the materials for set construction were so overordered that an apartment house was actually built with what was left over.

On the day I left Madrid to spend the Christmas holidays in Klosters with my family, six brand-new Rolls-Royces were delivered to the studio. For the use of the executives, I was told.

I never returned to Madrid. Word reached me in Klosters that Pierre S. Du Pont had, as he later put it, turned off Bronston's water. No more turkeys would be laying golden eggs. Happy New Year!

The money owed me by contract had not been paid. All I had received for my eight months work were my expenses. The main salary was to have started when we went into production. Legal actions were instituted by me against both Bronston and Du Pont. I had no choice.

There were some things I could never figure out about the whole business. Sam Bronston was one of them. He was a tiny, birdlike man with a ready smile and a mild manner. A mogul type he wasn't. His presence was hardly discernible in all the goings-on. He seemed to rely completely on Washinsky. I never saw or heard Bronston make a decision on his own. This question remains: Was he an innocent dupe, unaware of the stealing going on around him, or was he in on the plundering?*

The other puzzler was Pierre S. Du Pont. Could anyone be so unbelievably naive as to keep on signing those completion guarantees, picture after picture? Didn't he want to know what was happening to the money he was so generously supplying?

A clearer picture of Du Pont's concern about how his money was being spent comes from the deposition he gave my lawyer, Stanley Handman, in Wilmington, Delaware, on February 1, 1967. A limited partnership called Bronston-Bengal had been formed for the production of *The Nightrunners of Bengal*. Du Pont was a limited partner in that company.

> Q. Do you know of any activities of Bronston-Bengal, the limited partnership, other than what you testified to about the formation?
> A. No.
> Q. You don't know that there was any activity com-

---

* Phil Yordan kept his skirts clean in the ensuing litigation. He had a valid contract with Bronston to deliver screenplays for a fixed price. If that price was high, it was still perfectly legal, since both parties had agreed to it.

menced with the respect to the production of the picture itself?

A. No.

Q. Did you ever ask Mr. Bronston for any type of reports regarding production?

A. No.

Q. Did you ever receive budgets in connection with proposed productions?

A. No.

Q. You had no idea how much Mr. Bronston intended to spend in connection with this film?

A. No.

Q. Had you any idea of how the film was to be cast and who was supposed to play the leading parts?

A. No.

[Du Pont's lawyer, Mr. Costikan, asks the next question.]

Q. Do you know whether they had a script?

A. No.

Someone once said, if you want to know what the Lord God thinks of money, you have only to look at those to whom He gives it.

Things were not looking too great for me. For the past three years I'd worked on two films and, outside of expenses, had been paid for neither. Equally discouraging was the fact that I had had no screen credits in all that time. It's bad enough that in Hollywood out of sight is out of mind, but out of the country is even worse. I needed a job, fast. Something to put me back in the mainstream. The first person I thought of was my old friend, my colleague, my pal Elmo Williams. He was now the head of the Fox office in London and making a lot of movies. I'd saved his bacon innumerable times with Darryl Zanuck; now it was time to call in some markers.

I could have saved myself the trip to London. Elmo listened to my story the way an eminent surgeon listens to a patient's minor complaint, polite but distracted. When the director of his next production walked into his office, he hurriedly ushered me out.

I headed for California.

Things had changed in Tinseltown. And for the better. Dick Zanuck was now ensconced as head of production at Twentieth Century-Fox. I got no short shrift there. When I headed back to Rome I carried with me the treatment of my next film, *Fantastic Voyage*, to be made in Hollywood.

So the circle was complete. I was getting kicked around in Hollywood, so I ran to Europe, where I got kicked around some more. Now I was running back to Hollywood. Professionally, the sum total of my accomplishments after five years away was: one big, good movie; two small, fair movies; three pending lawsuits; and a partridge in a pear tree.

XVII

The Hotel Splendido, in Portofino, is indeed *splendido*. Located partway up a steep mountainside, it commands a spectacular view of the Mediterranean. It is one of those hushed, elegant hotels that seems always empty, even in the high season, when it's full.

Five of us had arrived from Hollywood earlier that mid-August morning, in 1965, to have lunch with Rex Harrison. He lived in Portofino in a villa not far up the mountainside from the Splendido. His American agent, Jack Gordean, had traveled with us and was now at the villa, along with Harrison's English agent, Laurence Evans. They were visiting their client while the rest of us waited at a table in the hotel's dining room. It was well over an hour that we'd been sitting there. Jet lag was setting in, and conversation was desultory.

I was the only one in the group who had never met Harrison before, and I was a little uneasy. This lunch, I realized, was crucial for me. It was the culmination of another lunch that took place in the commissary of Twentieth Century-Fox Studios in Los Angeles.

About ten days earlier Arthur Jacobs, an up-and-coming young producer, had asked me to have lunch with him. I knew Arthur casually and liked him. Everybody who ever met him liked him. It was hard not to. Jacobs had been a highly successful publicist and owned his own public relations company. He sold the company when he became an independent producer and, since his full name was Arthur P. Jacobs, he called his new production company Apjac. Almost immediately he and his company's name became synonymous and forever after he was called Apjac. I preferred the name Arthur, however, and mostly used it instead.

Arthur was a bundle of energy, vitality, and wild enthusiasm. His appearance always gave me the impression of a stick of dynamite enclosed in a thin turtleneck sweater covered by a handsome sports jacket. The impression was completed by a black, cigarette-sized cigarillo he was never without that looked like a smoldering fuse. With his raspy voice; close-cropped black hair; intense, deep brown eyes; and his publicist's persuasiveness, he could sell oil to Iranians. Besides all that, he had charm and taste.

We had no sooner sat down at our commissary table in the studio when Arthur led off in his classic PR style. "This is a lunch," he announced hoarsely, "that will change your life." There had been plenty of changes in my life in the past few years. What now? I wondered. "I want you to direct *Dr. Dolittle* for me."

That was quite an announcement. I'd known for months that Apjac was preparing a big musical based on the Hugh Lofting books about the tubby little English doctor who could talk to animals. After the tremendous success of *The Sound of Music*, Fox was looking for a follow-up, and this was it. *Dolittle* was to be the studio's major effort for the year. It never occurred to me that I would ever be considered to direct this project, since I'd never done a musical. Still, there it was, an offer. And not only an offer, but also the plum of plums. It took me by surprise.

Arthur went on to fill me in on some details. The leading role, the part of Dolittle, would be played by Rex Harrison. The tall, thin Harrison to play the short, fat Dolittle? Why not? I rationalized to myself. Anything is possible. Particularly if a star like Harrison wanted to do it.

In spite of his reputation of being a temperamental, ruthless perfectionist and impossibly difficult to handle, Harrison was a talent I would give anything to work with. This was an opportunity not to be missed. It wasn't really necessary for Arthur to go on with his pitch, since I was already well sold, but he continued. Leslie Bricusse, who had written, along with his partner Tony Newley, the hit musical *Stop the World I Want to Get Off*, and the smash song "What Kind of Fool Am I?," was writing the script, music, and lyrics. In fact, Arthur continued, Bricusse had already written and made demo recordings of several of the songs. Apjac was swinging into a full-blast, all-out frenzy of enthusiasm. Suddenly he jumped up from the table. "To hell with lunch. Let's go to my office and listen to the music. I can't wait for you to hear it," and then walked briskly out of the commissary.

I found the recordings wonderful, and the story line, which he ran through, enchanting. When he was finished he turned to me. "Well," he asked, "what do you say? You want to do it?" I couldn't believe my luck. There had to be a hitch somewhere. "Arthur," I replied, "I'm overwhelmed. When do I start?"

"Great! I knew you'd love it." We shook hands. Then he said, "There's one little problem, however." I knew it. The hitch. "Rex has director approval."

He could read my disappointment and concern. "Now, don't worry about it. I'm sure we can make it work. Rex wants to meet you, so you and I will go to Portofino next week and we'll bring some heavy artillery with us. We'll take along Bricusse, who's a fan of yours, and Jack Gordean. He's Rex's agent and also a big fan."

"Jesus Christ, you're bringing my entire fan club."

"Wait, there's more. We'll also take along Doc Merman." Doc was second-in-command of the production department at Fox. He was an older man, with a tough-as-nails appearance and a "deez," "dem," and "doze" manner of speaking. Underneath, he was a soft-hearted marshmallow and a cherished friend of mine.

"That's fantastic, Arthur, but Doc Merman? Do you think Harrison will even say hello to him?

"Didn't you know? Doc and Rex are great pals. Rex met him on *Cleopatra* and absolutely loves him. So you see, there's nothing to worry about. Still, with Rex, you never can tell."

"That's right." I smiled wanly. "You never can."

Patience, it has been said, is a minor form of despair disguised as a virtue. As we sat around the big table in the Splendido dining room waiting for Rex and his agents, I felt myself losing my virtue as my despair rose. My fate was in the hands of a man with seemingly divine right, and the longer we waited, the less reason I could think of for him to want me as his director.

It was now almost an hour and a half that we'd been sitting there. We'd begun to wonder if he'd ever show up, or should we order lunch and would he be offended if we started without him if he did show up. I was feeling like a slave in the marketplace waiting for the bidding to start.

We'd just signaled for the waiter when there was a commotion at the dining room entrance. *Maître d*'s, waiters, and busboys seemed to be moving in that direction, bowing and smiling and murmuring soft Italian greetings. Rex had arrived. An unmistakable aura of charm, grace, elegance, and urbanity radiated from the tall, slim figure. Loose, tan cashmere sweater over an open-necked sport shirt, sleeves pushed halfway up the forearms, tan twill slacks, tan

Gucci loafers balanced by a tan patrician face. A presence had entered and filled the room.

He swept toward our table, hand outstretched to greet his friends, his agents trailing behind, dimly visible in a misty wake of stardust. I rose to my full height of five feet, six and a half inches to be introduced, and Rex gracefully bent down from his approximately nine feet, eight inches to take my hand. "My God," I thought, "what if he doesn't like short directors?"

An empty place setting was on my left, and Rex slid into it. No one had much to say. It was an extremely awkward moment, tinged with embarrassment and somehow humiliating. This was, after all, not to be a value judgment. He could have screened some of my films for that. This was a director-judging contest and I was acutely aware of it.

A hush settled over the table while everyone waited to see how the prospective groom would react to the mail-order bride. Who was going to make the opening gambit? I decided it had better be me. "Rex," I said, "I hate to say it, but I've got something to tell you." The tension from the group was palpable. They all leaned forward to catch my every word. Rex turned toward me, his eyebrows slightly raised, a slight smile on his face. I took a deep breath. "I'm sorry," I said, "but I just don't think you're right for the part."

We stared at each other. Arthur was in my line of sight, on the other side of Rex, and I could see him pale. The social smile on Rex's face froze. But from across the table came a burst of laughter from Bricusse, who realized I'd reversed roles with Rex. A hint of recognition of what I'd done crept into the eyes I was staring into and the frozen smile started to melt and warm into a grin. "Perhaps you're right," he said, and we both started to laugh.

We had a marvelous lunch, full of wit, wine, and lasagna.

The Villa San Genesio was perched on a rock outcropping on the side of Mount Portofino, about a half mile up the mountainside from the Hotel Splendido. How Rex ever managed to get the place built, God alone knows, since the only access to it was an extremely steep and narrow goat trail with jagged boulders on one side and a sheer drop on the other. This rock-strewn, rutted, and potholed path was dangerous even for goats. But build the house he did, and once you got to it you found yourself in a villa of comfort and informality whose architecture gave full recognition to the Mediterranean that took up more than half the vast panorama visible from various terraces on different levels. Getting there, however, was not half the fun. It was all misery. There were only two ways to climb the path. One was on foot, with its dangers of sprained ankles, coronary attacks, and collapsed lungs. The other was far more dangerous: the dreaded jeep.

The road from the harbor of Portofino winds its way up the mountain in a paved and civilized manner and ends at a junction where it connects with the paved driveway leading east to the hotel. At that point the Harrison goat trail takes over. The goat trail terminated at the side of the villa in a complete dead end with no turnaround area, and that's where the jeep usually rested, facing downhill. This was a real World War II jeep, not one of those cushy limousines that are known by that name today. It had no top or doors or springs, for that matter. Seating was more theoretical than actual.

Using the jeep to go down the mountain from the villa, to either the hotel or the harbor, was always a hair-raising, kidney-dislodging, nerve-racking ride. Only Rex could drive the jeep, which he did with complete abandon, paying as little attention as possible to the steering and no attention at all to the brakes. It was a thrill-a-second journey on this iron bucking bronco, which Rex could barely keep from either lurching into the jagged rocks on one side or leaping into the abyss on the other as it rocketed headlong down the mountainside on a trail only marginally wider than itself.

The trip up to the villa from the port or hotel, however, was considerably worse. When you reached the end of the paved road, at the turnoff to the hotel, the jeep would be headed uphill. At this point Rex would turn the jeep around and, in reverse, back the rest of the way up the goat trail. Usually this was at night, after a few drinks and always with the accelerator jammed to the floorboard. It was a repeat of the downhill ride except in pitch darkness, with even more abandon by the driver, more erratic steering because of being in reverse but now augmented by the screaming of tortured gears and terrified passengers plus the knowledge of certain, imminent death. It was like riding with one of the Valkyries, only you were sitting backward on the horse.

All of this, of course, gave Rex his much-valued privacy, because few visitors were in good enough shape physically to take the walk up to the villa, and absolutely no one wanted a ride in either direction. Somehow we managed to survive several days of meetings, mostly by getting an early start and walking slowly up the mountain, firmly refusing rides at all cost. Rex approved of my being the director and we were ready to leave. However, he wanted a last chat with Arthur and me. We were in the living room of the Villa San Genesio, Arthur and I, catching our breath and trying not to pant too loudly, when Rex said, "Now about Sammy Davis, Jr. I absolutely will not have him in the picture!"

Bumpo Kahbooboo, crown prince of Jolliginki, was a delightful character Hugh Lofting had created for *The Voyages of Dr. Dolittle*, and Bricusse had incorporated him into the developing screenplay complete with songs and musical numbers. Bumpo was the son of a black African king and had been sent abroad to study at Oxford where, he said, he liked everything except algebra and shoes. The algebra hurt his head and the shoes hurt his feet. We all thought Sammy Davis, Jr., would be great casting, and Sammy had actually committed to play the role before the script had been finished. It was an unusual thing for an artist to do, but Sammy respected Bricusse's talent, had been a close friend of Arthur's for years, knew and liked my work very much, and was absolutely thrilled by the thought of acting with Rex Harrison. So it was all set until this sudden "No Sammy Davis, Jr.," edict was handed down.

"But why, Rex?" Arthur was genuinely puzzled, and so was I. "Sammy is perfect for the part. He can sing. He can dance. He's one of the world's greatest entertainers."

"That's it exactly," Rex shot back. "I don't want to work with an entertainer. I want an actor. A real actor, not a song-and-dance man."

We argued the point for quite a while, but we had lost this battle from the opening mortar burst. Rex was adamant. No Sammy Davis, Jr., and that was that, finished, over, period. Arthur and I sat there deflated, our banner in tatters. Rex paced the room for a moment, then turned to us with his most charming Cheshire cat smile. "Why don't we get Sidney Poitier?" he asked. "He would be splendid, don't you think?"

Sidney Poitier? What about all the singing and dancing? Acting, yes, of course, but would an actor of his stature play a secondary role and one not ideally suited to him? All of this Rex blithely brushed aside. Bricusse could rework the musical numbers to make them conform to a nonsinger. He'd done it for Rex, hadn't he? And there was always dubbing, voice replacement, you know. It could all be worked out, and Rex would be playing with a real actor and not an entertainer. The discussion, if it could be called that, finally worked its way around to a position where Rex was insisting on Poitier. If we didn't get Poitier he wouldn't do the picture. It was

Poitier or nothing. We said we'd do our best. We'd try to convince Sidney Poitier to play a character named Bumpo.

The whole Fox deal was based on Harrison committing to do the picture, and now the Harrison commitment was in grave jeopardy unless we accomplished a task that seemed more difficult than Jason stealing the Golden Fleece. None of us could see Sidney Poitier accepting the part of Bumpo in our picture. It was too ridiculous to contemplate. But contemplate it we must if we wanted to keep the picture from foundering.

The others left for California while Arthur and I went to New York. We had planned to do this right from the start. Our original plan, before we'd gotten Rexed, was to go to New York from Portofino and meet with Sammy Davis, who was playing the lead in a musical version of *Golden Boy*. It was the hottest ticket in town. Also, Herb Ross had done the choreography for the show and, since Arthur was pushing for him to do the same for us, it was a perfect opportunity for me to see his work. We were still sticking to the plan, although our goals were somewhat changed.

I was in my room at the Sherry-Netherland, in Manhattan, when Arthur phoned from his apartment on East Eighty-third Street the morning after we arrived. He had been in touch with Sammy Davis but didn't have the heart to tell him about the fatal development over the phone. Sammy had suggested that we see the show that night and have dinner with him later, and Arthur had gone along with the suggestion. Dinner, he figured, would be the best time to drop the bad news on the unsuspecting Sammy.

There was more to tell, though. Sidney Poitier, he'd learned, was staying nearby in New Jersey, and he had tracked him down. In fact, he had already talked with Poitier and had set up a meeting for that very afternoon in Arthur's apartment so we could tell him all about *Dr. Dolittle* and the great role there was in it for him. I had never heard anyone sound so depressed.

There was always a frenetic aura around Arthur, even in the calmest of times. Now, as we waited in the apartment for Poitier to arrive, he was almost manic. If his hair had been long enough to get a grip, he would have been pulling it. "I can't do it!" he kept repeating, "I just can't do it! How am I going to face Sammy? What am I going to say?" Arthur had been Sammy's press agent, and they'd become close friends. The prospect of hurting Sammy seemed to concern him more than what we were about to face with Poitier. He would have loved to be able to tell Rex to buzz off, get lost, go screw yourself, but he couldn't. There was too much at stake.

I wasn't looking forward to breaking the news to Sammy myself. Even though I had never met him, Arthur's dread had rubbed off on me. It would have been extremely painful telling him in any event, but Arthur's anguish was compounding it. "Why do I have to be there, Arthur? He's your friend, you tell him."

Arthur reacted in pure panic. "No, no, no! If you don't show up at the theater with me he'll know something is wrong," he shouted. "My God, he's sent me house seats. He'll know where we're sitting. If you don't come it'll be a disaster. Besides, you've got to see Herb Ross's work, don't you?" The doorbell rang. Arthur muttered "Oh, shit" to himself and went to answer it.

The arrival of Sidney Poitier changed the atmosphere in the apartment from gloom and foreboding to cheer and enthusiasm. We were like quick-change artists switching the Greek mask of Tragedy to Comedy in a flash. If we didn't sell the handsome, debonair, charismatic Poitier on the role of Bumpo we would be in deep trouble. Introductions weren't necessary, as we'd all met before. We thanked Sidney for making the trip from New Jersey to meet with us. It was no trouble, he graciously explained, since his sister lived in Manhattan and it was a good opportunity to visit her after the meeting.

Arthur summoned up all of his old press agent wizardry and, with me aiding and abetting, launched into his pitch. We told him all about the project and the character of Bumpo, but mostly we leaned very heavily on the point that we wanted an actor, a *real* actor, to play the part, not a song-and-dance man, not an entertainer. And we told him how much Rex wanted him and how much we wanted him and he was our first choice, our only choice, for the part. Then came the ear-splitting rendition of the score, accompanied by a running commentary describing the action, with Arthur and me playing all the parts. It was a solid gold, sixteen-cylinder pitch with all stops out and no holds barred.

Sidney sat immobile, chin in hand, listening. You could see him concentrating, visualizing, but his face was as unreadable as a professional poker player's. Our performance finally came to an end and we waited, drained, for a signal from Sidney. There was a heavy pause before he changed focus from inside himself to the two expectant clowns in front of him. "I like it. I like it very much." We still held our breath. "Yes, I'll do it."

He probably said a lot more, but I don't think Arthur or I heard much. We'd done it! We'd gotten Sidney Poitier to play the part of Bumpo! It was a triumph.

When the blood stopped pounding in our ears enough so we could hear again, he was saying something about how important it was for him to meet with Leslie Bricusse to discuss his character and musical numbers. We agreed and set up such a meeting for him and Leslie the following Friday at the Russian Tea Room. Leslie would have to fly in from Los Angeles, but that was okay with us. Anything was okay with us.

We shook hands all around, told him how thrilled we were, and Sidney left to meet his sister. As soon as the door closed, Arthur went back to his torment about Sammy Davis, Jr., just as though there was no Poitier interruption at all. I poured us a couple of drinks to celebrate our achievement and to bolster us for the coming ordeal that would begin at the Majestic Theater later that same evening.

We were just settling into our seats in the theater when a deep, authoritative voice poured over us. "Mr. Jacobs? Mr. Fleischer?" We both looked up, awestruck, at an enormous, menacing-looking black man resplendent in a richly gold-braided uniform that was straight out of *The Student Prince*. There was an unmistakable aura of Idi Amin about him. "When the intermission comes, please do not leave your seats. Wait until I come and get you." He bowed slightly and disappeared up the aisle. Arthur looked at me, a hint of fear in his eyes. I shrugged back. We had no intention of disobeying orders. Not from him, anyway.

The lights dimmed, the curtain raised, and the show began. From the moment Sammy made his entrance I knew something was wrong. It took a few minutes to realize what it was. He was playing the whole thing to us! Whenever he could manage a line, or a look, or a gesture away from the other players it came zinging right at us. It was as subtle as a derailed freight train. Each time it happened Arthur would groan as if he'd been hit in the stomach. At one point Sammy picked up a hat and ad-libbed, "I'm putting on my Rex Harrison hat," then beamed a dazzling smile our way. Arthur groaned and we both slunk down in our seats. A lot of Sammy's lines were being read with a British accent, either upper crust or cockney. It didn't do much for the play, but it had a hell of an effect on us. We were slipping lower and lower in our seats and people were beginning to look around to see where the groaning was coming from.

The first act passed with glacial speed and we didn't see Idi Amin when he came to get us, because our heads were practically resting on the bottom of the seats. "Mr. Jacobs. Mr. Fleischer. This way, please." The command in the voice could not be ignored. We pulled ourselves up and followed. He bulldozed a path through the crowded aisle, then across the packed lobby to a small door on the far side, which he held open for us. We scuttled in and he followed, closing it behind him. It was a small, round room, elegantly decorated with gilt moldings and furnished with spindly, gilt chairs. It was a room to which heads of state or royalty might repair to avoid the common throng in the lobby. In the center of the room a small, round table held two champagne glasses and a silver ice bucket in which a bottle of Dom Perignon lay chilling under a draped napkin. Idi went over to it, expertly popped the cork, and poured out two glasses. Replacing the bottle, he turned to us and said, "I will come back for you later," and left us alone in the gilded tomb. Arthur sank onto one of the chairs, put his head in his hands, and groaned.

The second act held even less joy for us than the first, and it seemed no more than a decade had past when Idi showed up to escort us backstage to Sammy's dressing room. It was a very small, L-shaped room with a tiny worn sofa facing the door, which was about three feet away. The short leg of the L was curtained off, and that was where Sammy made up and changed. Naturally, the greetings were effusive, and Sammy couldn't wait to get to the restaurant to talk about his role in the picture. He'd given it lots of thought and had many ideas. Also, it turned out, he was a much greater fan of mine than I'd ever dreamed. He'd seen every film I'd made and could remember camera setups from many of them. Arthur and I sat on the sofa while Sammy disappeared behind the curtain to get cleaned up and changed, but still kept up his description of a particular camera angle he greatly admired in *Compulsion*.

There was a knock on the dressing room door. Sammy interrupted himself to call out, "Come in!" And who should come in? The last, the absolute last person in the whole world we would want to meet in Sammy Davis's dressing room, Sidney Poitier!

There he stood, facing us, three feet away. I stared at him unbelievingly, stunned. The situation was rife with danger. If he mentioned our meeting about him playing Bumpo, the effect on Sammy would be devastating. On the other hand, if Sammy mentioned that he was in the picture, Poitier would surely conclude that the reason we were there was because we didn't want him and had gone to Sammy instead. The chance of losing Poitier was fantastically good.

Sammy came out from behind the curtain, saw who it was, and rushed over to embrace him. "What a surprise! What a wonderful surprise!" he said. There was no argument there. "Oh, I'd like you to meet my sister," Sidney said, gesturing to the very attractive young woman behind him.

Sammy kissed her, then indicated the two hapless figures on the sofa. "You know these guys, don't you?" "Sure," replied Sidney, holding out his hand. "Hi, Apjac, Dick." We staggered to our feet and shook hands with him and his sister. We were tiptoeing through a minefield, but so far, so good.

"I didn't know you'd be here tonight," Sammy said, resuming his dressing behind the curtain. "Why didn't you let me know?"

"Well, the whole thing was really spur-of-the-moment. I had some business in town today," he said, walking toward the curtain. I held my breath. This could be it. "And then I visited my sister," he went on, not mentioning our meeting, for which I silently blessed him. "We decided to try to see the show, so we went to the box office and by sheer luck we got a couple of last-minute cancellations." Arthur and I sat back down on the sofa. We were both breathing easier. The danger seemed to be passing.

"Listen, Sidney," Sammy said from behind the curtain, "I'd love to ask you and your sister out for a drink, but I've got to meet with these two guys about a part I'm going to do for them in *Dr. Dolittle*."

That was it. The whole minefield had gone off in our faces. This was total, complete disaster. After the song and dance we'd given Poitier a few hours earlier about wanting a real actor and not an entertainer, here we were in Sammy's dressing room and he's announcing that he's in the picture. Obviously, Sidney would assume he had caught us in the act, *in flagrante delicto*. I turned my head to look toward Arthur on my right. He felt the look and turned toward me. His expression mirrored mine. It was one of, "This is all a dream. It can't be happening." Slowly his eyes rolled up into his head.

I looked toward Poitier. What a magnificent actor. What great control. There wasn't the slightest indication of any kind that Sammy's words had any significance for him. He was completely cool and unaffected. "Don't worry about the drink," he said to Sammy. "I understand. Don't worry about it. We still have our golf date tomorrow morning?" "You bet," Sammy replied, appearing from behind the curtain, wiping his face. There was a flurry of good-byes and nice-to-see-you-agains, and Sidney and his sister were gone.

Dinner at the Italian restaurant was a nightmare. The whole

thing was very Mafioso. After all, they traditionally give an intended victim a nice dinner before they knock him off. By the time Arthur got around to the fatal moment, I was sick. I just couldn't sit there and see this wonderfully talented, delightful elf have his dream blown to smithereens. Arthur was so distraught and embarrassed that he found he couldn't break the news to Sammy in my presence. He asked me to leave them in private for a few minutes. I went to the bar and watched the pantomime between Arthur and Sammy in solitude. I could tell from watching Sammy's face exactly where Arthur was in the story. Marcel Marceau couldn't have been more expressive. By the time Arthur waved me back to the table the worst was over, but Sammy was hurt and very angry. He was going to sue Rex, denounce him to the NAACP, and give the story to the newspapers. Arthur was brilliant. He got him simmered down enough to agree to tell Sidney the whole story when they met in the morning to play golf, to make it clear that we were not replacing him with Sammy, but the other way around.

The following day Sidney phoned Arthur. Sidney wasn't angry. Sammy had explained everything and he understood the situation, but he'd decided he wasn't going to take the part. He wouldn't take a role that Sammy wanted. They were too good friends for that. It would be, he felt, disloyal. Arthur did his best to convince him otherwise, but Poitier was firm, he wouldn't play the part, no way, absolutely not. "Then I'll cancel your meeting with Leslie Bricusse," Arthur said. "There's no point in going ahead with that now." "Oh, no, don't do that," Sidney replied. "I'd like to keep that date. I really admire Bricusse's work. I've always wanted to meet him, so please don't call it off."

Arthur and I returned to Hollywood, licking our wounds and cursing our luck, while the studio was deciding what to do about the whole project. We were close to despair when Leslie Bricusse called us from New York on Friday. He'd had his lunch with Poitier at the Russian Tea Room. I never did find out exactly what took place, but it must have been pure magic. By the time lunch was over Sidney Poitier had agreed to play the part of Bumpo in *Dr. Dolittle*.

Leslie Bricusse delivered the first draft screenplay of *Dr. Dolittle* on October 22, and we all thought it was pretty damn good. The details of Poitier's deal were still being negotiated, but his price had been agreed on, $250,000. This was a not inconsiderable sum in 1965. Stars playing leading roles didn't do much better. Poitier was a star, all right, but Bumpo was not much more than a minor character who appeared only in the last third of the story. If we were going to spend that much on Poitier, the studio was determined to get its money's worth, so the part of "Bumpo Kahbooboo, crown prince of Jolliginki" had to be expanded. We thought up all sorts of expensive ways to enlarge the role, like a big musical flashback number of his days at Cambridge, a mammoth coronation sequence that takes place on a lake, with a hundred boats filled with revelers, singers, and dancers, that sort of thing. We pumped the part up until it looked like a balloon in the Macy parade. If, in the tradition of Hollywood, nothing succeeds like excess, then we were surely headed for a triumph.

You can get used to anything, even giantism, and after a while the grossly inflated Poitier part began to seem normal to us. The budget was beginning to look like a bloated stomach ad for Alka-Seltzer, but we hardly noticed it. We had Rex Harrison, we had Sidney Poitier, we had a wonderful screenplay, we had nothing to worry about. It was all consistent with the peculiar, self-delusionary insanity that unfailingly overwhelms the most levelheaded of film-makers. Maybe flatheaded is a more accurate word.

Everyone was eager to send the hot-off-the-press *Dolittle* script to Rex, who was just finishing another picture, *The Honey Pot*, in Rome. Apparently that production had not gone well at all. His wife, Rachel Roberts, had tried to commit suicide just before filming started, and word had seeped back to us at the studio that Rex and Joseph Mankiewicz (the writer, producer, and director of the film) were not getting along.

I had great misgivings about sending the script to Rex at that particular moment. Just getting through any picture is physically exhausting, but this one had a lot of emotionally debilitating problems, too. You didn't have to be a qualified psychic to figure what mood he'd be in. Even if we were sending the final draft of *My Fair Lady* he probably would have found fault with it. I pleaded my case with Arthur and Leslie and finally Dick Zanuck. Let's wait, I said, give him some time to recover from making the movie. Give him a few weeks. What difference does it make? Sending the script to him now is just asking for trouble.

No one agreed with me. Rex would love it. They couldn't wait for him to read it. O thou of little faith, they said accusingly to me.

Three weeks later I was in my office at Fox when the phone rang. It was Dick Zanuck's secretary. "Can you come over right away? Mr. Zanuck's waiting for you." There was quite a mob scene in Zanuck's office when I walked in. Arthur and Leslie Bricusse were there, and so were Stan Hough, the studio's production chief; Harry Sokolov, a lawyer and Zanuck's executive assistant; and Owen MacLean, head of casting. A cheerier group could probably be found as witnesses to a gas chamber execution. Dick was pacing the room much as his father did before him. When I came in he stopped and grabbed a cablegram off the desk and held it in the air. "He hates the script," he said bitterly, "and he's not going to do the picture!" Cassandra, I said to myself, move over.

"Has anybody talked to him?"

"I've been on the phone all morning with his agents and his lawyer and he's out of the picture."

"Well, shouldn't *someone* talk to Rex himself? Find out what bothers him?"

"NO!" Dick shouted, fuming. "I don't want anyone talking to that son-of-a-bitch. He forced us to get rid of Sammy Davis, who would have been terrific in the part, or he'd walk off the picture. So we hire Poitier, because *he* insisted on him, and he walks off anyhow. We've been jerked around enough. Fuck him! I don't want him in the picture. We'll find somebody else."

Finding somebody else wasn't all that easy, not after you'd gotten used to the idea of Rex Harrison playing the part. We went through the usual lists of available artists, but none of them seemed right, none of them was Dolittle. Bricusse had written a sophisticated, literate, urbane comedy that called for charm, warmth, and wit from the leading actor. It was tailor-made for Rex and didn't seem to fit anyone else. Apjac was getting more nervous by the minute because, once again, the whole project was in jeopardy. *Dolittle* was going to be one of the most expensive pictures ever made by Fox. If they didn't get an actor they believed in for the title role, who could blame them if they pulled the plug?

Just before Christmas Zanuck called Arthur, Bricusse, and me into his office. He was all smiles, full of enthusiasm. "I've got it!" he declared. "I know who would be perfect for Dolittle. Absolutely perfect! It came to me last night. Why didn't I think of it before?" We held our breaths. "Christopher Plummer!" he announced.

Christopher Plummer for Dolittle? I couldn't see it. I looked at the others. There wasn't any great reaction from them either. We were all, I suppose, trying to visualize Plummer in the part, but the picture wasn't coming in too clearly.

Dick Zanuck didn't seem to notice the signal lack of enthusiasm on our part and kept right on with his pitch. "He was great in *The Sound of Music*, and he's a wonderful actor, and he can sing," he said. "He'd be ideal! Maybe even better than Rex!" He was getting wound up, just as Darryl used to do, convincing himself that he was absolutely and completely right. "Well, what do you think?" he asked, looking at us for confirmation.

Arthur responded first. He was the producer, he had to. "Yeah, that's a good idea. That's a damn good idea!" he said, as though warming to the concept. "He could do it." It was, I felt, a desperate move on Arthur's part. We hadn't been able to come up with a suitable "name" for the picture, and here was the head of the studio rapturously endorsing Christopher Plummer. If Arthur disagreed, the whole project might go down the drain. Then Bricusse chimed in. "I hadn't thought of Plummer," he said, "but you're right, Dick, he could do it." Leslie didn't want to lose the picture either.

Zanuck turned toward me. "What do you think?" he asked. I just couldn't see Plummer in the part. He was a fine actor, he had all the qualifications, but to me he wasn't Dolittle. My being negative about him at this moment, however, could doom the production. I took the diplomat's way out, I weaseled. "Well, he's no Rex Harrison," I said, "but it's an interesting thought. He's a terrific actor and he could probably do a good job with the character. I'd like to talk to him about it and—"

I wasn't fooling Zanuck one bit. "I've got to know right now," he interrupted. "Do you want him, or not?" "Yes," I answered, without hesitation, "I want him." "Good!" Dick said with a big smile. "I think he'll be wonderful." I looked at Arthur and Leslie. They were smiling happily, too. I knew I'd done the right thing. There was no way that I would let either of them down. And maybe I was wrong. Maybe Plummer wouldn't be so bad after all. That old self-delusionary insanity was setting in fast.

The crisis about whether the picture would be made wasn't quite over, however. Plummer was appearing on Broadway in *The Royal Hunt of the Sun*, and no one had yet spoken to him about whether he wanted to star in our film. His agent, however, kindly pointed out to us that Plummer had a run-of-the-play contract. If we wanted him we had to be prepared to buy out his contract, or even buy out the play and then close it. In either event it was going to be an expensive proposition. But such is the way of Hollywood. A few hours before, Christopher Plummer couldn't have been farther from our thoughts. Now, suddenly, having leapt full grown from the head of Zeus, he was all we could think about and pay any price for.

Immediately after Christmas, Apjac, Leslie, and I flew to New

York to meet with Plummer and convince him that it would be sheer madness for him not to star in our movie. Arthur and I were seasoned hands at this business and we wheeled out the old Sidney Poitier routine. Our hearts may not have been completely in it, but we gave it plenty of soul. Plummer was no pushover, though. He wasn't at all sure that he was right for Dolittle, and even with the steam calliope going full blast it took us four long meetings before his defenses crumbled and he was ours.

The good news was flashed to the studio, Arthur and Leslie took off for foreign climes, and I returned to Hollywood in time for New Year's Eve, with a nagging conscience that what I had done was not right. Anyhow, there wasn't anything I could do about it, since we had made a definite commitment for $250,000 to Plummer, but I felt I had compromised myself and the picture.

The second week in January there was another big meeting in Zanuck's office. Jacobs, Bricusse, and the palace guard—Hough, Sokolov, and MacLean—were there. We were called together so all the final details of Plummer's contract could be tied down. The more we talked about him, the unhappier and more desperate I became. I felt there was something I should do about it. But what?

The meeting finished, we said our good-byes and started to troop out of the office, with me in the lead. When I got to the door and opened it, I realized it was now or never. If I left without making some last-ditch effort to derail what was happening with Plummer there would be no turning back. An actor I didn't believe was right for the part would be starring in a film I treasured, and I not only had done nothing to stop it, I also had aided and abetted in putting him there. I knew I was inviting the wrath of the gods, but I had to speak out.

I stopped in the doorway and turned. "Dick," I called to Zanuck, who was standing behind his desk, "I want to ask you something." Everyone stopped in their tracks. Dick looked toward me. "Do you *really* want Christopher Plummer in this picture?" I asked.

My eyes were fixed on Dick, but I heard some exasperated groans from the others and an "Oh, no," and a "My God." Dick's face went dead white. He stared at me for what seemed like a long time, then very slowly sat down behind his desk and put his head in his hands. This is where I get fired, I thought, kicked out of the studio. There was a heavy silence as we waited for him to speak.

Finally he did. To his everlasting credit, he said, "No!"

The palace guard went into shock. Arthur's and Leslie's eyes sparkled for the first time in weeks. Dick motioned everyone to sit down, looked at us all and our various expressions, and then did an astonishing thing. He laughed. He had a high-pitched laugh, almost a giggle, and actually said, "Hee, hee, hee!" like the characters in a cartoon strip. It was the kind of situation he loved, unexpected, seemingly impossible, and heady with the smell of a high-stakes gamble. He looked like he was thoroughly enjoying himself. "Well," he said, "what do we do now?"

"Let me ask you this," I said. "Would you take Rex back if he changed his mind?"

"Yes," he said and looked toward Arthur and Leslie. They shook their heads in agreement, as though they were in the grip of a violent chill.

"I'm sure he rejected the script because he was exhausted from making *The Honey Pot*," I said. "Let me get him on the phone and see if I can talk him back into it?"

"Okay, but I want you to make the call from this office. Eight o'clock tomorrow morning."

Harry Sokolov, the lawyer and executive assistant, finally found his voice. "But what if he accepts? What do we do with Plummer?"

"Pay him off," Dick replied.

Shortly before eight the next morning the same group was back in Zanuck's office, the only difference being that now everyone was equipped with an extension phone. The call was placed to Harrison at the Villa San Genesio, in Portofino, and when it came through I picked up my phone, and the six eavesdroppers in the room picked up theirs. It became without doubt one of the weakest phone connections on record. Rex was almost inaudible. He sounded as far away as he really was, and I sounded the same to him.

What should have been a relaxed, informal, confidential conversation became a series of hollered, yelled, and shouted statements. "How are you feeling?" I shrieked. "You must have been exhausted after the picture!"

"Yes, I was," the faint reply came back.

"Could that have affected your reaction to the script?" I screamed.

"I daresay it did" was barely discernible through the earpiece, but I could hear hope in those words, loud and clear.

"That was only the first draft," I hollered. "I'm sure we can make changes that will please you."

"I'm sure you could," the faraway voice said.

"Would you reconsider coming back on the picture?"

"What about Christopher Plummer? I understand he's replaced me," Rex responded from somewhere on Neptune.

"Don't worry about Plummer. That can be taken care of."

Then he asked a most surprising question. "Do you think they'll take me back?"

"I'm sure I can convince them," I yelled, my voice starting to crack. "I'll talk to Dick Zanuck and Arthur as soon as we hang up."

"Is there someone in the room with you?"

I looked at the mob of people all glued to their phones, hands covering mouthpieces, and then at Zanuck. He shook his head "no" vigorously. "No, Rex," I lied at the top of my lungs, "I'm all alone. This is strictly a personal call. No one knows I'm making it. But I just need to know one thing right now, before I go any further. If the studio calls you with another offer to come back on the picture, will you accept?"

"Yes, I will," the distant voice replied.

After we all hung up, the mood in Zanuck's office was jubilant. The only one who remained sober-faced was the lawyer, Harry Sokolov. "What," he asked, "if we get rid of Plummer and rehire Harrison and he quits again?"

Dick Zanuck, Apjac, Leslie, and I were unanimous in our response. "Oh, no," we said, "he'd never do *that*. Not after this. *Never.*"

Little did we know.

I became the go-between for Rex and the studio, shuttling back and forth from Hollywood to the Villa San Genesio. My relationship with Rex was strengthening and, as an added bonus, I was getting to know Rachel Roberts. I found Rachel, with her small, penetrating eyes, chunky pug nose, and too long upper lip completely captivating. There were stories about her violent Welsh temper and devastating battles with Rex, but I saw none of that. We had good times at the Villa San Genesio, and I always looked forward to being there. Rex and I would discuss and analyze the latest batch of script pages and songs and I would carry the results back to Apjac and Bricusse.

On March 7 the venue was changed to Rome, and I met Rex and Rachel at 8:00 P.M. in their suite at the Excelsior Hotel. We were going to have a drink and then go to dinner. By the time I arrived, many drinks seemed to have been put away by both of them, and the atmosphere was definitely not what I had grown accustomed to in Portofino. I sensed a certain hostility and tenseness between them.

No dinner reservation had been made, so I thought I'd show off a bit, impress the Harrisons. I would take them, I boasted, to a restaurant in which I was an investor, a part owner. It was called L'Elefante Bianco, an offshoot of The White Elephant in London. They knew me well there, but when I phoned I learned they were fully booked. However, for Signore Fleischer they promised a table for ten o'clock. I wasn't too happy about that because it meant almost two hours to kill before dinner with the heavily drinking Harrisons. Given enough alcohol, whatever was simmering between them could easily come to a boil. But I did want them to see my elegant restaurant.

The Rex-Rachel situation didn't develop as I anticipated. Something else did. It came out of left field when Rex said, "I hate the songs Bricusse has written for me and I won't do them." We'd been over the songs many times in Portofino and there hadn't been any major problems. Now, all of a sudden, he hated them. It was particularly alarming to hear him flatly refuse to do any of the songs that Leslie Bricusse had so artfully crafted for him (including "Talk to the Animals," which eventually won the Academy Award for best song). I listened to him nonplussed while he ripped into Leslie, describing how he was turning Dolittle into a nanny; composing banal music and lyrics; and, worst of all, how he was writing better songs for the other characters.

Rex was working himself into a frenzy of insecurity and jealousy. Now he not only refused to accept any of Bricusse's material, he also didn't want Bricusse. He wanted somebody else to write all his musical numbers. Once more we were getting into the thing we all feared so much, "ultimatum" time. I thought of Sokolov's words "What if he quits again?" and shuddered.

I tried reasoning with him, defending Leslie, but the conversation mostly consisted of my saying, "Yes, but—" Rex started suggesting other composers. "How about Comden and Green? Don't you think they'd be wonderful, Rich*ahd*?" (He always accented the last syllable of my name.) I started to respond, "Yes, but—" when he went on. "Or how about Flanders and Swann? They'd be splendid, don't you think?" I'd never heard of Flanders and Swann.

"Who?" I asked.

"Flanders and Swann," Rex repeated, looking shocked that I could be so *déclassé*. "Why, they're the hit of London. I'm surprised you haven't heard of them. They're doing a two-man show in a theater on Shaftsbury Avenue. It's all their own material. Extremely clever and brilliant stuff. Very sophisticated. They're the ones I want to write my songs."

"You may be right about them, but I don't know their work, and I don't know if Arthur or Dick Zanuck does either. Besides, they may not even be available."

"I've already checked that. They're available and they'd be delighted to do my music and lyrics."

"I don't know what to say, Rex," I said, trying to hide the rising outrage I was feeling about this high-handed treatment. "It's not at all fair to Bricusse. How can you do this to him?"

"Well, perhaps he can do some of the material," he said magnanimously, trying to show a heart bursting with charity, "but I want Flanders and Swann. I'll talk to my agents in the morning and have them phone Hollywood and tell Apjac and Zanuck what I've decided. Then you should go to London and talk to Flanders and Swann. You're the only one who knows exactly what I need in my songs." What he needed, I thought, was a good kick in the head, but that wasn't up to me.

The scotch bottle was almost empty by the time we left for L'Elefante Bianco. Vitorio, the *maître d'*, greeted me effusively and tried not to show how impressed he was with Rex. As he led us to our table, at the very back end of the room, I did what any part owner would do, I checked the house. L'Elefante Bianco was exceptional among Roman restaurants in that it attracted mainly Italian aristocracy and not many American tourists.

As we made our way down the long, marble aisle between the tables, I was pleased to see that it was full that night with an elegantly dressed, conservative-looking, older crowd. However, something started to happen that didn't please me at all. Rachel went into her basset hound imitation, a series of long, mournful howls and loud, throaty "WOOFs" for which she was justly famous among her friends. She would do this whenever the mood struck her—it didn't matter where she was. Apparently the mood struck her as she was sashaying down the aisle of this elegant restaurant. It did not augur well.

We were seated at a table that was so filled with sparkling crystal and gleaming silverware it looked like a display in a Sotheby auction room. Vitorio snapped out the heavy linen napkins, draped them across our laps, took the drinks order, and passed out the menus. Pasta is supposed to be calming to the soul, and as I studied the menu I hoped that Rex would order a large dish of it so that maybe I could start talking some sense into him.

Then it happened.

There was a horrendous, appalling crash of glass and silver smashing onto the marble floor. I looked up, startled. With her left arm Rachel had swept everything off the table in one fell swoop, except for a large, sharp dinner knife, which she now clutched in her right fist. Her appearance had undergone a Dr. Jekyll-Mrs. Hyde transformation. Suddenly her face was wild, nostrils flared, mouth twisted into a nasty snarl. Then the cursing started, a screeching torrent of coarse abuse directed at Rex, some of which I couldn't understand because it was either gibberish or Welsh. Whatever I had sensed simmering in the hotel room had now come to a scalding boil.

Rex looked as appalled as I was and sat there with both his hands flat on the table, staring at her. She tried to stab first one hand and then the other with the table knife, but he snatched them out of the way in time. She wasn't kidding. If she'd connected she would have pinned him to the tabletop.

I glanced away from the action and found that all the waiters had gathered together and formed a complete circle around our table. They were shielding the swanky patrons from this sordid display of Hollywood life.

Rachel started to make jabbing and slashing motions with the knife toward Rex's face and chest. He kept dodging and making ineffectual attempts to grab her arm, saying, "Rachel! For God's sake, Rachel," as though she were being an extremely naughty girl and should start behaving herself at once. There was no doubt, though, that he was terrified, and rightly so. Occasionally, just for variety, she would give the table a good, satisfying stab.

I knew this had to stop before either Rex got stabbed or the police were called and the *paparazzi* got hold of it. Slowly I moved around to the chair next to her and started talking quietly, comfortingly, joshing her along. "Come on, Rachel, take it easy," I said with a chuckle. "You don't want to get Rex's blood all over these fine chairs. All that blue blood will clash with the decor. We'll have to redo the whole damn place." I kept on ad-libbing and she started listening and calming down. When I felt it was fairly safe I put out my hand and said, "Now that's enough, Rachel, give me the knife." I couldn't have been more surprised when she gently handed it over. Just like in the movies.

I slipped the knife into my pocket and returned to my seat while Rachel lit a cigarette. The waiters disappeared. Rex grabbed my arm. "Good Lord, Rich*ahd*, how on Earth did you manage that?"

he said. "That was bloody mahvelous." "It's a way I have with women, Rex," I said, "but I could have done it quicker with a gun. Now, why don't we get the hell out of here?"

"Oh, yes," he said, "good idea. Let's do that."

As soon as we got on our feet I realized that Rex and Rachel could hardly stand. Both had been taken suddenly drunk. The predinner bottle of scotch and the rush of adrenaline they'd just experienced had done their jobs. I threw a fistful of heavy-duty lire notes on the table and started herding the Harrisons down the aisle of tables toward the entrance. Rachel pulled herself together, tossed the long, cashmere stole she'd brought with her around her neck, and haughtily staggered down the aisle, looking like Isadora Duncan as she ricocheted violently off the backs of several unsuspecting diners' chairs.

Rex followed through the gauntlet of irate local nobility, but he couldn't walk without support. He got it by putting a hand on the top of any well-coiffed, or barbered, head within reach, using it as a stanchion as he lurched his way out of the restaurant. Vitorio was not there to say good night.

Luckily there was a taxi parked right outside the door. I poured the Harrisons into it, handed the driver some lire, and told him to get them to the Excelsior Hotel. I have never been back to L'Elefante Bianco.

Zanuck and Apjac phoned me the next day. They had heard from Rex's agents and were furious. It was a slight case of blackmail. Hire Flanders and Swann, or else. Rex had the power at the moment and knew how to use it. So hire Flanders and Swann they did. They weren't giving up on Bricusse but were hoping that the new writers wouldn't come through. Only in Hollywood do you hire people and hope that they fail. I went to London and conferred with Flanders and Swann.

About a month later I was back at the Villa San Genesio with the Harrisons and, as luck would have it, a tape arrived from London with the first three songs. Rex was very excited and we played them about a dozen times each. Before we started listening to them Rex said to me, "I'm not going to make any comment. I want you to tell me what you think first." This was not a position I relished being in. If he loved the songs and I didn't, who knew what could happen? There could be a nasty argument, which he would undoubtedly win. If I tried to backtrack I would lose all credibility. Or I could be taken off the picture.

The songs struck me as being lightweight and "precious," the sort of things you used to hear in pseudosophisticated cocktail lounges. Next to what Bricusse had written it was like comparing a prime Stephen Sondheim score with an inept dilettante's imitation of Noël Coward. There was no clue as to what Rex thought. If anything, he appeared to be enjoying the songs. Rachel listened, too, and seemed delighted because they were about animals. The moment inevitably arrived when Rex said to me, "Well?" Let the chips fall where they may, I decided, and hope that they don't fall on me. I took a deep breath and told him exactly what I thought.

There was silence for several seconds while Rex thought over my comments. Then he looked at me and said, "I think you're right, Rich*ahd*. They do sound rather cheap."

Good-bye, Flanders and Swann. Welcome back, Leslie Bricusse.

As it must to all pictures, the time came when we ran into that hard wall of reality called "the budget." We were way over. A million and a half over. The picture was now menaced with the threat of destruction from opposite directions, Rex on one side with his Damoclean sword of quitting, and Zanuck on the other with his vow of canceling the production if we didn't bring the budget into line.

Getting a million and a half dollars out of a production is not a matter of simply cutting some lines here and there, or excising an occasional scene. That's like cutting some twigs off a tree branch when what is needed is to lose the branch itself.

We spent several days trying to solve the problem, but whatever solution we came up with made as much impression on the budget as trying to break into an armored car with a can opener. We couldn't get anywhere near the money until one day, while poring over the script alone, it came to me. A revelation! I had the answer! It was radical and fraught with danger, but it was the only way.

Get rid of Sidney Poitier!

We had made a mountain out of a Bumpo. The lavish production numbers, the additional songs, the added sequences we had force-fed into the screenplay were appropriate to the star quality of Poitier but not to the importance of the character he was playing. I did some quick figuring. If we got rid of all the extraneous nonsense we had been obliged to put in, and replaced Poitier with a good but less expensive actor, we could get the million and a half out. Great! But then again, maybe not so great.

The reason Poitier was in the picture in the first place was because Rex had insisted on it. No Poitier, no Rex was the way he had put it. We were now in a perfect *Catch-22* situation with Poitier. If we got rid of him, Rex would quit and there would be no picture. If we didn't get rid of him we would be way over budget and there would be no picture. We couldn't make the movie with him and we couldn't make it without him.

Arthur Jacobs and Leslie Bricusse wholeheartedly agreed with my analysis, but this was a dilemma worthy of executive dilemma-solving. Only Dick Zanuck could make the decision of which way to go. He didn't hesitate a fraction of a second. "Get rid of Poitier! Pay him off," he said. "We'll try to make Rex see reason, but if he won't, then that's it. End of picture."

The only good thing about this situation was the fact that the Harrisons were in Hollywood at the moment. Rex had been in town for the past few weeks for costume fittings and other preproduction chores and was going to leave for England in two days' time. If there was any convincing to be done it would be immeasurably better to do it face-to-face rather than over a transatlantic telephone connection. We all agreed that *how* we broke the news to him about Poitier was of the utmost importance. It was like approaching a skittish stallion. Any sudden move could cause some wild kicking and thrashing. No, we had to sidle up to him, nice and quiet-like, pat him on the neck, and slip a piece of sugar into his mouth. Keep him gentled down. Since I was throwing a farewell party for the Harrisons at my home the night before they left, it was decided that would be the perfect environment to slip him the piece of sugar, heavily laced with whiskey. Toward the end of the evening, at the *moment psychologique*, Arthur, Leslie, and I would take Rex aside and as casually as possible mention that Poitier was no longer in the picture and try to explain why. Not because of the money. No, no, no. Rex would never accept mere money as a proper reason. It was because the part of Bumpo just wasn't important enough to give it so much screen time, which happened to be true. Surely he would see the reasonableness of what we were doing.

Now, back in his office after the Zanuck meeting, Arthur was beset with some bedeviling concerns. What if Rex turned out to be not so reasonable after all? He hadn't displayed much of that noble quality so far. How do you break the news to Poitier that he's off the picture? This could be a Sammy Davis replay, and who needs that? Arthur hated the idea of paying off Poitier. Another two hundred and fifty grand down the tube. After Christopher Plummer, and whatever was paid to Flanders and Swann, it was getting pretty pricey. And all of it caused by Rex Harrison. He was living up to the nickname Bricusse had bestowed on him: Tyrannosaurus Rex.

It was five months since we had committed Poitier to do the picture, but his contract was still not signed. The main elements had all been agreed on, but a flock of minor pesky points were still unresolved. Arthur thought for a moment that maybe there was a way of getting out of the contract. A call to the legal department put that idea to rest. "No way," Harry Sokolov told him. "You've got a deal, like it or not." Arthur didn't like it. Being a producer, the thing that aggravated him above all else was having to pay off Poitier.

I had never seen an occurrence of *deus ex machina* except in a revival of an ancient Greek play. Now I was about to witness it in real life. You could almost hear the old stage machinery creaking when the messenger arrived with a telegram for Apjac. It was from Poitier's agent. It said something like: "There are twenty-two points still open in the Sidney Poitier contract. If they are not resolved within twenty-four hours we will consider the contract null and void."

Hallelujah and amen! Confetti filled the air. Twenty-two points still open? We will never give in to them! Never!

The farewell party at my home went according to plan. Rex was relaxed and enjoying himself. He even sang some of his songs from *My Fair Lady*, with Bricusse accompanying him on the piano, a rare and memorable event. There is no one in the entire world as charming and delightful as Rex Harrison being Rex Harrison.

Toward the end of the evening Arthur gave Bricusse and me the high sign, took Rex by the arm, and led him into an adjoining room. It was a crucial moment. The survival of the picture hung in the balance. Arthur came right to the point and told him that, with great regret, Poitier was no longer in the picture. He handled it beautifully, and Leslie and I backed him up wherever possible. We didn't know what kind of reaction to expect from Rex, so we were prepared for almost anything but what we got. He was completely understanding and *reasonable*. Yes, he said, he could see the problem. It was unfortunate that we had to lose Poitier, but the Bumpo role *was* tending to become a bit top-heavy. Yes, it was quite understandable that someone of Poitier's stature wouldn't want to play such a part after it had been reduced to its appropriate size. Perhaps a less stellar actor could bring it off. The collective sigh of relief given off by Arthur, Leslie, and me caused a ripple in the drink Rex held in his hand. It struck me that we were right back where we had started, all those many months ago in Portofino, when Rex had said, "No Sammy Davis, Jr.!"

He had just one request to make: He would like to know precisely how the Bumpo part would be changed. Of course, we couldn't do that this evening, but could I come to his bungalow at the Beverly Hills Hotel first thing in the morning and go over the script with him? Since he and Rachel were leaving the hotel at 9:00 A.M. for their flight to London, we agreed that I'd be there at eight.

The moment Rex opened the bungalow door for me the next morning it was clear that something was wrong. Very wrong. He was in his underpants, unshaven, hair tousled, face glowering. You could feel the anger emanating from him.

"The sewer rats are taking over!" he shouted at me.

"What? Who's taking over?"

"The sewer rats! They're coming out of the sewer and taking over."

"Taking over what?"

"The picture, of course! You know what I'm talking about."

"I'm sorry, Rex, but I haven't any idea what you're talking about. Just who do you think is taking over this picture?"

"Newley. Bricusse and Newley. They're working together. Ganging up. First they got Newley on the picture and now they've gotten rid of Poitier. The sewer rats are taking over!"

This was incredible. Anthony Newley was Leslie Bricusse's longtime partner and a highly talented actor, singer, writer, and composer. Together they had written successful Broadway musicals and many hit songs. Newley was ideal casting for one of the film's three leading parts, the role of Matthew Mugg, the cat's meat man, and we didn't hesitate in signing him to play it. Although it wasn't contractually necessary, Apjac had even cleared it with Rex, who voiced no objection at the time. But that was then and this is now.

"Newley's only an actor in this picture," I objected. "He has nothing to do with decision-making or anything else."

"Oh, yes, he does. I've heard all about it."

"From whom?"

"From Terry Rattigan. I had drinks with him in the Polo Lounge last night and he told me all about it."

So that was it. Terence Rattigan, a famous British playwright and old chum of Rex's, was also staying at the hotel. Out of pure, inebriated mischievousness he had concocted this mad theory and Rex had believed it.

"What in God's name does Terence Rattigan have to do with this picture? This is sheer nonsense."

"No, it isn't," Rex replied nastily. "Newley has crawled out of the sewer and joined his chum, Bricusse. He's helping to write the songs. That's why they're so rotten."

There is no one in the entire world as charming and delightful as Rex Harrison being Rex Harrison.

"Now, wait a minute!" I was beginning to lose my temper. "First of all, the songs are not rotten. They're terrific. Secondly, I've worked with Leslie Bricusse right from the beginning. I've been in on the creative process. I've watched him create and revise and change things in my presence. And I can assure you without a shadow of a doubt that Newley has not written one word or one note of the music."

"I wouldn't believe you any more than I'd believe them."

The words struck me like a slap in the face. Rex was going on about the sewer rats, but I interrupted him. "Let me say something right now," I said with controlled fury. Rex stopped and looked at me. "What we've been talking about up to now, about sewer rats, and who's writing what, all that is completely unimportant. What *is* important is my honesty and my integrity. If you don't have absolute faith in what I tell you, then we have no relationship. And if we have no relationship, then there is no possible way that I can work with you. You'll have to get somebody else to direct this picture." I picked up my script and walked out of the bungalow.

By the time I got to the path, a few yards away, I heard Rex's voice. "Rich*ahd*," he called. I stopped and turned toward him. It was a ludicrous sight, Rex standing there in the doorway in his drooping drawers and with his hung-over look. "I'm sorry," he said. "I apologize. Now come back in and let's talk about the script."

Rex was in and out of the picture three or four more times before principal photography started. He was like a Humpty-Dumpty who kept falling off the wall and each time all the king's horses and all the king's men would put him back together again. If he was this temperamental and fractious before we started shooting, I dreaded to think of what he'd be like after we got into production. I was expecting the worst.

My fears were groundless. Once the cameras started turning, in late June 1966, Humpty-Dumpty turned into a good egg. No more complaints, no more demands, just pure, creative professionalism. Not that the picture didn't have its problems. It was rife with them.

But they didn't come from Rex. They came from Newley, from Samantha Eggar, from the hundreds of animals, and from the weather, but not from Rex.

Even people outside the production dedicated themselves to making life difficult, particularly one young gent with the unlikely name of Lieutenant Sir Ranulph Twistleton-Wykeham Fiennes. This twit decided that the big, bad American movie company was going to ruin the charm of Castle Combe, the most beautiful village in England, where we were working. To protect the village from our destructive hands he planted bombs in various strategic places the night before we were to commence shooting. It was his idea, apparently, that the way to save the village from the marauding Yanks was to blow it up. Luckily the police ended this punitive expedition when they apprehended him and an accomplice on their way to the church tower where they were going to hang a banner that read, "Go Home Twentieth Century-Fox." Two of the bombs exploded the next morning, doing very little damage, but most of our first day of production was taken up with the bomb squad searching for and defusing the others. Lieutenant Sir Ranulph Twistleton-Wykeham Fiennes was eventually fined 500 pounds for putting our lives, and those of some of the villagers, in danger. English justice must have figured that a name like that was punishment enough.

Rachel stayed with the company through most of the shooting. She was, presumably, seeing to Rex's needs and comforts, helping him relax after a hard day's work on the set. From all outward appearances, she was doing her job well, and they both seemed content and happy. "It is only shallow people," Oscar Wilde said, "who do not judge by appearances." Well, we were deep people and believed what we were seeing. One night on the island of St. Lucia, in the West Indies, we learned that Oscar Wilde was wrong.

The Harrisons didn't stay in the hotel in Castries, with the rest of the company. Instead they hired a yacht and had it anchored some twenty-five miles away, in Marigot Bay, which was our shooting location. It was a nice, nonair-conditioned yacht and provided the convenience of not having to travel to and from the location every day. It also effectively isolated them, during those long, steamy nights, from contact with anyone except each other. There were two tiny hotels tucked away on the shores of the bay, but the Harrisons never left the boat. Perfect conditions for cabin fever.

Late one night the people onshore heard a terrible scream coming from the yacht, followed by a loud splash. They rushed outside in time to see Rex jump off the boat into the water. There was some thrashing about, then Rex climbed back on board. This was followed by the sounds of a loud, shrieking argument.

Over the following few days the story of what happened got pieced together slowly. Apparently there had been some fairly heavy drinking and a rather violent argument during the evening. Rex went to bed but was awakened by a terrifying scream from Rachel and then the sound of a body hitting the water. He rushed to the deck, where he found Rachel's shoes at the rail. In the water he saw her motionless body, still clothed in the dress she'd worn at dinner. After her previous attempts at suicide Rex had good reason to believe that she was trying it again. Panic-stricken, he dived overboard.

Only it wasn't Rachel's body, it was a log she'd wrapped in her clothes. For whatever pixilated reason, she had set it up to look like a suicide: the scream, the splash, the shoes on the deck, the clothed body floating in the water. Rex had just discovered the log when Rachel leaned over the rail of the yacht and started laughing hysterically. Rex failed to see the humor. When he got back on deck they had a wild screaming match.

All in all, it was a good way to help Rex relax after a hard day's work on the set. Better, even, than playing cribbage. It put him in a jolly mood for the rest of the week.

In April 1967, several months after principal photography on *Dr. Dolittle* was finished, Rex was back in Hollywood to do postproduction chores on the film. We didn't anticipate that it would be much of a job, just revoicing some faulty lines of dialogue here and there. However, after he screened the picture he had other ideas. He was dissatisfied with the way he'd performed all seven of his songs. The style he had employed during filming was the famous "speak-sing" that had become uniquely his own—it was his trademark. Using this technique, he spoke most of the lyrics, but sang some carefully selected words or phrases. We all thought he'd done a magnificent job, but Rex was not satisfied. He should have spoken some words he'd sung, and sung some words he'd spoken, he said.

The consummate professional. It was typical of him. All through the picture he had driven us crazy with his intolerance of the slightest deviation from professionalism that might affect his performance. That is why he thought Newley and Eggar were, as he put it, twits when they clowned around on the set and disturbed his concentration. And that is why, when he had to play a scene directly to an animal, he insisted that he have eye contact with it.

He actually couldn't do the scene unless the seal, or the pig, or the monkey was giving him its complete attention and looking him right in the eye. Sometimes he'd stop in the middle of an animal scene that appeared to be going well. I'd ask him what was wrong and he'd usually say with great frustration, "It isn't *looking* at me!" In spite of the time consumed in trying to satisfy Rex's demands, and the bruised feelings that sometimes resulted from his acerbic tongue, he was right. Every time.

It was very difficult for any of us to see how he could improve on the performance of his songs by merely singing or speaking a few words differently, but after my experience with him on the picture, I was a believer. If he felt that way, I was sure he was right.

When Lionel Newman, the flamboyant, profanity-prone head of Fox's music department, heard what Rex wanted to do, he exploded. It was a crock of shit, he insisted, there was no way it could be done. Harrison may be a fucking genius, Lionel raved, but that much of a genius he ain't. We'd be spending weeks of time and a fortune of money and we'd end up with nothing. The main problem, he explained, was that he had refused to record his songs to a playback like any other normal, fucking actor so that the tempo and the key would always be the same, no matter how many times the song had to be sung. But oh, no, that wasn't good enough for Mr. Rex fucking Harrison. He had to record the songs *live*, when he performed them on the set, and the tempos were all over the place. They varied as the mood struck him on every single take. Now, how are you going to vocally reproduce that *exactly* and change singing to speaking and speaking to singing as well? No way, brother. It can't be done.

We listened attentively to Lionel's expert opinion and then told him to go ahead and prepare the songs for rerecording. I can't remember what his response was to that, but I can guess.

It was going to take about a week to prepare the sound tracks for the fucking impossible job, but in the meantime the Directors' Guild Annual Awards dinner was going to take place. I had sent in my reservation for a table weeks before, along with the names of my guests. When the Awards Committee saw that I had invited Rex Harrison, they phoned me. Would Mr. Harrison consent to being the main presenter—that is, to present the award for best director to the winner? It would be the highlight and climax of the event. Naturally, he'd be expected to say a few words. Also, we'd have the best table in the room.

Rex very graciously accepted.

The Awards dinner is a formal affair. I bought a new tuxedo, and Mickey splurged on an expensive evening gown. After all, it isn't every day that you have the center table at such a prestigious event and have the main presenter as your guest. Arthur Jacobs, whom I had also invited, arranged for a chauffeured limo to pick Mickey and me up at our house in time to collect the Harrisons at six forty-five. The dinner started at seven.

The Harrisons were staying in Beverly Hills, on North Bedford Drive, in the old Greta Garbo house, which was being rented to them by Jean Negulesco, its present owner. The limo pulled into the driveway precisely on time, and Mickey and I walked up the path to the door. The house was about five minutes from the Beverly Hilton, where the dinner was being held. If the Harrisons were ready, as they promised to be, and the inevitable traffic jam at the hotel entrance was not any worse than it usually was for this event, our timing would be perfect.

I rang the doorbell and we waited. It was still broad daylight and we felt a bit foolish standing there in our evening finery. No one came to the door. I rang again and waited. Still no reply. I looked nervously at my watch. A couple of minutes had passed, we hadn't made a mistake in the hour. I rang again, this time keeping my finger on the button for what seemed like ten seconds and probably was. Nothing happened. We looked at each other, perplexed. Had they forgotten and were out someplace? We tried peeking through the windows. The rooms we could see into were empty. The minutes were ticking away and we didn't know what to do. Wait? Leave? Make a phone call from someplace? Phone whom?

We had just started to turn back toward the car when the door flew open, accompanied by a gale of laughter and shouts of, "It's the Fleischers!" "We thought we heard the bell!" "Been here long, dahlings?"

The sight that greeted us looked like a typical Peter Arno drunken society cartoon that used to appear in *The New Yorker*. There were four of them, Rex and Rachel, and Leslie and Evie Bricusse, joyfully soused and soaking wet. They had just thrown Evie into the pool, fully dressed, and then all had jumped in to rescue her. I didn't recognize Evie at first with her oversized, false eyelashes plastered on her cheeks and her long hair looking like overcooked spaghetti dangling over her face. Leslie, with his arm around her shoulders, was creating his own puddle as water poured off his cotton slacks and out of his tennis shoes. Rachel was hanging on to Rex's neck for support. Her bikini bottoms were barely hanging on, the tops had turned into a waistband. And Rex? He stood there with a happy grin on his face, *sans* toupee, in sloppy swimming trunks out of which hung his left ball.

It is a picture that lives in my memory: the dripping, drunken, disheveled merrymakers facing the two refugees from the top of a wedding cake.

Some quick, damp farewells were said as the Bricusses left and the Harrisons waved us into the house. "Make yourselves comfortable," Rex told us as we all entered the living room. "We won't be a moment," he continued as he and Rachel dashed up the stairway to the upper floor. Mickey and I looked at each other and shrugged. How they could be ready in less than an hour and a half was a mystery to us. I figured we'd be lucky if we got to the dinner in time for Rex to hand out the award.

In less than fifteen minutes they regally descended the stairs, immaculately dressed and coiffed. We hadn't realized that, at their behest, the studio had sent over what is known as a "wrecking crew": two wardrobe people to help them dress, two makeup people, a hairdresser for Rachel, and another to apply Rex's toupee. They had been there, waiting, since noon.

Our entrance into the hotel was as auspicious as I'd hoped it would be: plenty of photographers and flashing bulbs. If anything, being a little late burnished the glow of glamor. We just had time for a quick drink before they started serving dinner, and I was thinking how well the Harrisons had shaped up after such a boozy start.

I was wrong. They hadn't shaped up at all. Rachel wouldn't sit next to Rex but insisted on sitting several places away. It wasn't long before she started one of her bitter verbal attacks, shouting obscenities across the table. My God, I thought, this could turn into another L'Elefante Bianco. Luckily, the near-deafening music from the dance band covered her voice from the neighboring tables.

Apjac was sitting next to Rachel and tried to distract her, but that was hopeless. You could see that Rex was burning with humiliation, attempting to ignore her by pouring himself a drink and sort of carrying on a conversation with Arthur's wife, Natalie. But Rachel was determined to make a proper scene and finally threw a roll at him that fell short, bounced, and scored a bull's-eye on a water glass. Arthur stood up, took her firmly by the arm, saying, "Let's dance, Rachel," and whisked her onto the floor.

Rex's humiliation turned to anger. When she had gone, he got unsteadily to his feet, threw his napkin on the table, and said to me,

"I'm leaving!" and started to walk out. I leapt to my feet and grabbed him. "No, Rex!" I fairly shouted. "You can't! You're the main presenter! There are a couple of thousand people here tonight. It'll be a major scandal if you go."

He hesitated and looked around at the dressed-to-the-nines crowd. "Arthur's got her under control," I went on. "Look! She's dancing. She'll be okay when she gets back to the table."

Slowly, grudgingly, he sat back down and poured himself another drink. Mickey was sitting next to him, but I asked her to change places with me so that I could be closer to hand and better able to keep an eye on him. It was a good thing I did.

A few minutes later Danny Thomas, who was the master of ceremonies, stopped by and introduced himself to Rex. It was an effusive, loud greeting, and Rex rose and shook his hand warmly, a big, charming smile on his face. "I want to tell you how honored I am being on the same stage with you tonight," Thomas said sincerely. "This a great thrill for me." Rex laughed delightedly, thanked him for the compliment, and told him how pleased he was to be there. They shook hands again. Thomas said, "I'll see you later!" and left. Rex sat down.

He poured himself another drink, downed it, then turned to me. The happy smile was now replaced by an angry scowl. "I'm not going to be on the same stage with a fucking comic!" he announced. "I'm leaving!"

He started to rise, but I grabbed him by the sleeve and pulled him back down. "No! No! Rex," I said frantically. "You're not going to be on the stage with him. He's just the master of ceremonies. He's going to introduce you, that's all. Then he'll get off."

Rex poured himself another drink. And kept pouring them as the dinner progressed. So did Rachel, but she kept herself cheerily engaged in conversation with another of my guests, Edward Anhalt, an outrageous raconteur and Academy Award winner for the screenplay of *Becket*. The amount of booze being consumed by Rex worried me. He had become taciturn and sloppy in diction when he did speak. I didn't know how he was going to get up from the table, let alone make a speech.

Dinner finally ground to an end, untouched by Rex, and the awards ceremony began. That year the Directors' Guild tried out a new format. Instead of starting off with the television awards, as was usually the case, it was decided that this time the ceremony would commence with having the five nominees for best motion picture director come to the podium, one at a time, and be introduced.

Later, at the end of the evening, the final award, for best director, would be presented to one of the five. It was a simple enough procedure that was clearly explained at great length by Danny Thomas, but it led to one of the most distressing moments in Hollywood history.

The first nominee to be called to the stage was Mike Nichols for his direction of *Who's Afraid of Virginia Woolf?* It was one of those terrible, awful, ghastly things, but either Nichols hadn't been paying attention, or there was, somehow or other, a dreadful misunderstanding. Amid generous applause he bounded up to the podium, shook hands with Danny Thomas, and, thinking he had won the best director award, launched into a heartfelt acceptance speech.

When they realized what was happening the audience groaned and writhed in an agony of embarrassment. We sat there listening to Mike Nichols tell us how he never expected to win the best director award for his first picture and how surprised and grateful he was to us for bestowing this signal honor on him. I looked around the room. Some people were watching him dumbfounded, but most were either looking away from the stage or had their faces covered in their hands. It was one of the most painful blunders imaginable.

He had no sooner finished and left, to a smattering of confused applause, when Rex turned to me furiously perplexed, high dudgeon writ large across his face. "This is an outrage!" he declared. "I thought *I* was the main presenter. I'm leaving!" Again he started to rise and again I lunged at him and pulled him back down. "No, no, no! It's all a mistake!" I pleaded. "Don't go! You're still the main presenter!" and I tried to explain the inexplicable to someone who was already somewhat befuddled by drink.

As the time approached for the presentation of the main award I became more and more apprehensive. Rex hadn't slowed up on the scotch, his eyes were bloodshot, and he was visibly drunk. I doubted that he was able to stand up unassisted, and if he did stand up, could he walk? The image of Rex staggering drunkenly across the stage to the microphone horrified me. But there was an even worse image in my mind.

When the awards ceremony began and the dancers cleared the floor, foot-high brass stanchions connected by a thick, velvet rope rose automatically around the perimeter of the stage. It was a perfect trap for the unwary. Whether Rex was aware of the velvet rope didn't matter. In his present condition I could see no possible way for him to clear this hurdle. There was no doubt in my mind that he was going to end up flat on his face on the floor. That was the dreadful image I kept seeing in my head.

With growing concern I heard Danny Thomas make a glowing, respectful introduction of the main presenter, Mr. Rex Harrison. There was a huge burst of applause. The spotlight swung to our table and singled out Rex.

A dazzling smile, brighter even than the spotlight, lighted his features. He sprung to his feet, took a few light, supple steps to the dance floor, and leapt over the velvet hurdle with the grace of a gazelle. He then delivered one of the wittiest, most delightful speeches I'd ever heard. The crowd was enthralled. They loved it.

With all the aplomb and savoir faire that one would expect from either Professor Higgins or Rex Harrison, he opened the envelope and announced Fred Zinnemann as the winner of the best director award for *A Man for All Seasons*. Very early in the evening Rex had asked me to point Zinnemann out to him, since he had never met him and didn't know what he looked like. Now, as Zinnemann approached the podium, Rex flung his arms around him and greeted him like a dear and precious friend. He presented him with the award and quietly left the stage.

I don't know how he managed to do what he did. The only explanation I can offer is that it was a demonstration of supreme acting ability. It was a well-oiled Rex Harrison portraying a sober Rex Harrison. An Academy Award-caliber performance if ever there was one.

He never made it back to the table. Zinnemann finished his acceptance speech, the velvet ropes descended back into the floor, and the music and dancing started again, but there was no sign of Rex. We didn't think too much about it. He was probably being interviewed, having his picture taken with Zinnemann, something like that.

Meanwhile, Rachel was plastered and having a ball. Edward An-halt, arguably not the greatest dancer in the world, had her out on the floor. "You know," she said to him, "I was an Apache dancer." Anhalt sensed that something was about to happen. "Well, I'm not," he assured her. With that he found himself being flung across the room on his back. It caused quite a stir among the dancers. Evidently Rachel had earned a Black Belt in Apache.

Anhalt limped back to the table and Rachel attached herself to a new partner, a 350-pound photographer who happened to be standing nearby. She couldn't throw him the way she did Anhalt, but she got him moving faster than anyone thought possible. They didn't cut a figure on the floor, it was a swath. To add to the evening's entertainment Rachel now went into her basset hound imitations, howling, barking, and WOOFing all over the place. Their dancing, if you can call it that, became wilder and wilder.

The situation was getting completely out of hand when Doc Merman, the studio's assistant production manager and Rex's friend, came over to me. "We've got to do something about this," he said, indicating Rachel. "Where's Rex?"

"I don't have any idea. He's disappeared. He never came back to the table."

"Okay. Now, you go out and get the limo and I'll drag Rachel off the floor. I'll meet you in front of the hotel."

"But what about Rex?"

"Don't worry. I think I know where he is."

The timing was perfect. By the time the limo pulled up to the hotel entrance, Doc appeared with a limp, bedraggled Rachel under one arm. The crowd of celebrity-hunters looked on curiously.

The doorman opened the limo door. Inside was Rex, stretched out asleep on the backseat. "See?" said Doc. "I knew where he was. I've been through this before." He started to move toward the door with Rachel when Rex suddenly came awake. He looked around, blinking, then tried to get out of the car. "Oh, shit!" Doc said, as he grabbed Rex, struggling to keep him from getting out while still keeping a collapsing Rachel from sinking to the pavement. I got hold of Rachel and between us we managed to push her into the car. I got a quick image of a tangle of arms and legs flailing around on the floor of the backseat before Doc slammed the door. It all happened so fast the autograph hounds never even got to open their pads.

Doc turned to me and said, "It's all under control. I'll take them home."

"But I brought them, I should take them home."

"Let's not stand on ceremony. You go back inside and have a good time. Let me handle this." He got into the front seat, next to the driver, and off they went.

There was no doubt about it: If you wanted to have a stimulating, fun evening all you had to do was take the Harrisons to dinner.

Mickey and I hitched a ride home with the Anhalts.

A few days later, with great misgivings, we started to do the impossible: lip-synch Rex's *Dolittle* songs. Lionel Newman watched with a jaundiced eye as Rex stepped into a soundproof recording box on the Music Stage. He had already given Lionel and me instructions about how he intended to record, and it sounded more impossible than ever.

Lip-synching ordinary, spoken dialogue is difficult enough. It's usually done a few words at a time with the actor watching that bit of the scene projected on a screen. This piece of film is run over and over again until the actor feels ready to try a take. Almost never does he get a perfect synch the first time. Sometimes it takes dozens of tries. Then he moves on to the next few words. Revoicing a song is much more difficult because you can't sing a song a few words at a time.

When Rex told us what he wanted to do, Lionel looked heavenward, as though asking for God's help. Rex wanted to do half of an entire song in one piece. He was going to attempt perfect synch, stay on key, keep in tempo, and change the way he had originally sung or spoken certain words, all at the same time. "If he can do that," Lionel said to me, "I'll kiss his ass in Macy's window on Christmas Eve."

After two rehearsals Rex announced he was ready to try a take. Lionel looked at me as though the inmates had taken over the asylum. We started to record. After the first take we played it back.

It was perfect. Lionel was, for a change, speechless.

Rex felt he could do even better and asked for a second take. Again it was perfect.

Rex was completely wrung out. The concentration required was exhausting. He could only manage half a song a day, with a day off between songs. Each time it was the same: two rehearsals, then a take. He always got it right on the first or second try. It was a bravura, dazzling display of virtuosity and talent. It was Rex Harrison being Rex Harrison.

Four weeks later, when we finished recording, Lionel walked over to Rex and said, "I gotta tell you something, Rex: You're a fucking genius."

And so he was.

XVIII

There are some events in our lifetime that are so memorable that everyone can remember exactly where they were, what they were doing, and how they felt when they first heard about them. The John Kennedy assassination was one of those moments. The first lunar landing was another. And so was the December 7, 1941, Japanese attack on Pearl Harbor.

There are big pictures and there are *big* pictures, but when Fox decided to make *Tora! Tora! Tora!*, the story of that attack, it was going to be a BIG picture. The idea for making the film was Elmo Williams's, but Darryl Zanuck had adopted it as his own, personal, pet project and wanted to duplicate his (and Elmo's) triumph with *The Longest Day*, the film that saved Fox. Williams would be the producer.

It took Elmo five years to get around to offering me a job, but when he offered me *Tora!*, it was a doozy. By that time we were both back at Twentieth Century-Fox Studios in Hollywood and I'd had a rapprochement with Darryl Zanuck.*

It was to be a vast, complex project that told the complete and accurate history of the events, on both the Japanese and the American sides, that led up to the United States's violent entry into World War II. To ensure the film's evenhanded authenticity, the Japanese part of the film would be made by them, the American part would be made by us. This meant two complete and separate production

---

* While it may have been Elmo who actually offered me the job, he was a reluctant bridegroom. Dick Zanuck, as head of production at the studio, had no faith in the project but went ahead with it for Darryl's sake. Dick's main proviso, however, was that I direct it.

units—one in the United States and directed by me, and one in Japan and directed by Akira Kurosawa.

The task of preparing the production was almost beyond imagination. Research material alone filled several rooms jammed with filing cabinets. Most of it had been assembled by Dr. Gordon Prang and his staff at the University of Maryland. Prang had been appointed by General Douglas MacArthur as official historian of the Pacific war and had spent years collecting logbooks of every ship involved on both sides, as well as interviewing every Japanese and American participant he could find (he spoke fluent Japanese). The events leading up to the attack were broken down into month-by-month accounts for about five years prior to Pearl Harbor. Then they were broken down into daily accountings for the last year, then hourly, and finally into a second-by-second account for the day preceding, and the day of, the attack. All of this encompassed witnesses on both sides.

Every one of the hundreds of incidents in the film came from those files. Some information we came across was so incredible that we didn't use it because audiences might simply not believe it. During the attack, for instance, a Navy officer at Pearl Harbor saw some wounded sailors who had been blown overboard floundering in the middle of the channel. The officer dived in, swam to the nearest of the group, and got him back to shore. Then he went in a second time and did the same thing. The third time, he was tiring fast and could barely make it out to the last sailor still afloat. He grabbed him and started swimming. Halfway back to shore he stopped and said to the sailor in his arms, "I'm sorry, son, I'm exhausted. I can't go any further." The wounded young sailor replied, "I understand, sir," saluted, and sank beneath the water.

Production problems loomed large and intimidating. The three hundred fifty-three Japanese planes that attacked Pearl Harbor got there on six carriers in a thirty-three-ship task force. However, there was nothing left of the original Japanese Navy for us to photograph. With the exception of one destroyer, the entire fleet was on the bottom of the Pacific. The only way out for us was to build a complete aircraft carrier and a battleship (along with several other bits and pieces) out of plywood and have them set up on a seashore in Japan.

There wasn't much left of the American Navy either, since almost all of those pre-Pearl Harbor ships were now part of the Mothball Fleet. For the action we needed we had to build a set that was half of a battleship, sheathed in metal, that actually floated and could be towed through the water. That one set alone cost $1 million.

The only way we could possibly show the ships necessary for the reenactment of the attack on Pearl Harbor was to build miniatures. The Fox miniature department built models of nineteen Japanese ships and ten American ships. At three-quarters of an inch to the foot, the average length of the "miniatures" was forty feet. They also had to build the Battleship Row docks and the surrounding land areas.

Then there were the airplanes. There were no flyable Zeros left anywhere in the world. We rounded up twenty-eight Vultee AT-6's, "stretched" them six feet so they would be the same size as the Zero, and fitted them with the appropriate cowlings, windshields, and wheel skirts. Other aircraft had to be found that could be adapted for the Japanese dive bombers and torpedo planes. And all the other pre-World War II airplanes for the U.S. side had to be found and reconditioned: Flying Fortresses, P-40's, and North American VT-13's.

Finding cars from the 1941 era that could run and looked good enough to use in the Honolulu sequences became a major problem. One hanger on Ford Island, in Pearl Harbor, was converted into an automobile production line to repair, restore, and repaint the dozens of wrecks salvaged from various junkyards.

It took two years to prepare the film, and Elmo did a herculean, magnificent job. I had nothing to do with all that formidable effort. I was called in for the last six months of preparation before shooting began in Pearl Harbor. Elmo did all the hard work and I got to play with all the toys.

Kurosawa and I were supposed to coordinate our work before production started so that the Japanese and the American styles would intercut smoothly. I didn't honestly know what that meant. Was I supposed to tell him what to do, or was he going to tell me? It didn't sound too likely either way, but I was looking forward to meeting this legendary movie master. Elmo arranged for us to meet halfway, at the Ilikai Hotel in Honolulu.

Meeting him was a surprise. Whatever it was I was expecting, it wasn't a six-foot-tall, cadaverous, non-Oriental-looking Japanese wearing thick, dark glasses. He didn't speak a word of English, but his interpreter, Tetsu Aoyagi, a short, very Oriental-looking fellow, was completely bilingual, with a New York accent and the glibness of a Hollywood press agent. Elmo and I didn't trust him. We had no way of knowing if he was translating us or Kurosawa accurately.

276 • *Richard Fleischer*

The only time I ever heard Kurosawa speak anything but Japanese was in the lobby of the hotel one night when we met for dinner. My wife was there, and when she was introduced he kissed her hand and said, *"Buona sera, signora."*

We had a few meetings that were entirely about his half of the screenplay, but they were far from productive. There were several scenes that seemed extraneous, disconnected from the story. Kurosawa was gently insistent on keeping them in the script, but Elmo was argumentative and adversarial. It got a little embarrassing. I couldn't see how shouting at Kurosawa would change his mind. It came as a shock to me when Kurosawa agreed to make the changes. Maybe Elmo was right, I thought. Maybe this was the way to handle Kurosawa. Maybe.

We had one other meeting, this time in Darryl Zanuck's bungalow at the Beverly Hills Hotel, in Los Angeles. Besides Darryl, Elmo, and me, there was Kurosawa with his interpreter, and another man whom I'd never seen before who was taking notes. Darryl introduced him as his secretary. When Darryl saw me looking curiously at the notetaker, he gave me a surreptitious wink. The "secretary" turned out to be Darryl's interpreter, who was secretly checking up on Kurosawa's interpreter. He checked out okay.

The discussion finally got around to the question of how Kurosawa and I were going to cooperate directorially. The discussion came to an awkward halt. Nobody had any idea about how to do it. I'd been mulling it over for months, however, and put forward my concept. Forget about cooperation, I suggested. To try blending the dozens of sequences together was not only impractical but also a mistake. Instead of the Japanese and American sequences intercutting smoothly, they should do just the opposite. They should emphasize the differences between the two cultures. Kurosawa confirmed that the Japanese military would be shown as all spit and polish, formal, correct, obsessed with protocol and ceremony. On the other hand, I intended depicting the American military as relaxed, laid-back, a bit sloppy, and as casual as they could get away with. Everyone agreed that this was the way to go, and we stopped fretting about cooperation.

Because of Elmo's unbelievably detailed organization and preparation, the shooting in Pearl Harbor went more smoothly than anyone thought possible. Not that it was easy. There couldn't have been a more complex film to make. Almost every shot involved smoke; flames; explosions; planes diving, bombing, and crashing;

torpedoes running; hangars, planes, and ships blowing up; antiair-craft and machine guns firing; and actors acting.

Everything about this production was expensive. The Navy and the Army gave us nothing free. Everything we used we paid for. The hundreds of soldiers and sailors in the film had to be off-duty and were paid regular Hollywood extras' fees. We paid rental for space, ships, equipment. None of it came cheap.

Of all the expensive items we used, one in particular was the most surprising: tugs. The hourly rental of tugs was astronomical, and we needed them frequently. As one wit put it, "If the Japanese had attacked Pearl Harbor with tugs, we couldn't afford to make the picture!" Our accountants came up with an ironic bit of information: We spent more money reenacting the attack on Pearl Harbor than the Japanese had spent in actually doing it.

We had a large and wonderful cast of outstanding actors, but there were dozens of bit parts that I tried to cast with nonpros. Whenever I found a sailor who had the right look and could say a line or two, I used him. We were shooting on the deck of our half battleship when I spotted a great face: rugged, tough, broken-nosed, everyone's image of a real Navy sea dog. I cast him to play a tiny but funny role. He is on the deck firing a big machine gun at the attacking planes. Suddenly there is a huge explosion, and a great gout of water rises from alongside the deck next to his position, deluging him and everyone around him. He reacts by ducking, folding his arms over his head, and shouting, "Jesus Christ!" He turns, sees the ship's *padre* standing next to him, and says, "That wasn't cussin', Padre, that was prayin'!"*

Rigging water explosions was a difficult, time-consuming process usually taking about an hour. Sometimes, if you took too long to trigger it after it had been set, it could get waterlogged and not go off at all and you'd have to start all over again.

I wasn't about to let that happen. I was going to rehearse the scene over and over again so that the sailor I'd selected would be letter perfect and not forget his lines at the crucial moment. I explained to him how we'd practice the scene. "Now, first I say, 'Action!' and, just for now, you pretend to fire the machine gun. Then, when I yell 'BOOM!,' that's the water explosion and you react and say your line. Got it?" "Yes, sir," he replied. "Okay," I said, "let's

* This is a true incident taken from our research files. It was the same *padre* who uttered, during the actual attack, the immortal line "Praise the Lord and pass the ammunition!"

try it. Action!" I called and he pantomimed firing the gun. "BOOM!" I yelled, and the sailor reacted and said the line. "Good!" I said. "Now let's do it again." For the hour it took to set the charge I kept repeating the scene with him. He had it down pat.

The special-effects man signaled that he was ready. "Okay!" I called out. "This is the real thing! Firing the gun and everything!" The camera rolled. "Action!" I yelled. The machine gun started firing. Great! I pressed the button in my hand. There was a mighty explosion that shook the deck, and a huge geyser of water erupted out of the sea. It cascaded down in a drenching torrent exactly where I wanted it. The man at the machine gun sat there, staring at me, dripping, saying nothing. I waited. So did he, mute as a lump of meat. I cut the camera and walked over to him.

"What happened? Why didn't you say the line?"

He looked at me with innocent eyes and said, "You didn't say 'BOOM!' "

Working with the airplanes was the most difficult, nerve-racking thing of all. We had the AT-6's tarted up to look like Zeros. Something was always falling off them in flight. We'd constantly get radio reports from pilots on their way to a rendezvous point that said things like, "I've got to go back to base. My engine cowling just blew off," or, "Turning back. The windshield fell out." The planes were flown mostly by older American ex-fighter pilots who were now either heads of small airlines or important business executives. All of them were wildly enthusiastic aviation buffs, and they loved flying those little machines.

Next to me, during flying sequences, was a pilot who communicated my orders to the planes by radio. Only designated group leaders among the fliers could communicate with him; the others were supposed to keep off the air. Coordinating the groups of planes to come in at the proper height, crisscrossing with other groups coming in at different angles, and timing their action with explosions, flames, bullet effects, actors, and clouds that might come in and cover the sun at the wrong moment was purely ulcer-making time.

Whenever one of these complex sequences came off particularly well I'd tell my radio "talker" to tell the guys in the planes that I thought they did a hell of a job. Invariably this brought an immediate response from all the pilots, and my earphones would be filled with "Great!," "Wonderful!," "Thank you!," "We had a ball!" And always, after they all got off the air, the mystery voice came on.

There was a description in the script of the reaction of a Japanese pilot named Watanabe as he looks down on Pearl Harbor blowing up. It read, simply, "Watanabe smiles!" The phrase seemed to have captivated one of the pilots. We never knew who it was, but after every good scene we did with the planes, when all the voices had quieted down, the mystery voice would come on and say, "Watanabe smiles!"

There is a narrow pass in the mountains on the west side of Oahu, called Kolekole Pass. It was through this gap that one large group of Japanese planes flew undetected on the morning of December 7, 1941. As they came through the pass they made a sharp right turn and were on their way down to Pearl.

The morning that this scene was reenacted, our planes came through the pass in a perfect, tight formation, banked hard right, and found themselves faced with a small private plane coming right at them. All hell broke loose! The group broke up in every direction, like an exploding grenade. The radio was filled with the frantic shouts of the pilots: "Look out, Freddie, I'm coming up!," "Watch out, Charlie!," "Get out of my way, I'm diving!," "I'm banking left, I'm banking left. Look out!"

Finally things settled down. Nobody had run into anybody. Everyone expressed their relief. Then the mystery voice came on the air. It said, "Watanabe shits!"

During the entire attack on Pearl Harbor only one battleship actually got under way and attempted to escape, the USS *Nevada*. Once it started down the channel, the Japanese planes were all over it, machine-gunning and dive-bombing. Outside of the *Arizona* blowing up, this was the most spectacular naval action at Pearl Harbor. It was going to be our most difficult and, we hoped, most spectacular naval action, too. This particular sequence was going to be our *chef d'oeuvre*.

The plan was to tow our half battleship a mile up the channel, then, since it had no engines, take advantage of the tide and the current and let it drift down past our five strategically placed cameras. The channel itself would be filled with dozens of huge water explosions, synchronized to go off as the dive bombers released their bombs. Giant firebombs were planted all over the ship, to explode at certain specific moments. Scores of stuntmen were to be blown overboard. Groups of sailors would be seen scrambling all over the decks and superstructure, firing antiaircraft guns, machine guns, pistols. The air would be filled with shells exploding. The Japanese planes would be swarming, attacking from all angles. The cameras would frame the action so that only the built portion of the battleship would be photographed.

Every item was meticulously planned and rehearsed. The preparation took weeks. It was a choreographic job of staggering proportions. And it was dangerous, too.

The big day arrived, and the half battleship was towed to its starting position and tied off to a pier. Once the ship was set loose it would have to float downstream for almost a half mile before it came into camera range. Elmo and I walked to the set and did a last-minute check. We didn't want anything to go wrong with this shot. It would be next to impossible to redo.

Everything was ready to go. I sent word for the airplanes to take off and form up, ready for the attack when I gave the word. Then the order was given to wire the explosive charges. It was necessary to cut off all radio contact with the ship for fear of a stray radio signal accidentally detonating some of the explosives. We had to rely on flag signals to communicate with the set: a green flag for "stand by," a yellow flag for "cast off," a red flag for "action." Elmo and I started to walk back to the first camera position, almost a half mile away.

We were nearly there when we looked back. We couldn't believe our eyes. The ship was under way! It was floating down the channel, and there was no way to stop it!*

Then the nightmare started.

The circling planes saw the ship sailing down the channel and, thinking they had somehow missed their action cue, attacked the battleship. The special-effects men onshore, seeing the planes drop their bombs, started setting off the water explosions. The special-effects men aboard the ship began detonating their explosives. Stuntmen were being blown off the deck into the water. Sailors on board were firing guns and running everywhere.

And the ship had not yet come into camera range!

The battle was about half over before the first cameras were able to start photographing anything, but they got what they could. Elmo and I were ready to throw up. As far as we were concerned it was an unmitigated disaster.

But there was worse news. Tugs went out to stop the ship and push it back to its regular pier. Radio silence was lifted, and we learned that a group of sailors had been burned in a fireball explo-

* We never found out why the ship got under way. It could have been something as simple as someone merely moving a flag from one spot to another.

sion. In the excitement of the action they had run into a roped-off area where they shouldn't have been. By the time the half battleship was back at its berth, a fleet of Navy helicopters was ready to transport the injured to the hospital.

Elmo and I were devastated. We were worried sick about the injured sailors. How could we ever explain this colossal foul-up to the studio?

The film of what we were able to shoot was sent to the labs in Hollywood that night. The next morning it was screened by the studio executives. That afternoon we received a telegram from Dick Zanuck congratulating us on one of the most magnificent sequences ever put on film.

Ulysses S. Grant's biographer wrote, "Grant began a vast campaign that was a hideous disaster in every respect save one . . . it worked."

We had our difficulties and our problems working in Oahu, but we were making progress. In fact, we were well ahead of our shooting schedule. The word from Japan, however, was not so good.

In my mind I'd always questioned the wisdom of using Kurosawa for this film. It was neither his style nor his genre. It just seemed like bad casting, although it wasn't too difficult to see why Darryl Zanuck wanted him. Besides being an acknowledged filmmaking genius, a bone fide master of his craft, his publicity value was enormous. It would be fascinating to see what he would do with this film.

Even before shooting started in Japan, he was in conflict with the five American production people who had been sent by the studio to oversee how things were being run. Kurosawa felt this was a gross intrusion and an insult to national honor. He seemed to see a threat to national honor in almost everything the Americans did.

Since the place where Kurosawa was going to shoot his interior scenes, the Toeiga Studios, in Kyoto, was not quite large enough, Fox authorized the building of a two-story prefab structure that would serve as an administration building. Kurosawa hated it because it was built to American standards. It was an affront to national honor. He resented the doorways being six feet, six inches instead of the standard Japanese five feet, eight inches. You'd think a six-footer like Kurosawa would welcome not having to duck every time he went through a door. He particularly despised the toilet. It wasn't Japanese style, and he was affronted. The Americans, however, observed that he had his clothes made in England and that his personal car was a Jaguar.

His first real conflict with the unit production manager came when he decided to shoot all the interior scenes from 4:00 P.M. to midnight. The production manager couldn't understand this scheduling. Interior scenes are always shot during the day, during normal working hours. Decent American directors don't shoot at crazy hours like that. There was a bitter argument about it. Kurosawa won.

He refused to cast regular actors for all but the top leading roles. Instead he used businessmen friends of his. They weren't ordinary businessmen, either. They were heads of large corporations, leading industrialists. For sure, they weren't actors. The studio in Hollywood objected vigorously and warned him what the consequences would be. But go argue with a genius. The business barons stayed in the picture.

To establish a proper working atmosphere for his businessmen-actors, Kurosawa had special *Tora! Tora! Tora!* jackets and regulation Navy caps made for the entire crew. Everyone, without exception, not only had to wear them at all times but also had to salute the actors every time they passed one of them. He passed along the word that the Americans were not exempt from the jacket and cap rule. They confronted him and explained that they didn't think it would be proper for Americans to go around wearing Japanese Navy caps. Kurosawa agreed with them. They didn't have to wear the jackets and caps, but then they shouldn't come on the stage, either, he suggested. Naturally, the Americans ignored his suggestion.

The first day of shooting was memorable. Kurosawa had red carpets laid from their dressing rooms to the set, with an honor guard standing at attention lining the way.*

The scene took place in a small, white shrineroom on board a battleship. Kurosawa didn't like the shade of white. He had every member of the crew get a small brush, and they spent the rest of the day repainting the set a different shade of white. The studio in Hollywood didn't take kindly to this at all, and they told him so. But it was all part of his excessive preoccupation with detail. When he discovered that the books in the back wall of a set he was shooting

---

*It was said the reason he used the tycoons was to flatter them, make them feel important, in the hope that they'd finance his next film.

for another scene were not accurate for the period, he shut the production down for a day while this mistake was corrected.

While he may have been obsessed with detail, some of the larger things seemed to have eluded him. Like the 550-foot plywood battleship that was being constructed on the shore of a bay. The idea was to build the ship on land and have it backed up with water so it would look as though it was at sea. A very practical concept.

After Kurosawa picked the location, he never went out to check on the construction of the ship. But the Americans did, and what they saw appalled them. The ship was being constructed in such a way that it wasn't being backed up by the water, but by the hills and forests on the opposite shore of the bay. They became alarmed and took photographs of what was happening.

When they tried to show the photos to Kurosawa and explain the situation to him, he went into a fury. He refused even to look at the pictures. "I know what I'm doing!" he shouted at them and stalked off.

One million, six hundred thousand dollars later the battleship was ready, and Kurosawa still hadn't seen it. But it was a major event and cause for a celebration. He arranged to have the local mayor and many government dignitaries, as well as the press, attend the dedication of the battleship. They arrived in a fleet of limousines and were greeted with flying flags and a Navy band.

The ship was hidden from view by a large building that had been constructed on the site. Kurosawa led the group around a corner of the structure and got his first look at the ship. He came to a dead halt and stared at it. There it was in all its glory, backed up by hills and forests on the opposite shore. "It's all wrong!" he snapped at his assistant, "Tear it down!" He turned on his heel, got back in his car, and drove away.

It didn't get torn down. Not at that price. The studio in Hollywood sent him a message: You built it, you live with it.*

Work on the picture proceeded at a pace that even snails would ridicule. The amount of negative film exposed each day was minuscule. The filming was barely under way, and it was far behind schedule. The Hollywood studio was pressuring him, the production manager was pressuring him. His behavior became more and

---

* The only usable angle was straightforward, which faced the wide mouth of the bay. For all other angles, huge drop cloths had to be hung to block out the background.

more emotionally bizarre. One day, when he was questioned about a bill for something he'd ordered, he flew into a tantrum. His office in the offensive administration building became the victim of his anger as he vented his rage by kicking in its doors, throwing a chair through a closed window and smashing all the rest and demolishing all the office furniture. The detested, national honor-offending toilet came in for special attention: He destroyed it.

Probably with good reason, he started to believe his life was being threatened. There were a lot of politically important people in Japan who didn't want him to make this picture. He hired two bodyguards and a bulletproof limousine, with a chauffeur who looked like a sumo wrestler. His arrival for work each morning caused amused astonishment among the Americans. The limo would pull into the studio with the passenger section apparently empty. Suddenly Kurosawa would appear from below the rear windows. He had been driven to the studio lying on the floor of the car.

The atmosphere on the set was anything but happy. People were constantly running from the stage, weeping. Finally there was an incident that brought everything to a head. The stages in the Toeiga Studios had dirt floors, which meant that sets had to be built on platforms. During the preparation of a particular scene, before the director showed up, it was found necessary that someone crawl under the platform to make a simple electrical connection. Kurosawa's assistant of many years volunteered. Not wanting to soil his *Tora!* jacket and cap while crawling around in the dirt, he took them off. The job completed, he emerged from under the platform just as Kurosawa walked on the set. Kurosawa was outraged. Here was his own assistant, in spite of his specific orders, jacket and capless! His wrath knew no bounds. He rolled the script he held in his hands into a club and proceeded to beat the offending culprit about the head. When he finished, he handed the rolled-up manuscript to the hapless scofflaw and ordered him to beat every member of the crew with it. When the assistant refused, Kurosawa said to him, "You'll never be a great director unless you understand discipline!" and fired him on the spot.

The mood on the set turned ugly. The crew hated Kurosawa and became threatening. His bodyguards had to take him off the stage.

Word of the goings-on seeped out to the Japanese media. They had a field day: banner headlines and front-page stories. Darryl Zanuck (accompanied by his latest girlfriend, Genevieve Gilles) flew over to put pressure on him. When Darryl walked on the set, Kuro-

sawa called a halt to production while they, along with an interpreter, held a meeting on the stage. They huddled for a long time,
and when it broke up, one of the Americans loitering nearby heard
Darryl say, "You can have anything you want!" Not a very effective
way of bringing Kurosawa to heel.

Darryl left, and Dick Zanuck and the studio production head,
Stan Hough, showed up. Kurosawa wouldn't even meet with them.
They departed, and soon after, Elmo Williams appeared. He had
been given the hatchet job of firing one of the world's greatest
directors. The deed was done.*

The blame for this catastrophic turn of events lay on both sides,
although Twentieth Century-Fox must carry most of the burden.
Kurosawa had always been his own, completely autonomous, boss.
Now he had many bosses, all of whom he surely felt were his inferi-
ors, all of whom were tearing away at his autonomy, his dignity. His
way of operating was totally unlike anything they were used to. He
had a different set of rules: his own. Kurosawa was a master precisely because he went his own way. They made a major mistake in
how they treated him. It was folly to try to squeeze him into the
Hollywood studio mold. You don't hire Kurosawa to give you just
another movie or even behave like just another director.

You don't hire him to make you go bankrupt, either. I don't
know why Kurosawa took the assignment in the first place, but the
use of his businessmen friends as actors certainly casts some doubts
on his motives. Perhaps when he was faced with the reality of actually making the film his heart may not have been in it. As H. L.
Mencken put it, "Conscience is the inner voice that warns us somebody may be looking." On top of that he couldn't cope with the
pressure from Darryl, and the production manager, and Elmo, and
Dick Zanuck, and the cables from the studio, and the clamoring of
the media. It was probably something he'd never faced before in his
career, and it was all too much.

It wasn't easy to replace Kurosawa. Japanese directors of any
stature wouldn't think of stepping into his shoes. Two commercial
directors, Toshio Masuda and Kinji Fukasaku, took over.

It is interesting to speculate on what Kurosawa's part of the
movie would have looked like if he'd been left alone. He may have
turned out one of his masterpieces and made the American section
look terrible by comparison.

The only indication of what might have been was the one

* The official story given to the media was that illness forced him off the picture.

salvageable piece of film he shot that was used in the movie. It was a short scene about the American ambassador in the U.S. embassy in Tokyo, and it was done in English.

It is the worst scene in the picture.

Epilogue

The Sorrento-Naples International Film Festival is held each September in Italy. It is a big, gala affair, with lots of media and celebrities. *Tora! Tora! Tora!* was selected by the festival people as one of the films that would be in competition for the grand prize. Fox considered it important enough to organize an elaborate junket and brought Elmo and me, the two Japanese directors, and various and sundry studio executives, dignitaries, public relations people, and anyone else who didn't seem to be busy at the moment, to the festival.

The awards were to be announced and awarded at a black-tie soiree at the theater in the Royal Palace in Naples. Elmo and I and our wives were in the throng shuffling into the glittering auditorium on the big night. As we came through the doorway, one of the festival officials took my arm and pulled me away from the crowd. "This way, Signore Fleischer, you must come with me," he said as he guided me through a doorway. I had no idea what it was all about. We walked down a passageway that led backstage, where a small group of recognizable movie personalities were gathered. He told me to wait, and he left.

The ceremonies started. People made speeches, awards were awarded, and the backstage group thinned out as they made stage appearances, until I was left alone. I thought that they'd forgotten me.

Then came the announcement: *Tora! Tora! Tora!* was the winner of the grand prize and, as director of the picture, I was to receive the award. I didn't think I heard correctly when they said "receive" the award. I thought they must have meant "accept" the award. But no. When I came onstage and looked at the plaque at the base of the statuette that was handed to me, there was my name and no other.

It struck me immediately that this was wrong. If anyone should have received an award, it should have been Elmo. I looked down where he was sitting among the enthusiastically applauding audience, and it was clear he thought so, too. There was a smile on everyone's face in that auditorium except his.

Afterward I explained to him how badly I felt and how inequitable the award was. I reminded him of something he already knew, that it was the typical European fashion to give directors more credit than they usually deserved. I also told him that the whole business of even accepting the award was a total surprise to me. If I'd known about it beforehand, I would have insisted that he receive it, or I would have refused to go at all. Elmo listened quietly and said he understood.

When we returned to the studio in Hollywood, Elmo's attitude toward me became decidedly frosty. In fact, he stopped talking to me altogether. He wouldn't even return my phone calls. I wrote him a letter once again explaining that what happened in Naples wasn't my fault. Also, I mentioned that if it wasn't that incident that brought on the present situation, if it was something I'd done, either deliberately or inadvertently, I wished he'd tell me what it was so we could get it straightened out. He never acknowledged my letter.

So everything had come full circle. We all seemed to be players in Arthur Schnitzler's *La Ronde*. When I returned to Hollywood after my five-year European stay, Elmo and I were still friends, but Darryl and I weren't talking. Now Darryl and I were friends and Elmo and I weren't talking.

XIX

Think of Edward G. Robinson and you think of a short, tough-as-nails gangster, dapper in a double-breasted suit, grim-visaged, speaking in a whining, nasal voice, saying something like, "Yeahh! Yeahh! All right, you guyyys!" Think like that and you think wrong. That wasn't Eddie at all, see? That was the actor, not the real guy. The real guy was . . . like . . . lovable, you know what I mean? And I gotta tell ya, I loved Eddie Robinson.

We were preparing to shoot *Soylent Green* at Metro-Goldwyn-Mayer Studios in 1973. Charlton Heston was already committed to play the lead, and we all wanted Robinson to portray his mentor/sidekick. But there were difficulties. One of them was his health. It was fragile. He was eighty, and he had cancer. We couldn't hire him unless we were able to get health insurance for him, and he'd been turned down by the insurers in the recent past.

Another difficulty was the money. He wanted more than Metro was willing to pay. They offered him a lower fee, with a deferment for the remainder. Eddie's answer to that was, "At my age, I'm not sure I'd be around to collect it." Metro came up with the money. Somehow or other the health insurance was arranged (or Metro went without the insurance; I don't know).

Everyone was delighted, most of all Robinson. After all those years, the Hollywood blacklist still haunted him. For a long time moviemakers didn't want to know anything about him. He was a pariah. The boycott eased somewhat over time and he started getting parts in small, completely undistinguished pictures. He hated what he was doing, but he loved doing it. Acting was his life. He was happiest on a sound stage. Now, what with his illness and the continued resistance of many producers, he hadn't worked in three years. *Soylent Green* was his salvation. He loved the script. It was not only a wonderful role in an important film but, as he kept telling his wife, Jane, it was *about* something. He knew he was dying and he knew this would be his last picture, and he was happy. He was going to exit, if not laughing, at least smiling.

Once he was set to do the picture, the press finally got around to giving him the attention he'd deserved but hadn't been getting. The trade and public newspapers carried story after story. He had been rediscovered. Eddie was sadly impressed with what was happening. He said to his wife, "Now I know I'm dying. I've never gotten so much press."

I had never met Robinson before working on the film; in fact, I'd never even seen him in person. One day, shortly before we started production, I was on the stage making tests when the producer brought Eddie over to meet me. As soon as he walked in, all work stopped. The blasé, know-it-all, seen-it-all Hollywood crew stared at him, gawking like a bunch of tourists. Then they crowded around him to shake his hand, most of them trying to remind him of some picture or other that they'd been on with him.

The producer finally broke him loose and brought him over to me for introductions. Eddie grabbed my hand and pulled me down to him so he could whisper in my ear. "Well," he said conspiratorially, "I'm still fooling them!"

Love at first sight.

Eddie had another physical problem: his hearing. He was about a pebble away from being stone deaf. Still, if you got up real close and spoke directly into his ear, he could hear remarkably well. It was distance that defeated him.

The first scene I had to do with Eddie was a conference room sequence. He sat at the head of a long table with five very elderly actors seated on each side. Each of them had to address some question to Eddie while he was studying the contents of a huge volume on the table in front of him. He couldn't see who was speaking because he had to keep his eyes on the book. It was soon apparent that he couldn't hear them either. My heart sank. This could be a disaster.

I started to do some mental editing to see if I could salvage the scene with a bunch of close-ups. It wasn't the way I'd planned on shooting it, but it was at least a solution. However, I hadn't counted on Eddie. After a few messy rehearsals, he figured out who was speaking, and when, and got the rhythm of the dialogue. Suddenly he was playing the scene perfectly, answering each question, reacting to what was being said, even overlapping lines where I'd asked him to. And he couldn't hear a word anyone was saying! It was awesome and it was inspiring.

At the end of the scene, Eddie closes the big book, rises, and walks down a long, long passage and exits through a large, heavy door. The set was laid out so we could take advantage of the actual, foot-thick, heavily soundproofed stage door and have Eddie exit through it.

I commenced shooting. Partway through the scene something went wrong. I called, "Cut!" Eddie went on with the dialogue. "Cut!" I called, louder. He paid no attention. "CUT!" I yelled, cupping my mouth with my hands. He continued answering questions that no one was asking. I stood up and started waving my arms to get his attention. "EDDIE! CUT! CUT! STOP!" I screamed. Eddie closed the book, rose, and started the long walk down the passageway. There was just no way to stop him, even with my yelling, "EDDIE! COME BACK! WE'RE NOT SHOOTING ANY-MORE!" On he went to the end of the corridor, grabbed the out-sized latch on the stage door, and with a great deal of effort slowly swung it open and exited from the stage. The door closed heavily behind him.

He was wearing a radio mike and I could hear him through my earphones. Someone was outside of the door waiting for the red light to go off so they could come on the stage. Eddie said to him, "Do you think I can go back in now?" I sent my assistant to get him. Over the earphones I heard Eddie ask him, "How was I?"

We did the scene again. The same thing happened. Somebody (not Eddie) blew a line. I yelled, "Cut!" and we went into the same routine, with me yelling at him to stop and he doggedly plowing through the scene, closing the book, walking down the corridor, and out the doorway.

The third time it happened, when I called "Cut!" the camera-man, Dick Kline, yelled, "Lock the door!" It became a byword on the set. Whenever anything went wrong and I called, "Cut!" some-one would yell, "Lock the door!"

Eddie had a five-o'clock stop time in his contract, and I was obligated to dismiss him at that hour. He invariably ignored that restriction. I'd say, "It's five o'clock, Eddie, time to go," and he'd always respond with, "No, no. I want to finish this scene." Even when he wasn't involved with working, he liked to hang around the set, lounging in a director's chair, swapping stories with whoever was free. "Good night, Eddie," I'd say, "it's time to leave." "But I'm not working," he'd reply. "I like it here."

I could never get over his humbleness. We were working on a local location, in the Los Angeles Forum. At the lunch break the company trouped down to the cafeteria in the basement, where our meal was being catered. By the time I arrived, there was a long line of extras and crew members waiting to be served. Somewhere near the end of the line, trays in their hands, were Eddie and his wife, Jane. I walked over to them, took their trays away, and led them to a table that I'd had set aside for them. Eddie was genuinely embarrassed. He didn't want to jump the queue and kept looking around the room to see how the others were reacting. I assured him that it was perfectly all right and insisted that he and Jane sit at the table with me and be served. After we sat down, he leaned over to me and said, "This is what starts revolutions."

One of the high points of the story was the euthanasia sequence in which the Eddie Robinson character dies. We approached it with great unease. Although he never showed one moment's illness or weakness on the set, Eddie's frail health was always in the back of our minds. None of us working with him actually knew he was dying. Still, all of us felt that there was something prophetic and terribly touching about him playing a death scene. Jane visited the set every day to bring him his lunch and to check on him. On the day we shot the scene she wouldn't come near the studio.

The idea of the sequence was that Eddie, having chosen to die instead of having to live in the foul and corrupt future world depicted in our story, goes to a center where euthanasia is routinely carried out. He is placed on a gurney, hooked up to various valves and tubes, and wheeled into a large, domed room. To help make his termination as pleasant and peaceful as possible, beautiful music is played and lovely images are projected on the domed ceiling.

When Eddie was rolled into the room for rehearsal I walked over to the gurney where he lay to explain what would take place during the scene. Other than his just lying there, nothing much would actually happen. The music would be put in later, and so would the various ever-changing images that were supposed to be projected on the ceiling. He would be looking at a blank, white dome for the entire scene.

I bent low over him, my face close to his so he could hear me, and tried to describe what he should be seeing in the dome. The images, I told him, would all relate to nature, pure and unspoiled, the way it used to be: unpolluted waves crashing on a pristine beach;

forests, lush and green; fawns, unafraid, nibbling leaves; mountain streams, crystal clear, rushing against rocks; limitless fields of golden wheat swaying to the horizon.

Eddie watched me, his eyes wide in wonder, a gentle smile on his face. I felt as though I were telling a quiet bedtime story to a child. When I finished, it was clear that he was moved. He raised his hands to both sides of my face, slowly pulled me down to him, and kissed me full on the mouth. Then, still holding my face, he said, "You're very nice."

Watching him do the scene was unforgettable. He lay there, looking at the ceiling, his face expressing wonder, awe, sheer delight, aching nostalgia. Just as he reacted to actors he couldn't hear, he was now reacting to images he couldn't see. It was a phenomenon called acting.

When I cut the scene, the crew was completely silent. I turned and found Chuck Heston standing directly behind me. His eyes were brimming. Later, when it came time to do a close-up of him watching the scene, the tears were still there.

When I started to write this chapter I contacted Chuck Heston and asked him if he could give me his feelings as he played that particular scene with Eddie. He wrote me the following note: "As we played it out, I rose to his performance. When we finished, I thought, 'OK . . . if they want it better than that, they have to get another fella.' What really happened, I came to understand, was that Eddie, knowing that he was playing the last scene he would ever act in his life, somehow communicated that to me, unknowing, lifting me to his unspoken reality. It's a great scene . . . and I had nothing to do with it."

Shortly after we finished the picture, Eddie and Jane invited Mickey and me to their house for dinner and to view his art collection. Mickey was running an art gallery at that time and he knew she'd appreciate it. It was a lovely evening, but Eddie seemed tired, more tired than he'd ever been when we were working. He guided us through the collection before dinner, and we were overwhelmed. All the great Impressionists were represented.

After dinner Mickey made another tour of the collection while I chatted with Eddie and Jane. It was plain that he was fading, so I got Mickey and we said our good-byes. Eddie was too tired to get out of his easy chair, and we urged him not to try. Jane saw us to the door. As we were leaving, Eddie called out from across the room, "Mickey!" She turned.

"Yes, Eddie?"

"Please come back. My pictures want to see you."

A few weeks later, he was gone.

I gotta tell ya: I loved Eddie Robinson.

XX

The first time I met Laurence Olivier was in London on April 20, 1978. I had a dinner date with my longtime friends Laurence and Mary Evans at their charming flat just off Grosvenor Square. I arrived to find Laurence Olivier stretched out in an armchair, drink in hand, tweedy, rosy-cheeked, thinning white hair, looking robust and fragile at the same time. I was surprised to see him, since Laurie Evans hadn't mentioned he'd be there, but since Laurie was his agent, it wasn't too surprising. Seated in another chair was Olivier's sister Sybil, a short, plump, fluttery, gray-haired old lady looking as though she'd just stepped out of *Arsenic and Old Lace*.

Laurie introduced us, and Olivier struggled to his feet, took my hand in both of his, and greeted me as though he had been waiting all his life for this moment. "I am *so* delighted to meet you," he said warmly, in that rich and famous voice. "I can't tell you what a pleasure it is." It was impossible not to feel flattered. "Thank you, Sir Laurence," I replied, "I'm truly honored." "Please," he said, "call me Larry."

It turned out that Olivier and his sister had come up from Brighton, where they lived, for a day's shopping but had grown weary and decided to drop by the Evans's place to rest before getting the train back home. The sister was a complete delight but scatterbrained. She kept insisting that she'd left her shopping bag with all her purchases in the taxi. Everyone kept reassuring her that she had done no such thing and that, in fact, the bag was right there in the other room. Mary Evans would have to bring it out and show it to her before she was satisfied. Within five minutes she'd start telling me again that she'd left the bag in the cab and how in the world could she ever track it down. Olivier couldn't have been kinder or more tolerant and seemed genuinely amused by her.

We all had dinner together, and by the time we saw Olivier and his sister off on the train to Brighton he'd had a few too many drinks and was pretty much in his cups. Because of his numerous well-publicized illnesses, walking was difficult enough for Olivier, but now it was virtually impossible. Laurie and I had to take him under each arm as we walked down the station platform. In front of us Mary and Sybil walked calmly and sedately, chatting away, while we lurched and staggered along behind, with Olivier giving a splendid imitation of rubber-legged Ray Bolger. But Olivier never lost his wit or his charm or his dignity, and I was thoroughly enchanted.

We were almost to his car when he suddenly stopped walking altogether and stretched out his arms, holding Laurie and me back. Oh, please, I thought, don't pass out, please don't throw up, please, please don't destroy my illusions.

We waited, watching him. He was staring straight ahead at the two ladies, who were still walking regally onward. Finally he spoke, sounding very grieved. "You know," he said, "it distresses me to see my sister so unsteady on her feet." At that moment he endeared himself to me forever.

My second meeting with Olivier was also initiated by Laurie Evans. I was half asleep in my home in Los Angeles early on the morning of March 3, 1980, when the phone rang. It was Laurie calling from London. Was I available to do a film? What film? The film that Larry Olivier was doing with Neil Diamond, *The Jazz Singer*. Big trouble. After seven weeks of shooting, the director had been dismissed and production had come to a halt. Would I be interested in taking over? If I was, he'd suggest me to the producers.

I'd taken over pictures from other directors twice before, and I knew what a difficult and tricky job it was. It isn't something anyone in his right mind relishes doing. And I had doubts about the story. Could that old-hat, passé tale of a cantor and his son be updated, given a modern treatment? Maybe. Still, the prospect of working with Laurence Olivier and Neil Diamond was tempting. I told Laurie I was interested.

Two days later I renewed my fleeting acquaintance with Larry Olivier in his suite at the l'Ermitage Hotel in Beverly Hills. If on our first meeting the greeting was effusive and flattering, this time it was more like something reserved for the Second Coming.

There was good reason for it. The picture was a basket case. I had run some of the film already shot to see what the problems were. (It wasn't possible to see it all, since over 250,000 feet of film had been printed, and that would take more than forty-eight hours of nonstop running time to screen.) What I saw, and learned from the producers, was hair-raising.

Normally major motion pictures are shot with one camera. In this case (I never could discover why) the director had shot every scene with five to seven cameras. Even telephone booth scenes, or someone crossing a street. Seven cameras (and seven crews) in any sort of confined space are self-defeating. The most you can hope for is that they don't end up photographing each other. No camera is able to squeeze into the proper position for a good composition. Frequently the reverse angles on over-shoulder shots were never made, so that they ended up with seven extremely awkward angles over an actor's shoulder, angles that couldn't be cut together. There were almost no close-ups. Usually there were ten to fifteen takes on each setup, and the director printed every take on every camera. Dailies took three or four hours to screen.

The screenplay was being constantly rewritten by the director himself. The actors would turn up on the set to find that the scene they'd learned the night before was no longer in the picture and a new scene was being written at that very moment. And not only new scenes, but also new concepts, or no concepts at all. For the first weeks of shooting, Catlin Adams, who played the part of Rivka, had to play her scenes not knowing whether she was married to Neil Diamond's character, Jess, or was merely his girlfriend. She was not happy about that. Neither was Diamond.

The result of all this was that the actors had given less than sterling performances. It was a textbook example of how actors protect themselves when they feel they have been abandoned by the director.

Olivier, the most experienced of experienced actors, did what he did best: acted. He acted all over the place. This very gentile gentleman had done his damndest to portray a very Jewish cantor by using every broad cliché in the book. Rolling eyes, grimacing, gesturing, it was a performance worthy of the Yiddish Art Theater at its worst.

Neil Diamond, the most inexperienced of inexperienced actors, a true neophyte, never having acted before, had done exactly the opposite. Not having the confidence of an Olivier, he'd withdrawn into a shell and tried to make himself as inconspicuous as possible. He barely moved a muscle. When he spoke, he was almost inaudible.

Olivier was getting fed up. It was his practice to learn his lines first thing in the morning, when his mind was fresh and retentive. Then he found he was getting three or four new pages delivered to his dressing room while he was making up or having them shoved through his car window on the way to the set. Once, as he was wandering around the Goldwyn Studios on foot wondering where the set was, a production secretary pushed a page and a half of new dialogue into his hand. Still walking, he had glanced through it and then remarked, "You know? This piss is shit." It was a comment that everyone thought very funny and got wide currency on the set. That remark turned out to be a delayed-action bomb. Eventually it went off with a nice loud bang.

Things got steadily worse on the production. Scenes that had never appeared in any version of any script were entirely ad-libbed without any idea of where they would fit into the story. It became impossible to plan any kind of schedule or make any kind of budgetary estimates. EMI, the English producing company that was financing the picture, sent one of its executives over from London to discuss the situation with the director. The director flatly refused to meet with him.

Finally EMI threatened to close down the production unless they received a finished screenplay from the director and the writer within a week. This new version was delivered on February 28, 1980. It was quickly determined that it could not be shot without doubling the time left on the original schedule and doubling the budget as well. Besides, nobody liked it. The high point of *The Jazz Singer* story is the singing of "Kol Nidre" on Yom Kippur. In this version not only was Neil Diamond not going to sing it, but also there was no "Kol Nidre" at all! It was left out of the script entirely. *The Jazz Singer* without "Kol Nidre"?

The director was replaced.

Exactly two weeks after getting that phone call from Laurie Evans, I commenced shooting, and reshooting, the picture. I felt reasonably sure that I could salvage it and make myself something of a hero in the bargain. (Jerry Leider, the producer, later called it "the greatest rescue operation since Entebbe.") There was great pressure for me to finish Olivier as soon as possible, before his contract expired. Since he was getting $1 million for the picture, his compensation, if we exceeded the time allotted in his contract, would be $166,666 per week or $33,333 a day.

Working with Larry under these circumstances required more

than just being knowledgeable, technically proficient, and creative. It required United Nations-class diplomacy.

The very first scene I did with him made me sweat when he said, "We've already done this scene. Why are we doing it again?" How could I say a nasty thing to him like "You overacted"? Instead I told him a different truth. I said that I didn't like the way the scene had been staged previously.

There were other major problems with Olivier. Like most actors of his age, he suffered from the terrible scourge of a faltering memory for dialogue. Getting through a moderately long speech was agony for him. You could see him falter and grope for the lines. Sometimes they wouldn't come and he'd blow up and castigate himself unmercifully. "You old fool," he'd mutter, his face turning red with mortification and self-anger, "don't you know when it's time to quit and get out of the business?" I began to wonder about that myself.

The Jewish accent he affected for the part was yet another problem. He was very proud of it, and he described to me in great detail how it was different from the one he'd used in *The Boys from Brazil*. I thought it was a terrible accent and hated it, but decided that it would be foolhardy to try to change or modify it. Ordinarily I wouldn't hesitate to do such a thing, but I felt that if I attacked his cherished accent now I'd lose any relationship I'd established with him. We'd just have to live with it. I hoped that he'd perhaps forget about the accent as we went along, but no such luck. He was too much of a pro for that.

So how do you tell the world's greatest actor, a legend in his own time, that he's overacting? That he's got the words wrong? That you don't like the accent he's using? There's a little poem that goes: Diplomacy is to do and say/The nastiest thing in the nicest way.

That's how.

Neil Diamond presented a much different problem. It was a matter of bringing his performance up, rather than down, and giving him some self-confidence about acting. Before we started shooting I had a long meeting with Neil in his office at Archangel, his recording studio on Melrose Place. I wanted to get to know him a bit and find out how he felt about acting.

When I asked him if he'd ever had any acting lessons, he said, "Oh, yes." "Really? Who from?" I asked. "From Laurence Olivier," he replied with a smile. He had been studying him, watching him, trying to learn from the foremost actor of his time. I was touched by that. I knew that I was going to like Neil Diamond.

Neil made great progress during the picture. Toward the end of shooting he even got into Method acting. We were doing a scene in a sound studio where he storms into the recording booth in a rage and has a furiously angry argument with his pregnant girlfriend, Lucie Arnaz. We worked all morning on the sequence, but Neil couldn't get up a proper head of steam. He just wasn't angry enough to make the scene work.

The recording booth was separated from the music recording stage by a soundproof window. Neil's band was in there, on the music stage, as part of the background, and that's where he would wait until I called "Action!" over the microphone. I could see him in there, pacing nervously, while we reset the camera to do another take.

Suddenly, Neil seemed to go berserk. I couldn't hear him, but I could see that he was ranting and raving. The band was cowering and backing away from him, covering their heads with their instruments for protection, as he picked up and smashed microphones, music stands, chairs, anything he could get his hands on. The room was becoming a shambles. He was in a real fury. "Roll the camera!" I yelled at the camera crew and grabbed the microphone. "Action, Neil! Action!" I screamed into it. "Action, goddamn it!"

Neil blasted into the control booth in a blind rage. I was afraid he'd blow the lines, but he didn't. The dialogue got a little mangled, but it was right for the scene. He was wonderful. A dynamite performance.

After I yelled "Cut!" I grabbed Neil and asked him what had happened in the other room that had set him off like that.

"Well, I was feeling so lousy that I couldn't give you what you wanted, I asked my band to play something that would make me angry."

"And what did they play?"

"A Barry Manilow number."

The last day of work with Olivier took place on the last day of his contract. It also happened to be my biggest and most difficult day on the entire picture, a "live" concert with Neil Diamond at the Pantages Theater. The Pantages holds fifteen hundred people, and we had arranged to have the theater filled with young rock and roll enthusiasts. Olivier was to be in the audience for reaction shots.

Neil was going to do three songs for parts of two different sequences, including the big climactic number, "America." I had just one day to shoot it in, so I positioned the most cameras I've ever used on any film, thirteen of them, in various strategic locations in the audience, behind the bandstand, and in the wings. There was radio communication with every camera crew so I could call the shots as I saw them. I had just this one crack at the concert, and I was trying to protect myself in any way I could in case something went wrong, like a camera failure or an out-of-focus shot. But I was very nervous about the day's work because of what had happened the day before.

I had asked Neil to give me a full rehearsal, with his band, of the three numbers we were going to shoot. It was vitally necessary for me to know just where he'd be moving on the stage and exactly when he would make those moves so I could cue the cameras properly. Late in the afternoon we were ready for the rehearsal.

Neil asked that the entire auditorium be cleared. He didn't want anyone there except me. I was planning on having the cameramen watch the rehearsal, too, but Neil wouldn't have it. He was going to give a concert just for me, an audience of one.

I sat there alone in the middle of the big, empty theater, and the rehearsal started. Neil began with a number I hadn't heard before. Very catchy. The next song was familiar, but it wasn't from the picture. Neither was the next. Or the next. I liked the music and Neil was great, but I was getting impatient. "How about 'Louise'?" I called out as he finished another unfamiliar tune. "Louise" was one of the songs we were going to shoot the next day. Neil paid no attention and sang another of his standards.

The "rehearsal" went on for a full hour without one song from the picture being played. I kept calling out requests, but he didn't pay any attention to them. When it ended Neil gave me a big bow, I applauded, and the band left. I had no more idea of how I was going to photograph the songs the next day than when I started.

I followed Neil into his dressing room at the side of the stage. Bob Gaudio, his music supervisor, was there reading a magazine. "Neil," I said, "that was a great performance. I loved it. But what happened? Why didn't you do the songs we're going to shoot tomorrow?"

"I just didn't feel like it," he replied, taking a long drag on an unfiltered Camel cigarette. "I thought this would be more fun." Fun for whom? I wondered. I realized then that I'd just have to wing it. The climax of the picture, thirteen cameras, and I'm going to wing it! Great!

"Now," I went on, "about the order of the songs. Do you want to start with 'Summer Love' or 'America'?"

"I want to start with 'Louise,' " Neil replied.

I explained why we couldn't do that. We needed to erect a special bandstand for "Summer Love" and "America." Since it took more than three hours to put up and less than an hour to take down, it made sense to start with it already up. We were planning to take it down during an intermission.

Neil still wanted to start with "Louise," and it took a lot of persuasion to talk him out of it. Then it became a matter of which of the two remaining songs to start with. We all agreed that "Summer Love" would get him and the audience warmed up so that he could do justice to "America," the centerpiece and climax of the movie. Just so there would be no confusion about it, I made up two lists of the order of the songs. I gave one to Neil and I kept the other.

The audience started filing in at noon. They were mostly Latino and black teenagers. Olivier was called for 1:00 P.M. His contract limited his working to eight hours a day, including the lunch hour, so that I could keep him until 9:00 P.M. that night before his contract expired. If we needed him past that time we had no way to force him to do so. He had to agree to stay. But I felt I was safe. I expected to be finished well before that time.

During the morning, while we were still setting up the cameras, the film's producer, Jerry Leider took me aside. "I've got a small favor to ask of you," he said. "I'd like you to make an extra close-up of Olivier that we hadn't planned on. It's for the 'Kol Nidre' sequence in the synagogue. You can probably do it anywhere backstage after the concert." This request puzzled me. I couldn't see what it was for.

The Kol Nidre sequence takes place at a point in the story when the cantor and his son are estranged. The father has renounced him. During the solo singing of 'Kol Nidre' in the synagogue at Yom Kippur, the son, unbeknownst to the father, slips into the synagogue and takes over the singing. Olivier, sitting directly below the platform where this occurs, recognizes his son's voice and turns to look at him. For a second his eyes light up, but then a bitter, stern expression covers his face and he stonily turns away.

The conventional approach would be to have the anticipated reconciliation occur when the cantor recognizes his son's voice. I thought that was too pat and obvious. It would be far better not to give the audience what it expected, but to delay the reconciliation between father and son for the following scene, when they find themselves unavoidably alone together. Everyone agreed, and that's the way it was shot. It proved to be immensely powerful and moving.

So what was this extra close-up for?

Leider explained that the EMI office had gotten cold feet and wanted to protect itself with a close-up of Olivier turning, when he recognizes the voice, and smiling when he sees it's his son. *Smiling!* In that way, so the thinking went, if we ever wanted to fall back on a grand, old, hoary cliché, we could. No one would ever be able to accuse us of not being as cornball as humanly possible.

I told Leider what I thought of the idea: pure vomit.

"I know, but do it anyhow. It's only a close-up. Keep them happy. We'll never use it."

I reminded him of an old directors' adage: "If you shoot it, they'll use it."

"We won't, we won't, but please, do me this favor."

"The idea not only stinks, but I don't have time to make unnecessary close-ups when there is so much vitally important stuff to do."

"You'll have time. You have until nine o'clock tonight."

"Have you talked to Olivier about this?"

"Not yet, but I will as soon as he gets here." I knew Larry loved the way it was shot, and I was sure he'd refuse to make the close-up. I was counting on that.

"Okay, if there's time."

"Thanks."

Olivier arrived on time, along with the other actors required in the scenes, and they took their places in the audience in seats set aside for them. Then we waited. And waited. No Neil. I sent word backstage that we were ready. Word came back; he wasn't. More waiting. The audience started to get restless. Still no Neil. We were beginning to worry that we'd start losing the audience.

To fill in time, Leider took to the stage and did some amusing Borscht Circuit *shtick*. Still no sign of Neil. Leider was running out of routines, so he began introducing the actors who were present. Lucie Arnaz was the only one there the audience had halfway heard of. She got a nice, polite hand. The others didn't do as well. Then a terrible thought grabbed me: What did this particular crowd know about Laurence Olivier? They probably never heard of him, and if they did, their attitude would most likely be "So what?" I was sure he'd get the kind of mocking, kidding reception audiences give to unimportant actors. I could see a huge humiliation coming up.

Leider saved the Olivier introduction to last. I held my breath and gritted my teeth for the coming ordeal. I hoped Larry would understand and not be too hurt. "And now, ladies and gentlemen," Leider announced, "I am honored to introduce to you one of the stars of our picture, Lord Laurence Olivier!"

The audience audibly gasped, rose en masse to its feet, and gave him a standing ovation.

Shortly after that, still waiting for Neil, Leider came over to me. He was smiling. "Olivier says okay for the close-up. As long as we get it before nine." I was disappointed in Larry for agreeing. I couldn't understand why he did. "Well," I said, "it may all be academic. If Neil doesn't get out here pretty soon we won't finish today." "We have to," Leider answered. "We'll never be able to get this crowd back. Or the theater. Another show moves in tonight as soon as we wrap. Maybe you ought to go back and talk to him."

I'd been reluctant to do so earlier. This was his venue. He knew how to handle a concert, I didn't. I felt it wasn't proper for me to pressure him just before he had to perform before an audience. But now I had no choice. I had to see what was holding him up.

Neil was in his dressing room in the wings, dressed, made up, but not ready to go. Bob Gaudio was there with him. There seemed to be an ample supply of booze bottles and soft drinks. The air was thick with cigarette smoke. I could never understand how a singer like that could smoke so much, but he did. He told me it made him sing better. Go argue with Neil Diamond. "What is it, Neil?" I asked. "What's holding us up? What's the problem?"

"I don't know what songs to sing," he answered, "or in what order to do them."

"What!" I said, shocked. "You must be kidding. We laid the whole thing out last night, right here in this dressing room!"

"No, we didn't. I don't remember doing that."

"Well, I do," I said, feeling as though I'd wandered into a nightmare. I turned to Gaudio. "Bob," I said, "you were here. How about it?"

Gaudio hesitated a moment and swallowed hard. "I hate to say it, Neil," he said, "but at the risk of losing my job, he's right."

"Oh," Neil said. "Well, what did we decide?"

I pulled the list out of my pocket and gave it to him. He looked it over and then said, "Yeah, this is okay."

"You start with 'Summer Love,' right?"

"Yeah. Okay. I'll be right out."

"Please," I said and left.

I came out of the dressing room, gave Leider the high sign that everything was now okay, and alerted the thirteen camera crews to stand by, we'd be starting any minute.

Fifteen minutes later we were still standing by when one of my assistants came running up to me, breathless. "Mr. Diamond says he doesn't want to start with 'Summer Love,'" he said, gasping. "He says to tell you he's going to do 'Louise' instead."

At that moment I would have gladly killed Neil Diamond and the messenger, too. I clutched my assistant by the shirt. I could feel my face flushing. "You tell Mr. Diamond," I yelled at him, "that he's starting with 'Summer Love,' not 'Louise,' and that I expect to see him on that stage in exactly two minutes!"

A few minutes later Neil Diamond walked on the stage to thunderous applause and absolutely wowed the audience with "Summer Love."

By intermission we were running late. Leider came to me and asked what the Olivier situation looked like. I told him I thought we'd be pushing nine o'clock and that he'd be wise to get a time extension from him. He agreed that it wouldn't be practical to interrupt what we were doing just for a simple close-up.

Twenty minutes later Leider came back, shaking his head. "He'll give us the extension, all right," he told me. "He'll stay past nine, but if he does we'll have to pay him for a day's work. Thirty-three thousand, three hundred and thirty three dollars for a close-up! Can you believe that? And after he's already gotten a million for doing the picture!"

I felt as outraged as Leider. Suddenly I understood why Olivier had agreed to do the close-up in the first place: for the money. We were dealing with not just an avaricious actor but also with a wise and knowing director who'd been playing the "Don't Teach Your Grandmother How to Suck Eggs" game. He could see right away that we were going to have problems that would delay us and was counting on our running late so he could grab some extra bucks.

It was the money-grubbing that got to me. It didn't fit the lofty image of Laurence Olivier, and I felt disappointed, let down. If he'd agreed to do the close-up because he believed in it, and could get some extra money too, okay, I could accept that. But he was doing it for the money alone.

I was seeing a side of Olivier I didn't like, the side that was commonly recognized in Hollywood in his later years, that he'd accept a role in *any* movie if the price was right. I never wanted to believe that, but I did now.

Neil was late again for the second part of the show, and it was a quarter to nine when I finished the last shot. Leider said to me, "How about Olivier? You've still got fifteen minutes." "Impossible," I told him. "We haven't done anything in fifteen minutes on this picture yet." "It's important to me that we give it our best shot," Leider pleaded, "so go for it. If I see we're going past nine I'll signal you and you can call it off. We're not going to pay him any thirty-three thousand dollars."

I told the cameraman to set up for the close-up and that he only had fifteen minutes, but not to knock himself out trying. If we missed it, we missed it. The cameraman must have been inspired by the challenge. Exhausted as he was after a brutal day's work, he worked like lightning.

Olivier was dressed in his synagogue outfit and pacing up and down near the camera with a watch in his hand, counting the minutes. Leider was in the background with a watch in *his* hand. At eight fifty-nine I asked Larry to rehearse the turn and the smile. He sat in the chair that had been prepared and did it, still with the watch in his hand. The cameraman adjusted a few lights, I checked the setup through the lens, Larry looked at his watch, my assistant called "Roll it!" and Olivier's close-up (smiling) was immortalized on film.

It is customary, when an actor finishes his last shot, that the first assistant announces it, the crew applauds, and handshakes and hugs are exchanged. Not this time. Larry was sitting in the chair with his yarmulke, prayer shawl, and watch. There was dead silence. Slowly he stood up. "I have never been so badly treated on a film in my entire career!" he said, and stalked off to his dressing room.

About fifteen minutes later I entered his dressing room. I just couldn't let Larry finish his stint this way. The least I could do was try to say a proper good-bye to him, whether he was angry with me or not.

The small room was pretty crowded with his wife, Joan Plowright; his son, Dickie; and several friends. Larry was sitting in the center of the room on a straight-backed chair in his underpants, with his trousers down around his ankles. "Larry," I said, "I've come to say good-bye and to thank you."

Olivier stood up and took my hand in both of his, just as he'd done in the Evans's flat in London. "Working with you was like a blessed redemption, my dear Dick," he said. "I've been happier in my work than I've been allowed to feel for a long time." Then he put his arms around me. It made a nice tableau, me standing there in my work clothes being embraced by Laurence Olivier with his pants down.

The close-up was never used in the picture.

Larry didn't go directly back to England. Instead he made a short stopover in New York where, one evening, he had dinner in a restaurant with some friends. It was, as he explained to me later, "a fatally jolly dinner." During the course of the evening he repeated the remark he'd made during the shooting of the picture that everyone found so amusing, "This piss is shit." Larry is certain that a reporter was deliberately placed at the table next to his to pick up what she could, and the next day, with the word "shit" changed to "trash," and an appropriate euphemism for "piss," the remark hit the fan as well as the media. New York's *Daily News* gave it a big play in its entertainment section, and the major wire services picked it up. The time bomb he'd constructed in Hollywood a few months before finally exploded.

The thrust, and clear implication, of all the stories was that Laurence Olivier thought *The Jazz Singer* was a total piece of rubbish, and that he hated the producer, the director, and his costar, Neil Diamond.

EMI went right through the roof. The telex wires burned with threats of lawsuits and challenges to saber duels. Poor Larry was totally appalled by what his amusing, indiscreet remark had wrought. He finally had to issue the following statement to New York's *Daily News*, United Press International, and the Associated Press:

> I have nothing but respect for the way in which the film is now being handled. The brilliant ideas instigated by the producer, Jerry Leider, were expertly directed by Richard Fleischer and as for my leading man I am quite sure that the American public or shall I say the world public have a great and delightful surprise in store for them.

Larry wasn't aware of it at the time, but the main course at that New York restaurant turned out to be crow.

Two weeks after this incident I received a ten-page handwritten letter, dated April 20, 1980, from Olivier in England. It was an extraordinary document that began as an "apologia, explanation—discussion," as he put it, of what happened at the restaurant. "What a goddam shame anything should be allowed to intrude between us," it began, "I am quite anguished by the present situation and can only pray we can sleep it off or dream it away."

But there was something else that was much more important to him than a gossip columnist's extravagant reportage. He was apparently tormented by his behavior during the "close-up" incident and his demand for the thirty-three thousand, three hundred and thirty-three dollars. The bulk of the letter was devoted to an apologia, explanation—discussion (rationalization?) of his entire philosophy of making movies for money, movies he didn't particularly care for. It was his defense against the onus that he'd do any picture offered to him if the price was right.

He wrote:

> It's all to explain why I undertook *"Jazz Singer,"* not for any nobler reason than, "Oh, well—just think of the money." (My schedule was only originally 6 weeks) "& then you can forget it—like Dracula & such"—Good, worthwhile ones usually turn up just in time to keep the situation from getting chronic. The best possible education for my beloveds is naturally my main concern at this time of life. . . .

The last sentence, of course, was the crux of the matter. Although Olivier was the most acclaimed, celebrated, and respected actor of our time, he was never a big money earner. By Hollywood standards, at least until his later years, his fees were modest, he was a bargain. England, certainly, is not renowned for its wanton lavishness in rewarding its leading artists, and England is where Olivier spent most of his career. As time and life-threatening illness overtook him he began to sensibly, and surely apprehensively, think of his beloveds. The time left to provide for them was getting frighteningly shorter, so he did what Hollywood so glibly criticized him for, made movies for money, as many and as quickly as he could. For someone who had spent his life in pursuit of artistic and creative nobility, this was not an easy transition to make. Whenever he played a role in a picture he didn't like, his wardrobe included a hair shirt. Why else would he feel the need to expiate himself to me, the most recent of his friends?

The letter continued:

Must we always incline to feel hurt by the suggestion that every job of work we ever assay—is a shameful thing if not inspired by the most highly principalled motives?

The first films ever were thought up to make money. The first people to clamber up a platform in a small village market-place—the same reason.

. . . There are roughly 2 main emphases of balance in the promotion of our Art/Science/Business. In the making of an ostensibly wonderful film, the choice varies (with all of us, I think) between the intention to make money, with, hopefully, good likelihoods of elevating the thing to a standard which lends it sufficient interest for the more serious minded public not to dismiss it as commercial; or, to determine to make as artistically perfect (a) piece of work as may lie within our gifts, hoping to find human or humourous observations that will help your commercial public to find enough enjoyment in it, not to relegate it to the arty-crafty syndrome.

I don't find anything to be ashamed of in an avowed intention to make a profit, if only in an attempt thereby to achieve sufficient trust among the money bags so that you can continue exercising your talent so that you *may* one day find that you have made a masterpiece incorporating all things.

When Jerry L. was first hit by the dazzling flash of an idea of combining Neil with the 1st talking picture ever made (forever a household word) it is beyond credence that his first thoughts were primarily concerned with high Artistic purpose, the early script disallows that belief; he simply knew immediately that he had something that no backer could refuse. And why not? If our business fails to achieve profits it will die, & pretty quickly too. Yours & my generation can easily discern the diminution over 60 years of the public craving for this medium. I don't want it to die, I think it is a wonderful medium, possibly the most resourceful and limitless in capability ever devised in the history of Entertainment, and Entertainment is in my book, an Art in itself.

Why was I so outraged that Olivier wanted as much money as he could get? I don't believe I was motivated solely by some form of altruistic aestheticism. Were his motives so much less noble than mine?

The last time I saw Larry was August 4, 1980, in London. EMI had sent me over from Hollywood to do some looping with him. Certain of his dialogue sound tracks had too much background noise and needed to be redone. Larry, however, couldn't work in England because of tax reasons, so it was decided to do the loops out of the country. The plan was for me to meet him in London and accompany him to the Wagram-Audio Transfer Studio in Paris. Ordinarily I could have accomplished the amount of work to be done in an afternoon, but to be on the safe side EMI booked the recording studio for two days. One of our sound editors flew directly from the Coast to Paris with the necessary film.

We were supposed to start work at the Paris studio at 2:00 P.M., but we were a little late getting there. Larry had insisted we stop on the way from the airport to have his favorite French meal, a *jambon et fromage sandwich* on a *baguette*. And a bottle of red wine, of course. It was a two-drink flight from London, so with the bottle of wine and the sandwich nicely tucked away, Larry was fast asleep when we arrived at the studio.

The reception room of Wagram-Audio is on the ground floor. The actual recording room is underground, two floors below and no elevator. We started the long trek down. Larry's legs were not in the best possible shape, and he had to negotiate the stairs one slow, painful step at a time. Both feet had to be on the same tread before he could take the next step. I kept wondering how we would ever get him back up. Carry him? A block and tackle? Well, I thought, I'll worry about that when the time comes.

It took a long ten minutes before we reached the door to the recording room at the bottom of the stairway. Larry hung on the banister to catch his breath, then looked around and said, "Where is the little boys' room?" I looked at the French technicians who had accompanied us on the journey. They blanched and pointed upward. It was on the ground floor, off the reception room. He refused my offer of help, turned, and resignedly started to clump his way back up. Forty-five minutes later he returned. He was looking peaked. I could see now the wisdom of booking the studio for two days.

Some actors are good loopers (Charlton Heston is a whiz) and some are not so good. But good or bad, fast or slow, anyone can do it. On the very first loop it became clear that this whole trip was an exercise in futility. Olivier found it completely impossible. He couldn't even come close to getting it right. We worked on it for almost an hour. The loop must have gone by a hundred and fifty times, but he was unable to start in synch, and if you don't at least start in synch, you're dead.

Larry was getting frustrated. He would turn to me after missing the start mark and say peevishly, "I'm not Gary Cooper or Jimmy Stewart . . . I'm not one of your American actors who can do this mechanical stuff. I can't reproduce a performance on cue the way they do. I have a different sort of training." He repeated that statement three or four times.

I found the whole thing unbelievable. Olivier didn't know how to loop after all the films he'd directed and acted in? Come on! There wasn't anything I could do about it except have him read all of his lines "wild"—that is, without trying to synch them to the picture and hope that we could make some words or pieces fit later. Then we called it a day and clumped slowly back up the stairs.

We had dinner that night at Lucas-Carton, one of the most expensive restaurants in Paris. Larry invited a friend along and ordered two $150 bottles of wine. I said good-bye to Larry at his hotel, The Lancaster, and went on to mine, Le Crillon. The next morning I got the Concorde to New York and connected with a flight to Los Angeles.

Flying over the Atlantic at twice the speed of sound, I reflected on what had just happened. I did a little quick figuring. What with the air fares for me and the sound editor, hotel suites in London and Paris, two days' rental of the sound studio, Lucas-Carton, limousines, and various and sundry expenses, it was a tidy sum.

As near as I could figure, it came to $33,333.

Short Ends

Movie film in 35mm comes in thousand-foot rolls because that's all a camera magazine will hold. Under normal conditions, that gives you about ten minutes of filming. It's very rare, however, that the entire thousand feet get used up committing some scene to film (unless you run out of film during the shooting, in which case you strangle the camera assistant who is supposed to see that such catastrophes don't happen). Usually there's some unexposed film left over. This is called a "short end." If it's very short it's just thrown away. The longer pieces are saved and used for short scenes or quick takes.

In spite of the fact that Dick Zanuck wanted me to direct his first movie, *Compulsion*, getting the job was not easy. Dick's boss, Darryl Zanuck, was against it. He felt I wouldn't be suitable because, as he put it, "Fleischer's only good for those big, complicated, action pictures, like *Twenty Thousand Leagues Under the Sea* and *The Vikings*. He wouldn't be right for an intimate, psychological drama like this." Darryl was in Paris at this time, running DFZ Productions. The argument about my doing the picture was conducted by cable for several weeks until Darryl finally gave in and reluctantly said okay.

The first time he saw a frame of *Compulsion* was on one of his rare visits to the Hollywood studio after the movie was finished. He screened the picture and thought it was terrific.

A few days later Darryl and Dick had a meeting about the next DFZ production, *Deluxe Tour*, an expensive, large-scale movie written by Irwin Shaw. Darryl was wondering whom he should get to direct it. Since Darryl had loved *Compulsion* so much, Dick said, "Why not ask Dick Fleischer?" To which Darryl responded, "No, no. He's only good for those small, psychological dramas. He couldn't handle a big, complicated picture like this." You're only as typed as your last picture.

The following day Darryl offered me the screenplay. I thought it was terrible, and I turned it down. It was a decision I didn't regret, since it never got made.

"If you've made more than one picture you've made a bad one."

Walter Mirisch, producer,
generalizing on movie careers.

Compulsion was based on a true story, the thrill killing of an innocent boy by the young scions of two of the wealthiest, most distinguished Chicago families. Their names were Nathaniel Leopold and Richard Loeb. "Dickie" Loeb had already been murdered in prison when we were preparing the film, but Leopold had been released on probation and was working as a research lab technician in some remote Puerto Rican jungle.

The legal department of Twentieth Century-Fox was more than a little nervous about the possibility of Leopold bringing suit against the company, and they bombarded us with memos and communiqués urging us not only to change all the names in the script but also never, never even to mention Leopold and Loeb in any statements or interviews. We cooperated completely. Their names were changed to Artie Straus and Judd Steiner. We didn't even speak the forbidden names in private. Sometimes we all felt a little foolish during interviews denying that the movie, which was adapted from Meyer Levin's best-selling novel, had anything to do with Leopold and Loeb. But we did as we were told.

There seems to have been a monumental lack of communication between the legal department and the publicity department. When the picture was released, newspaper ads appeared carrying the eye-catching line "Based on the famous Leopold and Loeb murder case."

Leopold sued Twentieth Century-Fox and won. I wouldn't be surprised if some of the members of the publicity department eventually found work with a government security agency.

Darryl Zanuck and I did quite a bit of traveling together during the time I made pictures for him in Europe. When leaving France it was necessary to fill out an "exit form" and hand it in at Passport

Control. One of the questions listed was "Occupation." Unfailingly, Darryl would come over to me with a big grin on his face to show me how he had answered that question. It was always filled in with one word: "Idiot."

No one at Passport Control ever questioned it.

Since we worked only until noon on Saturdays and had Sundays off during the shooting of *Bandido* in Mexico, I arranged to have my wife arrive in Mexico City on a Saturday afternoon so I could meet the plane. I figured we'd spend the night there and do some sightseeing on Sunday before heading back to Tepitzlan, about an hour and a half away. When Gilbert Roland, one of our leading actors and a well-known Mexican-American personality, heard about it, he said, "Great, Ricardo, I will come there, too, and we'll go to the bullfights." He was a great aficionado, he told me, because his father had been a famous Mexican bullfighter. I would see how well loved he was by the people. He would have the box of honor, at least one bull would be dedicated to him, we would be treated like kings. Why not make a real day of it? he suggested. The flea market in the morning, the racetrack for lunch, and then the bullfights. There'd be plenty of time. The bullfights didn't start until four in the afternoon. And why don't we bring along your friend Earl Felton? It sounded good to me.

Sunday morning at the flea market was exciting. It was a great start for Mickey's Mexican holiday. Amigo (Roland's universally used nickname) got us a beautiful table at the racetrack's clubhouse terrace for lunch. We ordered and as soon as my enchilada was placed in front of me, I suddenly became light-headed and fell onto the plate face first. Altitude sickness. At 7,347 feet above sea level, Mexico City is the place to get it.

I was out for only a few seconds, but it scared the hell out of Mickey. She wiped the rice, beans, and salsa off my face and wanted to call an ambulance, but Amigo convinced her that would be worse than the altitude sickness. It would go away in a short while, he assured her, and then I'd feel fine again.

I was too dizzy to raise my head, much less walk, so I stayed with my face resting on the table for over an hour while the others dined and placed bets. As Amigo predicted, I started feeling better and by the time we were ready to go to the bullring I was completely recovered.

As advertised, Amigo turned out to be a popular figure with the bullfighting audience. The crowd loved him. There was much waving and cheering and applause as we filed into what must have been the presidential box. Amigo took his bows more like a visiting monarch than a native son.

It was the day of the *novilleros*, the semiprofessional novices. Amigo thought that was great. Now, he said, we'll see some really exciting, daredevil stuff. These kids take all sorts of chances just to attract attention.

The first fight began. There was a shocking disembowelment of the picador's horse, followed by the goring of a banderillero. So far the bull was ahead, 2–0. When the time came for the kid matador to start the part of the fight called "The Hour of Truth," he selected the most prominent person there to whom he would dedicate the bull. He tossed his hat up to Amigo. Who else? There was a great yell of approval from the crowd. Amigo stood up with a huge grin on his face and displayed the hat, looking very much like the pope dispensing blessings from his balcony overlooking St. Peter's Square. The matador would be back, after dispatching the bull, for his hat. Tradition requires that it contain a substantial wad of money.

The matador did his best to imitate the Three Stooges, but he lacked their grace and artistry. It took only four or five jabs with the sword before he was rewarded with a fountain of blood shooting from the bull's nose. The bull died of anemia. Everyone in our group looked pale. Altitude sickness was better than this.

Amigo turned to me and said, "That bum doesn't deserve anything, but I've got to be generous. They expect it of me." I watched him count out a hundred dollars in pesos and stuff them into the hat. The matador, when it was tossed back to him, accepted it with great dignity.

The second fight wasn't any better than the first. Another horse got disemboweled, the bull chased everyone all over the ring, and the matador dedicated the bull to Amigo. Who else? Amigo pasted a big smile on his face and accepted the hat gracefully. The crowd cheered. It was another lousy kill and it cost him another hundred bucks.

When the third matador dedicated the bull to him, Amigo was starting to look pretty grim. "Can't these bums find somebody else?" he said to me. "I'm running out of money."

As the fourth matador headed our way, hat in hand, Amigo groaned. "Oh, shit," he said, "not again." Amigo accepted the hat and turned to me, saying, "Maybe he'll get killed and I won't have to pay him." He didn't get killed, but he did get tossed like a rag doll. Still, he recovered and managed to stagger toward our box for his loot. Amigo bent way down below the railing to get the hat, which was on the floor. Then he grabbed my arm and pulled me down, too. "Ricardo," he said frantically in my ear, "give me some money, quick!" I gave him all I had and he put it into the hat. Again Amigo stuck a big false smile on his face, and as he tossed the hat down to the waiting matador Amigo said, "Go fuck yourself." What with the band playing and the crowd cheering, no one heard it but me.

When he accepted the hat from the fifth matador, Amigo bowed solemnly and said to him, "May you get a horn up your ass." The noise in the arena covered it nicely, and the matador bowed deeply in return. This time Amigo put the bite on Felton.

Just before the sixth and last fight was about to start, Amigo turned to us and said, "When they open the gate to let in the bull, we've got to get the hell out of here. We're not going to let the next thief rob us, too."

When the big gate opened and the bull charged into the arena, we picked up our belongings and slunk out. It was the end of a fun day in Mexico City.

Getting a small child to swallow a large dose of castor oil was a cinch compared to getting Earl Felton to sit down and write. After working with him on five pictures in a row I knew him for what he was: a terrible procrastinator, a practiced malingerer, a lazy lout, and a wonderful screenplay writer. The worst struggle of all was just to get him to show up at the office in the morning.

Most mornings I'd get a phone call from him about 10:00 A.M. "I'm sick," he'd groan in a voice thick with the effects of too much scotch and too many sleeping pills. "I need a couple more hours and I'll be fine." "Goddamn it, Earl," I'd say, "you be here in an hour, you hear me!" To which he'd reply, "Honk!" and hang up. He never, at any time, used the word "good-bye." He always said "Honk!"

An hour later he'd drag himself into the office on his crutch and cane, call out that classic line of the doctor's in *Mutiny on the Bounty* so I could hear it, "Reportin' fer duty, sar," collapse into his desk chair, and drink the first of an endless number of ice-cold Cokes. Then came the ritual of reading the trade papers, several slow trips to the men's room, and long phone calls to friends, until finally I'd stand in the doorway of our adjoining offices and glare at him. "Okay, okay," he'd say, stuffing a piece of paper into the typewriter in a bustle of activity. I'd return to my office, knowing what would happen next.

There would be a hoarse cry and a series of terrible groans from Earl's office. Once again I'd come to the doorway and look at him. "I'm having a seizure," he'd gasp, clutching his chest. "I'm a goner." And with that he'd fall out of the chair with a terrible clatter and lie moaning on the floor. That was my cue. I'd calmly pick up his desk phone and dial a number. "Hello," I'd say. "Is this the writers' pool? Well, my writer's broken. Would you send me up a new one right away?" "All right, you bastard," Earl would say, scrambling back into the chair. "Now get out of here and let me work." He might then write four or five lines of dialogue before we'd go to lunch.

Lunch was always a restorative. Earl would come back to the office with plenty of bounce, rip up what he'd written in the morning, and go to work in earnest. By the end of the day he'd have two, maybe three pages of dialogue. But what dialogue. True, it was like waiting for maple sap to drip into a bucket, but it was so delicious after you got it.

Earl told stories about his crippled childhood with a vicious relish. He was twelve years old when his mother left him in front of an apartment building, where he'd just come from a saxophone lesson, while she went to get the car. As he waited there, saxophone in hand, a kindly passerby dropped a dime into the open end.

His mother despaired of medical help for his useless, polio-crippled legs and took him to revival meetings hoping for a miraculous laying-on-of-hands cure. "Dragging myself up to the pulpit was embarrassing enough," he used to relate. "It was the crawling back down the aisle that was so humiliating."

Even when he was an adult and working as a writer in Hollywood, some poor, misguided soul would try to offer him hope for a miraculous cure. One evening he had a few people over for drinks at his apartment. There was a young lady present who urged him to put his faith in Mary Baker Eddy and Christian Science. After a while Earl excused himself and went into the kitchen. He returned twenty minutes later and served her a copy of Mary Baker Eddy's *Science and Health with Key to the Scriptures*, the Christian Science bible, which he had baked and basted in his oven.

Felton hated cripples. He would mock and even imitate them at every opportunity. One of his pet peeves was Herbert Marshall, a suave, popular English actor who had lost a leg in World War I. Marshall hid his handicap exceedingly well, and people commented on how effortlessly he moved about, particularly his ability to rise gracefully from a chair, something Earl could do only with great awkwardness. Somebody brought this sore topic up after dinner at my home one night, and Earl immediately took the gambit and started blasting Herbert Marshall. "Here," he said, "let me show you my imitation of Herbert Marshall getting out of a chair." He made a powerful lunge out of his seat, his feet slipped, and he shot under the coffee table with a mighty crash, breaking the big toe of his right foot against the table leg. We had to call an ambulance, and he was taken to the hospital, bellowing in pain. So much for Herbert Marshall imitations.

As time went on, Earl's friends gradually disappeared, either from natural causes or from the lack of ability to keep up with his fun-loving debaucheries. He had a meeting with his lawyer one day and told him, "If I have to spend another Sunday alone I'll blow my brains out." The following Sunday he found himself alone and he blew his brains out.

During the location scouting for *Dr. Dolittle* I found myself stuck in Dublin with three of my colleagues. We needed to get to Shannon, near the opposite Irish coast, but we'd missed all the commercial flights for that day. Twentieth Century-Fox was shooting a big World War I flying movie near Dublin, *The Blue Max*, and I thought they might be able to help us out if they had a spare plane. Elmo Williams was the producer of the film as well as being the head of production of Fox in Europe, so I phoned him in London to see what could be done. He was very obliging. All we had to do was go out to their nearby private airfield where they were working and we could use the camera plane, the only craft large enough to hold four passengers and a pilot. He'd make all the arrangements while we were on our way out to the field.

The private airfield turned out to be nothing more or less than a grassy pasture. Dinky little cloth-winged, open-cockpit biplane and triplane fighters were scattered about like toys. There was only one larger plane, a single-engined biplane relic with a fabric-covered, enclosed fuselage that was dramatically decorated with the insignia of the Iron Cross and the German Imperial Eagle, indicating that it flew in the service of the World War I Deutschland Luftwaffe. The Red Baron would have been proud to fly it.

We gathered around it a bit skeptically and watched some workers remove the camera mount and install the flimsy seats. After a while I walked over to what appeared to be the engineer. "Tell me,"

I asked him, "is this thing really safe to fly in?" "Oh, absolutely safe, sar," he replied with a reassuring laugh. "You've got nothin' atall ta worry about. We've put a rosary under every seat!"

It was late in the afternoon when we were finally hustled aboard. The flight would take about two hours, we were told, but we had to get there before sunset. The plane wasn't equipped for night flying. There should be ample time, though. Not to worry. Not to worry, that is, until we got a look at the pilot, a pimply-faced youth who looked fifteen but was probably younger.

The flight plan was simplicity itself. Once you're airborne, fly directly west until you come to Shannon. We didn't do that. Once we were airborne the kid in the cockpit rummaged around until he found a beat-up map, which he spread across his lap. I was sitting right behind him so I got a good look at this navigational aid. It was an old Esso motoring guide.

We headed west for a while, then banked to the north. A few minutes later we were headed south. Then west. Then south again. I was puzzled. Why all this jinking around on what should be a straight-line course? I finally figured it out: He was following the railroad. When the tracks turned north, we turned north. If the tracks looped south, so did we. At one point we started to circle. The tracks had disappeared into a tunnel and he couldn't find where they came out. For almost ten minutes we circled before he picked them up again. I watched the sun getting closer and closer to the horizon. The two-hour flight time came and went. Finally the Shannon River came into view. He abandoned the railroad tracks for the river and we followed its meandering course, the sun sinking relentlessly in the west, twilight spreading threateningly over the green landscape.

The city appeared in the gathering dusk and, by some miracle, the airport hove into sight. We didn't make any attempt to land but flew over it, wagging our wings. I asked the kid what was going on, why we weren't landing. We had lost our radio, he told me. We could receive but we couldn't send. He was acknowledging orders from the tower by wagging the wings!

As we descended slowly over the hangars we could see people running out, gathering in small groups, pointing up at us. After all, it isn't every day that you see a World War I German warplane, complete with an Iron Cross on its tail, coming in for a landing.

As we rolled to a stop near the terminal I looked out the window and saw an elderly Customs official running toward us, a shocked look on his face. He grabbed the door of our little plane and yanked it open. "Where on Earth have ya cum from?" he asked in genuine bewilderment. Our production manager, a man who I don't believe until that moment ever said a funny thing in his life, answered him in a rich, beer-hall German accent, "Ve haff bin fly-ink a long time," he said. "Who von der vohr?"

> "Every wheel has ball bearings. You can take out the ball bearings and you'll still have a wheel . . . but it won't run so good."
>
> Earl Felton, writer,
> responding to my attempt
> to cut some of his dialogue.

It's just as possible to miscast a writer for a film as it is an actor (or even a director). A prime piece of miscasting was done when Terence Rattigan, one of England's most respected playwrights, was hired to do the screenplay for *The Boston Strangler*. Rattigan was a good friend of the film's producer, Robert Fryer, who felt we might get a superior, literate screenplay from him. It sounded good to me. In spite of the mischief he'd wrought during *Dr. Dolittle*, I looked forward to working with this distinguished writer whose plays I had admired for many years. Still, I had a slight, nagging misgiving. This subject matter, the brutal rapes and strangulations of thirteen women in Boston, wasn't his genre. Why was he so interested in doing it?

I got the first inkling that something might be amiss when we had a meeting—Rattigan, Fryer, and myself—at the Beverly Hills Hotel with Gerold Frank, the author of the very detailed and factual book on which our film would be based. Having done all the research into the long series of gruesome murder-rapes with meticulous care, Frank was a true expert on the entire case and we had a lot of questions for him. There was one question, however, that seemed to fascinate Rattigan, and he kept coming back to it time and again: the size of the Boston Strangler's penis.

It took Gerold Frank aback the first time Rattigan brought it up, as it did Fryer and myself. Frank had no ready answer. But Rattigan seemed preoccupied with it. After a few minutes of conversation he'd ask, "How long do you think it was?" A little later he'd ask, "Do you think there was anything unusual about it?" It became obviously and embarrassingly apparent that this subject held a great fascination for him. For a literary man he seemed inordinately concerned about a dangling participle. This went on until finally Frank

said, "But he's just an ordinary, normal little guy." To which Rattigan responded, "Jesus! How normal can you get?"

Rattigan went away to some Caribbean island, where he had a
house, to write a treatment of the screenplay. A couple of months
later Fryer and I received the forty-or-so pages he had written and
we were appalled. This totally confused treatment bore very little
relationship to the book. Worse still, and most puzzling, it was
written as a comedy! Heavy-handed and lame, but a comedy. Then,
to top it all off (he must have thought this would be a wow when he
wrote it), he had a computer come up with the name of the chief
suspect for the grisly crimes, and it turned out to be Darryl Zanuck!

A thoroughly embarrassed Bob Fryer was obliged to turn in this
treatment to the front office. Terence Rattigan was summarily removed from the picture.*

There was no way for us to figure what could have been in
Rattigan's mind when he wrote this treatment, until a long letter
from him arrived. It was a truly tortured document of a talented
man facing the fact that the subject matter was beyond him, that he
was the wrong man for the job. He said, in part,

> You have a wonderful subject for a film, and it will make a
> wonderful film, told, as dear Gerry Frank has already told it,
> factually and in the strict order of events.
>
> I say this not to demean it at all, for that is precisely the
> way that I saw that I, if producer, would have ordered it
> done. In fact I wouldn't have hired myself. Or Tennessee.
> Or Pinter. Or Albee. Or—well perhaps I *might* have hired
> Arthur Miller and resigned myself to that "Social Con-
> science." After all the Strangler might just have been under-
> privileged, and Arthur Miller might, just, perhaps, have
> been able, for once, to subdue his rather limited powers of
> dramatic invention to a purely objective end.
>
> But I can't! I can't! I can't! I can't! I invent. It is the only
> reason for my existence. When that minor and unimportant
> gift leaves me—any minute now, which I don't believe or I
> wouldn't write it—I will leave the world. . . .
>
> I live, I thrive, by invention. With The Boston Strangler
> . . . you need none, but simply an honest telling of the
> horrifying facts. And that I could never give you.

* He was replaced by Edward Anhalt, who came up with a brilliant screenplay.

So what was it that induced him to take the job? Surely not just curiosity about the size of the Boston Strangler's penis alone. Was it nothing more than just a prurient interest in the case itself? We'll never know.

What we do know, though, is that after admitting his complete inability to write the screenplay, which was something he surely recognized even before starting, his conscience didn't bother him quite enough to return any of the money he was paid for not being able to do the job.

"Never be funnier than the director."
Peter Herald, associate producer on *Mandingo*,
instructing the crew on behavior on the set.

Crossed Swords (actually *The Prince and the Pauper* under an assumed name, or *Koldus Es Kirialfy*, as it was called in Hungary, where we were shooting the picture) could modestly be described as having an "all-star cast." George C. Scott, Charlton Heston, Rex Harrison, Raquel Welch, Oliver Reed, and Ernest Borgnine go to make up a pretty fair passel of names. Everyone on the picture seemed to be a star, even the two young, handsome French boys (in their late teens) who were our gofers. Their names were Laurent and Olivier, and when anyone needed anything they would always call out both their names so that it sounded like "Laurence Olivier!" Being summer, and stiflingly hot on the ancient, decrepit stages of Mafilm Studios, their main job was to plunge their hands into a large tub of ice water, dredge up the coldest bottle of soda pop, open it, wipe off the neck with their fingers, and give it to whoever had called out "Laurence Olivier!"

Just before we were to move the company from Budapest to Sopron, a small town about ninety-five miles away, one of the two boys became ill. The company doctor, bless his heart, diagnosed it as syphilis. The company panicked. All they could think of was all the cold drinks they had consumed whose bottles had been so lovingly opened and wiped off by those syphilitic hands.

The doctor reported the case to the Hungarian health authorities and just as the entire company, about 150 of us, were about to embark in a fleet of buses, cars, and trucks to Sopron, the police arrived and called a halt to the proceedings. The authorities had decided that everyone connected with the production, which included secretaries, bookkeepers, accountants, wives, and children who had nothing whatever to do with the actual shooting of the picture, would have to have a blood test before we could leave for our location.

So instead of heading for Sopron, we piled aboard our vehicles and headed for the State Hospital. There are probably more depressing, grim, menacing buildings to be found in a federal penitentiary than the monolithic, decaying, concrete lump known as the State Hospital, in Budapest, but it is doubtful. By the time the supernumeraries arrived, our mob of apprehensive refugees had swollen to about 200. We were herded down a flight of grimy, stone steps into the basement and through a maze of crumbling corridors that reeked with rancid chemical smells. We were beginning to feel that the Hungarian government had decided on a decidedly unpleasant fate for this syphilis-ridden lot.

The corridors led to a large, dingy room furnished with ramshackle, beat-up tables and an assortment of old-fashioned, disreputable-looking lab equipment. Daylight feebly groped its way through tiny barred windows high up near the flaking ceiling.

Eight technicians in filthy, stained lab coats stood two to a table and beckoned us over. We formed lines and shuffled toward them. When we got a look at their blood-taking technique some of our game troupe passed out.

There was nothing fancy or modern about this operation, no syringes or any newfangled contraptions like that. You rolled up your sleeve, a tourniquet made the vein pop up, a likely spot was swabbed with antiseptic. Then one of the technicians jabbed you with what appeared to be a horse needle. The other end of the needle—the less pointy end—had a short plastic tube attached to it, through which the blood fountained out and was caught by the second technician in a test tube. If the victim moved, or flinched, some of the blood would spill onto the technicians' hands, coats, and shoes. The test tubes were then labeled (with names completely misspelled) and stored, unsealed, in a wooden rack. After the first few people passed through the process, the place resembled a slaughterhouse.

The company was a total wreck by the time we arrived in Sopron that night. We had several lovely young British actresses with us who were completely unnerved and close to hysteria with worry. I decided to try to reach my doctor, Hy Engelberg, in Los Angeles, and get his opinion.

I was lucky. I got Hy after only a three-hour wait, and the connection was perfect. After I told him what had happened he said, "If somebody does contract syphilis, don't tell anybody, but call me first. It would make medical history and I'd want to be the first to announce it. It would make me famous!" He assured me that it was totally impossible to contract the disease in the manner I'd described and to forget the whole thing.

I passed this information along to the girls and to anyone else who wanted to listen. They were relieved but still uneasy. They wouldn't feel comfortable until they had the test results.

A week later the producer arrived from Budapest with the results, which he showed me first. They were incredible. About half the company showed positive, and they were the least likely group imaginable, mostly the accountants, secretaries, and wives, even our cameraman's eight-year-old son, who had arrived with his mother for a visit only the day before the bloodletting and had never even been on the set. The whole thing was a farce.

I took the list into the hotel lobby and gathered the young actresses around me. "Well," I said, "here's the list with the results. I'll read them to you." Their eyes widened, their faces tensed, and they drew in very close to me. You could see them holding their collective breath.

I pointed to the first girl. "You don't have it," I said. Then, in turn, I pointed to the others. "You don't have it! You don't have it! And you don't have it!" They gave squeals of delight, threw their arms around me, and covered my face with kisses. That's when I said, "*I* have it!"

The whole thing was such an obvious foul-up that the Hungarians demanded everyone take the test over again. The company revolted. They wouldn't hear of it, even if it meant shutting down the picture and deportation or jail. The government kept insisting and we kept refusing, until they gave up and we never heard from them again. The beauty part of the whole thing, of course, was that "Laurence Olivier" never had syphilis in the first place. It was a severe case of misdiagnosis.

Doing any scene with an animal is difficult. Doing a scene with a lot of animals is a nightmare. Doing a *musical* number with a lot of animals makes the nightmare seem like a midsummer's night's dream. *Doctor Dolittle* had a lot of musical numbers with a lot of animals.

"The Reluctant Vegetarian" was one of the trickiest musical sequences of the picture. It is dinnertime in the Dolittle household. Horses, cows, goats, chickens, ducks, rabbits, and birds are assembled in the living room, waiting to be fed. Among them are our principal animals, Che-Che the Chimp, Polynesia the Parrot, and Gub-Gub the Pig. Dolittle has to walk among them, handing out various kinds of feed while singing a song that relates that although he is a vegetarian he is a reluctant one. It seems he would much rather be eating the animals than feeding them, but being the great humanitarian, his "life's much the same as any English horse./I eat every flowering shrub there is/except for gorse./Sometimes I get luxuries like beetroot leaves,/of course."

It was not easy to do. The animals had to hold their positions for at least two and a half minutes without biting or kicking each other, or doing something that had to be mopped or shoveled up, and, toughest of all, not only had to eat what Rex Harrison handed them but also more or less pay attention when he sang to them.

Rehearsal after rehearsal the positioning and feeding of the animals was a complete shambles. Tie a goat down here, get a cow turned around there, move the pigs farther from the ducks so Rex had a better passageway. Slowly, *very* slowly, the scene took shape. We had started early in the morning and it was well along in the afternoon before I felt we were in a position to try making a take. We had rehearsed ourselves silly. Technically there wasn't anything more I could do except give it a try, trust to luck, and pray like hell.

Bells rang, "QUIET!" was shouted, the lights came on, the animal trainers hid themselves as planned. The camera rolled and I called "Action!"

The animals were magnificent. Their deportment was perfect. They ate what was handed to them and actually made eye contact with Rex when he sang at them. And Rex was at his charming best, his timing perfect, his performance superb. We were about halfway through and absolutely nothing had gone wrong. We're home, I thought. This is it! And on the first take! It's too good to be true!

I was right. It was.

Rex suddenly stopped singing. He looked at me startled, puzzled. I cut the camera and asked him what happened, why did he stop?

"I heard you call, 'Cut!' "

"*I* called 'Cut!'? The scene was going perfectly. Why should I call 'Cut!'?"

"That's what I thought, too. But I heard you call 'Cut!' "

"Impossible! Not when the scene was going like that."

"Well, *somebody* called 'Cut!' I distinctly heard it."

"I didn't hear it. *Nobody* called 'Cut!' "

Things were starting to get a little tense between us when suddenly a voice rang out—loud, clear, and sounding exactly like me. "CUT!" it shouted.

It was Polynesia the Parrot. She had heard me say it enough times and had decided to give it a try herself.

Rex looked at me, one eyebrow raised. "That's the first time I've ever been directed by a parrot. But she may be right. I probably can do it better."

Casting Glenda Jackson to play Sarah Bernhardt was a brilliant idea. Who else to play the world's greatest actress than the world's greatest actress? We hadn't yet started shooting *Sarah* (later retitled, incredibly, *The Incredible Sarah*) but were still early in the preproduction stages of the picture at Pinewood Studios, on the outskirts of London. As great an admirer of Glenda as I was (and still am), I had a distinct worry about her. The script called for her to range in age from eighteen years old into her thirties. The latter part fitted her like a glove. The girlhood part—well, up close, or even not so up close, Glenda was no longer eighteen. It didn't seem to be of any concern to her, but every time I thought of it my stomach gave a little lurch.

The time came for the first costume fittings. I was in the fitting room with Glenda. The costume designer, Anthony Mendleson, was also there along with a couple of seamstresses. It was at the end of a long, tiring day of fitting the heavy period costumes, and Glenda looked a bit dragged out and less like a teenager than ever. The final outfits were those for the early part of the film, the girlhood part. I was concerned about what might happen when she saw herself in those youthful frocks. I was convinced she would see that it just wasn't going to work, and where would we be then? That part of the story was essential—there was no way of dropping it. Shooting her through scrims and filters wouldn't help much and would be too obvious. Maybe we'd have to find a look-alike, young version of her, but I discarded that idea as soon as I thought of it. There's nobody like Glenda Jackson.

The seamstresses helped Glenda into her outfit. A pull here, a tug there. She ground out her cigarette, exhaled a large lungful of blue smoke, and turned to face the big mirror. I watched as she stared at the image facing her. She stared a long time. Then something happened. *She started to get younger!* In front of my eyes a metamorphosis was taking place. She became eighteen. Isn't it strange, I thought, how your imagination can play tricks on you? I desperately wanted her to look eighteen, so I was seeing her as eighteen. This is self-delusion of the first water, I said to myself.

Mendleson and I made our comments about the outfit, then left the dressing room while she changed into her next costume. I closed the door behind me as we stepped into the hallway. We were both silent for a moment. Then Mendleson said, "Did you see what I saw in there?"

"What was that?"

"When she looked into the mirror she became eighteen."

"Yes, I saw that, too."

"I cannot believe it. I just cannot believe I saw it happen."

I thought of something Stanislavski once wrote: "Our type of creativeness is the conception and birth of a new being—the person in the part. It is a natural act similar to the birth of a human being."

What we had just witnessed was the world's greatest actress giving birth to the world's greatest actress.

> "Directing is a democratic process in which everyone cooperates in doing exactly what I tell them to do."
> Anonymous director
> explaining how the system works.

The only way to describe Charles Bronson is "Mr. Charm." The United Nations could use his suave diplomacy. He demonstrated this considerable talent for making friends and influencing people on the first day of shooting on *Mr. Majestyk*.

The entire company was parked along one side of a lonely back road several miles outside of La Junta, Colorado, early one September morning. The strung-out trucks, buses, and cars covered about a quarter of a mile. This was the spot where we were supposed to make the first shot of the movie, but we were stymied. The transporter carrying the cars that worked in the shot hadn't arrived. Without those cars there was nothing we could do. Either the transporter had broken down or there was a dreadful foul-up in the transportation department. Whatever it was, there was nothing to do but wait and pace. Bronson started complaining to me about the inefficiency of the whole company, even though we had yet to find out what had happened.

After about an hour everyone was out on the road, chatting, playing cards, lounging. I found myself at one end of the line of parked vehicles with my first assistant, Buck Hall. Charlie Bronson was at the other end. The entire cast and crew stood between us.

Suddenly Charlie called out, "Hey, Dick!" I turned and shouted back, "Yeah, Charlie?"

"You know what this company needs?"

"No, I don't. What does it need?"

"It needs a European first assistant and a European crew!" he shouted back.

The entire company froze. This was an insult beyond compare or repair. The redneck coefficient of American movie crews is notorious. Compared to them the Ku Klux Klan and the Skinheads are the radical left. To be contemptuously compared to Europeans was a stunning slap in the face.

Luckily, the transporter with the cars showed up at that moment and we went to work.

As soon as we got back to the motel that evening, Buck Hall came to my room. Buck had been my assistant on many pictures over the years, and we were close and devoted friends. There were tears in his eyes. "The crew is leaving the picture tonight. They're going back to the studio and I'm going with them." Thank you, Charlie Bronson.

We talked for a long time. I pleaded with him and begged him not to go. Out of loyalty and friendship he finally agreed to stay and to try to keep the crew from leaving.

Buck came through for me. He and the crew remained on the picture, but they did something I'd never seen before, nor have I seen it since. They gave Bronson the silent treatment. Unless it was absolutely necessary, like calling him to the set, no one ever spoke to him again for the entire picture. Not a word. Not a "good morning" or a "good night."

Charlie must have been aware of what was happening, but he never mentioned it to me. The only reference he ever made that something peculiar was going on was one day when he said, "I just don't understand it. Nobody calls me 'Charlie' on this picture. They only call me 'Mr. Bronson.' "

A few nights later, Bronson and I had dinner together in the barnlike dining room of the motel in La Junta. I thought it might be a good idea if we got to know each other a little better. Across the room from us was a long table with about fourteen men in business suits; the men also were having dinner. They kept glancing over at us, trying to get a glimpse of a real, live movie star feeding in their presence.

Eventually the man at the head of the long table got up and strolled over to us. He was a tall, youngish chap with a bland, pasty face and very nervous. Obviously this was one star-struck local boy. He never even glanced at me; his eyes were riveted on Charlie as he hesitantly apologized for interrupting his dinner (not mine). Then he explained that the group he was with were the presidents and officers of several of the local golf clubs in the area. They got together like this every month or so. Anyhow, he said, they couldn't help noticing that Mr. Bronson was here making a movie and that they would like him to know that if he wanted to play golf he would be more than welcome at any of their clubs. They'd be honored, in fact.

I thought it was a very nice gesture and looked to Charlie for his reply. So did the shy, smiling young man. And Charlie did reply. "You know," he said, "where I live in Los Angeles the back lawn of my house is part of a golf course."

"Really? That's wonderful."

"And you know what I do with that golf course?"

"Why, no, I don't, Mr. Bronson."

"I let my dogs shit on it," he informed the young man and returned to eating his steak.

As I said, there's only one way to describe Charles Bronson: Mr. Charm.

> "Confucius say, 'When feast is finished, who has use for spoon?'"
>
> > Earl Felton, describing the position of screenplay writers after they have turned in their scripts.

Take a clutch of scientists, put them in an experimental submarine, reduce the whole thing down to the size of a microbe, and inject it into someone's bloodstream and what have you got? *Fantastic Voyage*, of course. And you've also got a movie heavily laden with special effects, which means a long, slow, tedious production. The waits between setups were interminable and boring, so we tried to amuse ourselves by making up appropriate song titles, such as, "There's a Long, Long Entrail Awinding," "Liver Come Back to Me," and "When an Antibody Meets an Antibody Coming Through the Eye." Actually, it was the antibodies that provided one of the few lighter moments on the set.

The "attack of the antibodies" sequence involved these rope-like, crystalline, nasty creatures wrapping themselves around the bosomy Raquel Welch while she's outside the sub and almost squeezing her to death. Antibody, in this case, was a misnomer.

They weren't anti her body at all, and who could blame them? In any event, Raquel is taken aboard the sub and the scientists try to save her by pulling the tight-clinging antibodies off her form-fitting white diving suit.

Other than to set the actors' positions, I didn't want to rehearse the rescue scene because of the amount of time involved. Each of the dozens of antibodies had to be hand-sewn onto the diving suit while Raquel was wearing it, and that took a couple of hours. Better just to say, "Action!" and let the actors tear away at them.

So I called, "Action!" and Stephen Boyd, Arthur Kennedy, and Donald Pleasance went to work on the antibodies, pulling, tearing, ripping. Then I realized that maybe a rehearsal would have been a good idea after all.

The actors were being gentlemen. No one wanted to be the first to make a grab for one of Raquel's splendid boobs, so they grabbed everywhere else. The result was, when I finally called "Cut!," a de-antibodied Raquel except for her bosom, which was thickly encrusted with them and looked like a Las Vegas showgirl's rhinestone-bedecked brassiere. Obviously we had to do the scene again.

The seamstresses went to work laboriously sewing more glittery antibodies onto Raquel while I urged the actors to shed their inhibitions and just pull the damn things off no matter where they happened to be.

An hour and a half later we were ready again. I called "Action!" and Messrs. Boyd, Kennedy, and Pleasance all made a dive for Raquel's tits, grabbing handfuls of antibodies. They looked like a pack of lustful scientists gone mad with sexual desire. They also looked ludicrous. I called "Cut!"

I finally had to rehearse the shot more carefully, giving the actors a choreography of where their hands should go and when. In the end it was a simple shot, really, and it took only six hours to shoot. However, we did come out of it with a new song title: "Thanks for the Mammaries."

I was on location in Bisbee, Arizona, shooting *Violent Saturday* for Fox when Buddy Adler phoned me from Hollywood to tell me that he'd been able to get Sylvia Sidney to play the role of the librarian in the picture. We were due back in a week to continue working in the studio, and she would be in the first scene I'd be doing there.

When I was growing up, Sylvia Sidney was a big star. I mean a *big* star. Superstar class. She was a fine dramatic actress famous for her deeply emotional scenes. Her tears were always a source of wonder to me. What depths of feeling she must have plumbed to make her cry the way she did.

The aura of her stardom still overpowered me. I couldn't imagine in my wildest dreams ever being permitted to direct Sylvia Sidney. I'd already worked with some pretty fair names: Robert Mitchum, Kirk Douglas, James Mason. But this was *Sylvia Sidney*, for God's sake. And now I was going to work with her and I hadn't even met her. The idea made me very nervous.

The morning of our first day back in the studio I arrived early and took my first assistant, Buck Hall, aside. "Look," I told him, "there's no way in the world that I'm going to meet Miss Sidney for the first time, on the set. I haven't even had a chance to discuss the part with her. I'm going to her dressing room now and talk to her. I don't care how long it takes or how much it holds up production. And don't start getting nervous and knocking on the door to tell me what time it is. I don't want to be disturbed, understand?" He understood, and I went in to see Sylvia Sidney. She was in a portable dressing room parked just outside the stage entrance. It was really a big wooden box on wheels. The room inside was tiny. I hoped she wouldn't be offended by this as I entered and introduced myself.

There she was, a delicate, birdlike lady huddled in a corner of the couch, knitting. She looked at me with her enormous dark eyes through even more enormous reading glasses, a sweet smile on her face. Her hair was up in curlers covered by a gauzy violet kerchief. She was not as young as when I'd last seen her on the silver screen, but the beauty, the sensitivity, the intelligence were all still there.

In Hollywood, from the moment you're introduced to someone it is taken for granted that you're on a first-name basis. I just couldn't bring myself to call her Sylvia, however. I had to call her Miss Sidney. We got over the usual amenities quickly and I launched into a long monologue about the story. Miss Sidney turned her attention to her knitting. She was listening, but she was knitting and not looking at me.

I told her everything I could about the plot and how she fitted into the story. She knit. She didn't look up. I told her about her character, where she stood in the community, her psychological makeup, why she was the way she was, her relationship with the other characters in the story. She kept on knitting, never looking up, never asking a question. Just knitting. I was beginning to sweat. Maybe I was being too shallow for her. Maybe she needed something more, like another director. Someone more experienced, more profound. I got deeper and deeper into the psychological character motivations, the things that probably shaped her child-hood and were carried over into her adult life. I invented her mother and father, what they were like, their influence on her. Then I invented *their* mother and father. I went on and on and she kept knitting, never looking up.

Finally I ran out of steam. I had nothing more to say. I couldn't have given a more complete analysis of the story and her character if I had a Bunsen burner and litmus paper. I looked at her. The needles were still clicking away, her head bent over her work. "Well, Miss Sidney," I said, "that's about it. What do you think?"

The knitting stopped, and she looked up, a serious expression on her face. "That was very interesting, Mr. Fleischer," she said. "I'll tell you what, though. When we get on the set, you just tell me where to stand and I'll be there." Then she smiled. A devilish, roguish smile.

All my reserve and nervousness vanished. "Sylvia," I said, "I could kill you." I kissed her and said, "I'll see you on the set," and started to leave.

As I opened the door she called to me. "Oh, and by the way," she said, "whenever you need tears . . . just tell me when to cry."

Fade Out

It's been a lengthy career and a lucky one, and much to my surprise I've lasted longer than the great majority of my peers. Most of them have been casualties of involuntary retirement. Indeed, as far as directing is concerned, I am a victim myself. It seems that in Hollywood there is a line drawn in the sands of time. You get on the wrong side of that line merely by living past the age of about forty-five. When that happens you automatically lose all your talent, experience, knowledge, taste, and the know-how of moviemaking. You may actually be at the peak of your abilities when the sand shifts and the line moves, and there you are on the wrong side, and the general perception is that you no longer know how to direct.

I'd been on the wrong side of the line for a good many productive years before the posse caught up with me. By that time I'd stretched a modicum of talent into an exceptionally long run. It's been an exciting, glamorous career, with many more ups than downs. The industry has been more than kind to me. Besides, I have a terrific family and, after fifty years, I'm still married to the same fabulous lady. (I sometimes introduce her as my first wife. Keeps her on her toes.) Hey, what's to complain?

But the fat lady hasn't sung yet. Along with my sister, Ruth Kneitle, I'm happily and successfully involved in the merchandising of my father's creation Betty Boop. She's fast becoming a worldwide merchandising queen. And then there is the Betty Boop animated feature that is now in production and of which I am an executive producer. I never thought I'd be carrying on in my father's tradition of animation, but here I am doing just that.

I really am lucky, starting four new careers at this time of my life: licenser, producer, author, and *bon vivant*. Involuntary retirement? Me?

I was looking through Bartlett's *Familiar* Quotations for an appropriate quote about retirement with which to end this book. I came across this one, by Lucretius: "Why dost thou not retire like a guest sated with the banquet of life, and with calm mind embrace, thou fool, a rest that knows no care?"

A good question. But then, what kind of fool am I?

Richard Fleischer
Filmography

1989   *Call From Space;* (Showscan Specialty film) James Coburn, Charlton Heston.

1987   *Million Dollar Mystery;* Dino De Laurentiis/DEG.

1985   *Red Sonja;* DDL/MGM/UA; Arnold Schwarzenegger, Birgit Nillsson.

1984   *Conan the Destroyer;* Raffaella De Laurentiis/Universal; Arnold Schwarzenegger.

1983   *Amityville III-D;* Dino De Laurentiis/Orion; Tony Roberts, Meg Ryan, Tess Harper.

1981   *Tough Enough;* Twentieth Century-Fox; Dennis Quaid.

1980   *The Jazz Singer;* EMI/Columbia; Laurence Olivier, Neil Diamond, Lucie Arnaz.

1979   *Ashanti;* Columbia; Michael Caine, Omar Sharif, Peter Ustinov, Rex Harrison, William Holden.

1978   *Crossed Swords* (aka *The Prince and the Pauper*)*;* Ilya & Alexander Salkind/Columbia; Oliver Reed, Raquel Welch, Ernest Borgnine, George C. Scott, Charlton Heston, Rex Harrison.

1976   *The Incredible Sarah;* Reader's Digest Films/CIC; Glenda Jackson.

1975   *Mandingo;* Dino De Laurentiis/Paramount; James Mason, Susan George, Perry King.

1974   *Mr. Majestyk;* Walter Mirisch/UA; Charles Bronson.

1974   *The Spikes Gang;* Walter Mirisch/UA; Lee Marvin, Ron Howard.

1973   *The Don Is Dead;* Hal Wallis/Universal; Anthony Quinn.

1973   *Soylent Green;* MGM; Charlton Heston, Edward G. Robinson.

1972   *The New Centurions;* Chartoff-Winkler/Columbia; George C. Scott, Stacy Keach.

1971   *The Last Run;* MGM; George C. Scott, Trish Van Devere, Colleen Dewhurst, Tony Musante.

1971   *See No Evil;* Columbia; Mia Farrow.

1971   *Ten Rillington Place;* Columbia; Richard Attenborough, John Hurt.

1970   *Tora! Tora! Tora!;* Darryl F. Zanuck/Twentieth Century-Fox; Jason Robards, Jr., Martin Balsam, Joseph Cotten.

1969   *Che;* Twentieth Century-Fox; Omar Sharif, Jack Palance.

1968   *The Boston Strangler;* Twentieth Century-Fox; Henry Fonda, Tony Curtis.

1967   *Doctor Dolittle;* Arthur Jacobs/Twentieth Century-Fox; Rex Harrison, Richard Attenborough.

1966   *Fantastic Voyage;* Saul David/Twentieth Century-Fox; Raquel Welch.

1962   *Barabbas;* Dino De Laurentiis/Columbia; Anthony Quinn, Silvana Mangano, Vittorio Gassman, Jack Palance, Ernest Borgnine, Katy Jurado.

1961   *The Big Gamble;* Darryl F. Zanuck/Twentieth Century-Fox; Juliette Greco, Stephen Boyd, David Wayne.

1960   *Crack in the Mirror;* Darryl F. Zanuck/Twentieth Century-Fox; Orson Welles, Juliette Greco, Bradford Dillman.

1959   *Compulsion;* Richard D. Zanuck/Twentieth Century-Fox; Orson Welles, Dean Stockwell, Bradford Dillman.

1959   *These Thousand Hills;* Twentieth Century-Fox; Lee Remick, Don Murray.

1958   *The Vikings*; Kirk Douglas/UA; Kirk Douglas, Tony Curtis, Ernest Borgnine, Janet Leigh.

1956   *Between Heaven and Hell*; Twentieth Century-Fox; Robert Wagner, Buddy Ebsen.

1956   *Bandido*; UA; Robert Mitchum.

1955   *The Girl in the Red Velvet Swing*; Charles Brackett/Twentieth Century-Fox; Joan Collins, Ray Milland.

1955   *Violent Saturday*; Buddy Adler/Twentieth Century-Fox; Lee Marvin, Ernest Borgnine, Victor Mature.

1954   *Twenty Thousand Leagues Under the Sea*; Walt Disney/Buena Vista; Kirk Douglas, James Mason, Peter Lorre.

1953   *Arena*; Arthur Loew, Jr./MGM; Gig Young, Polly Bergen, Henry (Harry) Morgan.

1952   *The Happy Time*; Stanley Kramer/Columbia; Charles Boyer, Louis Jourdan.

1952   *The Narrow Margin*; Stanley Rubin/RKO; Charles McGraw, Marie Windsor.

1950   *Armored Car Robbery*; RKO; Charles McGraw, Adele Jergens, William Talman.

1949   *Trapped*; Bryan Foy/Eagle-Lion; Lloyd Bridges.

1949   *The Clay Pigeon*; Sid Rogell/RKO; Bill Williams, Barbara Hale.

1949   *Make Mine Laughs*; RKO; Ray Bolger, Jack Haley.

1949   *Follow Me Quietly*; RKO; William Lundigan, Dorothy Patrick.

1948   *So This Is New York*; Stanley Kramer/UA; Henry Morgan, Hugh Herbert, Rudy Vallee.

1948   *Bodyguard*; Sid Rogell/RKO; Lawrence Tierney, Priscilla Lane.

1947   *Design for Death*; Richard Fleischer-Sid Rogell/RKO; Academy Award-winning Documentary Feature.

1947   *Banjo*; RKO; Sharyn Moffett.

1947   *Child of Divorce*; Sid Rogell/RKO; Sharyn Moffett.

1942–1945: RKO-Pathe News: Wrote newsreel commentaries; wrote and directed *This Is America* documentary series; wrote commentaries for various documentary short subjects. Wrote and produced own series of comedy shorts, *Flicker Flashbacks*.

INDEX

"What Kind of Fool Am I?," 22, 236

White, Jacqueline, 34

Who's Afraid of Virginia Woolf?, 268

Wilde, Oscar, 262

Wilke, Robert J., 70

Willi, Arthur, 10

Williams, Elmo, 205-206, 209-212, 213, 214-215, 232, 275-276, 280, 281, 285, 286-287, 319

Williams, Tennessee, 322

Williamson, John, 106

Willingham, Calder, 143, 147

Windsor, Marie, 45

Wise, Robert, 12, 38

Wyler, William, 184

Wyndham's Theater, 197

Yiddish Art Theater, 297

Yordan, Philip, 25, 229, 230, 231

Zackary, 227

Zanuck, Darryl F., 161, 181, 205, 217, 232, 281, 287

   Ballad of the Red Rocks and, 178-180, 188-189

   Crack in the Mirror and, 182-183, 184-188

   Greco's breakup with, 213-214

   Greco's relationship with, 183-188, 206-207

   interference by, 185-188, 207-210

   Kurosawa pressured by, 284-285

   Kurosawa's meeting with, 276

   nom de plume of, 183, 191

   production ignorance of, 183

   production mistake hidden from, 210-213

   restoration of former stature of, 214-215

   on Richard Fleischer, 313-314

   Shaw's screenplay for, 189-191

   Tora! Tora! Tora! adopted by, 273

   Twentieth Century-Fox controlled by, 124-127

   Violent Saturday admired by, 15-16

   Welles and, 170

Zanuck, Richard, 16, 126, 161, 174-175, 232, 252, 254, 256, 257, 258, 273, 281, 285, 313

   Plummer and, 247-249, 250-251

   Welles and, 173

Darryl F. Zanuck Productions, 161, 178, 313

Zendar, Fred, 14, 15, 105-106, 107, 108, 110, 111-112, 145

Zinnemann, Fred, 269

Zukor, Adolph, 99, 100, 101